OLD TIPPECANOE

William Henry Harrison, in the dress uniform of the War of 1812.

The original portrait showed Harrison in civilian dress as Delegate from North-west Territory in 1800. The Major General's uniform was superimposed in 1813.

Old Tippecanoe

*William Henry Harrison
and His Time*

By

FREEMAN CLEAVES

KENNIKAT PRESS/Port Washington, N.Y.

For

L. B. S.

ACKNOWLEDGMENT

THE WRITER received helpful assistance in research from many persons. At the New York Public Library, Hugo S. Paltsits, Charles F. McCombs, Miss Dorothy P. Miller and Sylvester Vigilante were genuinely cooperative over a period of some years. Doctor Thomas P. Martin and D. H. Mugridge of the Library of Congress and Doctor Hunter Miller of the State Department rendered invaluable services. A partial list of those remembered pleasantly during a research tour of the Midwest would include James A. Green, Mrs. W. T. Buckner and Miss Eleanor S. Wilby of Cincinnati; Doctor Harlow Lindley of Columbus; Doctor Christopher B. Coleman, Miss Nellie C. Armstrong, Miss Florence Venn, and Miss Esther U. McNitt of the Indiana State Library and Historical Society, Indianapolis. John Scott Harrison IV of Helena, Montana, kindly placed his valuable collection of Harrison letters at my disposal, while the late A. G. Mitten of Goodland, Indiana, made available a wealth of manuscript material which recently has been turned over to the Indiana Historical Society. Walter R. Benjamin and the late Thomas F. Madigan of New York showed me several items of interest; also Forrest G. Sweet of Battle Creek, Michigan, and New York City.

Research assistants in the field were Doctor John Alexander Moore and Anna Betty Moore of New York who sought out Harrison items in Boston, and in Louisville, Kentucky. Joseph Shafer of Madison, Wisconsin, delved into the extensive Draper Collection at the Wisconsin State Library and sent me his findings. Miss Agnes Reeder was most helpful in locating Harrison letters at the Chicago Historical Society.

For special courtesies appreciation is due Mrs. Lucille U. Moore of Louisville, W. J. Burke and Doctor Charles W. Green of New York. Miss Sarah Bishop of Philadelphia, Thomas Robson Hay, Doctor Nelson F. Adkins and Robert Orr of New York read portions of the manuscript and offered me numerous helpful suggestions. To these and many others who rendered their assistance on various occasions I wish to extend my best thanks.

A study of General Harrison's services in the War of 1812 which is worthy of special mention is that of Beverly W. Bond in Volume 13 of the Mississippi Valley Historical Review. Mr. Bond is to be complimented for the accuracy and adequacy of his findings.

THE HARRISON FAMILY

Benjamin Harrison I, b. England——; m. Mary; emigrated to Virginia before Sept. 8, 1632; Clerk of Virginia Council; d. 1649.

Benjamin Harrison II, b. Southwark Parish, Surry County, Sept. 20, 1645; m. Hannah; Militia Colonel; County Sheriff; Charter Trustee Wm. & Mary College; member Va. House of Burgesses 1680–1698; member Va. Council 1698–1712; d. Jan. 30, 1712–13.

Benjamin Harrison III, b. Wakefield, Surry County, 1673; m. Elizabeth Burwell, dau. Lewis Burwell; Attorney-General 1702–1705; Acting Treasurer of Colony, 1705–10; Speaker House of Burgesses, 1705; d. April 10, 1710, Berkeley, Charles City County.

Benjamin Harrison IV, b. Wakefield, circa 1700; m. Anne Carter, dau. Robert (King) Carter; Militia Colonel; County Sheriff; member House of Burgesses 1734–44; d. July 12, 1744, Berkeley.

Benjamin Harrison V, b. Berkeley, 1726; m. Elizabeth, dau. Col. Wm. Bassett; Militia Colonel and County Lieutenant; member House of Burgesses 1748–75; member Virginia Revolutionary Conventions; Committee of Correspondence; Continental Congress 1774–77; Signer Declaration of Independence; Speaker House of Delegates 1778–81, 1785; Governor 1781–84; member Va. Constitutional Convention 1788; d. April 23, 1791. Children: Elizabeth, b. 1751; Anna, 1753–1821; Benjamin VI, 1755–1799; Lucy (d. 1809); Carter Bassett (d. 1808); Sarah, 1770–1812; WILLIAM HENRY, b. Berkeley, Feb. 9, 1773; m. Nov. 25, 1795, Anna Tuthill Symmes (b. Flatbrook, N. J., July 25, 1775, dau. John Cleves Symmes); d. Washington, D. C., April 4, 1841.

CHILDREN OF WILLIAM HENRY AND ANNA SYMMES HARRISON

Betsey Bassett, b. Ft. Washington (Cincinnati), Sept. 29, 1796; m. Judge John Cleves Short, June 29, 1814; d. Sept. 27, 1846.

John Cleves Symmes, b. Ft. Washington, Oct. 28, 1798; m. Clarissa, dau. Gen. Zebulon M. Pike, Sept. 29, 1819; d. Oct. 30, 1830.

Lucy Singleton, b. Richmond, Va., 1800; m. Judge David K. Este, Sept. 30, 1819; d. April 7, 1826.

Wm. Henry II, b. Vincennes, Ind., Sept. 6, 1802; m. Jane Findlay Irwin, Feb. 18, 1824; d. Feb. 6, 1838.

John Scott, b. Vincennes, Oct. 4, 1804; m. (1) Lucretia K. Johnson, 1824; (2) Elizabeth Ramsey, Aug. 12, 1831; d. May 25, 1878. Son by second wife, Benjamin Harrison, b. North Bend, Ohio, Aug. 20, 1833, United States President 1889–93.

Benjamin, b. Vincennes, 1806; m. (1) Louisa Bonner; (2) Mary Raney; d. June 9, 1840.

Mary Symmes, b. Vincennes, Jan. 22, 1809; m. John H. Fitzhugh, March 5, 1829; d. Nov. 16, 1842.

Carter Bassett, b. Vincennes, Oct. 26, 1811; m. Mary A. Sutherland, June 16, 1836; d. Aug. 12, 1839.

Anna Tuthill, b. North Bend, Oct. 28, 1813; m. Wm. Henry Harrison Taylor, June 16, 1836; d. July 5, 1845.

James Findlay, b. North Bend, 1814 (?); d. in infancy.

CONTENTS

ILLUSTRATIONS

MAPS

OLD TIPPECANOE

COLONEL BEN HARRISON

COLONEL BEN HARRISON, a giant in size and master of Berkeley plantation, had won his last election. For more than forty years Colonel Harrison had represented his county, colony and State, entering the Virginia House of Burgesses even before attaining the age required by law. After twenty-five years of service in the Virginia House, he had taken his place in the Continental Congress at Philadelphia where his warm, bluff personality helped smooth the way for General George Washington in the field. Later returning to Virginia politics, this "uncommonly large man," brusque and forthright in speech, resumed his seat as a Burgess, was twice elected Governor, and in 1785 was chosen Speaker of the House over his rival and neighbor John Tyler.[1] Again successful in the ensuing elections, the Colonel was being talked of as Virginia's next Governor when a celebration of his latest triumph, followed by a painful recurrence of gout, induced him to take to his bed.

The ancestry and accomplishments of Colonel Ben Harrison are well worth recalling for as an elder statesman of Virginia's Golden Age he had always maintained himself in the front rank. The Harrison family was one of the oldest in the Colony and was highly respected; none could boast of more extensive and influential connections. Five Benjamin Harrisons in succession had gained wealth and political prominence in Virginia since the year 1632 when one Benjamin Harryson, who hailed either from England or from the Somers Isles (Bermuda), signed his name to a land document, on September 6, as clerk of the Virginia Council.[2] Of his ancestry in England not one fact is known but this first Benjamin Harryson, or Harrison, became a man of considerable property in Virginia, acquiring land on both sides of the James River in four or five present-day counties. At the Harrison plantation of Wakefield in Surry County was born the second Benjamin, who became a sheriff, a Burgess, local justice, and a colonel of the militia. Benjamin II assisted his son-in-law, the Reverend James Blair, in founding William and Mary College and he attained a high and lucrative post as member of the Virginia Council, the supreme judges and collectors for the King. That he was highly respected can hardly be doubted, his tombstone marking him as one "who did justice, loved mercy, and walked humbly with his God . . . always loyal to his Prince and a great benefactor to his country."[3] The first traces of rebellion against the ruling power appear in his son Benjamin III, who, educated for the law in London, made common cause with his brother-in-law, the Reverend Blair, in assailing two royal governors, Edmund Andros and Francis Nicholson. Harrison and Blair appeared together at a Lambeth Palace conference in London to testify concerning the known manners and morals of Governor Andros and triumphantly obtained his dismissal.[4] Returning to the Colony, Benjamin III entered upon a brilliant career while still a young man. His attacks against the hot-tempered and rancorous Nicholson, successor to Andros, brought him no political misfortune, as he became successively clerk of the Virginia Council, attorney-general, treasurer, and Speaker of the House. Benjamin III assisted in the revision of the Virginia law code and was writing a history of the colony when he died at thirty-seven years. As affairs then stood, twenty-seven lines of Latin and one Greek word were inscribed upon his tombstone.[5]

One of the historic accomplishments of Benjamin III was the acquisition of a plantation on the James River founded in 1619 by Richard Berkeley of Stoke, England.[6] "Berkeley Hundred" was a rich tobacco area extending for miles along the James River, a good day's journey southeast of the future site of Richmond, and including within its boundaries a generous portion of the county named for King Charles I. The wealth of Benjamin Harrison IV, who was a militia colonel, county sheriff, and for ten years a Burgess, came to be measured in a dozen plantations extending along the James and Nottoway Rivers. Benjamin IV further extended the family influence by marrying the daughter of Robert (King) Carter, richest native-born American of his day. Since it was Carter's hobby to help build homes for his daughters when they were married, he probably took a hand in erecting the present Berkeley manor. The original Berkeley mansion, where Benjamin III and his family lived, stood north of the James River where it widens into Tar Bay; the present house, located somewhat nearer the river, at Harrison's Landing, was erected in 1725–26 by Benjamin IV.[7] This brick mansion is a dignified family dwelling, two and a half stories high, with richly embellished pediments for the doors and much hand-tooled woodwork in its spacious rooms. Benjamin Harrison's mills, shipyard and tobacco fields made work for many slaves and his own vessels carried the yield to England. In due time he became the father of ten children, but one summer afternoon "a violent Thunder Gust Arose" and lightning struck him dead as he stood with his two little daughters at Berkeley's front door.[8] The bulk of his vast estate, with slaves and stocks thereon, fell to the first-born, Benjamin V.

Of such baronial character and means was the ancestry of Colonel Benjamin V, who lay dying of the gout even while his fields were being prepared for the year's great crop of tobacco. The Harrison family was now in comparatively straitened circumstances although up until his very last hours the Colonel had won very nearly every battle. Nearly fifty years ago, this Benjamin, a youth of stalwart frame, had returned home from William and Mary College following an argument with one of his professors. Further schooling appeared of no consequence, however, for upon his father's death that summer—the year was 1745—he turned to the supervision of a vast estate. Attaining his majority about 1748 (the actual year of his birth is lost to history), he married Elizabeth Bassett of Eltham, "a niece of the sister of Mrs. Washington and noted for her uncommon beauty."[9] Benjamin V took his seat in the House of Burgesses as delegate from Charles City County in the fall of that year and until his resignation in 1775, when he was serving in the Continental Congress, he was invariably reelected.[10]

The trend toward rebellion, previously indicated in his grandparent, Benjamin III, reappears in the present master of Berkeley. The Sugar Act, the Stamp Act of 1765 passed by Parliament, and the later depredations of the iron-fisted Lord Dunmore, the royal Governor, naturally provoked conflicting shades of dissent. A colonel of militia and a Burgess of influential connections, Harrison added a famous name to those who framed taxation protests and organized Virginia's Committee of Correspondence and the Non-Importation League. The views of Colonel Ben Harrison were not as radical as those of Patrick Henry or Richard Henry Lee but were highly respected. On the preamble of the ballot which listed the names of delegates to the First Continental Congress, Peyton Randolph (Harrison's brother-in-law) was nominated to preside in Congress, Henry and Lee to display the eloquence for which they were renowned, George Washington to command the army, Harrison "to utter plain truths."[11] Virginia thus made known her assurance that her great men would be foremost and the assignments were filled as indicated. While Randolph filled the President's chair, Harrison's tongue and temper and his "many pleasantries," according to John Adams, helped to steady a groping Congress.[12] Respect for the Colonel's moderation and conciliatory views brought him the chairmanship of Foreign Affairs, Marine Affairs, the Board of War, and Militia. Friend and supporter of Washington, Colonel Harrison was named official correspondent for the Congress with the General in the field. Harrison also served as chairman of the Committee of the Whole which debated the Declaration of Independence and reported that document as agreed to. His jest which accompanied the Signing has often been repeated in the history books.[13]

Affairs at Berkeley did not flourish during his absence. The Colonel's oldest son, Benjamin VI, was serving with the Southern army as paymaster-general; Carter Bassett, the second son, was in his early teens; William Henry Harrison, youngest in a family of seven, including four daughters, was not yet of school age. Resigning from the Third Congress, in 1778 Colonel Harrison regained his seat in the Virginia House of Burgesses, defeating Thomas Jefferson for the Speakership. Jefferson was made Governor and then the war came close to Virginia. Throughout most of the year 1780, the depredations of Colonel Banastre Tarleton and Lord Cornwallis, as they swept through the Carolinas, were draining the Colony of men, money, and arms; in December, finally, when the enemy threatened from below, the Virginia Assembly nominated Harrison as special agent to seek instant assistance from Congress. Harrison removed his family to a place of safety—for Berkeley lay directly on the land and water routes to Richmond, the infant capital—then rode once more to Philadelphia.[14]

Invasion came first, however, from the fleet of the traitor Benedict Arnold, then dropping anchor in Chesapeake Bay. Early in January, Arnold landed a detachment of Hessians and American loyalists at Westover, near Berkeley, and hastened to Richmond to plunder warehouses where powder was stored. Returning then to Berkeley he paid his respects to a Signer. The mansion was dismantled of family portraits, furniture and wardrobes which the soldiers heaped upon a bonfire blazing in the backyard. Grazing cattle were made targets for muskets; forty negroes and all the horses were stolen. The loss to Colonel Harrison was very considerable at this difficult time; his house and furniture were so damaged, according to a document of 1785, that he did not resume his residence there "until January last."[15]

The Harrisons were spared an immediate return to bare walls and empty rooms. Within the borders of the Colonel's several plantations were other homes and other branches of the family resided along the James. In the fall of 1781, Colonel Harrison succeeded Thomas Nel-

Benjamin Harrison V, Signer of the Declaration of Independence.

From a portrait in the State Capitol, Richmond, Virginia.

From a portrait attributed to Chester Harding in the possession of Elizabeth Irwin Harrison Buckner,

From a painting by Thomas Sully, Jr.

William Henry Harrison.

This painting hangs in the Union League Club of Philadelphia.

son, Jr., resigned, as Governor and made his home at the executive mansion at Richmond, being elected to two full terms thereafter. Returning to Berkeley in 1785 he attempted to resume his seat in the House but was defeated by young John Tyler of Greenway. Harrison expressed some bitterness over this slight but at once took up his residence in near-by Surry County, where he maintained an estate, and triumphed in the local election held there three weeks later. Reentering the House, he was elected Speaker and was successful in the ensuing campaigns in his own county. Following the last election in which his name was submitted, April 21, 1791,[16] he took to his bed for the last time, directing that some medicine be prepared. A faithful domestic brought it to him, sobbing: "Here, sir, is the medicine." "And here, Molly, will soon be a dead man," was the Colonel's rejoinder.[17] Upon his death, April 24, his rival John Tyler succeeded to his seat in the House.

Time and political change, reaching over half a century, could not have devised a more striking coincidence than the presidential succession of 1841 when William Henry Harrison, the son of Benjamin V, was replaced upon his untimely death by the son of John Tyler. Later events also proved that of Virginia's first flight of great statesmen born in those early years, only Colonel Ben Harrison and Richard Henry Lee, a third cousin, left descendants who would add luster to the family name.

William Henry Harrison had been born at Berkeley on February 9, 1773, in the midst of a colonial boycott on tea and much revolutionary talk. Of his early adventures very little is known but at least there was swimming and good fishing in near-by Kimadges Creek and the River James, and good horses in the stable to ride. He undertook his first studies in a detached brick building at Berkeley. Indicative of the English mode of construction, two of these houses were erected on either side of the mansion; one being used as an office or school and to accommodate an overflow of guests from the manor, the other encompassing kitchen, pantry, storeroom and servants' quarters. From this kitchen, platters of food were carried to the mansion dining table by means of stairs and an underground passage. In the building to the south, the "Bachelor's House," Benjamin VI, Carter Bassett, William Henry and their sisters received instruction from private tutors. After the happy easy life at Berkeley was broken off by Benedict Arnold's raid, William Henry for a time attended Brandon School, an adjunct of another Harrison estate, Lower Brandon on the James. Lower Brandon, like Berkeley, was the seat of a provincial, aristocratic gentry, the home of Speaker Nathaniel Harrison of the Virginia Council, son of a descendant of Benjamin II. Lower Brandon still retains its standing as one of the finest houses in Prince George County, on the lower side of the James.[18]

The question of a higher education for William Henry arose when he reached his fourteenth year. The war was over and his older brother, Benjamin, had joined the mercantile firm of Willing & Morris in Philadelphia, while Carter Bassett Harrison, later a member of Congress, was studying for the law at William and Mary. The youngest of the family appeared inclined for neither of these pursuits. Possibly because he indicated some interest in natural history, William Henry, whose sympathies for the weak and suffering were marked, was persuaded to prepare for the study of medicine. And so in the fall of 1787, Massa Billy Harrison, as the plantation negroes knew him, took the stagecoach for Hampden Sidney College in far-off Prince Edward County.

Hampden Sidney, then a struggling little log college, was selected rather than William and Mary inasmuch as the fame of a local practitioner had made it the recognized training ground for future physicians.[19] The stagecoach journey over old Plank Road occupied the greater part of two days but in return for a payment of only four shillings, a "hot diett" and lodging "with featherbed and clean sheet" were available at an inn along the way.[20] Arriving at Hampden Sidney, on the edge of a pine grove, the youth applied himself to the study of rhetoric, geography, history, mathematics, Greek and Latin. He assisted in founding a Literary Society, but indicated a great passion for military history. According to his own testimony he read the "ponderous work of Rollin" three times before he was seventeen years old, a considerable labor in the aggregate.[21] Charles Rollin's *Ancient History,* translated from the French, was then published in eight volumes, a total of nearly 3000 pages of unattractive type.

But William Henry did not remain long at Hampden Sidney. A Methodist revival swept over the college and the Harrisons were sound Episcopalians. Thomas Jefferson probably expressed the general sentiment when he wrote: "Hampden Sydney . . . is going to nothing owing to the religious phrensy they have inspired into the boys . . . and which their parents have no taste for."[22] William Henry attended an academy in Southampton County for a few months thereafter and sometime in 1790 entered the office of Doctor Andrew Leiper in Richmond.[23]

In Richmond, however, another uplift problem was encountered. One of the early abolitionist organizations, peculiar to the South, appealed to the boy's natural sympathies. But this "Humane Society," a group of Methodists and Quakers, was led by one Robert Pleasants, who was outspoken against Colonel Harrison's policies in the Virginia House. Benedict Arnold's theft of forty negroes from the Berkeley plantation was only fit and just punishment. Pleasants had noted in his journal, inasmuch as Colonel Harrison always opposed abolitionist measures introduced in the House.[24] To enroll the Colonel's son in the Humane Society was to pluck a brand from the burning.

The incident must have been distasteful to the master of Berkeley. So William Henry came home again, this time to be transferred to the Medical School of Pennsylvania University at Philadelphia. It was just about the time of Colonel Harrison's final victory over John Tyler that the youth took the boat for Philadelphia, and the news of his father's death awaited him as he reached the city. According to the Colonel's request he was to remain in Philadelphia to continue his studies under the guardianship of Robert Morris.[25] Morris, the noted financier of the Revolution, was a boon companion of Benjamin V in Continental Congress days.

For a short time only, William Henry attended classes in Anatomical Hall, a square brick building in Fifth Street. A legacy of 3000 acres had been granted him by his father,[26] but when his brother Benjamin wrote that no funds remained with which to continue his schooling, he cast about for a means to earn his own living.[27] He endeavored without success to find a secretarial post in the Federal service, a tiny affair which employed but few men. In August, William Henry sought out Governor Richard Henry Lee of Virginia who was then visiting the city. Lee patiently listened to his tale and suggested that he join the army, promising to secure him a commission from President Washington, a visitor at Berkeley plantation in times past. The project was executed without loss of time. "In 24 hours from the first conception of the idea of changing my profession," Harrison recollected, but a little inaccurately since he had tried to find other work before, "I was an Ensign in the 1st U. S. Reg^t of Infantry."[28]

Somehow he neglected to consult Robert Morris who learned of the business a little too late. Morris sent for the youth to come and explain, but Harrison called at the War Office on the way, secured his commission, and took the necessary oath before a judge. Then he went to his guardian to receive a few words of advice. The banker painted the prospect in dark and gloomy tones. A youth reared in luxurious surroundings was about to depart for an Indian wilderness, he remonstrated, there to encounter endless fatigue, peril and hardship. Army pay was very small, moreover, and little glory could be gained in fighting Indians. However, Morris concluded, he was going to a fine country where, if he should leave the army, he might establish himself to advantage.[29]

Still a little stirred at the prospect, for there had been reports of Indian raids and some fighting in Philadelphia newspapers that summer, Harrison entered upon his first duties as a recruiting officer, casting about for such raw material as could be obtained for $2.10 a month. The American army was then at a low ebb and enjoying its leanest years; in 1791, the regular force comprised but a single infantry regiment and an artillery battalion, the military life itself being generally despised. However, eighty men were raised in Philadelphia and on September 20 the little company started overland for Fort Pitt, later known as Pittsburgh, thence to descend the Ohio River in flatboats.[30]

Over 300 miles of rough and mountainous country, his feet swollen and calloused, Harrison toted a volume of rhetoric and his *Cicero*. Arriving at Fort Pitt about the middle of October, the men built flatboats then traced the long meandering course of "Beautiful River." Fort Washington at Cincinnati, from which an Indian expedition had recently set out, was their assigned destination.

It was a long leap for the son of the late Colonel Ben Harrison.

STUDENT OF WAR

HARRISON's introduction to army life could have been more encouraging, his entrance upon the scene made at a rather more auspicious time. The flatboats from Pittsburgh bumped the Ohio shore one dark November afternoon when, to the astonishment of the newcomers, groups of worn and terror-stricken men and women came stumbling within the walls of Fort Washington. More than 100 miles away, the expedition against the Indians had terminated in disaster; an ill-supplied and poorly-disciplined army under General Arthur St. Clair had been surprised, bewildered, and cut to pieces by fast-moving redskins. More than 600 officers and men had been killed, many of them tomahawked as they lay wounded, and of 200 women camp followers, 56 were slain. A fleet-footed woman, her red hair streaming behind her, led the flight through a wilderness of forest and brush.[1] The clothing of the survivors, Harrison recalled, was "reduced to rags . . . their countenances exhibiting strong evidence of the Privations and Sufferings encountered."[2] Three mounts had been shot from under General St. Clair before he managed to escape on a despised packhorse. The disaster which befell the American army on the morning of November 4, 1791, was known thereafter as St. Clair's Defeat.

The men had lost all their tents and baggage and there were few supplies at Fort Washington. To revive their spirits as well as to obtain necessary food the survivors broke into the village grog-shops, which caused Harrison to observe that he saw more drunken men during his first two days at the post than he had seen before in all his life. As soon as the army settled down to its daily routine, which was marked by idleness, duelling, and more drinking, Harrison discovered that he was no welcome recruit. A political angle was involved. His ensign's commission had been awarded him at the expense of the son of the senior captain who stood next in line for the promotion. Naturally, there was jealousy. The tall slim youth from Berkeley was regarded as an interloper; scornful looks greeted him as he appeared

9

on parade. With an eye to his slight frame and candid manner, the veteran soldiers forecast an early end to his military career.

One of the officers, a captain, whom Harrison recalled as a visitor once at Berkeley, proved friendly, but his advice was for the youth to resign. The captain pointed out the lack of healthy amusement to vary the dull routine of camp duty while the mortality from drinking and duelling was very high. "At least four fifths of my brother officers died from the effects of intoxication," Harrison once recalled, and he resolved to observe the rules of temperance.[3]

Duelling also was so prevalent among the officers that it is difficult to see how the young ensign managed to escape its perils but "a short experience in the army convinced me that fighting a duel was not an undoubted test of true courage." Even desperate duels, Harrison observed, were occasionally fought by men who never would have been chosen to lead a "forlorn hope."[4] Nor did the youth view the custom as in any way honorable. After witnessing a sorrowful scene at the bedside of a dying officer who whispered a few last words of forgiveness to his triumphant and unashamed slayer, Harrison vowed to take no part whatsoever in the pastime. Thus were disposed of two potential problems. An early army friend later recalled another factor which helped to shape the ensign's dutiful attitude. "Though of an age peculiarly weak against such temptations, he was strengthened to successful resistance by an unquenchable thirst for knowledge." Up with the sun, Harrison thumbed his worn volume of rhetoric and his *Cicero,* picked up what history books he could find and read several treatises on military tactics. These last had been the property of an artillery officer slain in the recent battle. Duelling forsworn, Harrison managed to win respect from his "uniform urbanity and kindness."[5]

These virtues were indeed praiseworthy but the grim-faced regulars, many of them veterans of the Revolution, waited to see what might happen when the young ensign conducted his first march to an exterior post. General St. Clair had constructed two outposts during the fall campaign—Fort Hamilton, twenty-five miles to the north, and Fort Jefferson, which lay forty-five miles farther on. The November weather had turned cold and wet, and a considerable number of officers being laid up, Ensign Harrison, although not yet nineteen years of age, was selected to lead a detail of twenty men and a packhorse train carrying supplies to Fort Hamilton. The detachment climbed the hills back of Cincinnati, forded a creek and found shelter for the night in the deserted cabin of a settler slain by Indians.[6] No savages were sighted—they had seized enough loot from the beaten army to satisfy temporary wants—and Harrison's little command reached Fort Hamilton in good order and accomplished a safe return. Pleased with the ensign's attention to duty, the General rewarded him with a public commendation, indicating a desire to see him succeed.

Two other winter marches in which Harrison took part were actual tests of fortitude. As the successor of General St. Clair, who departed early in January to report to President Washington, General James Wilkinson of Maryland, a bustling brigadier, planned an active winter. Toward the last of the month he assembled some mounted militia for the purpose of recovering the lost equipment at St. Clair's Defeat, and further planned to destroy an Indian town several miles farther on. Harrison set out on foot with the regulars, the mounted militia following them the next day. Rain and freezing nights converted a soft, deep snow into a sharp crust which jammed uncomfortably into the tops of the soldiers' leggings. Icy winds blew, the frost nipped fingers and toes. At night the men slept beside burning log-heaps with their packs or saddles as pillows. When one of them, while asleep, moved his head from his saddle his long hair, tied in a cue, was frozen into the ground.[7]

The march to Fort Jefferson consumed nearly seven days. As supplies were rapidly diminishing, Wilkinson decided to abandon the expedition against the Indian town and sent the regulars back to Fort Washington. The mounted militia rode on to the scene of defeat. When they returned about ten days later, Harrison heard further details of the ferocious carnage and massacre. Miles from the battle-ground the militia had sighted the first rectangular mounds in the snow; farther on an area of forty acres was thickly covered. Some of the bodies had been disturbed by wolves and panthers but a greater mutilation was the handiwork of savages. Limbs and organs had been torn from bodies, stakes "as thick as a person's arm" had been driven into the women. The militia dug a large pit in the frozen ground and all bodies "exposed to view or . . . conveniently found" were laid to rest.[8] Indians who trailed the detachment upon its return made a surprise attack on Fort Jefferson but were beaten off.

Forts Hamilton and Jefferson were separated by a three-days' march in wintry weather and Wilkinson decided to locate a new outpost between the two. Early in March, Harrison was among a detachment of 200 regulars and militia which encamped upon the chosen site of Fort St. Clair, near the present city of Eaton in southwestern Ohio. The weather again turned cold which rendered the task of guard duty, necessarily maintained without tents or campfires, "particularly severe."[9] Ensign Harrison commanded a guard every other night for three weeks and completed his duty in good health and spirits although there were others, seemingly more robust, who were victims of pneumonia and pleurisy. The veteran soldiers, observing this fortitude, conceded that the ensign had passed the final test.

All was not marching and standing guard that winter; on three occasions, by rioting against the village shopkeepers, the soldiers created disorder and damage in the town. Returning from Fort St. Clair, General Wilkinson attempted to take matters in hand. Orders were issued that any private found drunk outside the walls of the fort would receive fifty lashes on the spot, and properly to enforce this edict, Ensign Harrison was selected to lead a patrol through the village "at irregular Hours."[10]

Harrison dutifully followed these instructions, but with a little too much zeal when he ordered the punishment for two army artificers, makers of powder and ball. One offender received fifty strokes and his companion ten when he tried to interfere. To the embarrassment of General Wilkinson, the artificers hired "two rascally lawyers" who obtained a warrant for the ensign's arrest. Wilkinson promptly issued an order which exempted artificers from punishment and forbade the service of the warrant within the walls of the fort, but the local magistrate, Judge William Goforth, failed to sympathize with the General and instructed his court officials to arrest the ensign wherever found. The deputy sheriff who attempted the task, according to the account of that day, "was promptly knocked down by the hardy young soldier, who, coming to his senses, subsequently delivered himself up, was soundly scolded and locked in McHenry's tavern for twenty-four hours . . . spent in Jollification with some boon Companions."[11] Wilkinson considerately summed up in this wise:

"As the Corps of Artificers are in General extremely seditious, I did not conceive the occasion rendered it necessary for me to offer further violence to the feelings of Mr. Harrison, one of the best disposed, & most promising Young Gentlemen in the Army."[12]

Actual solace for the ensign developed as an assignment as escort of General Wilkinson's wife and three sons who were returning to school in Philadelphia.[13] June 13, 1792, flatboats carrying the official party and a detail of troops started up the Ohio and arrived at Pittsburgh in about three weeks' time. At Fort Fayette, recently built, Harrison reported to the army's new commander-in-chief, General Anthony Wayne, a stern-visaged Revolutionary hero nominated by President Washington to vanquish the Ohio tribes. His first command to Ensign Harrison:

"You will please to proceed with the Lady and family of General Wilkinson to Philadelphia . . . taking particular care to inquire for the best and *safest* roads . . ."[14]

The Indian troubles which brought Mad Anthony Wayne to the command of the army had been chronic ever since the Revolution when the British transacted a separate peace without informing their savage allies that the fighting was over. "In that war," recounted Chief Tecumseh of the Shawnee tribe, "our father was thrown on his back by the Americans, and our father took them by the hand without our knowledge."[15] Certain excuses were made. A Canadian historian had suggested "Timidity, or oversight, or a feeling of helplessness" as reasons why the British ignored the Indians in making peace.[16] But just as long as the savages kept on fighting, a buffer state between Canada and the Ohio River would serve the Empire well.

Encouragement toward tribal unity, guns and ammunition for hunting, and presents in token of friendship were extended by the British. Three notorious Tories, Colonel Alexander McKee, Captain Matthew Elliott, and the renegade Simon Girty, were attached to the British payroll as Indian agents and interpreters. The post-war years were bloody. Scores of flatboats bearing immigrants were raided, hundreds of lonely cabins pillaged, and the wives and children of slain settlers made captives. At the outset the Indian peril was underestimated and insufficient preparation made to meet it until the defeat of General St. Clair served as a final warning that savage prowess was not to be despised. For weeks President Washington debated the problem. In the end the ambitious General Wilkinson was passed over and Mad Anthony Wayne, who considered the Indians to be far more dangerous than redcoats, was ordered to discipline a new army. Congress authorized an increase in force to 5414 men, offering bounties for new enlistments, and detachments of soldiers were brought from Fort Washington to Pittsburgh where rigid training was commenced.

Harrison returned from Philadelphia in August to find the nucleus of four regiments, or Sub-Legions, encamped about Fort Fayette. As a member of the First Regiment, Harrison was assigned to the First Sub-Legion, of which Lieutenant John Whistler, ancestor of a famous artist, was a fellow-member. Two young officers later known to history as explorers, Ensign Meriwether Lewis and Lieutenant William Clark, were also with the Legion, and Harrison struck up a lasting friendship with Solomon Van Rensselaer of Albany, a young lieutenant of dragoons.[17]

But for the first time since he had joined the army, Harrison began to taste the stern rudiments of drill. Mad Anthony Wayne, renowned as a hard taskmaster in the Revolution, had much green material for his officers to work upon. "The practicising was all the time, sir," complained a private, "and hang the play we could take out of it."[18] Harrison paid strict attention to duty and hopefully awaited a promotion. It came, by chance, in this wise. One evening a quarrel waxed warm in the tent of Captain Ballard Smith of the First Sub-Legion. Smith's mistress snatched up pistols and threatened to shoot a sergeant who was present. There was no shooting but the captain was found guilty of conduct unbecoming an officer and a gentleman.[19] Ensign Harrison, upon whom Wayne had a watchful eye, received the captain's command by brevet and a lieutenant's commission followed during the winter.

Meanwhile, the army moved down the river to a site called Legionville where the men waged sham battles and skirmished in the snow. Granted a furlough, Harrison revisited Richmond and Berkeley to find that his mother, Elizabeth Bassett Harrison, esteemed for her kindness and benevolence, had recently died. The second parental tie with Berkeley broken, the Lieutenant decided to link his entire future with the West. In March, 1793, he transferred his legacy of 3000 acres to his brother Benjamin, receiving in exchange a tract of land in Kentucky and notes for 1500 pounds.[20]

When Harrison rejoined Wayne's Legion late in May it was encamped near Fort Washington, the most pretentious army the West had yet seen. Nearly 3000 troops were on the ground or at the several posts, and twenty boatloads of hay had been brought down the river for the use of the dragoons.

The Lieutenant resumed the daily round of drill at the camp which Wayne had named Hobson's Choice. An appointment greatly prized came in June when he was named Wayne's third aide-de-camp. Not only the honor but the extra stipend was welcome. There were other mouths to feed. As aide to the General, Harrison received a major's pay and emoluments, or $64 a month, four rations, and $12 for forage. To help in fulfilling his important new duties the Lieutenant purchased two fine horses, an investment taxing upon the purse, yet only mounts "of great strength, activity & fleetness," in Harrison's own words, would answer for that service.[21]

Throughout the summer the army marked time at Fort Washington while Wayne awaited the result of a peace conference held with the allied tribes. The delay was protracted. Three American commissioners had expected to meet the Indians at Sandusky, west of Cleveland, in June but through the intervention of British agents they were obliged to proceed across Lake Erie to Amherstburg, in Upper Canada, where late in July they lodged at the home of Captain Matthew Elliott. The tribes were assembled on the Maumee River, the Miami of the Lakes, near the present site of Toledo, from which written and verbal messages came. Simon Girty, a large quill pierced through his nose, held forth as interpreter:

"Are you fully authorized, by the United States, to continue and firmly to fix on the Ohio River, as the boundary between your people and ours? . . .

"If you seriously design to make a firm and lasting peace, you will immediately remove all your people from our side of the river."[22]

After some days of unsatisfactory debate, conducted through runners and interpreters, the Americans received a final answer which stipulated that justice would be done only when the Ohio River was made the western boundary for the whites.

Autumn was fast approaching, meanwhile, yet General Wayne could do little but break out roads, keep the outposts well supplied, and drill his men. Late in September came a letter from Secretary of War Knox. Efforts for peace, wrote the Secretary, had "failed under circumstances which leave nothing for us to expect but war."[23] The army began to anticipate stirring events. Wayne promptly sent for General Charles Scott of Kentucky to bring on two regiments of mounted volunteer riflemen and without further waiting, on October 7, 1793, the Legion set out for the Indian country, encamping seven days later on a creek beyond Fort Jefferson.[24] Scott and the Kentuckians arrived on the 24th but with them came a dispatch bearer from Secretary Knox. On no account would President Washington risk a defeat during a season when supplies and forage were difficult to obtain; the army was to halt its advance and take up winter quarters. The volunteer Kentuckians turned back disappointedly while the regulars hewed out sufficient space, in the midst of giant elm and walnut trees, for a sizable stockade. Log huts were erected for the officers and a comfortable house for the General and his aids.

An epidemic of duelling infested the camp during the late fall and winter when the troops were less active. Abiding by military tradition, General Wayne made no attempt to check the practice. "There were more duels in the Northwestern army between 1791 and 1795," Harrison bore witness, "than ever took place in the same length of time and amongst so small a body of men."[25] A general favorite in the army, he continued to remain aloof from the code. Late in December Wayne stirred up some action by leading a thousand volunteers to the scene of St. Clair's Defeat. Harrison rode beside his General over a lonely route extending northwesterly about twenty-five miles through a region which is still thinly settled. The detachment arrived on Christmas Day to find that the bodies buried by Wilkinson's militia nearly two years before had been disinterred by the savages and the bones were strewn about so thickly that the men had to scrape them together before they could pitch their tents.[26]

Six hundred skulls were collected, the rite of burial solemnized by a salute from four of St. Clair's field-pieces found hidden in hollow logs and the creek. The troops erected a rugged stockade of logs which was christened Fort Recovery. Leaving there a garrison of 200 men, Wayne returned in January to the camp which he had named Greenville. The rest of the winter passed quietly. In February Harrison ushered in a delegation of Indian chiefs who solemnly complained of the army's warlike conduct and suggested a truce. There could be no basis for a truce, Wayne replied, until the tribes had surrendered all whites held prisoners. During the spring the British were reported building an outpost at the Maumee Rapids, well within the present Ohio border, and in June the savages launched a furious attack upon Fort Recovery to be beaten back after three days of fighting. Apparently the war was on. General Wayne dictated an order for Scott to bring up his mounted Kentuckians.

Late in July, Scott arrived with 700 men and reported that 900 more were making forced marches to catch up. Little time was wasted in getting started. On the 28th, 3000 regulars and Kentuckians under Wayne, Wilkinson and Scott headed northward into the heart of the Indian country; passing by Fort Recovery they crossed the St. Marys River where a small outpost was erected to accommodate a garrison and the sick. The rest of the Kentuckians coming up, the army cut through "intolerable thick woods and . . . almost impassable defiles," and swung toward the Auglaize River which traced a southerly course from its juncture above with the Maumee.[27]

Harrison often recalled this march in later years as it served as a valuable object lesson in wilderness campaigning. Wayne, he noted, exercised constant vigilance to guard against surprise, his "long flexible columns in files which enabled him to penetrate the woods with facility and to present a very extended front . . . on every point" while mounted spies and guides reconnoitered the country ahead and about in every direction.[28] Sweating copiously beneath the

August sun, the troops cut roads through trees and brush, and bridged swamps to accommodate the wagon train; nightly, at the scene of every encampment, scores of trees were felled and a log breastwork erected to cover the entire army. Harrison was continually occupied as dispatch bearer, maintaining contact with Generals Wilkinson and Scott, and paying sharp heed to the commands of General Wayne for whom he evinced great admiration.

The weather grew extremely warm, good drinking water scarce, the stings of long black flies and great swarms of mosquitoes "very troublesome." Officers who kept journals of the campaign recorded advances of only ten and twelve miles a day.

Near the juncture of the Auglaize and Maumee Rivers the country grew extraordinarily rich and fertile; fruit trees and Indian gardens were increasingly numerous and cornfields skirted the bank of the river for miles. The tribesmen had fled this abundance for the shelter of the new British fort at the Rapids. Wayne loaded wagons with corn and burned the deserted villages. At the "Grand Emporium of hostile Indians," only thirty-five miles south of the present Michigan border, he erected Fort Defiance, high-water mark of American invasion.[29] The army crossed to the upper side of the Maumee, following its course northeasterly toward Lake Erie, and on August 19 reached the foot of the Rapids where a temporary work was erected to house the sick and the heavy baggage. Spies reported the enemy assembled in force only a few miles away and posted near the British fort.

Harrison summoned the officers to attend a council held in Wayne's tent that evening. The enemy would be encountered, it was expected, early next day. When the General called for ideas relative to the order of march and battle, certain differences of opinion were expressed. General Wilkinson suggested that the dragoons and mounted riflemen, instead of occupying their usual positions along the front, rear and flanks, should move in the center while the regulars bore the brunt of the attack. Wayne rejected this idea, however, and approved instead a plan submitted by Lieutenant Harrison as combining the desired qualities of "compactness and flexibility and facility of expansion."[30] An aide took down the following general order:

"The Army will March tomorrow Morning at five Oclock agreeable to the constant order of March, with this difference; That the Columns shall March two deep and in as close Order as Circumstances will permit of, being totally divested of Baggage, the Center will be left free for the Artillery and spare Ammunition."[31]

Rain prevented an early start and when the weather cleared the going was difficult. On the left as the army marched were thick woods bordered by steep ravines; on the right tall grass covered the river bottom. Two or three miles in advance of the British fort lay hundreds of fallen trees uprooted by a cyclone, the trees and grass presenting admirable cover for a thousand Indians and more than 100 British regulars and Canadian militia. As the Legion advanced along the river bank a sudden burst of rifle fire routed the mounted riflemen and dragoons in front; scurrying backward they broke into the front line of regulars who dropped back in turn several rods. A mounted officer galloped back to inform the General to whom Harrison was solicitously remarking: "I'm afraid you'll get into the fight yourself and forget to give me the necessary field orders."[32] Wayne replied that the standing order of the day was to charge the enemy with the bayonet and sent Harrison away to re-form the broken line. The shortest route to the right, the point of first attack, took the Lieutenant diagonally in front of the infantry and for a few moments he was exposed to fire from both sides "but my gallant steed bore me onward with such rapidity that I escaped unhurt."[33] He shouted an order to an officer of dragoons then galloped to the extreme left where Captain Solomon Van Rensselaer nervously awaited the command.

The dragoons recovered from their perilous confusion and charged on either side. The Kentuckians took steady aim with their long rifles. Harrison, continually dashing about the field, was chiefly concerned with keeping the lines intact. Private George Will, shot through the body, lay helpless for some moments and when he struggled to his feet at last he found himself facing Harrison. "Soldier," exclaimed the Lieutenant, "why are you not fighting with your company?" The stricken private could only point to the blood oozing from his shoes.[34]

As the Americans drove rapidly forward the Indians made an effort to turn Wayne's left flank which extended far into the woods. Little Turtle of the Miamis, the Shawnee Blue Jacket, Buckonga-helas of the Delawares, and Turkeyfoot, beloved Ottawa chief, urged on the fighting. The British leaders, McKee, Elliott, and Simon Girty, although present on the field, remained "at a respectful distance near the river."[35]

Harrison rode back to meet his General who was bringing up support for the threatened left. Driving hard at the opposing flank, Wayne cut off the retreat of the Indians and no choice remained for the savages but to head toward the river. As they gained the open sector the Kentuckians blasted wide gaps in their line. A Potawatomie leader fell, the young Shawnee Tecumseh saw his brother slain, and Chief Turkeyfoot was toppled from the rock which bears his name. Picking up speed, the Legion advanced more than two miles in seventy minutes of fighting. Then the warriors raised their dead and wounded to their shoulders and raced for the shelter of the British fort.[36]

At the gates of Fort Miami they received an object lesson in British diplomacy. Only the regulars and militia were admitted, then the doors were slammed shut in the face of the exasperated Indians. They had nowhere to go now but back to the woods and their ruined villages. Wayne halted the advance about a mile from the fort as the American killed and wounded were scattered over a considerable area of broken terrain. Throughout the rest of that day and the next the army scoured the ravines and fallen timber to pick up their wounded and missing. The bodies of 31 dead and 102 wounded were recovered but not all could be rescued in time. Harrison described the fate of one officer:

"His body was not found until (though the Wound was mortal) he had lived many Hours, and must have died with Utmost Agony. . . . He has a very young brother who is a Corporal—I take a good deal of pains to make him a Good Soldier. . . ."[37]

The Lieutenant picked up Captain Van Rensselaer who lay seriously hurt, rendered first aid and brought him into Wayne's own tent where he "nursed and watched me with the tenderness . . . of a brother."[38] The enemy loss was not quite as severe as had been suffered by the Americans but such was usually the outcome in Indian fighting.

The scenery surrounding the Rapids was described as unusually fine. According to the view of General James Wilkinson:

"The Beauty . . . which presents in one front, cannot well be concieved, the River meandering in various directions thro a natural meadow in high cultivation & of great extent . . . bounded by noble eminences, crowned with lofty timber . . . with Indian Villages scattered along the Eastern & the British flag flying upon the Western bank, after a dreary Jorney of more than 200 miles from the Ohio, thro an uncultivated Wilderness, fills the mind with the most Interesting Emotions, and affords the most pleasing recreation to the Eye. Here we beat our Drums Blowed our Trumpets and went to Bed."[39]

The fly-speck on the picture was the British outpost. A captured drummer boy revealed that the British had been supplying the Indians not only with food but with arms and ammunition. According to Harrison's recollection, Wayne had received the authority "to dispossess the intruders, if . . . necessary to the success of his operations against the Indians" but first he decided to reconnoiter. On the morning after the battle, in company with Harrison and his other aids and a corps of light infantry supporting him, the General advanced to within pistol-shot of the garrison. Harrison pointed out a gunner who held a lighted taper in the ramparts, ready to commence firing, but a British officer then appeared and ordered the light put out. Wayne lingered undisturbed to appraise the full strength of the fort. Four artillery pieces were mounted on the side toward the river, eight on the less defensible rear. Furthermore, its massive earthen parapet and a deep surrounding ditch, with horizontal pickets, "afforded no prospect of the success of an escalade," wrote Harrison, "but at the expense of valuable lives."[40] The British commander, Major William Campbell, opened up an acrimonious correspondence to which Wayne's final rejoinder was to demolish the Indian villages across the river and all the standing crops in the vicinity and even the British trading houses and Colonel McKee's residence, destroying "every thing within view of the fort . . . even under the muzzles of the guns."[41]

First the battle, then the burial. August 23, three rounds of shells from army howitzers were discharged after a "solemn Dirge."[42] The army turned back from its scene of triumph and reached Fort Defiance in four days. Wayne further strengthened the work while mounted detachments were sent to burn more Indian villages. Tracing the course of the Maumee to its juncture with the St. Marys and St. Joseph Rivers, the Legion burned the surrounding Miami towns and threw up a massive outpost which General Scott christened Fort Wayne. To erect a fort upon this ancient site, the French and Indian village of Kekionga, had been the object of the expedition led by General St. Clair.

General Scott's Kentuckians, who had volunteered only for a three-months' service, were grumbling at their stern taskmaster Wayne and before the fort was entirely completed they threatened to desert in a body. Late in October, finally, they were told they could go home. November 2 the Legion again reached Greenville where the troops resumed the daily routine of common duties, whiling away the evening hours with long discussions of the campaign. Wayne's official report of the battle, it was noted, had singled out several officers worthy of special mention including "my faithful and gallant aids-de-camp, Captains De Butts and T. Lewis, and Lieutenant Harrison, who, with the adjutant general, Major Mills, rendered the most essential service by communicating my orders in every direction, and by their conduct and bravery in exciting the troops to press for victory."[43] Major Mills, however, ventured a more specific observation before a company of officers in his tent. You all know, he stated——

"that Captains Debutts and Lewis, remained with Gen Wayne to keep him from being two much exposed from danger, and Aid-de-camp Harrison did all the riding to give orders, from the commander in chief. And where the hosted [hottest] of the action raged there we could see Harrison giving the order."

"It's my candid opinion," added the officer who took down this statement, "if he continues a military man he will be a second Washington."[44] In his first Indian campaign and battle the young lieutenant had conducted himself as a soldier.

DELEGATE TO CONGRESS

ANOTHER dull winter was in prospect but until the signing of a peace treaty with the enemy tribes it was necessary that the Legion remain embodied. Lieutenant Harrison had been hoping to receive a captain's commission and his thoughts were occupied also by a certain "Miss M" of Philadelphia whom he had met during some one of his visits to that city. November 27, 1794, while at Greenville, the Lieutenant confided his sentiments to his brother Carter, then a member of Congress. In this first letter of Harrison's anywhere to be found, the Lieutenant mentioned only a few details concerning the late campaign, confining himself almost entirely, and pardonably perhaps, to Miss M. There were difficulties of time and place, if not of fortune, in the way of his suit. His small fortune could not be considered "equal to her merit," Harrison wrote, nor could he determine when he would be able to visit Philadelphia again. But if opportunity presented itself during the coming winter, he continued——

"I shall make my addresses to Miss M. . . . If I should not succeed, I will not be vexed or mortified for I have been long enough a Soldier to have learned that there is no Disgrace in a *Well Meant & Well Conducted* enterprise, even if it should fail. . . . My Sword is almost my only patrimony—but while I wear that Sword & the livery of my Country, I will not disgrace them by owning myself inferior to any person. . . .

"There is but one way of making my decline my Purpose . . . that is to be convinced that there was some other person who could make her happier and love her more than I do—I love her so ardently I would forego my own happiness forever to contribute to hers."[1]

Since Harrison had reason to regret his small patrimony it is apparent that his beloved was the daughter of well-to-do parents in Philadelphia. But the Lieutenant was afforded no opportunity to visit the city that winter. The business of transacting a temporary truce kept Wayne and his aides snowbound at Greenville where a number of Indian delegations, ill-clothed and hungry, were welcomed and fed. In February, 1795, a preliminary truce was arrived at and Harrison took down a proclamation from General Wayne bidding "all men" to keep the peace.[2]

Not another word is to be heard of Miss M, however, nor was her identity made known. An interesting event which took place in Philadelphia during the spring was the marriage of Hetty Morris, daughter of Robert Morris, and James Markham Marshall, younger brother of John Marshall, a union which the bride's father highly approved.[3] But if Hetty Morris ever fell in love with Lieutenant Harrison, the secret was thoroughly kept.

Harrison's duties prevented him from going to Philadelphia but he made a trip to Kentucky in the spring. About the time Hetty Morris was married, the Lieutenant arrived in Lexington to obtain printed copies of General Wayne's peace proclamation and at the home of Major Peyton Short he met "a remarkably beautiful girl," Anna Tuthill Symmes.[4]

Anna Symmes, dark-eyed and sedate, had been born in Flatbrook, New Jersey, July 25, 1773, the daughter of Colonel John Cleves Symmes, who was to become an important man in Northwest Territory. Mrs. Symmes died soon after Anna's birth and when the British made New Jersey their battleground, Symmes donned an enemy uniform, placed his child on the front of his saddle and rode with her through the lines to the home of her grandparents, Henry and Phebe Tuthill of Southhold, Long Island. While Anna and an older daughter were growing up, Symmes fought in the Jersey campaigns, remarried, and served for three years in the post-war Continental Congress. In 1788, while a member of Congress, he contracted for a million acres of land between the Great and Little Miami Rivers in present-day Ohio, and received a judgeship in that country then known as Northwest Territory.[5]

Symmes's second wife, Maria Halsey, lived but a few years and his older daughter, Maria, left him to marry Major Peyton Short of Lexington. Lonely for woman's companionship, Symmes journeyed to New York in 1794 and married Susanna Livingston, sister of Judge Brockholst Livingston of that city.[6] His daughter Anna, meantime, had attended an academy in Easthampton, Long Island, and a private school in New York. Together with her father and her new step-mother, Anna came to the judge's home at North Bend, a little settlement sixteen miles west of Cincinnati, and while a new house was being completed, the two ladies visited Major and Maria Short at Lexington, Kentucky.

Before Anna had become the belle of the town, Lieutenant Harrison made her acquaintance and paid the fair newcomer civilities due. Duty soon called him back to Greenville, however, where chiefs and headmen from a dozen tribes were assembling for a grand council. Throughout the month of June the tribal delegations continued to pour in until 1100 and more redmen were assembled. Harrison struck up a few friendships among the chiefs which were to prove useful in later years for several of the red leaders dined at Wayne's own table. After several weeks of palaver, Wayne proposed a treaty confirming all previous boundary lines between the Indians and the whites but asked also for a generous additional slice of Ohio—the line extending several miles into present-day Indiana —and sizable tracts about all new forts, from Greenville to Defiance. What was left to the redmen in Ohio comprised an area equal to only a third of the present state but the chieftains finally declared themselves satisfied. They were not stupid, these Indians. Chief Little Turtle of the Miamis listed two additional tribes, called the Weas and the Eel Rivers, as separate from his own in order that each would receive an additional share of the annuities.[7] Actually, these Indians all belonged to the Miami nation. In return for the land cession, goods to the value of $20,000 were distributed among the tribes and annuities worth $9,500 were promised as yearly payments. Harrison, an interested spectator of events at Wayne's elbow, carefully studied the additional treaty provisions by which all prisoners were to be restored, private retaliation for injuries forbidden, and any future offenders on either side to be delivered up to the state. On August 3, 1795, ninety-two chiefs and twenty-seven white men, including Lieutenant Harrison, signed.[8] It became part of Harrison's peace-time army job to report infractions of the Greenville Treaty.

The business of treaty-making finally done, Harrison was again anxious to be off, this time to Fort Washington, where after borrowing the sum of $300 from an army surgeon he took command of the packhorse trains carrying supplies to the neighboring village of North Bend. At the home of Judge Symmes the bronzed Lieutenant renewed his acquaintance with little Anna and discovered that she returned his love. But when he asked John Cleves Symmes for the hand of his daughter the judge said no. Possibly as the result of the affray with the two young artificers and the deputy sheriff some scandalous tales concerning the young man's conduct had been going the rounds, and Harrison was still a mere army lieutenant. So Judge Symmes commanded him to stay away from his daughter.

William Henry Harrison.

Anna Symmes Harrison.

From paintings of about 1840—Courtesy of John Scott Harrison 4th, Esq., Helena, Montana.

From a painting by Hoyt.

William Henry Harrison, Ninth President of the United States.

Despite this stern injunction from a man of influence in Northwest Territory Harrison still contrived to meet his love and after General Wayne gave the would-be bridegroom his blessing, a runaway marriage was agreed to. November 25, Symmes mounted his horse and rode from North Bend to Cincinnati on business and upon that day also a wedding party gathered at the home of Doctor Stephen Wood, a tenant of Symmes's. Wood, who was treasurer of Northwest Territory and a justice of the peace, married William and Anna in the parlor of his log house and watched them ride away to Fort Washington.[9]

Two weeks elapsed before Harrison encountered his father-in-law. The occasion was a farewell dinner given by General Wilkinson to General Wayne, who was about to depart for Philadelphia. "How do you expect to support my daughter?" inquired the judge. Harrison fingered his scabbard. "My sword is my means of support, sir!" Symmes and the Lieutenant became more friendly, and when his first son was born, Harrison named him for the judge.[10]

As aide-de-camp to the General, Harrison naturally would be expected to accompany that officer to Philadelphia, but Wayne was quite willing to excuse him from the tour, leaving him at the fort with Anna.

The town of Cincinnati had been growing; from the cluster of twenty or thirty log cabins which Harrison discovered there in 1791, it had increased to a village of 400 souls. As peace descended upon the frontier, the importance of Fort Washington diminished. A single company only was retained as a garrison and many officers and privates, even before leaving the army, were entering the business life of the town. When Captain Jonathan Pierce received a furlough, General Wilkinson placed Harrison in command but greatly disappointed in not receiving the captaincy he wished, the Lieutenant asked permission to resign as Wayne's aide. Upon the General's return from Philadelphia Harrison wrote, July 11, 1796:

"I hope your Excellency will not think me ungrateful in soliciting your permission to resign the appointment which I have the honor to hold in your family. Judge Symmes having lately entrusted to me . . . some business . . . and the delicate situation of Mrs. Harrison's health at present—have induced me to make this application . . . The very illiberal treatment which I have met with from the Government has determined me to abandon the profession of arms entirely in a short time—but in the interim it will be extremely convenient for me to have the command of this Post."[11]

Certainly this was a very frank letter yet General Wayne, who was about to depart for Detroit, responded cordially. The General replied he was "well convinced that Mrs Harrison's delicate condition . . . requires your presence & . . . attention," but he declined to accept the suggested resignation as aide.[12] Harrison continued in command of Fort Washington and there his first child, Betsey Bassett, was born on September 29. A payment of $450 for 160 acres of land at North Bend, however, indicated a desire to make a home elsewhere and when Harrison purchased a four-room cabin on the property it was evident that a return to civil life was in prospect.[13]

Save for duties as assistant quartermaster, Harrison found little to do at a fort garrisoned according to peace-time requirements. He entertained a few delegations of Indian chiefs who were bound for Philadelphia to take the retiring President Washington by the hand. He reported the movements of suspected Spanish spies and other foreign agents then active upon the thinly settled frontier.[14] Daily he paraded his company for morning inspection within the walls of the fort. But when the long-awaited commission as captain arrived in the summer of 1797, Harrison had transferred much of his activity to the business life of the town. With a partner, James Smith, he had recently purchased a whiskey distillery on Deer Creek, commencing operations on a fairly large scale.[15] The following spring, receiving an appointment as Land Office Register, he naturally decided to resign from the army. Another appointment appeared in the offing when Colonel Winthrop Sargent, Secretary of Northwest Territory, was named Governor of Mississippi Territory, leaving the secretarial post vacant. Sargent was a good friend of Harrison's and just before taking his departure he suggested in a letter to Secretary of State Timothy Pickering that the Captain might well be named as Territorial Secretary:

"I . . . determined to deposit the public Records with a Captain Harrison, a Young Gentleman of Virginia, and of Education . . . who for seven years I believe has sustained a fair, indeed unblemished reputation as a Military officer. . . . I may venture to Vouch, that he will not betray any trust, with which Government may honour him—Indeed, I think him a very deserving young man."[16]

The post of Territorial secretary paid $1,200 a year, reckoned a very welcome sinecure. A few days after Sargent had written to Pickering, Captain Harrison addressed a letter to the Federalist leader in Congress, Robert Goodloe Harper of South Carolina, whom he had met as a land company agent in Philadelphia some years before:

"The appointment of Colo Sargent . . . will of course make a vacancy in the Secretaryship . . . to obtain this is the object of my wishes. . . . I have been seven years a soldier during which period my exertions to render service to my country have been unceasing. . . . I have in no small degree enjoyed the confidence and friendship of all three Commanders in Chief and almost of all my superior officers. . . . My friend Colo Neville (who was here a few days ago) informed me that he had engaged Mr. Ross of the Senate in my interest—and that yourself and General Morgan of the lower House had promised your assistance. . . ."[17]

The question of the succession had evidently been brewing for some time. Harrison's letter had barely time to reach Philadelphia when, on June 28, 1798, President John Adams "was pleased to appoint . . . by and with the consent of the Senate, William Henry Harrison to be Secretary of the Territory . . . Northwest of the River Ohio."[18] Governor Arthur St. Clair, who was then absent, found his former ensign in charge of affairs when he returned to Cincinnati. Duties as Secretary proved not particularly engrossing to Harrison, however, and he proved a desultory record keeper. Apparently his farm and distillery continued to occupy most of his time. In October his second child, John Cleves Symmes Harrison, was born and the Secretary advertised his horse Fearnaught for sale.

The Territory was bubbling over with politics during the Federalist rule of John Adams. Secretary Harrison and Governor St. Clair, in their political beliefs, stood at opposite poles. St. Clair was an ardent Federalist who practised an autocratic rule; his assistant a republican admirer of Vice-President Thomas Jefferson. The two men failed to get along very well[19] and Harrison's reaction to Federalist doctrine is revealed in the tale of Griffin Yeatman, a Cincinnati innkeeper:

"Some time before the election of Delegate, a captain of the army . . . at a party of gentlemen . . . uttered a violent denunciation against the Republican . . . members of Congress. This was resented by . . . Harrison who insisted upon his making an exception of the Virginia delegation . . . violent language ensued, which would have terminated in blows but for the interference of the company. . . . The Captain expressed his regret."[20]

The election of delegate to which Yeatman referred was an important event in the annals of Northwest Territory which was yet to be represented in Congress. According to the Ordinance of 1787, which inaugurated territorial jurisdiction, any territory was entitled to second-grade government as soon as its population totaled 5000 free white male inhabitants. The advance to second grade, an intermediate step toward statehood, would give the territory a council appointed by the President, an elected House, and a delegate to Congress. Disfavoring any Republican voice in the government as well as a check upon his powers, Governor St. Clair openly opposed the advance in the Northwest but he could not argue with the census nor effectively counter-attack the voice of a free people. The census indicating more than the required number of free white males, in the fall of 1799 advance to second grade was officially inaugurated in the Northwest when the first Territorial House brought members together at Cincinati from points as far distant as Detroit and the Illinois country.

The lines of cleavage, political and economic, were clearly drawn. The existing public land law, it was felt, was most unjust to the settler, favoring instead the private speculator who was able to purchase the minimum amount sold by the government, a whole section of 640 acres, then turn about and sell it in lots at a stiff advance upon the original price of two dollars. Harrison's own quarter section of land in North Bend had been obtained from Speaker Jonathan Dayton of Congress, a partner of Judge Symmes, for but little less than three dollars an acre. From the town of Chillicothe, as members of the Territorial Assembly, now came an influential group of young Republicans, Colonel Thomas Worthington, Edward Tiffin, and Nathaniel Massie, all good friends of Secretary Harrison who made room for Colonel and Mrs. Worthington in his North Bend cabin. The scheme proposed to Harrison promised that the Republicans would unite upon him as their candidate for the post of delegate if he would agree to "obtain an amelioration of the laws for the sale of the Public Land."[21]

Harrison naturally took the side of the settler and his Republican partisans and consented to run. His opponent turned out to be Arthur St. Clair, Jr., attorney general for the Territory and a man who could be counted on to do his father's bidding in Congress. Apparently the nomination of Harrison came as a surprise to the Governor. Several days prior to the election Harrison received a communication from St. Clair asking that he superintend the October distribution of Indian annuity goods at Fort Wayne, but the assignment was declined in a formally worded note which may be considered as an indication of existing feeling. "Having been solicited . . . to offer

Mrs. (Jane Irwin) William Henry Harrison, Jr.

From a painting (about 1830) in the possession of Betty and Agnes Farrar, Kansas City, Mo.

William Henry Harrison, Jr.

From a pencil sketch, the only portrait.

Both by courtesy of John Scott Harrison 4th, Esq., Helena, Montana.

Berkeley, Charles City County, Virginia.

Redrawn from a photograph in the *Virginia Magazine of History and Biography*. The porches are modern additions.

The home of General Harrison at North Bend with the Ohio River and the Cincinnati and Whitewater Canal in the foreground. It was destroyed by fire, July 25, 1858.

From an engraving by W. Woodruff for *The Ladies Repository*.

himself as a candidate for . . . Congress," Harrison replied in the third person——

"& having made known . . . his intention of serving if elected & the time fixed on for the delivery of the Goods being so late as to make it impossible for him to attend to this business in the event of a successful election, he must request the Governor to appoint some other person."[22]

Harrison added that he would be willing to undertake the business if he lost, which was not the case, although the balloting was very close, eleven votes to ten.[23]

Delegate Harrison, sharp-eyed, lean and erect, rose again and again in Congress Hall, Philadelphia, to defend his Public Land bill. A few days after his twenty-seventh birthday, on February 18, 1800, he had presented his committee report to the House. The report and bill which followed could cut the existing requirements of sale in half:

"Resolved, That all townships directed to be sold . . . shall be divided into half sections, containing . . . 320 acres each.

"Resolved, That all the said lands shall be offered . . . at public sale in tracts of 320 acres . . . *Provided,* That the same shall not be sold under the price of two dollars an acre, and that the sale shall be at the following places . . . Pittsburgh . . . Marietta . . . Chillicothe . . . Cincinnati. . . ."[24]

Other articles provided that the settler could make a down payment of only a twentieth of the full price, then a fourth part within three months, and the rest within four years. The bill was sharply attacked by Congressman Harry Lee of Virginia, son of the man responsible for Harrison's army commission, and by other eastern Federalists who believed that the land should be retained in the hands of responsible parties if not by the government. Harrison, who had watched the troubled faces of settlers at foreclosure sales, was outspoken and forceful. The present system of land purchase, he argued, benefited only the wealthy. Foreclosures among farmers who bought in installments were painfully frequent; too much money was flowing out of the West, too many settlers emigrating to Spanish possessions along the Mississippi. Harrison's pockets were filled with petitions from distant settlers which the delegate presented at moments deemed most opportune.[25]

The House responded agreeably and passed the bill as written but the more conservative Senate, predominantly Federalist, decreed that only half the public lands should be sold in half sections of 320 acres, the rest in whole sections as before. Harrison and Albert Gallatin, managers of the bill for the House, closeted themselves with the Senate leaders and endeavored to thrust open the half-shut door. Their efforts were unavailing, Harrison reported; "all my exertions aided by some of the ablest members . . . of the lower house . . . were not sufficient to induce the Senate to recede."[26] But there was good reason, on the whole, to be pleased with the measure. "This law promises to be the foundation of a great increase of population and wealth to our country," he observed in a message to his constituents. Had it been delayed a year or two longer there was reason to believe the greater portion of Ohio would have been gobbled up by wealthy speculators. The Harrison Land Law was long and fulsome in its provisions; as published in the *Western Spy,* reaching lonely firesides, it became the settlers' favorite reading matter.

Although the Land Law was a measure of far-reaching importance in the Territory, another which Harrison introduced had a considerably greater bearing on his own political future in the West. Three more judges were desired in Northwest Territory, or possibly a division of that huge and unwieldy jurisdiction. Court was held so seldom in distant areas that criminals readily found sanctuary. Some of the delegates to the first Territorial Assembly at Cincinnati had travelled nearly a thousand miles over bad roads, going and coming, in order to fulfill their brief duties. To remedy these conditions Harrison asked first that Congress authorize the additional judgeships but because of the partisan nature of appointments the bill reached a deadlock. The delegate then withdrew it in favor of another measure which asked that Northwest Territory be divided into two parts, the line of division to be drawn due north from the juncture of the Great Miami and the Ohio Rivers, which, in fact, is the existing boundary between Ohio and Indiana.[27]

Among a number of ideas already formulated on the subject of division were those advocated by Governor St. Clair who was striving to shape legislative matters from the Territorial seat at Cincinnati. In a letter to Delegate Harrison the Governor had advocated division into three parts with Cincinnati as the capital of the middle district and Marietta of the eastern. Any other plan of division, St. Clair insisted, "would ruin Cincinnati."[28] But Governor St. Clair, who spent most of his time at his home in western Pennsylvania, was unconvincing in the role of a Cincinnati advocate. In a letter to

Secretary of State Pickering his greater interest was revealed. The Federalist administration, wrote St. Clair, "should procure a division of the Territory, so as to prevent any part from becoming an independent State; because . . . they would oppose the views of the administration."[29] St. Clair also confided his thoughts to Senator James Ross, Pennsylvania Federalist, but he urged Ross to include Cincinnati in the western division of the Territory, Governor St. Clair, in short, favored whatever plan of division would best checkmate the Republicans, preferably a tripartite scheme which would leave the three sectors small and weak and of no real political influence despite a preponderance of Jeffersonian sentiment. "A multitude of indigent and ignorant people," the Federalist governor set forth, "are but ill qualified to form a constitution and government for themselves. . . . The people think the division . . . would little retard their becoming a state . . . they expect that both the power & influence would come into their hands."[30]

That these views were really private was indicated in St. Clair's request that his sentiments be concealed from Colonel Thomas Worthington, who was then visiting Philadelphia. Secretary Pickering, however, permitted Harrison to read his letter and the delegate passed along the information for what it was worth. Naturally Republican sentiment was aroused. Harrison, who was not unsupported, arose but twice to answer critics of the bill and to read petitions from lonely inhabitants of the Illinois country.[31] March 31, the House passed the measure to which was affixed a provision vacating all the Territorial offices, thus disposing of Governor St. Clair. But to this the Governor's friends in the Senate strenuously objected. Harrison attended a number of committee conferences before the two Houses finally agreed to two-part division. A slight change was made in the boundary line which was pushed a few miles westward to the mouth of the Kentucky River, thence extending northeasterly to Fort Recovery and then due north. But as soon as the eastern division (Northwest Territory) became a state (Ohio), then the Great Miami line would apply. The town of Vincennes on the Wabash River was designated the capital of the western half, Indiana Territory, and Chillicothe, now occupying a central position, was made the new capital of the Territory of the Northwest.[32] Save for the loss of the provision which would have ousted Governor St. Clair it was a highly satisfactory transaction for Harrison and his friends from Chillicothe. "W. H. Harrison from *our* territory," wrote a Northwest army man, "has come forward very handsomely. . . ."[33]

The ensuing stroke of business was the appointment of a governor for Indiana. The sponsor of the division measure appeared to be the logical candidate. President Adams, on the eve of adjournment of Congress, nominated Harrison although the delegate demurred. Friends in Ohio had forecast that Governor St. Clair would be ousted within another year and his successor might well be Harrison. Before coming to a final decision on the matter, the delegate joined Mrs. Harrison who was visiting the widow of Benjamin Harrison VI in Richmond. There and at Berkeley the coming presidential election was a leading subject for discussion, the expectation being that Thomas Jefferson would surely be elected.

Harrison, who had been an occasional dinner guest of President Adams, had also made the acquaintance of Vice President Jefferson that spring, although the only record of their meeting was the latter's plan for a town so constructed, according to its designer, that it would be free from pestilential diseases.[34] An appointee of John Adams, Harrison took no active part in the campaign but was advised by Virginia kinsmen that Jefferson, when elected, would be likely to retain him in office. During the course of the summer he sent his acceptance to Secretary Pickering later notifying his friends in Ohio that if they so wished he was willing to abandon his "new dignity."[35] Vincennes on the Wabash was a long distance away, the governorship of Ohio a possibility still.

Harrison's third child, Lucy Singleton, was born at Richmond in September, 1800. Several weeks later the family set out on a stage-coach and keelboat journey for the Northwest, pausing at North Bend to collect the few family goods. Mrs. Harrison and the children remained at Major Short's in Lexington for the winter, while the Governor, following the Christmas holiday, went on to Vincennes.[36]

IV

A NEW FRONTIER

POST VINCENNES was now the capital of a jurisdiction extending from Northwest Territory to Wisconsin, the white population in this vast region numbering 5,640, with about 200 slaves. Four-fifths of the settlers classified as white were an intermixture of French and Indian blood, although half-breeds living in the woods were called redmen, in accordance with circumstances of birth. Nearly all the settlements in Indiana had been founded by the French in their explorations along the various waterways to the shores of the Great Lakes. As yet there were no good roads in the Territory. Indian trails and wide buffalo traces linked Vincennes with Kaskaskia and Cahokia in the Illinois country and with Clark's Grant, settled by Revolutionary veterans, in the East. However, the trails were a convenience in dry weather. The distance by land to Cincinnati, for example, was 200 miles; by the water route nearly 600.

The scenery about Vincennes, on the east bank of the Wabash, was often described as beautiful. The town was situated on the edge of a broad prairie bordered by uplands and a vast forest with near-by Indian mounds rising nearly 100 feet high. On the river bank, by the church of St. Francis Xavier, were the remains of old Fort Sackville, captured by Colonel George Rogers Clark of the Revolution. About 400 houses, of plain logs and bark, or clapboarded and whitewashed, occupied neat rows between the Wabash and the communal gardens back of the town. Wheat, corn, and tobacco were planted; hemp, hops and a variety of fruits were plentiful, and the life of the French settlers an indolent one. Over a well-trodden buffalo trace winding through the forest to the Falls of Ohio (near Louisville), the post-rider came from Lexington, Kentucky, once a week.[1]

Harrison arrived at Vincennes early in January, 1801, bringing a negro servant from Berkeley, and was lodged at the home of Colonel Francis Vigo, an elderly frontier patroon who had offered the builder of his house twenty extra guineas for its completion before the Governor came. Harrison accepted the use of the great parlor, richly panelled, the floor paved with alternating blocks of ash and walnut.

33

Inaugurating his duties on January 10, at the little two-story capitol, Harrison swore in William Clark, the Chief Justice, who in turn swore in the youthful Governor, also Secretary John Gibson, a veteran of the Revolution, and Judges Henry Vanderburgh and John Griffin. The five men then sat "for the purpose of adopting . . . laws" and Harrison's long rule over Indiana Territory was begun.[2] A number of routine measures—organization of the lower courts and militia, and the altering of county lines—were enacted. About the middle of February the Governor rejoined his family in Kentucky.

In May when he returned the fruit trees were in blossom, the prairie red with strawberries. The wife of Judge Symmes, who accompanied Mrs. Harrison on the journey by keelboat, was thrilled by the outlook. "This beautiful country, which I cannot sufficiently admire . . . would be injured by a comparison with any other," she wrote her step-daughter, Maria Short. "On one side we have the delightful Wabash, on the other the most enchanting landscape of elegant scenery."[3]

The inviting prospect was marred, however, by the rapacity of French and American traders, the drunkenness and degredation of the near-by tribes. As Superintendent of Indian Affairs, ex-officio, in the Territory, Harrison was early visited by a number of chiefs who enumerated many wrongs. They found the Governor accessible and sympathetic. In July, Harrison sent a lengthy report of conditions to Secretary of War Henry Dearborn, in charge of the Indian Office now removed to Washington. In a letter sprinkled with such phrases as "unprovoked murder . . . cruel deed . . . atrocity . . . these horrors" indignation stemmed from every page. The Indian chiefs, Harrison ·wrote—

"all profess and I believe that most of them feel a friendship for the United States . . . but they make heavy complaints of ill-treatment on the part of our Citizens. They say that their people have been killed—their lands settled on—their game wontonly destroyed—& their young men made drunk & cheated of the peltries which formerly procured the necessary articles of Cloathing, arms and ammunition to hunt with. Of the truth of these charges I am well convinced."

Harrison enumerated murders done, encroachments by hunters, the enormous "mischiefs produced by . . . Whiskey," and other "causes of irritation." Tribal intercourse with the white people had led to an "astonishing annual decrease of these unhappy beings." After trading their peltries for whiskey, the redmen, in a frenzy, would stab each other. Four were found dead in the street one morning.

Among the three small tribes nearest Vincennes, the Weas, Piankeshaws, and Eel Rivers, Harrison reported, only a few chiefs remained. The whites also suffered, although mildly in comparison. Resentful when peltries and whiskey were gone, the savages would break down fences and indiscriminately slay livestock. Harrison once ordered out the local militia to restore order but he held his own people responsible for these crimes. "Whether something ought not to be done to prevent the reproach which will attach to the American Character by the extermination of so many human beings," Harrison protested in his humane way, "I beg leave most respectfully to submit to the Consideration of the President. That this exterpation will happen no one can doubt."[4]

The Governor, young and idealistic, had national honor in mind. As an initial corrective Harrison issued a few prohibitory edicts and thereby gained the confidence of the Indian chiefs. In May, upon his return, all persons were forbidden to hunt, settle, or survey on Indian lands, and all trespassers were ordered at once to remove. In July, when the tribesmen convened at Vincennes for a council, the sale of liquor was forbidden to any Indian within a mile of the town and was banned altogether on Sundays. Harrison also warned against the bartering of liquor for an Indiain's common necessities, his clothes and weapons, for many were almost naked. Before the hunting season opened, traders were ordered to keep out of the Indian hunting camps.[5] The frontier watched and waited, meanwhile. Harrison could revoke traders' licenses for any infractions of these rules but to punish a white man for murdering an Indian, or even to keep him in jail while awaiting trial, was indeed difficult. Although the laws provided punishment for white and Indian offenders alike, Harrison observed in an early communication to the government, there was a wide difference in their execution. Of a party of three slayers who fled to Kentucky, two escaped the hands of the sheriff sent to extradite them while the third, arrested and brought back, broke jail in Vincennes. Harrison also reported the case of a settler who had cudgeled an Indian to death. "There were strong doubts that a jury could . . . be procured that would convict him, although the evidence was indisputable; such was the delusion under which the white inhabitants labored with respect to the crime of murdering an Indian."[6] The jury naturally freed the prisoner. Harrison's indignation would not be spent, however; after ten years in office he was still striving to prevent and to punish such crimes.

Taking advantage of the fine prospect afforded the agriculturalist,

Harrison occupied himself pleasantly during his first summer at Vincennes in clearing a 300-acre farm purchased, it appears, from Colonel Vigo. "I am much pleased with this country," he wrote in a proselyting vein to James Findlay of Cincinnati. "Nothing can exceed its beauty and fertility."[7] But until he could be assured of reappointment by President Jefferson two years hence, he postponed plans to build. In company with some regulars stationed at Fort Knox three miles up the river, the Governor would spend an occasional afternoon "making war upon the partridges, grouse and fish," the last being taken from the Wabash in a seine. By means of his industry and informality, if not by his edicts, Harrison won the good will of the frontier. "Mr. H. is a man of some merit, has handsome manners . . . in conversation he is sprightly and gay—can repeat a theatrical performance and mimmick a blackguard as well as I ever saw a man," a political critic conceded.[8]

When satisfied that his exertions had improved somewhat "the affairs of the wretched Indians," Harrison took up the problem of marking the Indian boundary line about Vincennes.[9] The basis for the American claim lay in an almost forgotten tribal grant to M. St. Vincent (or Vincennes), the first French commandant at the Post. The original tract ceded was enormous, describing an area 210 miles long and 72 wide, extending far into present-day Illinois. In a legal sense this land had been transferred to the Americans by the Treaty of Greenville but since the Indians had originally ceded this land to Frenchmen, their revered friends of the past, Harrison advocated a moderation of the existing claim. During the summer of 1802, he entertained a delegation of painted chiefs and headmen representing the near-by Wea, Piankeshaw, Kickapoo, Eel River, and Delaware villages.

Some of these tribes now numbered but a handful yet game had become so scarce that the warriors roamed over a wide expanse of country in order to supply themselves with food. After persuasively warning them against tribal bloodshed and the excessive use of whiskey, Harrison portrayed a new way of life for the Indian. Responding to the Governor's plea for a means of conservation, President Jefferson had advocated that the Indian lay aside his hunting weapons in favor of agricultural tools. The doctrine of hoe vs. bow was now explained:

"Your father, the President, wishes you to assemble your scattered warriors and to form towns and villages, in situations best adapted to cultivation; he will cause you to be furnished with horses, cattle, hogs, and implements of husbandry, and will . . . instruct you in management."[10]

The experiment had been fairly tried. In the South the Creeks and Cherokees were raising large herds of cattle and were harvesting bountiful crops. "This has had a most happy effect on their population" Harrison pointed out, "and all their wigwams are already filled with children." Harrison himself, a tiller of 300 acres, furnished the Indians an object lesson. September 6, 1802, while the council was still in session, his fourth child, William Henry Harrison, Jr., was born.

But when Harrison introduced the subject of a land treaty the chiefs for the first time became voluble. As he had anticipated they set forth the claim that they had ceded their lands about Vincennes only to the French. The tribesmen would not be hurried in any reconsideration of this plea. On September 17, five weeks after the council convened, they finally consented to cede an area about seventy-two miles long and thirty-six wide, extending the long way across the Wabash River into Illinois. Fifteen chiefs and ten white men placed their signs and signatures on an agreement to be ratified later at a council of the northern tribes, the intended meeting place Fort Wayne.[11]

A ride through the Illinois country that fall introduced the Governor to a strong Federalist group which wished to see the Territory divided, yet the expense of self-government at this time, Harrison pleaded, would bear hard on the present limited population.[12] The argument served for the time being although the question was to arise again. The Illinois country was not exactly in step with far-reaching Knox County, east of the Wabash, where a good class of immigrants was finding a new home. The more educated newcomers, many of them Virginia Republicans, were settling in or near Vincennes and the Harrison temperament proved to their liking. Nor was the Governor unpopular elsewhere. In December a caucus of citizens from four counties petitioned Congress to lift the existing ban on slavery in the Territory and recommended also, in a letter to Jefferson, the reappointment of Harrison who was quite willing indeed to remain.[13] "Devoted as I am to agriculture and domestic life," he notified Senator Jonathan Dayton, "my situation is far from being unpleasant; but the emoluments of my appointment are very important to me and this session [of Congress] will determine whether I am to enjoy them after the month of May or not. I have indeed, not much apprehension of being superseded."[14]

President Thomas Jefferson was sure to reappoint a man who held sway among the Indians as well as the people. Shortly before attaining his thirtieth birthday, Harrison received official assurance of continuance at Vincennes, also a "general commission for treating." A delicate international situation was forecast, Jefferson wrote. Spain had yielded up Louisiana to the Emperor Napoleon, ruler of a people whose friendship the Indians held in reverence. "The occupation of New Orleans, hourly expected, by the French," Jefferson advised, "is already felt like a light breeze by the Indians." Should a French army be landed, should French influence again become dominant, the tribes would "immediately stiffen" against further land cessions. Therefore, advised the President in a practical vein, "whatever can now be obtained must be obtained quickly." Interesting details of a broad plan, by which Harrison might offset the French menace, were outlined in this "unofficial and private" letter of Jefferson:

"Live in perpetual peace with the Indians . . . cultivate an affectionate attachment from them. . . . The decrease of game rendering their subsistence by hunting insufficient we wish to draw them to agriculture, to spinning and weaving. . . . When they withdraw themselves to a small piece of land, they will perceive how useless to them are their extensive forests and will be willing to pare them off . . . in exchange for necessaries. . . . We shall push our trading houses and be glad to see the good and influential individuals among them [the Indians] run into debt. . . . When these debts get beyond what the individuals can pay, they become willing to lop them off . . . by a cession of lands. . . ."

The supreme object in view was nothing less than the purchase of all the country east of the Mississippi to its northern regions, now held by the Indians, particularly the lands along that river. "I must repeat that this letter is to be considered as private," Jefferson concluded, "you will also perceive how sacredly it must be kept within your own breast . . . how improper to be understood by the Indians. . . ."[15]

The redmen were ever pawns in some game, particularly in counterplotting between nations. Napoleon was ready to use them, if feasible, in the fruition of his schemes against England and her colonies and his feeling toward America was by no means friendly.[16] However, the frontier was tremendously stirred over the transfer of New Orleans to France and before Jefferson's letter arrived Harrison had already acted. Late in March, as soon as the ice was out of the river, he ascended the Wabash in "a splendid barge" and summoned the Miami, Shawnee, Delaware, and Potawatomie chiefs to meet at Fort Wayne.

Secretary John Gibson, Attorney-General John Rice Jones, Thomas Freeman, a government surveyor, two army officers and twelve rank and file accompanied the Governor. Some thirty miles from the fort, where the river grew shallow, horses in care of other soldiers awaited. Harrison rested one night at the fort then continued on to Detroit to repair a tardy distribution of Indian annuities and obtain flour and other stores for the council. Riding past Fort Defiance and skirting the Maumee River he gazed upon scenes once visited with Wayne's Legion; at the Rapids a public barge from Detroit took him across Lake Erie. The Michigan country, organized as Wayne County, was now a part of Indiana, Detroit its only sizable town. Harrison lengthened his stay to administer the estate of Colonel John F. Hamtramck, late commandant at the fort, and attended a ball held in his honor shortly before departing in May.[17]

At Fort Wayne, Captain John Whistler commanding, Harrison faced a group of defiant chiefs and warriors who loudly protested the validity of the treaty signed at Vincennes. The atmosphere grew unfriendly when a number of Miamis clad in British-made garments and bearing imported weapons—distributed at Amherstburg in Upper Canada—arrived and joined the ranks of dissenters. Harrison's task was difficult. Chief Buckongahelas of the Delawares declared that nothing done at Vincennes was binding upon the tribes, the Shawnees arose in a body and walked out.[18]

As Harrison later discovered, his chief protagonist at the council was Captain William Wells, dark-faced interpreter and Indian Agent at the fort. Taken prisoner by the Indians at the age of 13, Wells had grown to manhood among the tribes and then had escaped to join Wayne's Legion on its march to the Rapids. For his commendable work as a spy he had been rewarded with a post at Fort Wayne but he was prone to enhance upon the methods of Chief Little Turtle, his father-in-law, who had secured additional annuities for the Miamis at the Treaty of Greenville. The argument was clearly presented that more annuities should now be made but Harrison could promise no further gifts since the government regarded the Vincennes tract as already ceded at Greenville.

Harrison prompted his surveyor to indicate the lines of the disputed cession while the Indians made "their own rough delineations . . . on the floor with a bit of charcoal."[19] By order of the Governor, annuities then due were withheld. After several days of councils, fifteen chiefs agreed to the boundaries defined at Vincennes and for the additional cession of a salt spring upon the Saline River in Illinois, the tribes were promised an annuity of 150 bushels of salt.[20] Apparently all was settled amicably. The tribesmen received their annuities and the Governor was about to depart when word was brought of a tribal council held by the Miami and Delaware tribes in the woods. Harrison awaited impatiently for the result. Respecting the proprietorship of the Indian lands lying between the Ohio and the White River in Indiana, the Miamis decided to acknowledge Delaware rights.

When news of French possession of Louisiana reached the tribes, Harrison discovered in descending the Wabash, "they could not conceal their joy." The happiness the Indians had once enjoyed with the French was "their perpetual theme . . . their golden age."[12] Aware of this fact, the Emperor Napoleon and Minister Talleyrand had been speculating upon their use against the settlements if occasion warranted; Jefferson, at this crisis, was ready to "marry . . . the British fleet and nation."[22] Then the American Minister to Paris made a timely stroke with the pen and purchased from Napoleon all of Louisiana. News of the transaction reached Harrison as he returned to Vincennes but that other plans had been brewing was apparent from an account of a traveller carrying a box of French guineas who had tarried briefly in town. The stranger may have been a St. Louis trapper to whom a British agent attributed "two Barrels of Dollars from the French Gov^t to be distributed among the wise and confidential Indians."[23]

Now that Louisiana had become American soil Napoleon had wasted his bribe and the French threat had vanished yet Jefferson gave no sign that the plan of land acquisition should be modified. Harrison received instructions to deal next with the Kaskaskias, the remnant of a once flourishing confederacy of five Illinois tribes. A long war with the Sacs had reduced them, whiskey and disease had weakened them, and the warlike Potawatomies now threatened their extirpation. Less than a score of Kaskaskias now remained, the Peoria representation among them numbering but a single chief.[24] According to Jefferson's original plan, Harrison met them in council at Vincennes and bargained for the whole of their tribal heritage, comprising nearly one half of the present state of Illinois. But the Kaskaskias were guaranteed the protection of the United States against all possible enemies, to them an essential provision, and their regular annuity increased to $1000 a year. Harrison reserved two sizeable tracts for tribal use and provided the sum of $300 for the erection of a Catholic church. For Chief Ducoigne of that tribe a new house was also to be built. The Indians remained at liberty to hunt upon the ceded land."[25]

This was a treaty emblematic of the fruits of original French penetration in America. Whiskey and disease had prepared the way for wholesale land acquisition along the Mississippi River and its tributaries in Illinois. Further up the Ohio, a bypath from early trade routes, the tribes had maintained much of their strength. Save for the Vincennes tract and Clark's Grant at the Falls of the Ohio (opposite Louisville), present-day Indiana was still in the hands of the tribesmen and thus the way to statehood was blocked. If the rich country along the Ohio could be obtained from the Indians and immigration thus encouraged, it was argued, funds to bear the expense of second-grade government would be forthcoming from additional taxes on lands. Certainly President Jefferson would not be adverse to the plan.

During the summer of 1804, while Harrison was building himself a brick house, the question of second grade government was "agitated with considerable warmth."[26] The newly established *Indiana Gazette* enlivened its columns with a lengthy and torrid debate between Benjamin Parke, advocate of the Governor's plan, and William McIntosh, a well-to-do Scotch land speculator, who appeared adverse to the contemplated Indian cessions inasmuch as he still had much property in the restricted area to sell. The argument ended in personal recrimination: "I pronounce and publish Wm. M'Intosh, a filcher, a pilferer, & thief."[27] The clique of Illinois Federalists, who originally proposed the move, also dissented, advocating division instead, and when the District of Upper Louisiana was temporarily attached to Indiana for the purposes of government they petitioned Congress to be joined to the new district as a separate Territory.

Congress declined to act on the plea, however. As an initial step to attain second grade, Harrison summoned members of the Delaware tribe for a council at Vincennes. The chiefs numbered a dozen half-breeds and Christians, peaceful and friendly in the main. Satisfied with their claim that the Miamis had yielded full rights to the land in the tribal council at Fort Wayne, Harrison outlined a broad tract extending nearly 300 miles east as far as the Falls of the Ohio. The council was still in progress and affirmation in sight when Harrison called for a plebiscite among the citizens to decide upon the question of second grade.[28]

The cession received a few days later for the government paved the way for a vote favoring the new step. It was easily Harrison's greatest triumph. For a million and a half acres or more, the Delawares were promised annuities of $300 a year for ten years and work horses, cattle, hogs, "implements of husbandry," and other goods to the value of $800 in hand. The Governor then drew up another treaty with the neighboring Piankeshaws, who although

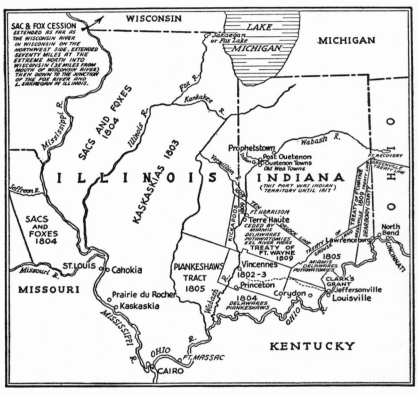

Indian Land Treaties, 1802–09. (Present state lines are shown.)

smaller in numbers had lived long in that region, in order to extinguish any remaining claim.[29] Vincennes and the ruling faction looked forward to better times and representation in Congress. "[This] acquirement . . . is of immense value," applauded the *Indiana Gazette,* "as it will facilitate the establishment of extensive settlements."[30] When the citizens met at their county polling places in September, second-grade government received a plentiful vote.

Harrison had the additional pleasure of seeing his new home nearly finished and "three-fourths of the expense . . . at end," when he was called to St. Louis to organize the District of Upper Louisiana, which had been attached to Indiana. Toward the last of September, 1804, Doctor John Scott of Lexington, formerly of Wayne's Legion, arrived at Vincennes. As at other times in the past, Doctor Scott had made the long journey to attend Mrs. Harrison who was expecting the birth of her fifth child.[31] The Governor and the Kentuckian had long been intimate. On October 4, when a son was born a few days after Harrison was called to St. Louis, it was named John Scott Harrison. A son born to Mrs. John Scott in the doctor's absence was to be christened William Henry Harrison Scott.

Harrison's visit to St. Louis was productive of new friendships and a famous land treaty. An escort of mounted regulars accompanied the Governor across the rusty-brown Illinois prairies. Among the party also were Colonel Francis Vigo, Attorney William Prince, Joseph Barron, interpreter, and Judges Vanderburgh, Griffin, and Thomas T. Davis of the Territorial Supreme Court. A cavalcade of citizens advanced from Cahokia, on the east bank of the Mississippi, to meet them and as they were ferried across the river another welcoming party approached from St. Louis. October 12, jurisdiction over the District was formally yielded by Captain Amos Stoddard, the military commandant.

The capital of Upper Louisiana was then a town of about 200 houses mostly built of stone and indicative of wealth. There was much more elegance there than at Vincennes. "The ladies," Harrison wrote, "are remarkably handsome, gentle, and well bred, and the society . . . altogether a polished one."[32] Harrison was entertained at the fine home of Auguste Chouteau, wealthy land owner and trader who with his brother Pierre owned a large part of the town. The Governor received a flattering offer of a partnership but could not accept. A republican in a former royalist province, Harrison chose to play the rôle of a Jeffersonian ambassador and even waived the customary fees for trading licenses.[33] The people of St. Louis were not unpleased. The Governor's "affability and easy access," commented a fur trapper, formed "a strong contrast" with what they had long been accustomed to.[34] Harrison laid down the law however in respect to British sympathizers. Hoping to break up a trading ring illegally operating along the upper Mississippi, he refused the license applications of all known Tories and subjects of the King.

After reorganizing the courts and militia and drafting a new law code with the help of the judges the Governor took up the matter of appeasement in lands. Present at St. Louis were members of the belligerent Osage tribe, who were dismissed with warnings and with gifts,[35] also five members of the allied Sac and Fox tribes of the Mississippi valley. Their principal purpose in coming to St. Louis had been to deliver up one of their warriors as the slayer of a white man who had been tomahawked for insulting an Indian girl at a dance in a frontier cabin. As public sentiment was outspoken against him, the offender was placed in jail while Harrison wrote to Jefferson for a pardon. The Chouteau brothers, meanwhile, extended the large sum of $2234 to these Indians in credit. Duly encouraged, the visitors had loaded up with fine coats, medals, and whiskey. Auguste Chouteau, acting as intermediary between the Indians and the Governor, promised them the release of the prisoner provided several million acres of tribal lands were yielded up, including some Spanish grants in Upper Louisiana claimed by the trader.[36]

At the council which ensued the undelegated chieftains signed away the greater part of the Sac and Fox lands in western Illinois, extending into Wisconsin, and ceded also a generous tract in Missouri to satisfy the debt to Chouteau. Altogether the ceded country comprised some 15,000,000 acres including a rich mineral region to the north. In return the Sacs and Foxes were granted the protection of the United States against all enemies, annuities valued at $1000 yearly, and extinguishment of their current debt.[37] The aftermath of the transaction, however, was calamitous. The pardon for the Indian prisoner, signed by the President, had not yet arrived when the warrior broke out of jail and was shot dead by a sentinel. News of the treaty, of Chouteau's whiskey and the shooting caused an uproar when the tribesmen returned to their native villages. An indignant delegation set out at once for the nearest British camp to relate their complaints and to receive understanding treatment. Tribal support for the British was not withheld during the War of 1812 and even thirty years later Chief Black Hawk chose to fight rather than yield up this land.[38]

Harrison returned to his family of five and his new home early in December. Erected on a gentle elevation in the midst of a walnut grove, Grouseland was the first brick mansion in all that region and sufficiently large to accommodate a growing family. Of a Georgian style, it resembled the Governor's native Berkeley, two and a half stories high, with four great chimneys, and thirteen large rooms. On the first floor, as at Berkeley, were two rooms of unusual size, one designed for council meetings and entertainments, the other the family living room illuminated by firelight and candles. Wainscotings of polished black walnut, hand-carved mantels, sashes and doors were the product of skilled workmen in Chillicothe and Pittsburgh; the window glass, ordered nearly two years before, had been brought from England. Under the semicircular staircase a closet for records was ingeniously hidden, not to be rediscovered until in recent years. Harrison paid particular attention to details of defense. The outer walls, eighteen inches of solid brick, were slit for portholes, the broad-silled attic windows designed for sharp-shooters. Most of the windows, all of six feet high, were fitted with heavy shutters both within and without. In the cellar was constructed a powder magazine with walls of heavy masonry and an arched brick ceiling, and a trap-door led to a look-out station on the roof. Shrubbery, handsome shade and fruit trees surrounded the grounds; in the spring Mrs. Harrison would plant her flower gardens. It was a home that could match any in St. Louis, although its cost prevented the Governor from becoming well-to-do through land speculation. To pay for the brick alone, Harrison bartered 400 acres of land with an estimated value of $1000.[39]

Indiana Territory's first election, of primary concern to the Governor, invoked his ready partisanship in behalf of Republican candidates for the legislature who had advocated the advance to second grade. In the Illinois country a number of Federalists and a minority clique of Republicans were still lined up for division of the Territory, which was one issue, and of the Republicans who presented themselves for nomination the Governor favored those who held pro-slavery views.

According to the Ordinance of 1787 which set up Northwest Territory, the country north of the Ohio River was to be forever free soil yet many of the old French residents held slaves and Harrison himself had brought one or two family servants from Berkeley besides indenturing others.[40] The spirit of growth in the Territory, stimulated by the arrival of a new class of citizens from the East and South, prompted the desire to import slaves inasmuch as many immigrating slaveholders were settling across the river in Kentucky. The convention of citizens which had petitioned Congress for Harrison's reappointment also asked that the free-soil provision in the Ordinance be suspended for ten years, a plea which met denial in a Jefferson-ruled House. But if Indiana could elect the pro-slavery legislature which the Governor wanted, such views could be further presented through its chosen delegate to Congress.

That Harrison ever advocated slavery for Indiana has been denied yet evidence favoring the opposite view appears to be complete. In the Illinois country, where the Governor made known his wishes, he encountered the active opposition of the Reverend James Lemen, privately a protégé of the abolitionist Thomas Jefferson. "Governor Harrison asked and insisted that I cast my influence for . . . slavery here," wrote Lemen in his diary. "I not only denied the request, but informed him that the evil attempt would encounter my most active opposition."[41] Another fragment of evidence is revealed in Harrison's own résumé of the election. Despite the efforts of Lemen and his friends, Indiana's first elected House stood six to one for slavery. Thus "the wishes of nine-tenths of the people" had been realized, Harrison notified the President, adding that those who had favored second-grade government also had favored slavery.[42] Harrison's own candidate for delegate, learned and outspoken Attorney Benjamin Parke, was also successful in the election and it was through him that petitions advocating the extension of slavery were presented in the National House.

None of these petitions were successful, it can be added. Slaves continued to be held under the guise of an indenture law passed by the Governor and the judges, but none could be bought or sold in Indiana and Harrison was adamant against any transportation for sale in Kentucky.[43] Jefferson paid little attention to the issue. Holding firm the reins of Congress, the President was quite willing for Harrison to have a further voice in the selection of Indiana's representative body whether or not pro-slavery. The Territorial Council, or Upper House, was to be appointed by the President from a list of nominees submitted by the lower body. Prior to rendering his choice, Jefferson mailed the Governor a document with spaces left blank so that Harrison himself might select a Council from the nominations submitted. The President offered a few words of advice as a general guide although without mentioning slavery:

"I can only recommend an adherence to the principles which would have governed myself in making the selection. 1—to reject dishonest men. 2. those called federalists. even the honest men among them are so imbued with party prejudice. . . . 3. land-jobbers are undesirable."[44]

So Harrison made his selections, which included only one Federalist, and on July 29, 1805, "with graceful address . . . [and] affable manners"[45] he delivered his first annual message before the Indiana General Assembly, an intimate little group of twelve men. Evangelical as usual in his republican zeal the Governor felicitated the lawmakers first upon "the important right of legislating for themselves," and extracted a point from the recent acquisition of Louisiana:

"The mighty river which separates us from the Louisianans will never be stained with the blood of contending nations; but will prove the bond of our nation, and will convey upon its bosom, in the course of many thousand miles, the produce of our great and united empire. . . . And if, in the immense distance . . . other laws and other manners prevail, the contrast . . . will serve the useful purpose of demonstrating the great superiority of a republican government, and how far the uncontrolled and unbiassed industry of freemen excels the cautious and measured exertions of the subjects of despotic power."[46]

That the French settlers at Vincennes had never regarded republican rule with much favor gave point to the remark. The subject of Indian welfare occupied a considerable portion of the message. Of all the colonizing civilized nations, Harrison declared, only the United States had passed laws seeking the aid and protection of the redmen. Yet there was much to be done. A Federal statute forbidding the sale of liquor to the Indians was considered to be in force in their own country only; elsewhere, barring Harrison's local restrictions, they could obtain as much as they wished. A compassionate observer of their unfriendly situation, Harrison pleaded for a thorough-going extension of the measure:

"The interests of your constituents, the interests of the miserable Indians, and your own feelings will sufficiently urge you to . . . provide the remedy which is to save thousands of our fellow creatures. You are witnesses to the abuses, you have seen our towns crowded with furious and drunken savages, our streets flowing with their blood, their arms and clothing bartered for the liquor that destroys them, and their miserable women and children enduring all the extremities of cold and hunger. . . . A miserable remnant is all that remains to mark the names and situation of many numerous and warlike tribes. . . . Is it then to be admitted, as a political axiom, that the neighbourhood of a civilized nation is incomparable with the existence of savages? Are the blessings of our republican government only to be felt by ourselves?"[47]

The Indiana legislature responded by passing an act prohibiting the sale of liquor to the Indians, but it was to be considered in force only as soon as all the neighboring States and territories, Kentucky, Ohio, Louisiana and Michigan, adopted a similar measure. Harrison forthwith sent copies of the law to the other western governors, emphasizing the unfortunate restriction. "The necessity of this provision arose from the great inconvenience which the citizens . . . would suffer if the prohibition to sell liquor did not extend to their neighbours as well," he notified Governor Edward Tiffin of Ohio, a State since 1803. Could the Ohio legislature also take suitable action? "The dreadful effections which have been produced among our Indian neighbors by the immense quantity of ardent spirits . . . poured in upon them . . . have long been known and lamented by every friend of humanity."[48]

Humanity lacked sufficient friends for prompt enactment of a prohibitory law elsewhere, however.

The Indians themselves were not so much concerned with the whiskey problem as with a scheme to gain further annuities from previous land sales. From Secretary of War Dearborn, Harrison discovered that William Wells and Chief Little Turtle had been fomenting over the Delaware Treaty of 1804. First, the Miami chiefs were induced to mark a statement that the Delawares had no right to sell, then Chief Billy Patterson of the latter tribe placed his sign on a protest that the Governor had "got them to sign a Deed for their lands without their knowledge."[49] These tribal messages, together with a plea that Harrison be removed from office, went directly to Secretary Dearborn over the Governor's head. Harrison, who had based his treaty upon the Miami-Delaware agreement at Fort Wayne, was incensed at this duplicity. Captain Wells, in fact, although in league with the Indians against the government, was known to be systematically cheating the tribes. Not another man in the Territory, the Governor declared, possessed as much unaccountably acquired wealth.[50]

Harrison sent two experienced frontier diplomats, Secretary Gibson and Colonel Vigo, to interview the Indian chiefs. Confronted close at hand by these agents, the tribesmen agreed that Wells had been talking too much and that his talk was unbecoming a white man. In fact, neither Wells nor Little Turtle was any longer trusted by the chiefs and the agitation against the Governor had been attended with suspicion of its sponsors. The principal Miami and Delaware leaders agreed to confer again with the Governor at Vincennes and the Potawatomie chiefs were also summoned to satisfy any remaining complaint.[51]

Early in August, Little Turtle and Peccon of the Miamis, Buckongahelas, Teteboxti, Richardville, and other principal Delaware and Potawatomie chiefs arrived with Captain Wells and stalked into the council room at Grouseland. Harrison and an imposing group of Territorial officials awaited them; Secretary Gibson traced the lines of the Delaware cession in charcoal as the redmen squatted about the floor. The Miamis declared at the outset that they had yielded only hunting and settling rights to the Delawares who could claim no right to sell. Uniting with the Potawatomies, a poor but numerous tribe, their first demand was for an increase in annuities. Harrison bided his time, pitting the Miamis against the Delawares to see which would first yield their claim. When the Miamis won, however, the Governor informed them that since the Delaware claim had been legally settled by treaty, further payment for the disputed cession was out of the question. To gain any additional annuities, the Miamis should consider cession of another strip of land.[52]

The ensuing Treaty of Grouseland brought in a cession of nearly two million acres extending easterly from the ceded Delaware tract, past Clark's Grant as far as the Kentucky River-Fort Recovery line. Harrison took due precautions to make the agreement binding. By the first article, the Delawares relinquished whatever claim they possessed to the land; Article Two acknowledged cession of the whole by the Miami tribe and its branches, the Weas and Eel Rivers. Considering the number of tribesmen involved, Harrison granted a slightly greater compensation than was usually allowed by the Indian Office; and it was politic to satisfy also the Potawatomies, even though their country lay miles to the north. Gifts of clothing, saddles and hunting weapons to the value of $4000 were delivered and $1600 in additional annuities for ten years promised. Harrison furnished some of the leading chiefs with suits of white man's clothes; George White Eyes of the Delawares received also a castor hat and a fine silk shawl; to Chief Lapoussier of the Weas went a tent, a suit, two scalping knives and other goods, to Winamac of the Potawatomies, a saddle worth $15. As a finishing touch to the transaction the personal annuity of Chief Little Turtle was raised from $150 to $200 and Captain Wells was commissioned to buy him a negro servant in Kentucky.[53]

The Treaty of Grouseland was climaxed by much good feeling and high praise for the Governor. From Cincinnati, gateway of immigration, came a comment: "The people are much pleased with the purchase made by your Excellency."[54] "Highly satisfactory & pleasing," was the response from the Secretary of War.[55] But the greatest compliment came from the friendly Delawares. In the future, declared their leader, they would hold the United States in the same regard as they had their former fathers the French.[56]

War between the Sac and the Osage Indians threatening, Harrison rode again to St. Louis late in September to enforce his promise that the former would be protected from all enemies. As the District of Upper Louisiana, reorganized as Missouri Territory, had been recently detached from Indiana, the timely arrival of General James Wilkinson as Governor, bringing a detachment of regulars, helped to prevent the outbreak of war.[57] The two governors negotiated a temporary truce between the tribes. Harrison returned to Vincennes to meet a delegation from the shrunken Piankeshaw nation which agreed that further annuities would be of greater benefit than a broad expanse of lands. A strip about eighty miles wide, adjoining the Kaskaskia cession west of the Wabash, was yielded.[58] Nearly all the Illinois country as well as southern Indiana had now been opened to the whites and before attaining his thirty-third birthday, Governor Harrison could survey many millions of acres peacefully acquired in accordance with Jefferson's wish.

V

TWO SHAWNEE BROTHERS

S PRING lifted the somnolent Wabash into a brimming laden stream. The softened earth of the cultivated prairie was ploughed for increasing crops. New cornfields and gardens, encroaching upon the fringes of the forest, refurbished the land in April. The recent land transactions were attracting many newcomers from the South and East, and Vincennes could very nearly gauge the seasonal prospects from the first few days of arrivals. Buffalo traces, widened into roads along the newly-acquired land on the Ohio, invited the immigrants to leave the winding waterway and travel overland. The principal route to Vincennes occupied a northwesterly course from the Falls of the Ohio, where Harrison had founded the town of Jeffersonville after the plan of his friend and patron at Washington.[1]

The town of Vincennes now contained nearly a thousand souls. With the arrival of a better class of immigrants from the East, the Governor and his associates, many of them Virginians, were endeavoring to introduce a degree of civilization to the frontier. During the sixth year of his rule, Harrison helped to establish a circulating library in the town, and at the opening service of worship for Methodists, he held the candle while the minister, the Reverend William Winans, read the text.[2] Plans for the organization of a university at Vincennes were also underway. A trading post and lonely frontier village for three-quarters of a century, Vincennes was taking on new importance as a Territorial capital. As long as the frontier remained at peace with the neighboring tribes the citizens could afford to cultivate a little learning. Primarily, of course, this progress was based upon the acquisition of land.

Naturally, there were countercurrents and reaction. Speculators with undesired tracts on their hands were reluctant to see new Indian lands opened. And among the tribesmen themselves were certain "interested and crafty individuals," as Thomas Jefferson described them,[3] who deprecated the furtherance of agriculture and domestic industry. This reactionary element, inculcating "a sanctimonious reverence for the customs of their ancestors," was revealed among the Indians just as the Territory was making its greatest gains. Two Shawnee brothers, one a statesman, the other a "Prophet," were at the spearhead of the movement, and duly encouraged by the British they threatened for a time to check the entire scheme of land acquisition and Territorial advance.

These Indian leaders had started their work in Ohio. Tecumseh (Shooting Star or Crouching Panther), was one of triplets born of a Creek mother, Methotase, near Old Chillicothe, now Oldtown, Ohio, early in 1768. As Methotase was giving birth to the third child a meteor flashed above and streaked the heavens. The attending squaws rushed from the hut to watch the blazing phenomenon and returned with their story of the shooting star—in the Shawnee language, also, a "panther." To her last-born Methotase gave this name.[4] Tecumseh became a resourceful hunter and leader of sham battles but when he was fifteen, after he had helped to capture a flatboat on the Ohio, he became strangely distressed at the spectacle of a white victim burned alive. As a young man in his twenties he persuaded his followers to abandon methods of torture. Tecumseh was then conducting a series of raids along the river. Alert and observant, very easily aroused from sleep, he invariably managed to elude pursuit and capture. He accepted few of the spoils. It was enough for him that he was preventing a few white men from entering his country.

Tecumseh would not sign the Treaty of Greenville and he frowned on those chiefs who "touched the quill." Making his camp at Wapakoneta, an Indian village on the St. Marys River, he made a few friends among the Ohio settlers and was welcomed into the cabin of James Galloway, in Old Chillicothe, where he learned to speak a little English. A substantial tradition relates that he fell in love with the settler's daughter, Rebecca. He broached his suit to Galloway who left the decision to the girl. When Rebecca interposed the provision that her suitor adopt white man's ways and dress, Tecumseh went his way and pitched his tent near Greenville.[5]

The Shawnees were a proud but landless tribe. Driven from the South by the Creeks and from Virginia and Pennsylvania by the encroaching whites, they found sanctuary among the Miamis and Delawares in the Northwest. News of the land treaties transacted by the Indiana governor was most disturbing to Tecumseh. Without first going to war, the white men had discovered a most efficient method of acquiring land. About the year 1805, Tecumseh adopted the principle that all the tribes should unite and that none should sell their lands without the consent of all. To enforce his beliefs he violently threatened, or undertook to depose, the treaty-signing chiefs. His was a restless energy and spirited address. "You see him today on the Wabash and in a short time . . . on the shores of Lake Erie or Michigan, or on the banks of the Mississippi," Harrison reported after Tecumseh's talents became known. "Wherever he goes he makes an impression favorable to his purposes."[6]

Tecumseh's one-eyed brother, Tenskwatawa or Elskwatawa, "Him With Open Mouth," was commonly known as a drunken and worthless forest vagabond until, emerging from an epileptic trance, he announced himself as a man of great works. This Prophet revived an old legend of Shawnee priority in the scheme of Creation and preached the ancient ways of life. He would disappear at intervals into the forest, there to receive the authentic revelations of the Master of Life, the Great Spirit, by whom was conferred the power to cure diseases, to stay the hand of death in sickness, and to penetrate secret heresies. In obedience to his divine master, The Prophet bade his followers to forego white man's dress, drink, cultivated foods, and customs; Indian women were forbidden to marry the white man and civilized ways were wholly ruled out.[7]

Early in 1806 The Prophet made himself known in Indiana by purging a Delaware town. Three Moravian missionaries, John Peter Kluge and his wife and the Reverend Abraham Luckenbach, had established their mission far up on the White River near the present site of Muncie. Here they were assisted by a Delaware preacher, Joshua, and Caritas, a squaw. For five years they labored almost fruitlessly in the wilderness, with only "5 baptized persons . . . 4 unbaptized persons" in their congregation.[8] Then The Prophet appeared, summoning all the Indians in that region to hear his revelations at the near-by village of Woapikamekunk.

First the old chiefs were deposed. The warriors held a grand council, resolving "to root out all witchcraft and poison-mixing and by fire to extort confession from all such as the Shawnee should accuse, and whoever would not confess should be hewn in pieces with their war-hatchets and burnt." (This quotation has a Biblical flavor; it is from the pen of the devout John Peter Kluge.) The Prophet then disappeared to commune with the Great Spirit while his followers carried on the work. First the venerable Delaware chief Teteboxti was accused of concealing a "fatal poison" and when he would not confess he was suspended between poles and tortured by fire. At last Teteboxti cried out that Joshua, the Delaware preacher, possessed the poison and "seven wild Indians" entered the Moravian settlement forcibly to remove Joshua.

The Delaware denied this accusation and Teteboxti was forced to recant. Then The Prophet returned to the council and commanded all the Indians to sit in a circle to hear him pronounce judgment. Teteboxti and other respected chiefs, all of whom, so it happened, had signed land treaties, were then accused of poison-mixing. Joshua had no poison—he had signed away no land—but nevertheless he was "possessed of an evil spirit." The warriors burned alive Caritas, the old woman. Ten ferocious savages, their faces painted black, now entered the Moravian settlement to seize and execute Teteboxti. The savages kindled a large fire, hit the chief on the head with a war-hatchet, and tossed him alive into the flames. Then they raided the mission for corn and tobacco and returning to Woapikamekunk, kindled a hot fire for Joshua. As the Delaware solemnly chanted his prayers in German he was struck with the hatchet and thrown into the blaze. Billy Patterson, a half-breed chief, singing and praying, was the last to be burned. When the missionaries learned of this final disaster "dread and terror took from us all power of speech and reflection, and we could do nothing but utter cries of lamentation and woe."[9] Soon they abandoned their mission and returned to the home church in Bethlehem, Pennsylvania.

The news came to Harrison about the latter part of March. It was all the more disturbing inasmuch as a Delaware warrior had been murdered by a settler near Vincennes. Harrison questioned witnesses, jailed the slayer in old Fort Sackville and ordered out a militia guard. During the night, however, the prisoner was assisted in making his escape. Indignant and outspoken, the Governor posted a reward of $300 for the apprehension of the murderer, expressing regret that the sum could not have been "doubled or even trebled."[10] He sent an aid to explain the situation to the Delawares and wrote out a warning for those tribesmen who had conducted the purge. "My children," exhorted the Governor, "tread back the steps you have taken and endeavor to regain the straight road. . . . Who is this pretended prophet who dares to speak in the name of the Great Creator? Examine him. . . . Demand of him some proofs . . . some miracles. . . . If he is really a prophet, ask him to cause the sun to stand still, the moon to alter its course, the rivers to cease to flow. . . . No longer be imposed upon by the arts of an imposter. . . . I charge you to stop your bloody career."[11]

By a curious mischance, the message fell into the hands of a British or Tory partisan who instructed The Prophet that he could cause the sun to stand still by forecasting an eclipse due on June 16. The Prophet summoned all his followers to witness the miracle. At the designated hour a shadow crept over the sun. The converts cried out in frenzy, doubters were terrorized, and a horde of Michigan tribesmen flocked in to witness further miracles until famine threatened the camp.

From the hand of Thomas Jefferson, Governor Harrison received another renewal of his commission during the summer of 1806 and Doctor John Scott, again a visitor from Lexington, ushered in a sixth arrival in the family, named Benjamin. Harrison alluded to these pleasing events, mentioning also the rising responsibilities of a father, in his letter of acknowledgment to the President:
"I received . . . the new Commission . . . and I beg you to receive my warmest thanks for this additional proof of your confidence and friendship—The emoluments of my office afford me a decent support and will I hope . . . enable me to lay up a small fund for the education of my children—I have hitherto found however that my nursery grows faster than my strongbox."[12]
The flurry of excitement caused by The Prophet's raid was now past. The neighboring tribesmen who assembled for the summer council gave Harrison their "solemn assurances" that they would always remain at peace with the United States. In his speech before the legislature, alluding to the recent murder of the Delaware, Harrison expressed his confidence that the near-by tribesmen would never take up arms "unless driven to it by . . . injustice and oppression." While the difficulties attending enforcement of the law were great, the territory was in no shape to withstand an Indian war. If juries and jailers would not assist in enforcement it was possible perhaps to mold the public opinion. Harrison begged the legislative members "to lose no opportunity of inculcating, among your constituents, an abhorrence of that unchristian and detestable doctrine which would make a distinction of guilt between the murder of a white man and an Indian."[13] For a time peace and quiet continued along the Wabash although one night a bullet crashed through the shutters at Grouseland as Harrison walked the floor with baby John Scott in his arms.[14]

Among the white settlers, meanwhile, doctrines seemingly respectably sponsored disquieted republican minds. Harrison toured the new purchase along the Ohio and harvested his crops in the midst of much speculation and anxiety concerning the affairs of Colonel Aaron Burr, the slayer of Alexander Hamilton, whose followers were building flatboats at the Falls of the Ohio and equipping them with arms and supplies. Of the true nature of the Colonel's plans and intentions, no one appeared to know. Some months before, Burr had visited Grouseland, apparently to enlist the Governor's interest and aid, but he never returned a second time and the true purpose of the visit was left vague.[15] In November, 1806, when public curiosity reached a state of alarm, Attorney-General Joseph Hamilton Daveiss of Kentucky asked that Burr be indicted on the ground of treason but the charge proved too sweeping for events attending mere organization. Following the trial, and Burr's triumphant dismissal, Harrison sent Judge Waller Taylor, a confidential associate, to pick up what intelligence he could find at Jeffersonville.[16] A detail of militia was then examining all passing flatboats, Taylor reported, but Burr had already gone down the Mississippi finally to be apprehended, by order of President Jefferson, in distant Alabama.

Harrison, at one with the administration, expressed his candid view of the Colonel's secret and shady motives even if a puny military expedition into Louisiana, which was all that came to light, was not in itself disloyal or treasonous. Although sharing in the common republican indignation against the unfortunate prisoner, the Governor was zealous in rehabilitating Burr's fugitive associates. "The grosest falshoods were Used to entrap those whose honesty he knew to be proof against any proposal to violate the Laws of their Country," he wrote in behalf of Major Davis Floyd of Jeffersonville.[17] Ordering out an escort of Indiana rangers for the protection of "four misguided men . . . their wives and helpless children," Harrison advised the commanding officer of the essential worth of human kind: "The people are guilty of no more wrong than that of being duped by one of the smartest Villian[s] in the country."[18] But as the result of this intervention, the Governor did not escape the charge that he, too, had been tarred with Burr's brush. In forthcoming political campaigns in Indiana, when Harrison brought forward his own candidates, the point was freely discussed.[19]

Except for what political capital that could be gained from the affair, the public furore over Burr was displaced by disturbing reports from the vicinity of Greenville, where Tecumseh and The Prophet had recently removed. Enraptured by The Prophet's declarations, the Indians abandoned their spring planting in favor of the manufacture of war clubs. During the early summer, 1807, when a "Banditti of Creeks" and other outlaw tribesmen grew bold, Harrison organized three companies of Indiana rangers, who patrolled the trails and by-paths where forays had been reported,[20] and he ordered Captain William Wells to send "two confidential Indians" to the camp of The Prophet. Wells reported in a pessimistic vein:

"The Indians have continued to flock to Greenville which increases the fears of our frontiers. . . . They appear deff to everything I say. . . . The Prophet tells them . . . the great spirit will in a few years distroy every white man in America. It is my opinion that the British are at the bottom of this business."[21]

Wells expressed nothing particularly new. British aggression off our coasts and on the high seas fostered this indignation. June 22 occurred the fateful *Leopard-Chesapeake* affair off the Virginia Capes, six Americans killed, nineteen wounded, and several others impressed into the British service. Harrison, reading the signs in the West, expressed the opinion that The Prophet's activities were motivated by the same hostility, that the tribesmen again were being enlisted in the British cause. Indeed, he came to consider the movement of British agents among the Indians as a "kind of political Thermometer" by which he could apprehend the disposition for peace or war across the sea.[22] Signs of British activity were plentiful. A party of rangers picked up a stranger who declared he had been held a prisoner by the Indians for two years yet his hair was newly-barbered and he wore a suit of clean underwear.[23] A trader long friendly to the Governor revealed that British Agent Thomas McKee, son of Colonel Alexander McKee, deceased, had recently voyaged down the Maumee to visit The Prophet; another trader picked up a message from McKee to the Indians that "a plan of operations was concerting." From Chicago came a trader's sworn deposition that the Michigan tribes were planning an attack on the settlements and traders along the Mississippi openly expressed alarm.[24]

Harrison promptly warned the legislature. The situation on the Atlantic Coast, the "unheard of outrage" of the *Chesapeake* affair, made immediate preparations necessary. "We are peculiarly interested in the contest which is likely to ensue for who does not know that the Tomahawk and scalping knife . . . are always employed as the instruments of British vengeance?"[25] Constant labor with the militia found the Governor engaged in the multiple roles of "Commander-in-chief, Adjutant and even drill corporal." Such duties were far from irksome, Harrison admitted, in notifying the Secretary of War of a disgraceful deficiency in arms. Although required by law to equip themselves the militia could not be depended upon to do so. "We have cavalry without swords, light infantry without bayonets or cartridge boxes, and battalions armed with a mixture of rifles, fowling pieces, broken muskets and sticks," remonstrated the Governor. To a regular army man, such things were "really shocking."[26] Secretary Dearborn was urged to make deposits of public arms at

Vincennes and elsewhere along the frontier. That the distant tribes would soon commence the war Harrison had little doubt.

Certain historians have chosen to castigate the Indiana Governor for linking British influence with The Prophet yet the tenor of mind of the Indian living south of the Canadian border was to the British always a matter of concern. Maintaining a wilderness colony across fresh water from an aggressive new nation, Britain's leaders eyed the Indians constantly in order to turn their grievances to their own account. This was a policy mutually helpful for neither the British army in Canada nor the tribesmen were strong enough to go it alone. When Governor William Hull of Michigan Territory transacted a land treaty which, in the opinion of one British agent, would "not be settled without the loss of some lives,"[27] steps were taken to organize this dissatisfaction and to retain it well within bounds. A Shawnee delegation from The Prophet's camp visited the British post at Fort Amherstburg in Upper Canada that fall returning with gifts of clothing and a verbal invitation ("no writing was trusted . . . for fear of accidents") for The Prophet to attend a general council at that post in the spring.[28] Concurrently, during the fall of 1807, Governor Harrison and Governor Thomas Kirker of Ohio sought to persuade The Prophet's following to disperse and Jefferson himself sent a warning message to which Tecumseh delivered an answer: "These lands are ours. The Great Spirit has appointed this place for us and here we will remain."[29]

However, neither the Indian outbreak feared by Harrison nor the conflict with England developed that fall. Although prompt to enlist the interest of The Prophet, British officials in Canada advised their agents to maintain the peace as long as possible for the reason that a state of war was not feasible, for the time being, on the western frontier. But the contrast in American and British policy toward the tribesmen at this juncture can be gauged from the instructions of Thomas Jefferson to the western governors and those of Governor General James A. Craig of Canada, sent to his Indian agents. Wrote Jefferson:

"A misunderstanding having arisen between the United States and the English war may possibly ensue . . . in this war it is our wish the Indians should be quiet spectators, not wasting their blood in quarrels which do not concern them."[30]

And Craig:

"No time should be lost by messages to the different nations and by every other means that are usual in our intercourse with them to remind them of our long subsisting friendship. . . . I shall be very glad to receive some information as to the history of the Prophet . . . and the extent of his influence . . . if this is great . . . it might be worth while to purchase it though at what might be a high price upon any other occasion."[31]

Such was Governor Harrison's thermometer.

A year or two following the completion of Grouseland, funds were available for investment elsewhere. His commission as governor renewed, Harrison further linked his fortunes with the Territory by purchasing a few hundred acres on Blue River, near Corydon in southern Indiana, where he erected a grist and sawmill and contemplated building a shipyard.[32] Tecumseh and The Prophet quit Greenville at last, moving in the spring of 1808 to a more convenient site near the junction of the Wabash and Tippecanoe rivers in Indiana. The village called Prophetstown was about 200 miles from Vincennes by the water route although somewhat nearer Fort Amherstburg, and within fifty miles of the principal Potawatomie, Miami, Chippewa, and Ottawa towns. Convenient portages led to streams linking Illinois, Michigan, and the Wabash, a proximity disquieting to Vincennes. Harrison sent some friendly Delaware and Miami chiefs to protest the encroachment but Tecumseh's "threats or persuasions" sufficed to drive them away.[33]

Indian councils held at Fort Amherstburg and Vincennes that summer were to indicate the contrast in British and American resource. Responding to the invitation originally sent The Prophet, who was then the better-known chief, Tecumseh arrived at Fort Amherstburg early in June. Colonel William Claus of His Majesty's service, who enjoyed a three-hour conversation with him, delivered "a handsome present to the Shawnees."[34] Then on the way to Fort Amherstburg, Claus announced, was Governor-General Craig, who made the long arduous journey from York, the Canadian capital, to preside over a grand council of seven nations. Upon his arrival, the assembled chiefs and warriors performed their war dances and games, receiving many bundles of presents. The Governor's speech, the text of which can be guessed at, was two hours in length while messages relayed to the tribes urged them to unite against the Americans but to refrain from any hostilities.[35] Much sympathy because of the loss of their lands was expressed. A council of chiefs and headmen agreed next day that the Americans were "always telling them lyes and taking their country from them."[36] The Wyandots, or Hurons, respected for their bravery and wisdom, were appointed to deliver the sentiments of all nations to the Governor who then sat down to dinner with "90-odd chiefs." Affairs were in a prosperous vein, Craig indicated to Secretary for War Castlereagh in London. "In America," the Governor-General explained, "fortunately the system of gratifying these people is not much in vogue."[37]

The ensuing transactions at Vincennes indicated that Craig's statement was susceptible of proof. While Tecumseh was visiting Fort Amherstburg, in the town of Malden, Harrison received a small party of Shawnees from Prophetstown and having fed them, gave them some seed corn to plant. The Indians gave notice of a contemplated visit by The Prophet and in August, despite Harrison's warning that he bring only a few of his followers, "some hundreds of famished Indians" descended upon the unprotected town.[38] Harrison, who had been entertaining the neighboring tribes, was then short of supplies. While near-by farms and storehouses were scoured for corn, The Prophet gathered his followers about him and harangued them daily in the presence of the Governor. "The art and address with which he manages the Indians is really astonishing," Harrison reported, his denial of being under British influence "strong and apparently candid."[39] Harrison bound The Prophet to give notice of any warlike intentions among the tribes and bade him farewell after a council lasting fifteen days. There were raised eyebrows at the Indian Office, however, when the bills for supplies came in. Secretary Dearborn wrote a letter of inquiry to the Governor. "I never knew an Indian that was not more grateful for having his belly filled than for any other service," Harrison responded. It is hardly necessary to state that no British official was called upon to explain the issuance of extra provisions at Malden. Upwards of 5000 Indians, according to the notations of Colonel Matthew Elliott, were welcomed and fed at that post in the fall.[40]

Quite unaware of the proceedings at Fort Amherstburg and Malden, Harrison expressed a favorable reaction to The Prophet's visit, predicting that on the whole his influence might prove "rather advantageous than otherwise to the United States." To the Indiana legislature that fall the Governor expressed renewed confidence that although European quarrels still menaced our shores, there was "every prospect of a continuance of . . . harmony and good understanding with our Indian neighbors."[41] Yet quite as much harmony and good understanding had been established at Malden where the British made Tecumseh's cause their own. At least the chieftain's marked preference for British friendship and councils boded no particular good for Vincennes.

THE TREATY OF FORT WAYNE

HARRISON had governed Indiana Territory for nearly eight years with but few evidences of internal turmoil except on the part of the Federalist faction, which naturally had been passed over, in large part, in the matter of appointments. But by 1808 Indiana's population had increased nearly fivefold since the Governor's induction into office, a growth which meant change and a re-shuffling of the political scene. Three factors of revolt symptomized growing pains. The list of civil appointees made by the Governor had an increasingly strong flavor of native Virginia. In the eastern part of the Territory, the antislavery party, opposed to indenture, had become relatively larger; in the West, in Illinois, an independent faction still clamored for division. Practical politicians realized that if these malcontents could get together, some kind of deal might be arranged. A special election to fill two vacancies in the Indiana House paved the way.

The special election of 1808 hinged upon complaints against the Governor's hierarchy of educated friends, among which were Chancellor Waller Taylor, Attorney-General Thomas Randolph, and Judge Benjamin Parke, the former attorney general and delegate to Congress. Moreover, populous Vincennes and Knox County still held the balance of power in the legislature where attempts to secure division had been blocked. When the special election seated two pro-division members from Illinois, a deal was sought by which the abolitionists would support division in return for assistance in repealing the indenture laws.[1] Both moves were direct thrusts at the Governor and the dominant party at Vincennes. Harrison had helped to write the indenture laws and he was naturally opposed to a division, which by cutting off Illinois and Wisconsin, would leave Vincennes on the western border of a shrunken Indiana. Michigan, organized early in 1803 as Wayne County, had become a separate jurisdiction.

The 1808 legislature proved to be the last to represent Indiana,

Illinois and Wisconsin at Vincennes. Convening late in September, that body promptly passed a resolution advocating division and elected Speaker Jesse B. Thomas, who was not only pledged but bonded to work for the measure, as delegate to Congress. Then the pro-division leaders, including those who once had voted to introduce slavery, combined with the abolitionists to repeal the indenture laws. The legislature also took a rap at Harrison's appointive power by voting that the office of Territorial attorney general should be made elective, a point which actually rested with Congress. Harrison replied with a blunt veto, for the legislature had exceeded its prerogative.[2] He was powerless however to prevent division. When Delegate Thomas entered Congress that fall, he secured a committee report favoring division and the bill was passed on February 3. The delegate was burned in effigy as the news reached Vincennes but his work was past recall.

An act making the post of delegate elective by the people, instead of by the legislature, was also secured by Thomas. After welcoming the birth of a seventh child, Mary Symmes Harrison, the Governor set the election for the following May. The ensuing contest disclosed the Governor's political ineptitude, his dictates of heart in these contests proving a little too strong. Harrison's nominee proved to be the Virginian Thomas Randolph, whom he recently had appointed attorney general, but by its vote to make that office elective the legislature already had gone on record against him. Opposing Harrison's candidate was a muscular and robust youth, the antislavery man Jonathan Jennings, who was properly skilled in the work and the sports of the farmers. There followed a humiliating campaign. Randolph was dubbed an "aristocrat," and "the Governor's man"; Jennings was hailed as a friend of the people. While Randolph made dull speeches, trimming on his known proslavery views, Jennings threw the maul, pitched quoits with men, set the pace in mowing hayfields and helped new settlers and voters roll logs.[3] Harrison entered actively into the campaign as usual, mounting the stump for his friend at Corydon and writing electioneering letters. All might have been well had not a third candidate, John Johnson, a Virginia lawyer who stood outright for slavery, drawn sufficient strength from Randolph to bring about his defeat by a plurality of twenty-six votes. Great was the disappointment at Vincennes. In view of his well-known principles of republicanism, Harrison could hardly object to the extension of the voting franchise but his feeling relative to Jonathan Jennings can be gauged by his pledge of $100, when a subscription paper was circulated at Vincennes, for the purpose of sending a man to Washington who would adequately represent the town ana county.[4] Except for measures designed to embarrass the Governor, Delegate Jennings failed to distinguish himself in Congress.

Whatever the significance of the election, which, save in respect to the slavery issue, was no progressive trend, Harrison continued to promote the higher learning in the Territory. The circulating library still flourished and the affairs of that modest seminary known as Vincennes University were promoted by means of public lotteries backed by the Governor and three associates. Harrison was the first president of the Vincennes Historical and Antiquarian Society, recently organized, and in 1809 the Society for the Encouragement of Agriculture and the Useful Arts, which the Governor founded, began to offer prizes for the raising of bumper crops.[5] Affairs at Prophetstown were not forgotten however. To make a show of strength at Vincennes Harrison called out two companies of militia early in the spring. The men were dismissed soon after a French trader sent to watch developments at Prophetstown reported that the Prophet's present activity gave little cause for alarm. An epidemic of illness had nullified his asserted power in staying the hand of death, the Frenchman reported, and the Michigan tribesmen had fled to their homes.[6]

Had Tecumseh and The Prophet kept abreast of political developments in the Territory they would have discovered that this was no time to allow their apparent strength to diminish. The cramping of Indiana's bounds resulting from division of the Territory naturally brought the question of land acquisition to the fore. A few days before the election of delegate to Congress, Harrison had confided a long-contemplated project to William Eustis, Secretary of War under President Jefferson's successor, James Madison. The Indian boundary, the Governor pointed out, lay only twenty-one miles north of Vincennes. Below the town the country was "sunken and wet," while to the west the land was "almost entirely Prairie and not of such quality as to be settled for many years." Unless the tracts higher up could be acquired, Harrison suggested, the existing settlements could expect little further growth nor would the Territory ever advance to statehood within its present narrow bounds.[7]

While Harrison awaited a response to his letter to Eustis, The Prophet appeared at Vincennes with a retinue of only forty men. He entered a strong denial of any plan to attack the settlements. "The result of all my inquiries on the subject," Harrison advised the War Office, "is that the late combination was produced by

British intrigue . . . in anticipation of war. . . . It was however premature."[8]

Vincennes still lacked adequate protection, however. Harrison advocated the erection of a fort within the limits of a new land cession extending up the Wabash. At high water, he pointed out, Indian canoes from Prophetstown could descend the river faster than a man could ride on horseback. President Madison, after six weeks of reflection, decided to authorize the cession. Harrison was advised "to take advantage of the most favorable moment," to restrict payment to "the rate heretofore given."[9] The Governor at once notified Indian Agent John Johnston, successor of William Wells at Fort Wayne, and runners were sent to summon the tribesmen to meet at that post.

Harrison prepared for an absence of six weeks. On the first of September, accompanied by Captain Peter Jones, his secretary; Interpreter Joseph Barron, a negro servant and two friendly Indians, he set out on a newly cut road to North Bend which was reached early on the seventh. Harrison summoned the "agreeably surprised" Judge Symmes from his farm work[10] and next morning visited Cincinnati, now a metropolis of 2000 souls. There was considerable interest in the contemplated cession. At the government land office it was said that hundreds of families were ready to move west of the Greenville Treaty line, which ran roughly northeast. Resuming his journey to Fort Wayne through Dearborn County in eastern Indiana, Harrison discovered the farms to lie rather closely together.[11] Most of the county, a gore-shaped stretch of land, fifty miles by twelve, was still hemmed in by the Greenville Treaty line.

September 15, Harrison greeted the Indian Agent and the commanding officer at the Fort. It had been a journey on horseback of some 350 miles. A few Delawares and their interpreter, John Connor, arrived with the Governor. Intent upon securing the attendance of every principal chief, Harrison again sent out scouts to bring in the rest. Chief Winamac and a delegation of Potawatomies were the next to arrive, then the Miami chief, Peccon, also The Owl, Osage and Silver Heels, Pinnewa of the Potawatomies, Charley, Eel River chief, and more Delawares. Blackhoof, recognized Shawnee leader, a signer of the Treaty of Greenville, was present to lend his influence in favor of the cession.[12]

Harrison, his approach quite informal, visited each tribal camp in turn. A friendly Mohican chief revealed that British agents at Malden had warned the tribesmen never to entertain another proposition to sell their lands. Five Medals, a Potawatomie, refused to appear because he had learned that the Governor wished to purchase the land only for himself and his friends. Other strange rumors were abroad and a few of the chiefs were still at Fort Amherstburg receiving British bounty. The Delawares and Potawatomies who were present agreed to favor the cession although the Miami and Eel River chiefs declared they would never yield another foot. William Wells had attended their tribal conference, however, and there was reason to believe "this was a mere finesse to enhance the price of their land."[13] When 1100 chiefs and warriors were assembled, Harrison lighted the council fire.

A company of regulars leaned on their rifles and watched the proceedings. Four sworn interpreters translated the Governor's speech for the tribesmen. Putting his strongest point first, Harrison urged the benefits to be received from annuities. There was little game in the contemplated cession and the embargoes brought on by warring powers in Europe had greatly decreased the price of pelts. That the Indians were poor and their game increasingly scarce, Harrison emphasized, was due not so much to the encroachments of white settlers as to the commerce with British fur traders who stimulated the redmen to kill for the skins alone. To offset this improvidence the tribesmen should adopt Thomas Jefferson's plan. The raising of hogs and cattle required little labor and would be the surest resource. The remnant of the Wea tribe on the Wabash was poor and miserable, habitually spending all hunting proceeds for whiskey. The branches of the Miami nation would be much more "respectable and formidable" if they assembled together in the interior. As the Governor concluded an outline of the proposed cessions was shown. First was proposed cession of a wide expanse bordering the Vincennes tract on the north and extending up the Wabash, also a twelve-mile strip west of the Greenville Treaty line.

The Owl, a principal Miami chief, responded briefly and promised an answer from the tribes. On the third day, the 24th, the Indians met by themselves in the woods, a stormy council at which the Delawares and Potawatomies, who needed further annuities, continued to urge the cession while the Miamis held fast to their land. When the tribesmen reassembled before Harrison, the Miamis were angrily reproached by their brothers. The Governor pleaded for good feeling between the nations:

"Miamis be not offended with your brothers the Putawatimies. If they have discovered too much eagerness to comply with the wishes of their Father, look at their Women & Children see them exposed to the winds & the rain . . . to the snows of the Winter. Putawatimies do not suffer . . . your own distresses to make you angry with your brothers the Miamies. . . . I wish a strong chain to bind you together in the bonds of friendship. I wish to hear you speak with one voice. . . . Consult together once more."[14]

Miami chiefs from two villages were induced to agree to the Governor's proposal that evening but constantly arriving were fresh numbers of tribesmen "loaded with gifts from the British . . . and charged also with strong remonstrances against the treaty." The vehement talk of the newcomers, some 300 Miamis from the Mississinewa towns in the interior, intimidated the wavering chiefs. When the Mississinewa tribesmen declared they no longer considered the Potawatomies as brothers, that the chain which united them would be broken by the tomahawk, an answering shout of defiance went up and the warriors all hurried to the council house to speak with the Governor. Harrison met them with a rebuke and a warning to keep the peace. The Miami chiefs were invited to visit him at his quarters that evening.

Harrison discussed with these painted savages the subject of present British kindness. It proceeded, did it not, only from a wish to embroil the redmen with the United States? In case of a war, as in times past, the British would seek to interpose the Indians between themselves and the Americans. The British would be unable to defend Canada by themselves. "A complimentary answer," Captain Jones made note, "was returned by the Head Chief." That was all, and Harrison could accomplish little during the next three days except to effect a reconciliation between the tribes. Then the Miamis began to suggest that the regular government price, two dollars an acre, be paid for the land. Some one had been coaching them in tactics and their "tenaciousness in adhering to this idea," Harrison observed, was "astonishing."[15] He countered with the assertion that if they sold their land by the acre, the government would take only what was good, leaving many scattered and useless tracts on their hands. On the seventh day of the council The Owl declared they had determined to sell only the land west of Dearborn County and the Greenville Treaty line. They did not want the Governor to go home empty-handed.

Fourteen hundred savages, more or less, were now assembled about Fort Wayne, a treaty assemblage exceeding in numbers that of Greenville in 1795. A defeat for Harrison at this juncture would mean an unhappy loss of prestige. Was the government's commissioner unable to cope with such a representative throng? Harrison talked for two hours in reply to The Owl, reviewing the known conduct of the British and Americans toward the savage tribes. The

British, he reminded the savages, had always encouraged them to fight the Americans, yet, if the lands they had lost in these wars had been sold the annuities thus gained would have satisfied their every want. The United States, on the other hand, had never asked for assistance in fighting. The Great Father had asked the tribes only to remain at peace. In respect to treaties, Harrison added, the United States was the only nation to purchase land from the Indians, for the French and the British had appropriated it for their own use. The Indians listened in respectful silence, concealing their thoughts. When Winamac, the friendly Potawatomie, arose to sustain the Governor's argument the Miamis arose and left the council house. The situation was not yet in hand.

Harrison sent his interpreters and the more friendly chiefs circulating among the Miamis in an effort to discover "the real cause of their obstinacy," but could learn nothing new. The army officers at the fort began to predict that they would never be induced to sign. Harrison would not yet admit defeat. Arising early next morning, he took Interpreter Barron and entered the Miami camp at sunrise. There, received "with the utmost complacency," he brought the headmen together in Chief Peccon's tent. He had come to visit them, he remarked, not as the Governor but as their friend. He was ready to listen to all their complaints. Encouraged by this deference, Charley, son of Little Turtle, first spoke his mind. The chief produced from his shirt a copy of the Treaty of Grouseland. "Father," said Charley, "here are your own words . . . you promised that you would consider the Miamis as owners of the land . . . why then are you about to purchase it from others?"[16]

Harrison saw the light. The old question of prerogative had arisen. Wondering if this indeed were all, Harrison soothingly agreed that the land was the Miamis' own, yet this single tribe could not cede it nor receive the entire compensation without offending their friends and neighbors. And so he had summoned representatives of all the tribes to the council. But to satisfy any doubts, Harrison promised to draw up the treaty in a manner which would show the Delawares and Potawatomies participating only as allies of the Miamis, not as having any rights to the land. Such a promise, freely given, was considered a satisfactory concession. Seeking out further complaints the governor learned that one chief had been ignobly swindled by William Wells, another by a trader from Detroit. Each of their claims would be satisfied, Harrison promised, and the Miamis agreed to meet him again at the council house.

Considering the difficulties involved in this treaty, terms of sale somewhat in excess of sums hitherto paid were agreed upon and Harrison was forced to shade his original demands for land along the Wabash until Kickapoo consent was obtained. In addition to the twelve-mile strip west of Dearborn County, he secured a broad tract bordering the original Vincennes cession, and a long narrow strip west of the Wabash was ceded on the condition that the consent of the Weas be obtained. If the Kickapoo tribe could be induced to yield still another tract higher up along the Vermilion River, said to contain a rich copper mine, $700 in additional annuities was to be granted. Annuities promised for the principal cessions totaled $1,750, and $5,200 worth of goods was then delivered, and $1,500 in domestic animals granted the Miamis to satisfy their exclusive claim. "I think . . . upon the whole that the bargain is a better one . . . than any made by me for lands south [east] of the Wabash," Harrison summed up for the Secretary of War.[17] Tracts of land totalling nearly 3,000,000 acres had been acquired.

A gathering of citizens and a public dinner awaited Harrison's return to Vincennes. Toasts were drunk to the treaty and statehood within five years was forecast. The Indiana legislature and the militia officers of Knox County adopted resolutions recommending his appointment for a fourth term as governor "not only because of his superior military talents but also his integrity, patriotism, and firm attachment to the general government."[18] President James Madison, awaiting the results of the proceedings at Fort Wayne, now signed a commission for another renewal in office.

Two more transactions then pending concluded Harrison's treaty-making in Indiana. Chiefs Lapoussier, Little Eyes, and sixty Wea tribesmen who assembled in the council room at Grouseland readily agreed to the terms arrived at and were awarded $1,500 in goods and $400 in additional annuities. A portion of the latter sum was dependent upon Kickapoo cession of the land along the Vermilion, and on December 9 these tribesmen also were induced to yield.[19]

QUICKENING OF WAR

TWICE a year in the Territory were held militia muster days when able-bodied citizens assembled on parade. From the peculiar nature of militia, a self-governing and self-supporting body, these were days when duty gave way to pleasure for, as Harrison once explained to the Secretary of War, the battalions were armed with a curious assortment of weapons, including broken muskets and sticks, and, as was generally understood, with firewater taken internally. Elected militia officers, as a rule, were men who could be counted on for easy-going disciplinary methods; muster days in the West had long constituted an enjoyable social gathering at which farming prospects and politics were discussed.

Harrison spent many hours with militia leaders in the legislature to repair existing neglects in the law and with much striving he drilled into the Knox County battalion a small degree of discipline. A psychological factor eluded correction, however. Harrison found it discussed in a Kentucky newspaper which came regularly to Vincennes. In the fall of 1809, Governor Charles Scott, one-time militia general with St. Clair, Wilkinson and Wayne, warned the Kentucky legislature:

"A fatal spirit of indolence, in one respect, has seized upon us; and while basking in the sunshine we think not of the tempest. . . . We have yet to learn to make our citizens soldiers by giving them weapons and discipline and having a sufficient portion of their strength actually disposable in a moment of emergency."[1]

These words touched a responsive chord in Indiana. Harrison, who reviewed his ancient history that winter, devoted many hours to the writing of two long and discursive letters sent to Governor Scott of Kentucky and later published as "Thoughts on the Subject of the Discipline of the Militia of the United States." The letters were well received in Kentucky. Harrison, who had read "the ponderous work of Rollin" three times before he was seventeen years old, took his theme from the historical triumphs of a well-trained citizen militia in ancient Carthage, Greece, and Rome. What of America? In a republic where "standing armies are universally reprobated," militia training should become the first rule. "We must become a nation of warriors, or a nation of Quakers. . . . No instance can be produced of a free people preserving their liberties who suffered the military spirit to decline amongst them."

"We have indeed, no militia," Harrison continued. "That term is properly applied only to citizens who are disciplined or trained for war. . . . We look at the returns and find that 680,000 men are enrolled; but we forget that not a fiftieth part of them are soldiers. . . . I have no idea . . . that England and France united could conquer America. But, in our present situation, if 50,000 of their best disciplined troops were landed in one of the Southern States, we should find it a work of much time and difficulty to get rid of them. . . . The storm which has so long desolated the old world, has never presented to us an aspect more threatening. . . . Why then is there so much indifference manifested upon this all-important subject?"[2]

It was difficult, perhaps, to convince a pioneer in quest of his fortune in a new-found land that he should prepare for war. But with three land treaties executed in quick succession at a time when the tribesmen in the north and west were being organized against him, Harrison was to make use of the militia before very long. From a French trader, Joseph Brouillette, who was sent to Prophetstown in the spring of 1810, came disquieting reports. Angered because of the recent treaties, Tecumseh and The Prophet served notice that the ceded land would not be surveyed. The Prophet appeared to be well informed of everything that went on at Vincennes, the Frenchman reported.[3] Rumors of war came also to Harrison. Winamac, the friendly Potawatomie, declared that The Prophet, when all was ready, would strike first at Vincennes; Fort Wayne, Fort Dearborn at Chicago, and St. Louis would be the next to fall. Grosble, Piankeshaw chief, issued warnings of danger to a French resident and then came to Harrison to beg that his little band of tribesmen be removed across the Mississippi to escape the threat of war. The Prophet, said Grosble, was planning to enter Vincennes in the guise of friendship and give the signal for a general massacre. Harrison was reminded of the famous tribal organizer Pontiac who, in 1763, had annihilated the British garrison at Michilimackinac by a ruse.[4]

Although Harrison made none of these stories public The Prophet's hostility soon became known. In June a pirogue loaded with salt—part of the regular tribal annuity—ascended the Wabash to be received at several villages. The boatmen delivered a few barrels at Prophetstown and continued up the river but as they returned the barrels lay still untouched. The Prophet had decided not to receive it, they learned. As these boatmen began removing the barrels Tecumseh strode up and shook them by the hair. Were they Frenchmen or Americans? They were Frenchmen, fortunately. But a swarm of Indians began to plunder Brouillette's cabin and the boatmen returned to Vincennes to broadcast a tale of hostility and approaching war.[5]

The alarm quickly aroused the frontier. Harrison called a public meeting to discuss prompt measures for defense and was urged to call out two companies of militia, which he obligingly did, although the principal value of such a force, the Governor knew, lay in military display. Bodies of undisciplined Indians, wherever collected, were often subject to "unaccountable paroxysms of terror," and would scatter at the first alarm.[6] Harrison sent Colonel Vigo to gauge the sentiment among the Miamis who were being solicited by a band of Wyandots to join The Prophet, and Touissant Dubois, French trader and guide, was detailed to Prophetstown as successor of Brouillette.

Vigo returned from his mission to state that only one Miami chief, as far as he could determine, had been seduced by The Prophet. No immediate danger appeared in prospect. At Prophetstown, Captain Dubois was reminded that the Indians had been cheated out of their lands, that no sale to the whites was good unless ratified by all. Harrison decided to reply through his most trusted interpreter, Joseph Barron, and wrote out a message, conciliatory yet barbed, for The Prophet. Arriving at the village Barron sought out that chieftain who scowled at him silently for some moments before speaking. "For what purpose do you come here? Brouillette was here, he was a spy. Dubois was here, he was a spy. . . . You, too, are a spy. There is your grave—look on it!"[7] The Prophet was still well informed. Chief Tecumseh soon came striding up. He assured the interpreter that his life was in no danger and asked him to state his business. Barron then translated Harrison's message into the musical Shawnee tongue:

"Notwithstanding the improper language you have used [and] . . . what bad white men have told you I am not your personal enemy . . . There is yet but very little harm done but what may easily be repaired. . . . A great deal of that work depends upon you. . . . You say [we] purchased land from those who had no right to sell.

Show the truth of this and the lands will instantly be restored. Show us the rightful owners of these lands."[8]

Tecumseh, a hospitable native, invited Barron to lodge with him that night and secluded within a well-furnished cabin, the two men talked in the dark until long after midnight. The great chief denied that it was his intention to make war. It was hardly possible, however, to remain on good terms with the white men unless their settlements were held within present bounds. The principle that the Indian lands were the common property of all should be universally acknowledged. "The great spirit said he gave this great island to his red children," exclaimed the warrior chief. "He placed the whites on the other side of the big water, they were not contented with their own. . . . They have driven us from the sea to the lakes, we can go no farther."[9] It was the eternal Indian soliloquy. Tecumseh declared that he himself would go to Vincennes, bringing a retinue of only thirty followers, and talk with the Governor. He remembered Harrison at the Greenville councils, "a very young man sitting by the side of General Wayne."

Meanwhile Harrison greeted a company of army regulars, dispatched by the War Department to erect the new fort on the Wabash. Harrison first set them to work on old Fort Sackville at Vincennes and the two companies of militia, their harvest season approaching, were temporarily dismissed. The Governor was satisfied with Tecumseh's assurance that he would bring only a few men although on August 12, 1810, Captain George R. C. Floyd, commanding at Fort Knox, counted eighty canoes filled with warriors "painted in the most terrific manner." Floyd halted the flotilla and examined the canoes. The Indians were well prepared for battle. "They were headed," the officer wrote his wife, "by the brother of The Prophet, who . . . is one of the finest men I ever saw—about six feet high, straight with large fine features and altogether a daring, bold-looking fellow."[10] Indian canoes carried from two to ten men each and the number of his followers was estimated at nearly 400.

Tecumseh, arriving at Vincennes late that day, was escorted to Grouseland where Harrison was sitting on the porch, reading and smoking. The Governor arose to meet an unusually handsome chief. The color of Tecumseh's eyes, deep-set, has been described as hazel, his nose somewhat aquiline, and he bore a cheerful, friendly air. The chief was neatly dressed in buckskin, his small arms—presents from the British—a tomahawk mounted in silver and a hunting knife in a neat leather case.[11] Harrison stepped down, extended his hand, and offered the chief the hospitality of his home, but Tecumseh asked merely to pitch his tent "under that elm tree."

A council which drew many spectators to Grouseland opened on the third day of his visit. Harrison had set out a neat row of chairs on the lawn which, on the side toward the river, was fenced in by catalba posts. The Territorial officials, including Interpreter Barron and Captain Floyd, were seated; Lieutenant Jesse Jennings and twelve regulars from Fort Knox were conspicuously present and a hundred militiamen were lodged within the house. Tecumseh, bringing possibly one half of his forces, halted at a distance and critically eyed the enclosure. The tribesmen ever hated the white man's fences. Harrison sent Barron to usher the chief forward but a request was brought back that the council be held in Grouseland's walnut grove. So the chairs were removed from the enclosure and set out in the grove.

Harrison courteously suggested that his distinguished visitor sit among the principal council members: "It is the wish of the Great Father, the President of the United States, that you do so." Tecumseh emphatically declined. "My Father?—The Sun is my father, the Earth is my mother—and on her bosom I will recline!" With these few words he stretched himself upon the ground.[12]

Few of the whites could understand this brief outburst delivered in Shawnee and puzzled spectators glanced quickly about to gauge the great chief's meaning. The effect, related one who was present, was "electrical."[13] Harrison quietly arose and opened the council with a brief talk. If Tecumseh had any complaints to make let them openly be known. There should be no concealment between the white chief and as great a warrior as Tecumseh. Let all transactions take place in an open path and under a clear sky.

Speaking rapidly in his native language, Tecumseh replied that the whites had encroached too far, that the tribes had been greatly wronged. Indian lands, he said, were held by all the tribes in common and none could sell without the consent of all. He was prepared to punish the chiefs who had signed the Fort Wayne treaties, his warriors would reduce them to the status of common men. None should escape his anger. Everything would be placed in the hands of the warriors who were determined to make a stand.

Harrison did not attempt to reply. Tecumseh's speeches during the first two days of the council, he reported to Eustis, were "sufficiently insolent and his pretensions arrogant."[14] Nothing could be accomplished toward an understanding. The chief poured a torrent of abuse on Chief Winamac, who was present, for having aided the transaction at Fort Wayne. On the third day of the council, following an exchange of speeches, a verbal explosion took place. Reviewing the whole course of the white man's conduct in America, Tecumseh recalled the happy tribal relations once enjoyed with the French who had never asked for lands nor fenced them in. He criticized the tactics of the British, however, in inducing the Indians to go to war. Then he recalled, Harrison related, "every instance of injustice and injury . . . committed by our citizens upon the Indians from the commencement of the revolutionary war." Could he now be blamed, protested Tecumseh, for placing so little confidence in the promises of the Americans? "Brother," the chief continued, "I wish you would take pity on the red people. . . . If you . . . cross the boundary of your present settlement it will . . . produce great troubles among us." Harrison, remaining seated, began to relate instances of "uniform regard to justice" shown the Indians, but before all his words had been translated, Tecumseh sprang up in violent anger. "Tell him he lies," he shouted at Barron.[15]

A number of warriors, armed with knives, tomahawks and war clubs, rose menacingly from the ground; a sharp click was heard as Winamac cocked his pistol. "Those fellows mean mischief, you'd better bring up the guard," Secretary Gibson called out to Lieutenant Jennings. Spectators scattered to find sticks and stones. William Winans, the Methodist minister who lodged at Grouseland, ran to the porch and stood guard at the door with a shotgun as Mrs. Harrison shooed her children into the house.[16]

Barron hesitated to translate Tecumseh's actual words and the chief marked the evasion. He insisted that the Governor be called a liar. Harrison arose from his chair with drawn sword and as the regulars came running up he warned them not to fire. He warmly reprimanded Tecumseh. There would be no more such talk, exclaimed the Governor; the council fire would be extinguished that very day. After a brief interval of silence Tecumseh turned away with his warriors and went back to his camp.

Harrison began to wonder if Tecumseh, in bringing so great a force, had been searching for an opening for actual outbreak. Two companies of militia from the neighboring settlements were ordered to assemble that night and were embodied next morning with those of the town. They paraded through the streets with a great clatter, a troop of of seventy-five dragoons in the van. Tecumseh summoned Barron to take an apology to the Governor and was granted another hearing in the afternoon.

Tecumseh's talk, as he reappeared in the walnut grove, was earnest

From a painting by Stanley M. Arthurs.

Harrison and Tecumseh meet in council in the walnut grove at Grouseland.

Grouseland, Harrison's home at Vincennes, Indiana.
The restored mansion is still standing.

although not wholly politic, revealing as it did the instigation of self-seeking whites. "Brother," said Tecumseh——
"There are many white people among you who are not true Americans. . . . A person came to our village shortly after the Treaty . . . and said . . . I am the Agent of a large party of white people who are your friends and will support you, they sent me here to inform you everything that . . . the Governor . . . is doing against you . . . but you must observe great secrecy and by no means inform me. . . .
"Brother. Another American told us lately at our village that you were about to assemble the Indians . . . for the purpose of making more proposals for more land. . . . This man told me that I must go to Vincennes and make my objections . . . and not be afraid to speak very loud to you."[17]

Tecumseh, as Harrison had knowledge, was referring to William Wells, deposed Indian Agent at Fort Wayne, and to William McIntosh, Tory land speculator who had belligerently opposed the move for second-grade government. McIntosh had consistently criticized the treaty cessions as they tended to cheapen the value of his own speculations. Of shady reputation in business dealings, he was the Governor's most active enemy at Vincennes.[18] It was hardly necessary to ask the identity of the visitors at Prophetstown. Harrison put two questions to the chief. Would the surveyors sent to mark the new purchase be molested? And were the Kickapoos to receive the annuities promised in the final land treaty? "When you speak of annuities I look at the land and pity the women and children," was Tecumseh's reply. "I am authorized to say they will not receive them. . . . I want the present boundary line to continue. Should you cross it . . . bad consequences."

Harrison could yield nothing. Since the land had been acquired by fair purchase, he answered, the government would support its rights by the sword. He promised to place Tecumseh's claims before President Madison. Then the council adjourned. Harrison arose early next morning to pay his visitor farewell. Why, inquired the chief in his tent, should the President seriously consider his claims? "The Great Chief is so far off he will not be injured by the war. He may still sit in his town and drink his wine whilst you and I fight it out."[19] Tecumseh and three principal chiefs then departed on a recruiting tour of the Illinois country and Michigan, entering Malden, across the Detroit River in Canada, early in November.[20]

"The brother of The Prophet . . . is the great man of the party," Harrison notified Eustis.[21] Disregarding the chieftains' warnings, he engaged two government surveyors to run the line of the new purchase and for a time the work was accomplished without incident.

The Indians were not at all dependent upon American annuities for their winter garments. Host to 6000 Indians at Fort Amherstburg during the fall months, according to record, Colonel Matthew Elliott marked their disposition as "ripe for war." The tenor of a speech flung out by The Prophet confirmed this view. "Our neighbors are on the Eve of War,"[22] he informed a superior, a disclosure so alarming that Governor Craig instructed the British Minister at Washington to inform our government that danger impended upon the frontier. With energies bent against Napoleon in Spain, Britain was not prepared to defend her Canadian border and wished to shoulder no blame. As Governor Craig put it: "A war so near our own frontiers would be very inconvenient . . . and would expose us to suspicion . . . which would sooner or later involve ourselves."[23]

Craig received a cogent analysis of the effect of British sympathy for the tribes from the military commander in Canada. "Considerations of prudence" having been neglected by Elliott, wrote Sir Isaac Brock, the Indians had retired from the November council "with a full conviction that they might rely with confidence upon receiving from us every requisite of war."

In the light of Harrison's charges of British support for the tribesmen this letter has further significance. "Our cold attempt to dissuade that much abused people from engaging in a rash enterprise could scarcely be expected to prevail," Brock went on, "particularly after giving such manifest indications of a contrary sentiment by the liberal quantity of stores with which they were dismissed."[24] That was the essential point. Even the British, at this juncture, were blaming their agents for inspiration and aid to the tribes.

Another sequel to Tecumseh's visit was Harrison's showdown with William McIntosh. Some one had been gossiping that the Governor not only defrauded the redmen in council but was profiting from the large quantity of Indian goods lately drawn. Harrison posted a reward for the apprehension of the slanderer and as soon as the evidence was in, brought suit for $9000 damages, the trial to be held in the April, 1811, term of court.

McIntosh bestirred himself in a countermove, mailing to Delegate Jonathan Jennings at Washington accusations against the Governor of bribery and collusion in public land sales. Bent upon laying "the groundwork for an impeachment,"[25] Jennings laid the documents before President James Madison but the plan brought swift rebuttals from citizens of standing in Indiana. While Harrison sought not to explain his conduct, his financial circumstances being no better than they should be, but to expose "a tissue of most barefaced falsehoods,"[26] certain testimonials were forwarded from which could be read:

"The undersigned have recently heard that attempts are making by a faction . . . to rob Govr Harrison of the confidence of the General Government—a Confidence which by his mild, just, wise and Republican administration he has eminently merited. . . . In no Country we believe can any chief magistrate enjoy in as high degree and Confidence, the love, respect of the great majority of the people than does Governor Harrison."[27]

Other voluntary depositions and letters in support of the Governor sufficed further to refute the charges. In the aggregate this testimony bulked large, of passing interest also was its indignant and outraged tone. President Madison acted no further than to have the documents filed by the State Department and nothing was heard of the matter on the floor of Congress. Also gratifying to the Governor was the result of the McIntosh trial at which the defendant was overwhelmed. "Every part of my conduct, and administration for ten years was scrutiniz^d," Harrison summed up with pride. "After twenty-five witnesses were examined the rascally calumniator begg^d for mercy."[28] The Governor had insisted on that number of witnesses.

His dealings with the Indians and his land transactions deemed fair, Harrison waived nearly two thirds of the $4000 damages awarded, accepting payment of the balance in lands much of which in late years was turned over to widows and orphans of soldiers.[29] The trial, however, only slightly curbed the machinations of McIntosh. Following a sudden clash of small arms with Attorney General Randolph, who was stabbed in the back, the Scotchman was revealed months afterward as having conducted "a treasonable correspondence" with the British at Amherstburg and during secret midnight councils at the home of a sympathizer, he induced the Wea chiefs to sign a declaration "that their lands had been taken . . . without their consent." McIntosh himself had lost his lands, he said, for attempting to take their side.[30]

Strained relations with Spain in West Florida took the additional company of regulars from Fort Knox that spring and construction of the long contemplated fort on the Wabash was deferred. News of

Indian depredations at last was reported as soon as the regulars had left. Two Potawatomie Indians had destroyed a hunting party of four whites on the Missouri River, settlers on the Wabash and White Rivers indicated an alarming loss of livestock, and on a farm in Illinois Territory another man was slain.[31] Harrison warned the settlers not to pursue the marauders because of their fondness of awaiting in ambush, and acted to avoid outright war. Two men were sent to recover stolen horses from Prophetstown and to apprehend the Potawatomie offenders reported to have taken refuge there. These emissaries brought back four horses, an unusual piece of work, but the Potawatomies, it was reported, had fled into Illinois. Then Harrison discovered that the neighboring Weas were proving difficult. Whereas in April (before the McIntosh trial) these tribesmen were "all submission," in May two surveyors of the new purchase were seized and tightly bound.[32]

The Governor chose to exercise forbearance with his red neighbors, writing frankly to Secretary Eustis what he could not admit to Tecumseh: "I wish I could say that the Indians were treated with justice and propriety . . . by our own citizens but . . . it is very rare that they obtain any satisfaction for the most unprovoked wrongs." A Vincennes innkeeper who had shot a drunken warrior was acquitted by a jury, Harrison reported, "almost without deliberation." When two Wea tribesmen were wounded by a settler's shotgun, Harrison sent them gifts of atonement and a surgeon to dress their wounds. The righteousness and virtue popularly attributed to slayers of Indians would not down. But caught between aggressiveness and violence on both sides, Harrison could not exempt the Indian from blame. "Encroachment upon the rights and property of those who will not resist," he advised the Secretary, "is a characteristic of every savage. 'Sooner shall the lover stop short of the last favor (I use a figure of the late Presd^t Adams) having obtained the rest' than an Indian cease to demand as long as there is a prospect of his demands being complied with."[33]

The seasonal crop of rumors concerning The Prophet's activity was a bumper one that spring. A Kickapoo chief "of excellent character" declared that the peaceful pretensions of Tecumseh and his brother were not to be relied upon. They had warned their young warriors against precipitancy in war, he said, but to those who joined their growing confederacy a rich harvest of plunder and scalps had been promised. Governor William Clark of Missouri reported that the Sacs had accepted the war belt and an Indian interpreter at Chicago declared it his certainty that the Michigan tribes were bent on immediate war. When the annual boatload of salt went up the Wabash in June another incident was noted. This time The Prophet seized the whole boatload, notifying the Frenchmen in charge that Tecumseh, who was recruiting forces in Michigan, would soon arrive at Vincennes with several hundred warriors.[34]

As long as Vincennes appeared weakly defended, Harrison feared a blow from some quarter. It was necessary to make a show of words if not of arms. The Governor summoned Interpreter Barron and Captain Walter Wilson, large-framed militia officer, and dictated another message for the Shawnee leaders at Prophetstown:

"Brothers, this is the third year that all the white people . . . have been alarmed at your proceedings, you threaten us with war, you invite all the tribes to the north and west . . . to join against us.

"Brothers . . . my warriors are preparing themselves, not to strike you, but to defend themselves and their women and children. You shall not surprise us as you expect to do. . . .

"Brothers, you talk of coming to see me attended by all your young men. . . . I must be plain with you; I will not suffer you to come into our settlements with such a force. . . .

"My Friend, Tecumseh, the bearer is a good man and a brave warrior, treat him well, you are yourself a warrior."[35]

Barron and Wilson, speculating upon what manner of reception might await them, reached the village after five days. There they were escorted to a cabin, fitted with rugs of bearskin, while The Prophet held a council. Barron grew doubtful of their present security, particularly so when he saw the village squaws, led by The Prophet's wife, file past the cabin while making unfriendly gestures. Dark came on and the men lay in silence, very watchful, until toward midnight there was a knock at the door. Tecumseh, who to their surprise now entered, revealed the result of the council. The two white men, he said, were to be turned over to The Prophet's wife and her squaws to do their bidding. Overruled in his protests, Tecumseh had now come to lead them to safety.

The two men placed their lives in his hands, following the tall chief out of the cabin and creeping silently through the town. A wild turkey gobble given as a signal halted them some distance away and Tecumseh led them to a prearranged spot where two young warriors guarded their horses. The chief declared in parting that he would arrive at Vincennes in eighteen days or less "to wash away all bad stories," and further promised to bring only a few warriors.[36]

While Harrison awaited the return of Barron and Wilson more disquieting news came from Illinois where Indians had shot a settler ploughing in his field and had massacred his family. Other families in the neighborhood were fleeing to the towns or gathering together for safety. Alarmed for the safety of Vincennes itself in the absence of a regular force, the Governor indited a terse note to the Secretary of War:

"I was informed four weeks ago that it was the intention of The Prophet to commence hostilities in Illinois in order to cover his principal object which was an attack on this place. . . . At present a majority of the best informed chiefs are for peace but every scalp taken . . . with impunity will add to the number of the hostile party. . . . No two days pass without some horses being stolen."[37]

Baron and Wilson now arrived with their story testifying that Tecumseh had promised to bring only a few warriors. Harrison dispatched a sentinel to keep watch along the river, however, and several days later that officer galloped into town with the news that a formidable war party was descending the Wabash while numerous Indians were approaching by land. But Tecumseh, strangely enough, had halted his followers some distance away for what purpose one could only speculate. These tidings quickly spread in Vincennes; suspense rapidly mounted. Reported the *Western Sun* of that village: "53 canoes have certainly been counted . . . and a number [of Indians] have come by land—we cannot estimate the whole at less than 250 or 300 men. . . . What can be the cause of this delay but to put us off our guard."[38] Harrison sent Captain Wilson to discover what was abroad but Tecumseh only temporized. After delaying five days to collect all his land forces he arrived at Vincennes late on Saturday, July 27, bringing an entourage reported by Harrison as 300 strong.

Once these savages were lodged about the village, Harrison realized, any mischief might occur. He had reason to recall the warning of Chief Grosble. If an attack was intended, furthermore, it was the natural wish of the Indians that the town be surprised. A victory by surprise would give the treacherous redskin "more éclat," in Harrison's words, "than the most brilliant success obtained by other means."[39] He summoned three companies of local militia, paraded them through the streets with a troop of dragoons, and "by some management in marching and changing quarters" made the three companies appear as four or five. Night and day patrols of horse and foot were active, the Indian encampment closely watched.[40]

The loud clatter of arms carried a soothing note, yet, for fear of a nocturnal outbreak, the citizens could hardly sleep. Harrison wished to finish the council quickly. He requested first that Tecumseh meet him on Monday but not until the day following did the chief send word he was ready. Tecumseh inquired if armed troops would attend the council, in which case his warriors would be armed. Harrison served notice that only the dismounted dragoons would be present but he judiciously concealed a force of militia inside his house while a body of riflemen loitered conspicuously along the path by which Tecumseh was to approach.[41] Not until late in the afternoon, as rain clouds threatened, did Tecumseh finally make his approach bringing nearly 200 followers armed with native weapons. Amenities were brief. Very sharply Harrison demanded an explanation. Why had the chieftain brought so large a force? What was the inspiration for the raids and murders in Illinois? Who was responsible for the seizure of the annuity salt?

Tecumseh was visibly confused. He neglected the plea he had planned to make and took up the last question first. It appeared impossible, he said, to please the Governor. This year he had been angry because the salt had been taken, last because it was refused. Tecumseh was making some further excuses when it began to rain and he asked that the council be adjourned.

At two o'clock next day he returned with some chiefs hitherto friendly to Harrison, together with his regular following, and called upon Lapoussier of the Weas to speak. The Wea chief, who had been cultivated quite surreptitiously by McIntosh, declared that the Miamis had been forced to sign the Treaty of Fort Wayne only because of Potawatomie threats of violence. It was perfectly proper, therefore, to discover the chief responsible and to punish him. Harrison impatiently brushed aside this quibbling. Miami consent, he truthfully could declare, had been gained through friendly means. Intent upon putting an end to the council he addressed himself to Tecumseh. The leader of foremost influence among the tribesmen, he declared, could prove the truth of his peaceful pretensions by delivering up the Potawatomies who had murdered the four whites on the Missouri.

Tecumseh replied with a lengthy speech in which he revealed all his plans. After great difficulty he had united all the northern tribes in his confederacy and now the southern tribes must be induced to join. The Seventeen Fires, the United States, had set an example of national union and no Indian complained, so why should the whites be alarmed at similar efforts of his own. The Potawatomie offenders were no longer at Prophetstown, Tecumseh added, yet why should they not be forgiven? He himself had forbidden revenge upon other tribesmen who had wronged his people. He promised to send out runners to warn against further forays, however, and in atonement for the murders done he presented some ceremonial wampum. As Harrison laid aside the wampum he asked his final question. Was Tecumseh still intent upon preventing white settlement in the ceded Wea country? The chief replied that he hoped nothing would be done until his return from the south when he intended to pay a call upon the President. It was possible that Indian hunting parties might interfere with the new settlements, he added.

The conversation had lasted until it was nearly dark. Harrison declared that the moon which they now beheld would sooner fall than the President suffer his people to be murdered with impunity, and he would dress his warriors in petticoats sooner than yield up this fairly acquired land. That was all. Tecumseh turned back to his camp.[42]

THE MARCH UP THE WABASH

T HE motive of Tecumseh, in hovering above Vincennes to collect his land forces, could only be interpreted as hostile. After
promising to bring only a few warriors he had descended
menacingly upon a town inadequately protected. Indians whom Harrison classified as neutral expressed the belief that some sudden blow
was meditated. In the opinion of the French traders and friendly
chiefs whom the Governor questioned, Tecumseh's intention was to
demand that the new purchase be abandoned. If this had been refused, he would have seized and put to death the treaty-signing
chiefs who were present, indicating Harrison as the man actually
responsible for bloodshed. Should Harrison have interfered there
would have been further outbreak. "Had he found me unprepared I
am certain that he would have found means to pick a quarrel," the
Governor contended. "That he had some design in view he thought
fit to abandon is most evident."[1]

Whatever his motive, Tecumseh had broken his promise to limit
his forces and had shown a singular lack of understanding of the
temper of the whites. As he made his departure, on August 5, he left
behind him a spirit of retaliation which he failed to comprehend.
Even before the council was over, a group of citizens had held an
indignation meeting. A committee headed by Samuel T. Scott, the
Presbyterian minister, drew up an address to the President urging
the "exertion of some rigor" against The Prophet's band, and
adopted a brace of stern resolutions:

"*Resolved,* That the . . . safety of the persons and property of
this frontier can never be effectually secured but by the breaking up
of the combination formed by the Shawanese prophet. . . .

"*Resolved,* That we are fully convinced . . . this combination
. . . is a British scheme, and that the agents of that power are constantly exciting the Indians to hostility. . . .

"*Resolved,* That the assemblage of Indians at this place . . . was
calculated to excite the most serious alarm, and but for the energetic

measures . . . adopted by our executive, it is highly probable that the threatened destruction of this place and the massacre of the inhabitants, would have been the consequence.

"*Resolved,* That a temporizing policy is not calculated to answer any beneficial purpose with savages. . . .

"*Resolved,* That we approve highly of the prompt and decisive measures adopted . . . by the Governor."[2]

The resolutions approved by Harrison were forwarded to Washington. News of action by the War Department now arrived. Responding to the alarms created in Illinois on July 17, Secretary Eustis ordered the Fourth Regiment of regulars—comprising about 600 men recruited in New England—to descend the Ohio from Pittsburgh "with all possible expedition." If The Prophet should seriously threaten hostilities he should be attacked, Harrison was advised, and the force to be employed should be "sufficient to ensure success." This left nothing more to be asked yet another dispatch, dated July 20, 1811, arrived in the same mail. It was the earnest wish of the President, Eustis now observed, that peace be preserved. He had ordered the main body of regulars to halt at Newport, opposite Cincinnati, while a single company advanced to receive the Governor's instructions. Harrison was authorized to bring on the rest of the regiment only "if indispensably required."[3]

Fuming at the vacillation of officials who lacked appreciation of Indian nature Harrison served notice that he was ordering on the whole regiment with a view to erecting the contemplated fort on the Wabash and quieting the frontier. The mere approach of an army would do much to quiet Indian hostility, although a runner sent to inform the hostile chiefs that an armed force was now on its way returned with an avowal that the Governor was only bluffing.[4] Since this was hardly the case, Harrison now circulated peremptory demands that the chiefs deliver up all tribesmen guilty of murder, all stolen horses, and that they summon their straying warriors from the fold of The Prophet. To prevent any outbreak or misunderstanding the tribesmen were instructed to remain in their villages and keep the peace.

These warnings availed little. General Wayne, whom the Indians still remembered, was now dead. The settlers along the frontier, including the Governor himself, had long contented themselves with farming and other peaceful pursuits. The Indians were confident they were no longer warriors. "Their hands are soft, their faces are white," commented Chief Shabonee (or Shaubena), friend of Tecumseh. "One half of them are calico peddlers. The other half can only shoot squirrels."[5] American prowess in the field, in short, had sadly decayed.

As a corrective measure, Harrison advised the War Office he intended to lead an expedition up the Wabash to build the desired fort and then conduct a military demonstration in the vicinity of Prophetstown, taking hostages if necessary. If the show of arms did not cause The Prophet's party to disperse, at least its presence would convince the Indians that the government was determined to protect its own.[6]

Tecumseh's visits to Vincennes had made news in the West. As Harrison prepared to return his call resentment against The Prophet and the British was mounting. A crisis was believed to be near at hand. Governor Ninian Edwards of Illinois expressed the opinion that "partial war" would continue as long as the savages were permitted to assemble at Prophetstown.[7] Governor William Clark of Missouri believed the crisis to be "fast approaching."[8] In Ohio, Kentucky, and Tennessee, public meetings were held, budding statesmen mounted the stump. Prophetstown, product of British perfidy, became a political issue, the Federalists dissenting; Vincennes, lonely beleaguered outpost, the symbol of a cause. Such at least was the popular sentiment in the West and despite the deprecatory gestures of the fading remnant of Federalists the current wave of martial feeling was to unseat nearly half the members of Congress, those called "submission men," in the fall. Kentucky, inclined toward an invasion of Canada on her own account, was to send young Henry Clay—foremost War Hawk—to Washington to be elected Speaker of the House.

Late August was at hand and the Ohio River falling rapidly as Harrison rode to meet the Fourth Regiment at Jeffersonville, rallying Indiana militia officers along the way. Because of tardy supply shipments the regiment had been delayed and Harrison was forced into days of impatient waiting while the river continued to fall, endangering the progress of keelboats. He reviewed the neighboring militia of Clark and Harrison Counties and, visiting Louisville across the river, was greeted by stalwart Kentuckians who acknowledged themselves ready to march anywhere at any time provided only that the route lay north. The question was merely how far they might go, inasmuch as a clash with England was being debated. Harrison was prompt in reporting this sentiment to the War Office. "The people of this Territory and Kentucky are extremely pressing in offers of their services for an expedition into the Indian country. Any number of men might be obtained for this purpose or for a march into Canada."[9]

A letter from Kentucky's famed attorney-general, Colonel Joseph Hamilton Daveiss, typified sentiment. Daveiss, who had fought at Fallen Timbers, was yearning for a renewal of military exercise and fame. Governor Harrison provided his only hope. "It is but rare that anything of the military kind is done," he wrote wistfully:

"it is still more extraordinary that a gentleman of military talents should conduct matters of this kind when they are to be done. . . . Under all the privacy of a letter, I make free to tell you, that I have imagined there were but two men in the west who had military talents: And you, sir, were the first of the two. It is, thus, an opportunity of service much valued by me. I go as a volunteer. . . ."[10]

Who, Harrison might reflect, was the other man of military talents in the West? Quite likely it was Kentucky's first governor, Isaac Shelby, "Hero of King's Mountain" in the Revolution. The military talents of Andrew Jackson, a major general of militia in Tennessee, had not yet become known.

Daveiss and his followers were to join the army at Vincennes. Declining offers of volunteer infantry from Kentucky, for Indiana could supply a sufficiency of troops of this character, Harrison wrote Governor Scott asking permission to accept a detachment of mounted militia, Captain Peter Funk of Louisville galloping in such haste with the letter to Frankfort as to ride his fine mount to death.[11] A small troop of mounted riflemen was organized under Funk and another was expected to march from Kentucky after the fall harvest, in about four weeks' time. The size of the Fourth Regiment, which arrived September 3 in ten keelboats, was disappointing. Sickness and desertion had reduced the regulars to scarcely more than 400 effectives. While the boats continued down the Ohio, Harrison rode overland to Vincennes with Colonel John P. Boyd, regimental commander. Boyd, a Massachusetts man, was famous for exploits in India where he had commanded an army of elephants and native mercenaries in the service of the Nizam of Hyderabad.[12] He told some tall stories. Much indeed was expected of the Colonel in the coming campaign.

According to orders Harrison already had sent out, all of Indiana's militia was to be mobilized even though the plan was not yet authorized by the Secretary of War. Unaware of the reduction of Colonel Boyd's force, Eustis recommended that only four companies of militia be used. Yet Governor Harrison's force, according to a previous letter, must be "sufficient to ensure success." Directly upon his arrival at Vincennes, Harrison asked Judge Benjamin Parke, a captain of dragoons, and Chancellor Waller Taylor, major of militia, to indicate the true situation of affairs upon the frontier. Two questions were put for these gentlemen to answer, their responses to be placed before Eustis. Would it be safe to penetrate the Indian country with such a force as already prescribed by the Secretary of War, and would not the object of the expedition be greatly promoted by enlistment of all the available militia? The responses furnished by Taylor and Parke substantiated to the full Harrison's own opinion and defined the policy underlying the contemplated expedition. To dissolve The Prophet's combination, Judge Taylor pointed out, would require "a force that would awe the turbulent and refractory, confirm the timid and wavering, and insure protection and safety to the friendly and well disposed."[13] Wrote Parke: "The smallest reversal of fortune on the part of the Government would instantly unite all the Indians against it and a five years' war would scarcely be sufficient to restore peace on the frontier."[14] Not only was The Prophet's party increasing, he added, but increasingly greater quantities of supplies had been furnished by the British at Malden. To give point to this assertion Harrison quoted the testimony of Captain Touissant Dubois. In thirty years of trading among the tribesmen, Dubois had never known "one-fourth as many goods given to the Indians as now."[15] Another trader lately at Amherstburg reported that the value of goods placed with the British Indian Department during the present year exceeded that of previous years by twenty thousand pounds sterling. Vast stores of gunpowder, flints, lead-bars and rifles had been requisitioned; blankets, shirts, and shrouds of cloth were also furnished. Profiting also by means of the American annuity system, the Indians had never been so well provided for.

Satisfied that Eustis would see the light, Harrison went ahead with plans to use twelve or fourteen companies of militia infantry, averaging sixty to seventy men each, and four of mounted riflemen and dragoons in addition to Boyd's regulars. Not all of the militia responded, but a letter from Eustis confirming his judgment was already on the way. By land and by water, the army was slowly converging upon Vincennes. Colonel Joseph Bartholomew, with three companies of infantry, sixty mounted riflemen, and a small troop of dragoons, was marching from eastern Indiana. Vincennes and Knox County contributed about 350 militia in addition to eighty dragoons under Captain Parke. Captain Peter Funk and Colonel Daveiss arrived with some forty Kentucky riflemen and more were to follow in October. Exclusive of regulars, the volunteer army numbered about 800 men of which 200 were mounted. Men of prominence in Indiana were the elected militia leaders; several had engaged in former Indian campaigns.

Coursing a distance of 160 miles along the shallow Wabash, the flatboats of regulars skirted rocks and sandbars while a rapid current obliged the men daily to wade into the river and haul. At dusk, on September 19, the smartly-dressed regulars landed their boats and were boisterously greeted by a motley militia, roughly clad in deerskin frocks, caps of bearskin, and carrying knives, tomahawks and hatchets in their belts. "Their whooping and yells and their appearance," wrote an astonished private from New Hampshire, "caused us to doubt whether we had not actually landed among the savages themselves."[16] Drums beat, flags were unfurled. Harrison jovially greeted the officers. Vincennes was quite taken by the array of brass-buttoned regulars, elegantly garbed in tail coats and skin-tight pantaloons with tall stovepipe hats, topped with red, white and blue cockades, tightly strapped under the chin. The army uniform of 1811, then in a period of transition, was probably the gaudiest costume ever to appear on the frontier.

As Commander-in-Chief of the army, General Harrison turned to details of organization and supply. He appointed as aides Major Henry Hurst, a Vincennes lawyer, Major Waller Taylor, Colonel Marston G. Clark, a member of the Indiana legislature, and Attorney-General Thomas Randolph, who volunteered as a private. Colonel Daveiss reported also as a private but was complimented with the rank of major over the dragoons and mounted riflemen.[17] Prominent among the latter was the colorful troop of "Yellow Jackets" under Captain Spier Spencer, an old Indian fighter, and the appointment of Daveiss was not according to their wish.

While the arrival of supplies was awaited, the leaders of the infantry corps were directed to drill their men. September 22 Harrison paraded the militia on Big Prairie, north of Vincennes, maneuvering the infantry in two long thin columns after the manner of Wayne's order of march and battle. The troops were instructed to face quickly to the right or left in meeting imaginary flank attacks, and to turn upon their center in changing direction.[18] The showing of these recruits was far from satisfactory, nor did Colonel Boyd at all distinguish himself in an attempt to maneuver the regulars.[19] A sham battle was held, the mounted riflemen and dragoons screaming and yelling as they galloped up and down the prairie. Rifles cracked sharply as the men took cover and deployed from the woods. Indians from Prophetstown who had come to spy upon the army were summoned to have a talk with the Governor.

Another act of insult and defiance had been reported, Harrison reminded them. Only thirty-five miles from Vincennes a band of Indians had stolen the horses of an army dispatch bearer.[20] The Governor was in no mood for further sufferance. Why had no stolen horses been returned, no Indian murderers delivered up? The time was too short to meet his demands, replied Chief Shabonee, a spokesman. Nothing could be done until spring. Unless the stolen horses were immediately returned, retorted Harrison, the army would start upon its march the very next day. The distance it would advance would depend upon the conduct of the Indians themselves. "I listened to his soft words," recalled Chief Shabonee, "but I looked into his eyes. They were full of fire."[21] The Indians promised to return to their village, achieve what they could, then return to meet the army. Harrison also sent Interpreter John Connor to escort a few leading Delaware and Miami chiefs to Prophetstown to bring their warriors under army protection.

Constant wading in the river while hauling flatboats had caused much illness among the Yankee regulars. Harrison estimated his available force at slightly more than 1000 men. Mrs. Lydia Bacon, wife of a confined regular officer, noted the details of the Governor's costume as he paid a final round of calls upon the sick. ". . . equiped for the March, he had on what they call a hunting shirt, made of calico & trimed with fringe . . . the ends were pointed instead of square & tied in a hard knot to keep it snug." A large ostrich feather decorated his beaver-fur hat. "The Governor," added Mrs. Bacon, "is very tall slender with sallow complexion & dark eyes, his manners are pleasing, he has an interesting family." Just after daybreak, October 26, she watched the army march. "It was a sad sight to see them depart, a great many fine young men . . . some very young, left their studies at college to go on this campaign."[22]

A drove of cattle and hogs and the wagon train made ready, the army advanced along the east side of the Wabash at about twelve or fifteen miles a day. Flatboats loaded with supplies were to follow as rapidly as the low water would permit. The regulars discovered their first blue grass in the prairie; the militia, entering the new purchase, speculated upon the richness of its soil.[23] Harrison flung out mounted detachments as flankers and posted a strong guard at night. October 1, the army reached a site known as Terre Haute, about sixty-five miles north of Vincennes, where the banks of the Wabash rose

steeply from the river. Just ahead was the little Wea village of
Weautano, or Rising Sun, where rich groves of fruit trees gave it
also the name of Old Orchard Town.[24]

Early next morning Harrison and his aides rode ahead to discover
a site for the fort, halting about three miles above Terre Haute where
a sharp bend of the river allowed a clear view up and down stream.
This was the site of Bataille des Illinois where a prolonged fight a
century ago between the Indians of the Mississippi and the tribes on
the Wabash had left a few warriors on each side. Harrison inspected
a light growth of oak and honey locust trees which would provide
wood for the army while near by stood a field of corn grown sere and
yellow, planted by his order during the previous spring. Returning to
Terre Haute Harrison ordered the army forward but remained a
while to consult with Chief Shabonee and his followers. Instead of
returning to their village, apparently they had been scouting the army.
Why had the Governor posted such a strong guard every night? inquired Shabonee, the Potawatomie. Did he actually distrust them?
The chief talked broadly of a willingness to treat. However, as Shabonee later admitted, the Governor "was wary, he was a great war
chief."[25] This was but "part of our way of making war." Harrison
again dismissed them with an order that they return with a suitable
delegation from Prophetstown to confer again. Shabonee thereupon
departed, not to his village but to recruit another war party in Illinois.

Harrison came up to Bataille des Illinois that evening to discover
that a fine feud between Colonel Boyd and the militia had come to a
head. A glittering reputation had preceded the Colonel to Vincennes
but that "his courtier-like manners before strangers covered the most
capricious violence and arbitrary temper which subjected his soldiers
to the most severe punishments . . . and insult and oppression to such
of the officers as would submit," was the summing up of his character by the militia officers.[26] The present trouble, Harrison discovered,
resulted from disregard of his edict against "all kinds of petty punishments, inflicted . . . for the most trifling errors of the private soldier,"[27] for Boyd had ordered an offending wagoner flogged. A militia captain assigned to the duty had refused to execute it and the
Colonel had ordered his arrest. Enraged by the Colonel's conduct,
the militia was carrying out encampment orders in a helter-skelter
of abandon. Harrison calmly surveyed the confusion and rode among
his men. "In ten minutes," the militia officers later reported, "the
army was comfortably encamped and every corps placed in its proper
position." The crux of the difficulty lay in the fact, unappreciated by
Boyd, that the volunteer two-thirds of the army was "composed of a

class of people who required on the part of their Commanders a union of address, moderation and firmness, to train them gradually to a . . . submission and obedience which violated all their former habits and opinions."[28] Harrison, Boyd discovered that day, was truly the army's commander, the militia a breed of soldier unaccustomed to dominance. In issuing his order against petty punishments, the Governor had sought to ward off trouble, an effort unappreciated by the Colonel.

However, militia shortcomings were bound to be encountered at some point in the campaign. Low water had held up the flatboats bringing provisions and the volunteer soldiers faced an irksome task. Maneuvers with shovels and axes at a time when rations became scanty fostered rebellion in camp. Harrison sent expert hunters in search of deer, wild turkeys and bee trees but returns were rather scanty.[29] After four days of cutting trees and logs, coupled with fatiguing drill, some of the men openly threatened to desert. They had enlisted, as they thought, to fight Indians.

Harrison made no threats nor ordered any floggings save one only to pardon the offender. October 8 he paraded the troops on the prairie and made a speech. Contemplating these ranks of long, lean men, many of whom he knew by their first names, the General admitted that they had enlisted for a difficult campaign. The work was proving hard and tiresome and so he wished to detain no one further against his inclination. Whoever wished to go home was free to do so, Harrison suggested, to encounter whatever blessings were due him from his neighbors, wife or sweetheart. It was for them to judge how the deserter had covered himself with glory. In respect to rations, the General was receiving no greater portion than the common soldier yet was quite willing to endure further privation in order to continue the campaign. All others who would choose to follow his example were asked to reveal themselves with a shout, raising their swords or rifles.[30] "All did," observed a young ensign, John Tipton. Harrison ordered the troops to wage a sham battle and the men sprang into action on the wet prairie. Dismissed at sunset, they drew an extra amount of whiskey, threw their hats into a ring and wrestled in front of blazing campfires. The work and the drills went on.

The distance the army would advance, the Indians had been warned, would depend upon their own conduct. An invitation to keep on marching was interpreted from a bold daylight theft of eight horses from an Illinois settlement not far away. Harrison's indignation had not yet subsided when, on the night of October 10, com-

motion struck the camp. The loud report of a rifle sent guards racing
for safety as a bullet from out of the darkness wounded a sentinel in
both thighs. Men sprang to arms promptly and took their positions
while Harrison and Colonel Boyd rode up and down the lines until
daybreak. Major Daveiss boldly insisted on being allowed to scour
the woods with dragoons, but could find no Indians.[31]

A courier came up that afternoon with a letter from Secretary
Eustis which confirmed Harrison's present intention to advance as
far as Prophetstown. Under the circumstances the instructions from
the War Office were most gratifying:

"The course to be pursued with The Prophet . . . must depend, in
a great measure . . . on his conduct. . . . You will approach and order
him to disperse, which he may be permitted to do on condition of
satisfactory assurances. . . . If he neglects or refuses . . . he will be
attacked and compelled to it by the force under your command. . . .
His adherents should be informed that in case they shall hereafter
form any combination of a hostile nature . . . they will be driven
beyond the great waters."[32]

The war talk in Congress probably lay behind this letter but the
instructions still left the loophole of "satisfactory assurances" open
to The Prophet. News of affairs at Prophetstown was brought by
Interpreter Connor and four friendly Delaware chiefs who had advanced to summon their warriors as instructed but had been met by
a party of Indians in war paint who had invited them to join forces
for the contemplated battle. The Prophet's men had expressed "positive assurances of victory," and it was indicated that 600 warriors
were then at the town.[33]

Following their conference with Harrison the four Delawares settled down to a game of cards with the militia but they began to voice
an opinion, which soon spread through the army, that the present
force was too small to be successful against The Prophet. While it
had long been an accepted fact that an American could lick two
Britishers, three Frenchmen, or four Spaniards, yet to insure even
"partial victory" in Indian warfare, Harrison pointed out, it was
essential to outnumber the savages by at least two to one. His present
army now comprised 1020 men of whom about 70 were sick, hardly
a force comparable to that of Wayne or even St. Clair. The militia
guards began to see Indian enemies in every shadowy bush and behind every tree; several times the camp was aroused by false alarms.
After consulting with his officers, Harrison sent back for four more

companies of militia, presumably already embodied, and cheered the troops with the announcement that they would see fighting. The Wabash was still falling and rations had been reduced to less than a pound of flour a day. Handicapped by axes of a brittle and worthless quality, the men continued their work on the fort and daily drill was not neglected. Heavy rains dampened the militia, who had no tents, but at last the river began to rise giving cause to expect the flatboats. Harrison remained continually active supervising every detail, building a rugged outpost as General Wayne would, and joking with the men as they worked. After three weeks of labor the finishing touches were applied to the fort. Stout two-story log blockhouses, connected by barracks, overhung each corner; a line of pickets extended high above a surrounding trench, dug four feet deep. October 27 the outpost was dedicated. Considering the fort in the nature of a temporary work, which it proved to be, Harrison permitted the officers to give it his name. Major Daveiss, famed for oratory in Kentucky, spoke fervently of glory and patriotism and broke a bottle of bourbon over the main gate: "In the name of the United States, and by the authority of the same, I christen this Fort Harrison."[34] There was much cheering. A sham battle in the woods further celebrated the day.

Next morning, after quarter rations were meted out to the men, Harrison greeted Captain David Robb of the Indiana militia who brought up a reinforcement of seventy-six mounted riflemen followed by flatboats loaded with corn, flour, and munitions. A troop of mounted volunteers from Kentucky was reported on the way. The remainder of the militia, due to Quakerism and anti-administration sentiment in eastern Indiana, had been prevented from turning out. The General was highly satisfied, however, with the army's progress in drill. "I am happy to inform you," he wrote Secretary Eustis on the 29th just before the army again set out, "that . . . the troops are in fine spirits and eager to come in contact with the Enemy. I have used every exertion in my power to perfect them in the maneuvers which they are to perform." He forwarded the latest news from Prophetstown where a few more Delaware and Miami chiefs, recently arrived in camp, had been "badly received, ill-treated and insulted and finally dismissed with the most contemptuous remarks." Although The Prophet was reported now to have but 450 warriors with him these were "desperadoes wound up to the hightest pitch of enthusiasm by his infernal arts . . . performing war dances day and night." The first white prisoner was to be burned, it was promised. Harrison, however, indicated renewed confidence. "I promise you Sir that all the objects intended by the Expedition shall be effected."[35] The Governor's good friend, Doctor John M. Scott, again visiting Grouseland, confined himself to military matters in a letter to the *Kentucky Argus:*

"The governor will not give up the point—he will bring them to his measures either by fair means, or hard knocks—they may have their choice—it would not do to relinquish the object now—the prophet would grow insolent beyond measure. . . . Colo Daveiss is a very active and vigiland officer. . . . When the fight begins we calculate that he will do wonders, or be killed—he is all for glory."[36]

If we may interpolate some family news at this point, Carter Bassett Harrison, the eighth child and the fifth son, had been born the day before the new fort was christened.

Leaving a garrison with the sick at the fort, Harrison resumed the march on the east side of the river and debated a choice of routes. To continue on his present course would be the shorter way but the country was heavily wooded while west of the river lay a stretch of wide prairie extending as far as the eye could reach. The ground to the west would better accommodate the army wagons and the drove of cattle and hogs and by crossing the river Indians on the east bank could be evaded. On the second day out from the fort, Harrison issued a temporary order to shoot any Indian on sight ("fine news," wrote John Tipton), and the army safely forded the river. Faster progress was made through this prairie country, its bluegrass withered by autumn frosts. Game appeared more plentiful; several deer and a prairie wolf, which the regulars examined with interest, were started up and shot.[37]

Reaching the mouth of the Vermilion River, an estimated three days' march from Prophetstown, the army halted to construct a small blockhouse for the protection of flatboats and the additional sick. On November 2, during clear and crisp weather, the men threw up a temporary work with breastworks extending to the river. Supplies were transferred from boats to the wagons. Harrison welcomed a detachment of sixty mounted Kentuckians under Captain Frederick Geiger of Louisville. Two veteran campaigners, General Samuel Wells and Colonel Abraham Owen of Kentucky, arrived with Geiger as volunteers. There were a few too many officers in this army. Harrison appointed Wells a major of Kentucky riflemen and enlisted Colonel Owen as a second volunteer aid. News of another Indian depredation came hard on the heels of Geiger. A party of savages on the east bank of the Wabash had killed a man lying asleep on the deck of a flatboat on its way back to Fort Harrison.[38]

Harrison sent his most expert woodsmen to trace the party but trails extending southward grew too faint to be followed. Had the savages scattered, the General wondered, later to unite and attack the settlements? Pondering the question late that night he arose from his bed and directed a militia officer to take twelve picked men and ride straight to Vincennes. The citizens were to barricade all public buildings and prepare to defend themselves at the first sign of alarm.[39]

The second day after leaving the Vermilion the army followed the course of the Wabash to the northeast and entered a rugged, broken country where Pine Creek coursed through rocks and wooded ravines. Harrison was determined to forestall any attempt at surprise, at least on November 4, anniversary of St. Clair's Defeat. Captain William Prince was sent ahead with a detachment of woodsmen to discover a safe place for a crossing. Returning, Prince reported the plain trails of Indians from Illinois who apparently were heading for Prophetstown. Inclining "a few miles to the left" Harrison prepared to meet an attack as the army forded the creek.[40] Mounted riflemen guarded the front and rear and both flanks but no savages were anywhere seen. Extra sentinels, however, were posted that night.

Harrison had covered about six miles the next day when a mounted detachment raised the cry of "Indians ahead." Again a body of scouts rode forward to examine the woods but could report nothing of alarm. But Harrison did not wish to take further risks that day. His present position could be easily defended. The men threw off their packs and encamped; Prophetstown would be reached on the morrow.

Another stretch of thick woods and ravines presented hazards on the last day's march. Captain Touissant Dubois, leading the spies and guides, was of the belief that The Prophet would attack that day if ever. Determined to get through safely, Harrison drew up his baggage train compactly, ordered the men to toss in their knapsacks, and placed them in the order of battle. The infantry, muskets ready, were formed now in two columns, now in four or five, the dragoons and mounted riflemen shifted back and forth three times within a distance of one mile.[41] That the dragoons became entangled in some heavy underbrush, however, necessitated some of this fine maneuvering. Yet not until the army emerged from the woods were Indians seen. Here and there, ahead of the army, they were riding about on horseback, hallooing and gesturing defiantly.

Harrison asked Captain Dubois to ride ahead with a flag but it proved useless to try to bring the Indians to a parley. They had tried to cut him off, Dubois reported, and since no parley could then be had, Harrison proposed again to encamp, only to encounter the strong protests of his officers. Major Daveiss, Colonel Boyd and several others urged an immediate attack. But, as Harrison explained, he had been instructed first to order the Indians to disperse. In any event, the ground ahead should be carefully reconnoitered. While Major Daveiss rode ahead with a detachment of dragoons, Harrison again took up the march. The army had covered perhaps a mile of ground, tramping through Indian cornfields, when three mounted warriors hove in sight with a white flag suspended from a pole. One of them, Chief White Horse, Harrison recognized as "a man in great estimation with The Prophet."[42] He invited the chief to come forward. White Horse expressed uneasiness and alarm at the manner of the army's approach. The Prophet already had sent out a delegation to meet him, he said, but it had gone down the east bank of the river and so had failed to meet the army. Harrison, who knew only of an assault upon a flatboat by any such delegation, replied that his army would not attack provided The Prophet met his known demands. White Horse—the point was important—agreed that a council would be held next day and a suspension of hostilities was solemnly promised. Major Daveiss, who had returned, interposed with a demand that hostages should be taken but Harrison, unfortunately, did not consider it necessary.

A suitable camp site had yet to be found. Five hundred yards below the town, where the army then waited, were cornfields and a large cultivatd area but wood and water were lacking. Again the troops advanced. Raising his field-glass, Harrison sighted a partially fortified village where the curving left bank of the Wabash provided landing space for many canoes. Indians were seen running about in every direction as if preparing for an attack, many taking positions behind a breastwork of logs. They had fortified their town, Harrison observed, "with care and astonishing labor," a task seldom engaged in by the northern tribes.[43]

Chief White Horse and his followers again rode up to protest the invasion. Harrison, plainly marked as he sat astride a gray mare, again assured them that their village was safe. He inquired where a camp site for the night might be found and White Horse pointed to the northwest where Burnet's Creek wound past the village, nearly three miles distant from the mouth of the Tippecanoe River. Harrison sent two aides, Majors Taylor and Clark, to survey the ground while Captain William Piatt of the regulars advanced to examine the situation north of the town. Piatt's search availed nothing but Taylor and Clark reported that wood, water, and some forage could be found on a partially wooded tract beside Burnet's Creek, three quarters of a mile west of the town.[44]

Early that evening the army halted on a ten-acre piece of ground shaped like a blunt flatiron, rising several feet above the wet prairie, and bordered on two sides by woods and the creek, on the short ends by a marshy prairie and thickets. The evening air was growing chilly and damp as Harrison traced the lines for the encampment. Mingling army regulars and militia along the outer lines, he placed about a third of his force on the side facing Prophetstown and directed as many more, about 300, to guard the opposite side bordering the creek. The mounted riflemen under Major Wells and Captain Spencer picketed their horses inside the lines and took positions at the short ends, the right and left flanks; the dragoons under Daveiss and Parke, carrying pistols in their belts, were instructed to act as a reserve.

Altogether a force of 950 officers and men, including 300 regulars, made camp for the night. The regulars pitched their tents, the militia gathered wood for fires with which to dry their damp clothing and to cook a scanty supper. There was still an insufficiency of axes, hardly enough remaining to cut firewood and construct a rude enclosure for the livestock. Although Harrison did not place entire trust in The Prophet still an attack was not anticipated and it was deemed unnecessary to fortify the camp. The troops received the usual order to lie on their arms with bayonets fixed and cartridge boxes ready. Should an attack occur, each corps was to hold its own position until relieved. A light rain began to fall as two companies under a field officer mounted guard. Before turning in Harrison again inspected the ground. Although well adapted for an action against enemy regulars, he decided, "it afforded great facility to the approach. of savages."[45]

TIPPECANOE

NOW THAT Tecumseh had departed south to enlist the Creeks and Cherokees in his confederacy the responsibility for what happened during the morning of November 7, 1811, must rest entirely with The Prophet unless the tale of Chief Shabonee concerning British influence is accepted. Shabonee, present on the ground, left testimony that the Battle of Tippecanoe "was the work of white men who came from Canada and urged us to make war." The urging was not unprecedented. The British had used similar tactics at Fallen Timbers and at St. Clair's Defeat. "Two of them who wore red coats were at Prophetstown," declared Shabonee. "It was they who urged the fight. They dressed themselves like Indians to show us how to fight. They did not know our mode."[1] The British, it appeared, wished to attack at daybreak; the Indians at midnight. Somehow a compromise was reached.

The Prophet played his role by rendering his warriors invulnerable. During the night hours while Harrison's army slept the one-eyed Shawnee mixed a sacred composition in a kettle and after pronouncing a mystic enchantment gave assurance that the powder of the Americans would be as harmless as sand, their bullets soft as rain. Half the soldiers were already dead, in fact, the rest in a state of distraction.[2] "They will all run when we make a noise in the night." Evidently there was to be little or no fighting. At about four o'clock in the morning the Indians crawled up to the American encampment, taking positions behind trees and clusters of thickets. A fatal spell having been cast over the army they intended to swarm in at a signal and take possession if possible without firing a shot.[3]

The early-morning sky was releasing trickles of dampness when a few soldiers arose a little earlier than usual in order to rekindle the fires and warm themselves before the reveille call. Harrison was up and was drawing on his boots as the orderly drummer stood at attention. The night, it seemed, was safely over. However, it was still very dark. On the left flank of the rear line, at the angle formed by

Captain Geiger's Kentuckians and Captain Robert Barton's regulars, a sentinel detected an indistinct rustling behind a thicket of willows. He ran a few steps toward the next man and whispered: "Let us fire and run in . . . there are Indians in those bushes."[4] The men listened for a moment but heard nothing more until the whiz and thud of an Indian arrow sent them flying into camp. Another sentinel, Corporal Stephen Mars of Kentucky, fired his rifle at an indistinct figure and dashed for safety. An Indian bullet dropped him in his tracks but at least the alarm had been given. The savages let loose an ear-splitting yell and rushed toward the lines. Another sentinel, closely pursued, cocked his rifle as he ran and turning suddenly, shoved the muzzle into a redskin stomach and let drive.[5]

The yells which re-echoed through the forest were calculated to scare the sleeping enemy into flight. A heavy burst of musketry ripped into tents and campfires, bouncing live coals high into the air. So violent and frenzied was the attack that a few of the Indians entered the tents to fight hand to hand with the enemy. Captain William C. Baen and two others were tomahawked and scalped during the first mad rush. Three savages who gained the tent of the powerfully built Captain Geiger were shot or otherwise vanquished, Geiger receiving a bullet in the arm. The Kentuckians at the angle, their line in disorder, could scarcely be distinguished from Indians in their midst. Barton's regulars formed a ragged front, a few taking positions behind tents.[6]

Harrison got his shoes on and called for his negro boy George to bring up his gray mare but the animal had broken loose from its picket and George was "confoundedly frightened." Waller Taylor's servant came up leading a black horse which was offered and Harrison mounted at once, summoning two companies of regulars, who assembled promptly, to reinforce the stricken line. That he was astride Major Taylor's dark mount was a stroke of fortune. According to the Indian plan a hundred warriors were to rush in and slay the white chief on the gray mare. Colonel Owen, following directly after Harrison, was toppled from "a remarkably white horse" almost at the General's side.[7] Harrison, who saw Taylor coming up on the gray mare, ordered him to get another horse.

Campfires were still burning brightly for it was worth a man's life to put one out. The men sought the protection of near-by shadows. Eyes blinded by the glare of rifle fire endeavored to discover the hidden foe. The red-skins, their faces painted black, could hardly be detected save by their shouts yet squirrel rifle cartridges of twelve buckshot capacity told among them with effect.[8] The savage yells and clash of arms spread clockwise around the left flank. A slashing second attack brought Harrison back to the line which faced Prophetstown but here the regulars under Boyd, plus Colonel Bartholo-

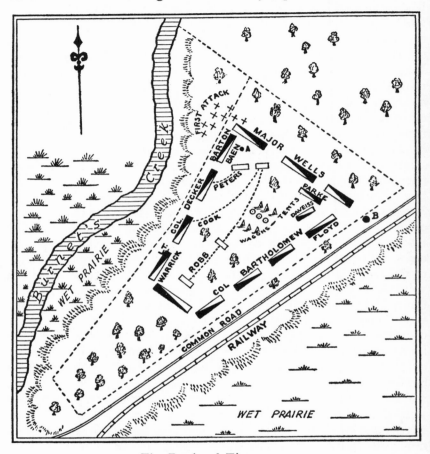

The Battle of Tippecanoe.
Map by Benson J. Lossing (1860).
A—Captain Baen tomahawked; B—Major Daveiss shot.

mew's sweating militia, stood firm against the assault. A third attack, very bloody, was launched against Spier Spencer's Yellow Jackets on the right where bullets came so thickly as to shower the bark from trees. The veteran Spencer, as Harrison approached, was shouting, "Close up, men! Steady! Hold the line!"[9] A bullet struck him in the head. He continued to shout but was struck in both thighs. He called for help and two men raised him up but a ball through the body finished him. When Harrison drew near he found Ensign John Tipton sighting down a barrel. "Where's your captain?" "Dead, sir." "Your first lieutenant?" "Dead, sir." "Your second lieutenant?" "Dead, sir." "Your ensign." "Here, sir!"[10] Harrison promised immediate assistance and turned to rally Captain Robb's militia company which showed signs of melting away in the immediate rear. With the aid of Major Taylor, now astride a sorrel horse of the General's, he lined up Robb's militia in support of Spencer's company and summoned a company of regulars to help brace the flank. As the movement was effected Thomas Randolph fell mortally wounded. Harrison dismounted, bent over him and asked if there was anything he could do. Nothing, replied Randolph, save to watch over his child.[11]

The Indians were fighting quite differently from their usual custom, Harrison noticed. "They rushed up to our lines in large bodies by signals from their chiefs, fired, and then retreated to load again."[12] He kept a sharp watch on the flanks, reinforcing every weakened part of the line. As bullets still spattered, the men expressed concern for his safety. Upon the General's survival, it was commonly believed, depended not only victory but the very existence of the army. "Harrison was seen where danger was most eminent [sic]," testified a volunteer. A bullet struck his horse in the neck, another passed through the rim of his hat and grazed the side of his head. "His voice," recalled one of the regulars, "was frequently heard and easily distinguished, giving . . . orders in the same calm, cool, and collected manner . . . which we had been used to . . . on a drill or parade. The confidence of the troops in the General was unlimited. . . ."[13]

Again on the line facing Prophetstown, Harrison was halted by Major Daveiss who could play no passive role in this fight. Indian snipers were doing much damage from cover at the left. "Will you permit me to dislodge those damned savages behind those logs?" Harrison declined to allow the dragoons to be drawn into the battle yet the Major persisted, selecting twenty men and again seeking out his commander. The fighting had continued some minutes longer when the impetuous Kentuckian was advised to "use his own discretion." Extravagant as to dress, the Major wore a white surtout easily distinguished and as he approached the Indian cover he received three balls in the body—mortal wounds. A few of his men gained the fallen timber and discharged their pistols, but no Indians were to be seen.[14]

Concerned with the safety and conduct of the militia, Harrison paid particular attention to keeping their lines intact. But with the exception of two men who fled at the outset and a few others who sought the shelter of wagons, militia and regulars alike indicated a wholesome willingness to fight. Officers were seen binding up their wounds amid the action, soldiers stuck to their posts even though mortally stricken and would not quit the field. Captain Jacob Warrick, shot through the body, was taken back to the surgeon to have his wound dressed but insisted upon walking back to his company to die on the front line.[15] Much of the enemy fire, aimed upward at the little plateau, passed harmlessly over the heads of the defenders but from fallen trees and near-by bushes the lethal hail still came. In the heat of the conflict Colonel Boyd, who bore himself capably, called for three cheers "to astonish the savages and silence their infernal yell."[16]

Daybreak was at hand yet the Indians, encountering surprisingly grim resistance, hesitated to make another charge. Harrison resolved to anticipate them as soon as it was light. With an idea to simultaneous charges from both flanks he shifted three companies of regulars to the left, under Major Wells, and two to the right under Boyd. Colonel Bartholomew, his militia armed with squirrel rifles, was supported with bayonets; Captain Parke and the dragoons mounted their horses and stood ready as a supporting line.[17] Harrison signaled the bugler and a simultaneous rush began on both flanks. The clamor of battle rose to new heights. A Yankee private receiving his baptism of fire described it: "The awful yell of the savages seeming rather the shriek of despair . . . the tremendous roar of musquetry—the agonizing screams of the wounded and dying, added to the shouts of the victors, mingling in tumultuous uproar, formed a scene that can be better imagined than described."[18] Past the charging regulars raced the dragoons until the Indians reached safety in a marsh where mounted men could not follow. The survivors picked up as many dead and wounded as they could recover and raced back to their village pursued by a yell of triumph "almost equal to that of the savages at the commencement of the battle."

The anticlimax to this expenditure of nerve, brawn, and blood came as an emotional release. Many of the troops were "weak for joy." Many offered up their prayers of thankfulness to heaven, but all, the militia officers united in saying, "acknowledged that the cool undaunted bravery of the c. in c. contributed more than even the courage of the army to defeat the ferocious . . . enemy that assailed us."[19] The survivors swarmed about their General in delight that he who had exposed himself "in a manner to make all . . . shudder for his life" had escaped unhurt. Congratulations were ex-

From a drawing by Louis Betts.

Closing phase of the Battle of Tippecanoe.

As daylight came on the dragoons and Kentucky mounted riflemen charged on both flanks.

WILLIAM HENRY HARRISON,

GOVERNOR AND COMMANDER IN CHIEF OF THE INDIANA TERRITORY,

To *Timothy Kibby, Gent.*

Greeting:

REPOSING special trust and confidence in your fidelity, courage, and good conduct, I have appointed you a *captain* in the _____ company of _____ in the _____ battalion of the _____ regiment of the militia of the county of _____ and you are hereby appointed accordingly. You are therefore carefully and diligently to discharge the duty of a *captain* _____ in leading, ordering, and exercising the said _____ in arms, both inferior officers and soldiers, and to keep them in good order and discipline ; and they are hereby commanded to obey you as their *captain* _____ and you ourself to observe and follow such orders and instructions as you shall from time to time receive from me or your superior _____

IN testimony whereof, I have hereunto caused the seal of the territory to be affixed, the *twenty-first* day of *December* in the year of our Lord one thousand eight hundred and *four* and of the independence of the United States of America the *twenty-ninth*

Will Henry Harrison

GOVERNOR's COMMAND,

Secretary.

Governor Harrison's commission to Timothy Kibby, Gent., captain of the District of St. Charles (Upper Louisiana) militia, December 21, 1804.

changed by the regular officers and militia. Colonel Boyd showed particular attention to the General and altogether much good feeling prevailed.

Harrison was very well pleased with the showing of the troops who were almost entirely green. One observation stands out in his own accounts of the battle. Although many changes of position, in respect to the numbers engaged, had taken place yet in each instance, notwithstanding the ferocity of the attack and the darkness, his commands had been obeyed with "promptness and preciseness," and every movement carried out "with military propriety."[20]

"The most of our men from Kentucky are safe or not badly wounded," a volunteer officer wrote on the field. "Such a battle has never been fought. . . . We are all in high spirits."[21] After caring for the wounded and partaking of a scanty breakfast, Harrison ordered a breastwork of logs erected. There was talk that Tecumseh was returning from the south with an army of followers at his heels. The drove of hogs and cattle had stampeded during the action; only half a pound of beef and a pound of flour could be issued as regular rations for two days. The westerners dined on the horses which had been killed in the action and while sentinels took potshots at Indian stragglers in the prairie, volunteers hunted for lost horses and cattle. The burial of the dead was a somber and arduous task. Graves two feet deep and sufficiently wide to accommodate several bodies were dug for the privates. Three Masonic brothers, Joseph H. Daveiss, Thomas Randolph, and Colonel Isaac White of Kentucky were buried together on the field.

In deaths and casualties Harrison had lost about a fifth of his fighting force. Thirty-seven dead, 151 wounded and two missing were reported at the outset but wounds at first considered trifling began to develop alarming symptoms. Harrison and the army surgeon believed that some of the Indian rifle balls had been poisoned, or perhaps chewed, which tended to enlarge the wounds and lacerate the contiguous flesh.[22] Fourteen men died within the first two days; fifteen more were to succumb on the long march home. Enemy losses, however, appeared to be as great. Thirty-six Indian dead were picked up on or near the battleground, others were found in cabins and in shallow graves next day. The proportion of Indian dead to the number engaged—which friendly chiefs variously estimated as from 560 to 700 warriors from eight tribes—had never been so large in any battle in Harrison's recollection. "It was a terrible defeat," admitted Chief Shabonee. "Nearly all the [American] dead lay unscalped.

Our women and children were in the town . . . waiting for victory and its spoils. . . . The Prophet had promised that every squaw . . . should have one of the white warriors to use as her slave. Oh, how those women were disappointed." Only three scalps had been taken by the Indians and of these, two were recovered. The Kentuckians gathered a rich harvest of enemy scalps, slicing them up so that all might share, each man cutting a hole in his piece to fit on the ramrod of his gun.[23]

Harrison, engrossed in a dozen duties, sent an aide to command the sentinels to cease firing at Indians lying wounded in the prairie. A Potawatomie chief was brought to the Governor and while a surgeon dressed his wounds he solemnly avowed The Prophet to be a man of pretension and deceit. The attack, he confessed, had been a great mistake. Meanwhile The Prophet was having a difficult time in the village. He sat with his head dropped down between his knees as exasperation and reproaches engulfed him. "You are a liar," shouted an angry Winnebago, "for you told us that the white people were dead or crazy when they were all in their senses and fought like the Devil."[24] The Prophet retorted that the virtue of his magic composition had been lost because his wife, with the way of women upon her, had touched the sacred kettle. He begged to be permitted to try his spell once more but his disillusioned followers would have no more of it. They bound him ignominiously with cords, slung him onto their shoulders and abandoned the town. Night on the battlefield found "every man mounting guard without food, fire, or light, and in a drizzling rain."[25] The tired soldiers kept themselves awake by passing the watchword every five minutes. Indian dogs prowling about in search of carrion created alarms but The Prophet's men had fled to Wild Cat Creek, twenty miles away.

In the morning, November 8, Harrison sent Captain Dubois with a detachment of spies to reconnoiter the village but it was barren of the enemy save for a few dead warriors in cabins and an old squaw left to die. Harrison and his aides with the dragoons and mounted riflemen rode over and from a storehouse filled with dried corn, beans, and peas, the men filled their knapsacks, Indian kettles, and loaded up six wagons. Inspecting the cabins before the torch was applied, Harrison discovered "an ample supply of the best British glazed powder," and some fine imported rifles still in their wrappings.[26] Clouds of smoke which rolled over the prairie signalized the destruction of Prophetstown.

The army prepared to take up the march early next day. To allow room in the wagons for the wounded, officers' baggage and the saddles of lost horses had to be burned. To set the example, Harrison tossed in his camp chair, bed, and small trunk and a fine saddle, his sorrel horse having been shot dead under Major Taylor. The army covered only eight miles that day, the wounded suffering grievously as the wagons pitched and jolted over the rugged terrain. The men were subsisting principally on a little parched corn when, on November 12, they reached Fort Boyd, the temporary blockhouse at the mouth of the Vermilion where flatboats awaited with supplies. As many of the sick and wounded as could be accommodated were placed on board and the outpost was abandoned. Harrison congratulated the sergeant in charge for arresting the two deserters who had fled. The weather turned bitterly cold. Undressed wounds festered and grew painful; one or two men died every day.[27] After stationing fresh detachments of regulars at Fort Harrison and Fort Knox, on November 18 the Governor was welcomed by a throng of anxiously waiting citizens at Vincennes. It had been a memorable campaign of fifty-four days.

As many generals have discovered, battles are only half won in the field, ensuing debating contests turning many a victory into defeat. Speaker G. W. Johnston of the Indiana House delivered the formal address of welcome for that body and Harrison received the private congratulations of men and officers who wished to fight again. Observers of the foregoing events, however, soon lined up on opposite sides. The first account of the battle to be published conveyed the idea of an army surprised and thrown into confusion. Harrison had entrusted his official account to Major Waller Taylor who set off in advance of the army to deliver it in person to Secretary of War Eustis at Washington. Stopping overnight at Louisville, Taylor described a few highlights of the encounter and it was this sketchy version, transmitted by letter to a Kentucky member of the House, which flared in the press several days before the release of Harrison's report.

According to the letter unwittingly inspired by Taylor, the savages "killed all the guards with arrows [said to be poisoned] and were in the camp before the whites had the least notice of them . . . Major Floyd fought like Caesar in his shirt tail."[28] Then came a bitter polemic from the pen of Humphrey Marshall of Kentucky, Federalist historian and brother-in-law of Colonel Daveiss. Daveiss, submitted Marshall, had been sacrificed to "jealousy and unmilitary orders" in nothing short of a "horrible butchery," and the disaster to Colonel Owen, who rode a white horse, was attributed to official carelessness.[29] Fathers who lost their sons in the battle likewise expressed resentment. Why, one might pause to inquire, should glorious war be anything like this?

The tempest which developed might have soon abated had not an unpleasant political situation developed within the army. Although Colonel Boyd remained deferential and obliging as long as the troops were far from home, a singular change in his temper was noted during the return march. The proud colonel could hardly forget that Harrison had forbidden the exercise of strict military discipline even among his own troops. A regimental order, therefore, praising the merits of the regulars whose "contempt of danger and determined courage saved the camp," was circulated at Vincennes thereby enlisting the interest of the anti-Harrison faction.[30] Boyd promised to make known the heroism of the regulars to Secretary of War Eustis, a man from his own State. All credit for bravery and promptitude in the action belonged to the Fourth Regiment, Eustis could learn from the Colonel's scrawl, the militia must be excluded from any share. Then Vincennes began to boil and the argument grew warm around Boyd. Even his own officers, with but one exception, were talking against him. Other cohorts, then, could be summoned and off to Washington went a more complete version of "the dastardly conduct of some whole militia companies," and in the next mail a letter to Congressman Richard Cutts, a Massachusetts man.[31] The Prophet beaten, the contest became sectional. "As second in command," wrote Boyd:

"I have had much to encounter with a Militia impatient of subordination. . . . Our Camp was attacked two hours before day in the midst of rains . . . the brave Yankees . . . supported every front, and incontinently moved and charged when the fire was most destructive, and . . . gained the Battle . . . but for them, the candid militia acknowledged, a defeat would have been inevitable. . . . Support the just honor of the Yankees."

Boyd enclosed some western newspapers for Cutts to show Secretary Eustis. The papers contained the formal thanks of the Indiana legislature extended Boyd and an address of felicitation by a group of Harrison's political opponents who tended to deprecate the performance of "the spirited but untutored Militia."[32]

This chaff became grist for the political mill. Jonathan Jennings became active in Congress as a disseminator of gossip unfavorable to Harrison. A letter written to a Virginia Congressman and printed anonymously in the newspapers charged that the actual object of the

Wabash expedition was simply to recompense Harrison's friends for the "dirty work" done in the McIntosh trial. Charges of graft and dishonesty in the distribution of annuities and the purchase of Indian goods were laid again at the Governor's door. The tribesmen were victims of a plot first and last. Although expenses were mounting at Grouseland Harrison offered a reward of $100 for the name of the writer, whose identity could only be surmised.[33]

The congratulations which Harrison did receive were indeed gratifying although they failed in the end to outlast the calumnies. After giving formal thanks to Boyd, a measure hotly debated, the Indiana House and Council united in an address of felicitation and praise for the Governor, and the high indignation of militia officers at the address of "7 or 8 persons" who publicly supported Boyd resulted in an articulate session of their own:

"1. *Resolved uamiously* [sic], that we canont consider the said Address in any other light than one amongst the *many* attempts which have flowed from the same source, to wound the feelings and injure the character of Governor Harrison.

"2. *Resolved,* That the said Address in attempting to bestow the merit of the *masterly conduct* in the direction and manoevering of the troops . . . to any other than the Commander in chief asserts a notorious untruth, which will be acknowledged as such by the whole army.

"3. That our indignation is justly excited at the false and contemptuous manner in which the Militia who served . . . are treated in the said address. . . .

"8. That we have the most perfect confidence in the Commander in chief and shall always feel a cheerfulness in serving him. . . .

"9. That we would prefer serving under him to any person that would be designated by the government for that purpose."[34]

And so on through number fourteen.

The Kentucky legislature accorded Harrison resolutions of "warmest thanks," two voices dissenting.[35] As grateful a response as any was a meeting held at the home of Samuel Wells in Louisville. The Boyd sentiment expressed in Indiana aroused high indignation among the Kentucky volunteers. Resolutions vying in spirit with those of the Indiana militia were passed. A toast to Harrison, "the brave and consummate General," was greeted with ten cheers. Hisses were directed at "the British Agents at Vincennes."[36] To the "friendly sentiment" expressed in a letter from Governor Charles Scott, Harrison replied at length. The army had not been "completely surprised," and the story of officers fighting in their shirt tails was "absolutely untrue." This was Harrison's explanation:

"It has been said, that the Indians should have been attacked . . . on the evening of the 6th. There were two reasons which prevented this, first the directions which I received from the Government made it necessary that I should endeavour . . . to accomplish the object of the expedition . . . without bloodshed and secondly—that the success of an attack by day upon the Town was very problematical. . . . If I had commenced an attack . . . after they had sent a chief to inform me that they were desirous of an accommodation . . . who can doubt but that a much greater clamour would have been raised . . . the cruelty of attacking those innocent people would have been pourtrayed in the strongest colors. . . . The order of encampment was the order of Battle for a night attack and . . . every man slept opposite to his post in the line. . . . A nightly incursion was precisely what I wished because from such a one only could I hope for a close and decisive action. . . . In night attacks discipline always prevails over disorder; the party which is able to preserve order longest must succeeed. . . . I am satisfied that all my weak powers were exerted to the utmost for the safety and glory of my Troops. Indeed no Commander had ever greater reason to do so. . . ."[37]

December 20, to the editorial regret of the *Western Sun,* Harrison resigned as Commander-in-Chief. The regular officers were reluctant to approve his withdrawal. Colonel Boyd had not yet left Vincennes —he departed January 23, 1812—when other Fourth Regiment officers declared it their duty publicly to state:

"The Commander in chief throughout the campaign and in the hour of Battle proved himself the soldier and the general. . . . Should our Country again require our services to oppose a civilized or savage foe we should march under command of General Harrison with the most perfect confidence of victory and fame. . . ."[38]

But with the departure of Colonel Boyd, whose regiment remained to guard Vincennes, the charges against Harrison were spread and multiplied. One of the most persistent criticisms insinuated that he had allowed the Indians to select his camping ground. En route to Washington, Boyd was feted in some quarters as a "hero of Tippecanoe"[39] and the Philadelphia *Aurora* threw open its columns to his complaints for the reason, perhaps, that the editor, William Duane, was a confidante of Jonathan Jennings. As late as August 15, 1812, when brigadier generals were being named to conduct the second war with Great Britain, the *Aurora* was still printing harsh criticisms concerning the Wabash campaign, setting forth such comment concerning the march and plan of encampment as could have been inspired only by Boyd.[40] For such reasons as these, sentiment against Governor Harrison was fostered in the Cabinet and in Congress. "I believe," remarked Harrison in the midst of it all, "the Greatest generals had admitted that they could fight a second battle upon the same ground much better than the first."[41]

Returning from the south by way of Missouri, Tecumseh visited the tribes on the Des Moines River then crossed to the Wabash through upper Illinois. He brought a dozen followers with him one night in midwinter to a dark and ruined Prophetstown. "I saw the marks of the great white general that I had defied in his own council house in every blackened brand of the burned town. I stood upon the ashes of my own home . . . and there I summoned the spirits of the braves who had fallen . . . and swore once more eternal hatred."[42] Tecumseh found his brother in a near-by Wyandot village and upbraiding him shook him fiercely by the hair. The Prophet, or possibly unofficial British participation in the battle, had ruined all his plans. Harrison offered Tecumseh an escort to present his complaints to the President but forbade him to present himself as the leader of any party of Indians. Since Tecumseh wished to take a large retinue if he went, the plan was abandoned. Delegations of hungry tribesmen entered Vincennes during the winter, bringing declarations of peace, but the Governor would not admit them too easily to favor. It was difficult indeed to distinguish those warriors who had fought in the late battle. Many who now professed abiding friendship were believed to have taken part.[43]

Harrison posed before Secretary Eustis the question of renewed peace relations, and, advised to take a conciliatory stand, he greeted ninety chiefs and warriors at Vincennes early in March. Their appearance brought stares from the wives of the Yankee regulars. One chief wore nose and ear jewels with one side of his face painted red and the other green; one had a pair of cow horns on his head. The chiefs were "good orators." Unanimous and vehement were their declarations that they would never again listen to The Prophet. Harrison suggested that they influence their tribesmen according to these heartily professed sentiments of peace. After receiving their annuities the Indians performed their dances before each principal house as drummers beat upon a deerskin stretched over a keg.[44]

The chiefs professing peace represented a majority faction but the lawless proved sufficient in number to carry out a series of bloody raids that spring. In March an Illinois family of ten persons was wiped out and on a farm thirty-five miles north of Vincennes, the wife of a settler, four children and her brother were slain. Early in April the family of Atha Meeks on Little Pigeon Creek was attacked. Meeks was shot and his son seriously wounded before the Indians were finally beaten off. Another settler was found dead and scalped on Driftwood Creek in Harrison County, another was slain while defending his home on White River near the forgotten town of Hindostan. The Indians treasured these scalps. Rivalry for prestige among them, Harrison knew, would likely produce more. The most harrowing account of murder and mutilation followed a raid upon the Harryman family living on the Embarrass River only seven miles from Vincennes. Harryman, a settler from Vermont, was about to remove his wife and family of five children to a place of safety when all were set upon, shot, stabbed, and tomahawked, and with the exception of the youngest, held tightly in its mother's arms, all were scalped.[45]

The scare grew widespread as Congress still debated war. Outlying fields and cabins throughout Illinois and Indiana were hastily abandoned even though it was corn-planting time. Wherever possible, groups of families banded together inside hastily constructed blockhouses. Many fled to Kentucky or to Vincennes where Harrison directed that log fences be thrown up about the principal houses.[46] An underground passage of escape was dug from the Grouseland cellar and a secret passage leading from the second floor provided a means of egress. At a time when danger still threatened, late in April, the Fourth Regiment received orders to march to Dayton, Ohio, leaving their sick and wounded safe in Kentucky. News of the recent Indian raids reached the War Office too late for an effective countermand. Harrison bid the troops a regretful farewell:

"Gentlemen, if you ever come to Vincennes you will always find a plate, knife & fork at my table; I assure you that you will never find the string to the latch of my door pulled in."

The departure of the regulars added to fear and insecurity at Vincennes. Congress had voted to raise six companies of rangers to protect the frontier, yet only one, yet to be heard from, had been assigned to Indiana. Meantime, Harrison did not feel authorized to call out the militia. "So much for the generalship of our wise men at Washington," commented the sympathetic *Kentucky Gazette*.[47]

But after May 3 there were no depredations and a company of mounted volunteer Kentuckians who rode in from Frankfort were confined to guard duty and drill. Harrison, meantime, had sent Mrs. Harrison and the eight children, the oldest now fifteen, to Kentucky for safety, thence to journey by stagecoach to Cincinnati.

The comparative quiet which descended upon the frontier Harrison believed to be only "one of those deceitful calms which frequently occur in Indian Warfare."[48] Assailed by the "violent party" in Congress as the instigator of hostilities on the Wabash, the British Ministry had ordered its Indian Agents to redouble their efforts for peace. Representatives of twelve tribes met together on the Mississinewa River and received from Colonel Matthew Elliott a message reproving the Shawnees for making war. The Wyandots, venerated by the other tribes as "uncles," declared that the outbreaks must cease. The British had "advised all the red people to be quiet." "Had I been at home [when the American army advanced]," replied Tecumseh, "there would have been no bloodshed at that time." He laid the blame for the recent murders on the warlike Potawatomies. "In spite of our repeated counsel to them to remain quiet and live in peace with the Big Knives [they] would not listen to us." The Potawatomies retorted that a few "foolish young men" of their tribe had followed the evil councils of a pretended Prophet. As the chiefs themselves could no longer control these scoundrels they hoped The Prophet would better instruct them.[49]

From present events in the western country it could be gathered that the British still shrank from open war. The Indian Agent at Fort Amherstburg reported that the tribesmen had received only 1200 pounds of powder during the last six months, less than one half the usual amount.[50] To Malden and Fort Amherstburg, The Prophet and Tecumseh now repaired. They arrived at a timely hour. A few days before, June 18, 1812, responding to the clamor of the War Hawks in Congress, the government announced the opening of hostilities against England. The Battle of Tippecanoe had played its part as a curtain raiser. Would Tecumseh and his allies now fight for Great Britain? After so great and intensive cultivation of the tribesmen there remained little doubt as to the answer.

X

KENTUCKY CROSSES THE OHIO

IN LINE with the republican system of popular election, the State of Kentucky, whose War Hawks were clamoring for conquest, sought to nominate a general to command in the field. The brigadiers originally appointed for northwestern service failed in certain respects to please. Both men were veterans of the Revolution. Governor William Hull of Michigan, then approaching his sixtieth year, was only slightly younger than General James Winchester of Tennessee. The Madison administration was reversing the old adage of Nestors for council, youth in the field. Henry Clay, Richard M. Johnson, John C. Calhoun and Felix Grundy, foremost among War Hawks at Washington, averaged less than thirty-three years of age.

General Hull, in advising against an invasion of Canada and declining of the proffered commission, had shown wisdom. British control of Lake Erie and of a strong force of Indians rendered invasion impracticable save under a vigorous, self-assured leader. Hull was persuaded, however, to accept the appointment on the ground that Michigan was in need of protection against Indians. Three weeks before the declaration of war, he took command of three Ohio militia regiments at Dayton, later to be joined by the Fourth Regiment of regulars recently at Vincennes. His gray locks, a commentator has noted, "commanded . . . respect."[1]

Throughout the month of June, Hull cut a road through the swampy Ohio wilderness to the north and erected Forts McArthur, Necessity, and Findlay along the way. It proved a long wearisome tour, the militia mutinous, the packhorses much worn. July 2, approaching the River Raisin, in present-day Michigan, he received belated news of war and five days later he encamped near Detroit, not yet certain as to his future course.

The other gentleman of respectable years selected to conduct operations in the Northwest was, like Hull, a veteran of the Revolution. But while Hull could be credited with services as Governor of Michigan, Colonel James Winchester had hardly stirred from his fireside at his magnificent stone house "Cragfont" near Bledsoe's Lick in

Tennessee.[2] Winchester was a kindly and humane personage but his fondness for good living and his aristocratic demeanor failed to command the respect of the western troops. Militia were likely to be critical of any regular officer sent to command them and to balk at a leadership untried and unknown. "Being a stranger and having the appearance of a supercilious officer, he was generally disliked," observed a Kentuckian.[3] There was much similar testimony. In conferring these appointments upon Winchester and Hull the government had passed over militia generals Harrison of Indiana, age 39, and Andrew Jackson of Tennessee, six years his senior. Did the wise men at Washington want a strong general?

The events leading up to the nomination of General Harrison were gratifying. As soon as a body of rangers had been embodied for the protection of Indiana, Harrison departed on June 19 for a tour of Kentucky, from Louisville to Lexington and thence to rejoin his family in Cincinnati. Escorts of citizens advanced to greet him as he approached the various towns and he was feted at numerous public dinners. A "federal salute" announced his arrival at Frankfort on the 26th, and celebrated by a gathering of citizens at a tavern. The *Argus* of Frankfort, which had printed Humphrey Marshall's vigorous onslaught upon Harrison following Tippecanoe, sought to redeem itself for this criticism. "Such were the agreeableness of the manners, conversation, and demeanor of the Governor as to attract the attention, esteem and friendship of all that were introduced to him," read the comment after a sparkling evening. ". . . Each member of the company vied in their attentions to a man so highly esteemed throughout the state."[4] Animated in bearing and appearing very fit, Harrison reviewed files of militia corps on Saturday afternoon and made many new friends among the officers.

Speaker Henry Clay, arriving home from Congress after Harrison had left Lexington for Cincinnati, reported a new surge of martial feeling in Kentucky. "I have almost been alarmed at the ardor that has been displayed," he notified Secretary of State James Monroe. Recruiting was being conducted with great success by militia officers. Colonel John Allen, distinguished head of the Kentucky bar, had raised a rifle regiment; Colonel James Simrall of Shelbyville had recruited several mounted companies, and Captain Nathaniel Hart, Clay's brother-in-law, had an infantry company of 100 "as fine fellows as ever shouldered a musket," all ready to march at a moment's notice.[5]

Clay took the occasion to remind Monroe of the availability, as a general, of Governor Harrison. "He was received in this State . . .

with a cordiality and attention which no public character ever before experienced in this Country. . . . No military man in the U. States combines more general confidence in the West . . . than he does. Everywhere I have been asked 'how come Harrison overlooked?' I hope the President will find it proper to bestow on him one of the Brigadiers' appointments lately authorized." Discovering small enthusiasm for General Hull in Ohio, Harrison asked Governor Scott of Kentucky to notify President Madison "that the volunteers from your state would serve under me as well as under any person."[6] Scott obliged by writing: "It would give me the highest pleasure to see a man promoted to an efficient command, who promises to be one of the greatest military men of the time."[7] Harrison would demonstrate the winning principle of republicanism as well as resolve a fatal stroke upon the enemy. At a dinner held in his honor at Cincinnati he offered the following toast:

"The American Backwoodsman—Clad in his hunting shirt, the product of his domestic industry, and fighting for the country he loves, he is more than a match for the vile but splendid mercenary of an European despot."[8]

For the accommodation of his family, Harrison rented a comfortable home on Broadway just below Fourth Street in Cincinnati. Opportunity for service was believed close at hand. Governor Edwards of Illinois reported the first British victory—capture on July 17 of the distant outpost of Mackinac, an island fortification lying between Lakes Michigan and Huron. As a result of this early triumph, which employed possibly a thousand Indians, hundreds more were flocking to the British standard. The British Agent in that region, energetic Robert Dickson, who for years had conducted unlicensed trading on American soil, arranged a truce between two warring tribes, the Chippewas and Sioux, and united them in the service of Great Britain. Throughout the West word was anxiously awaited regarding the fortunes of General William Hull. A victory by Hull would do much to prevent further British recruiting among the Indians; a defeat would undo the work of ten treaties.

Danger which threatened Fort Dearborn at Chicago and the Illinois settlements brought a call from Governor Edwards for help. Governor Scott offered Harrison any detachments of Kentucky militia the emergency might require. A plan of frontier defense which Harrison outlined at a public dinner at Lexington late in July was forwarded, at Clay's suggestion, to the Secretary of War.[9] This advice had its precedent. Three years ago Secretary Eustis had called upon Harrison for a plan of frontier defense. The Governor then emphasized the erection of a chain of forts commanding the straits between the Great Lakes, and naval control of Lake Erie where British vessels still ruled uncontested.[10] The advice, unfortunately, had not yet been heeded.

If not too late in the season, Harrison now advised Eustis, a chain of outposts should be erected along the Illinois River as far as Chicago. For the protection of supply convoys and reinforcements en route to Detroit a considerable body of troops should be marched immediately to Fort Wayne. Significantly, too, did Harrison point out the danger awaiting relief detachments en route to Detroit. As long as the British held command of Lake Erie, permitting free movement of an enemy force, supply convoys could be met and attacked at any chosen point on land.[11] Henry Clay reported the dinner gathering to Secretary Monroe:

"I was . . . a passive spectator of a very large body of Citizens assembled in Lexington to express their opinion on public affairs. A number of resolutions were proposed and carried. One affirmed our ability to bring the Indian war to a speedy conclusion under the guidance of Wm Henry Harrison. . . . It was carried by the loudest acclamation."[12]

For the protection of the Illinois settlements Harrison prepared for another campaign on the Wabash. After returning to Vincennes for two days he rode to Louisville to meet the expected regiment of Kentuckians. Brisk labors to forward supplies were interrupted by a courier from Governor Scott. The latest emergency was grave indeed. A dispatch rider from General Hull brought not only a request for reinforcements but some private messages from Ohio militia officers in the army. Although Hull had crossed into Canada he neglected to launch an attack on Fort Amherstburg and while he awaited battle in the open, General Isaac Brock approached with a strong force of regulars and Indians under Tecumseh. Hull retired moodily to Detroit. Brownstown in his rear was in enemy hands, the source of supply cut off. Indignation over the General's "apparent imbecility and cowardice" was mingled with the hope that Governor Scott would use whatever military authority he possessed to speed a new leader to the front.[13] "I observed that the Gen¹ was quite imbecile and that he paid more attention to parade than action," testified an officer concerning Hull's manner and conduct at the time.[14] The militia officers indicated Governor Harrison as a leader who possessed their confidence, "a man esteemed by the soldiery, and calculated to repair the errors of Hull."[15] The Fourth Regiment of regulars, "the Tippecanoe boys," united with the militia in the request that Harrison receive the command. "Oh! for a Harrison or the shade of a Wayne!"[16]

August 24, when Harrison again reached Frankfort, Scott had but one more day to serve in office. His successor, Isaac Shelby, and other public men had been summoned to a meeting at Scott's house. Harrison conferred there with Shelby and Scott, former Governor Christopher Greenup, Judge Thomas Todd of the State Supreme Court, Major General Samuel Hopkins of the Kentucky militia, Henry Clay, and Congressman Richard M. Johnson. Unanimous was the agreement that Governor Scott should appoint Harrison a major general of Kentucky militia by brevet.[17] During inaugural ceremonies for Governor Shelby a cheering throng greeted Harrison as a proclamation and general orders were read.[18]

News of Hull's surrender, on August 16, had not yet arrived as Harrison accepted the command of two regiments of infantry, plus another of mounted riflemen, under Brigadier General John Payne, already on their way to join General Winchester who was then at Cincinnati. Three more infantry regiments, one of dragoons, and one of mounted riflemen were to proceed in the same direction while a somewhat smaller force was directed to march under General Samuel Hopkins to Vincennes. As the soldiers were mustered before Harrison, ambition for conquest again mounted and Henry Clay wrote Secretary James Monroe that evening:

"If you will carry your recollections back to the age of the Crusaders . . . you will have a picture of the enthusiasm existing in this country for the expedition to Canada and for Harrison as Commander."[19]

Clad in a plain hunting shirt, Major General Harrison left Frankfort early next morning with the intention of taking command, if General Winchester would agree, of the forces destined for the relief of Detroit. While en route to Cincinnati he received first reports of Hull's surrender on August 16. And Fort Dearborn, which Hull had ordered evacuated, had fallen to the Indians, the little garrison massacred on the preceding day. It was as Harrison had feared. Instead of a confident march into Canada, the Northwestern army faced the grave problem of frontier defense. Danger from Indian attacks, Harrison realized, was more than serious. Tribesmen summoned to a peace council in Ohio early in August had remained noncommittal as to their war plans but with Hull's surrender and the fall of Fort Dearborn, their decision would be instantly made. Fort

Wayne and Fort Harrison were marked as the next points of attack, while "Up^r Canada," Harrison wrote John Gibson of Vincennes," cannot be conquered this fall."[20]

After two days in the saddle, Harrison reached Cincinnati where he learned of the perilous situation at Fort Wayne. One William Oliver, a young sutler at that post, said that a band of savages, at first apparently friendly but becoming murderous and incendiary, had surrounded the little outpost defended by only seventy men. A key point of western defense built upon a site selected by President Washington, the fort was no longer the strongly fortified work which Wayne had built, having been reduced to about one-half its former size. Young Oliver's offer to carry back word that relief would soon arrive was accepted with misgivings. Harrison feared for his safety and while expressing doubt that he would ever see him again, the General provided an escort of four Shawnee Indians from the friendly Chief Blackhoof's band. That Oliver and his Indians accomplished a safe return at a time when the enemy was holding council in the woods, as Harrison learned a week later, was considered "miraculous."[21]

The youth from Fort Wayne had gone not to Winchester but to Harrison. The two Generals, each in his own camp, exchanged letters throughout a day and an evening concerning the question of who should command.[22] It was a contest between a regular and a militia officer with the odds, if any, favoring Harrison. Upon receiving news of Hull's surrender, Winchester had assumed the command of the Kentucky reinforcement under Brigadier General John Payne. Naturally he had jurisdiction over the 17th Regiment of regulars under Colonel Samuel Wells, who had fought at Tippecanoe, and this was a regiment originally destined for the relief of General Hull. Then came Harrison, greeted with an outburst of cheering from the troops, and bearing the marked distinction, plus the accredited credentials, of a major generalship of Kentucky militia. The new general at once took over the three regiments of Kentuckians present, without which Winchester's regulars would be of little use. When he also asked for the command of the 17th Regiment, the Tennessean reluctantly conceded the point. Although in his letters to Secretary of War, Harrison acknowledged that his command was provisional only. Yet army sentiment was all for Harrison and it was essential that the troops march under one head. So on August 28 Winchester yielded the command and departed to resume recruiting service in Kentucky.[23]

An aggravating want of ready munitions and equipment delayed

Harrison two precious days at Cincinnati. What, indeed, had the War Department been doing during recent months of crisis? Just across the Ohio River was an army supply post at Newport yet only 1200 cartridges were available and only one piece of artillery, an ancient four-pounder, could be located for miles around. The dragoons had no pistols and hospital stores were few. The demands of Hull's army had put a great strain on local military resources yet no supplementary supplies had been shipped.

Harrison was not yet an officer of regulars and could obtain no money for drafts drawn upon the War Office. It is not at all clear at this juncture how a supply system was arranged. Altogether the confusion was such, the General informed Eustis, "as can only be expected from men who are perfectly new to the business."[24] He equipped the dragoons with muskets and appealed to Cincinnati citizens for homemade cartridges of which 12,000 were promptly made up and sent forward by wagon train. Orders went out to the army quartermaster at Pittsburgh to forward supplies and munitions in all haste.

There was no time to drill the army. While the available force comprised, in Harrison's opinion, "perhaps the best materials for . . . an army that the world has produced . . . no equal number of men were ever collected who knew so little of military discipline."[25] Early on Saturday, August 29, he put the first detachment of infantry in motion; starting with dragoons the next morning he overtook the marching men near Dayton and was greeted "joyfully" with cheers along the whole line.[26] At Piqua, eighty miles above Cincinnati and nearly halfway to Fort Wayne, an express rider from Lexington brought Harrison a brigadier general's commission signed by the President on August 22 and a letter from General Winchester.[27]

The new commission, if accepted, Harrison realized, actually tended to reduce his present rank. Assigned only to the command of operations in Illinois and Indiana, Harrison was advised by General Winchester that the latter was now authorized to take over the army originally destined to relieve General Hull. Harrison postponed his acceptance of the commission. According to his present instructions there was no escaping the fact that the wrong general was riding to the relief of Fort Wayne.

Harrison awaited the arrival of ammunition from Cincinnati and a regiment of mounted Kentuckians under Colonel John Allen as well as further word as to Winchester's plans. He set the militia to work making cartridges but when they proved restless a friendly lecture from the tail of a camp wagon aroused their willingness. "The backwoodsmen are a singular people," Secretary Eustis was advised. "From their affection and attachment everything may be expected but I will venture to say"—and here was a point—"they never did nor never will perform anything brilliant under a stranger."[28] Twenty-five or thirty miles ahead, near the St. Marys River, were encamped possibly 700 Ohio militia who hesitated to go on. Allen's regiment coming up, Harrison sent it ahead to reinforce the Ohioans and spur them on but the Shawnees who had accompanied young Oliver returned to report that about 300 Indians were laying siege to Fort Wayne. All the houses in the vicinity had been burned, the crops and livestock destroyed. The garrison was determined to resist to the last, they reported, but the commanding officer, Captain James Rhea, was nervous, fearful, and frequently drunk.[29] Further advised that a detachment of 550 British had set out from Fort Amherstburg, Harrison sent back word to Winchester, then somewhere along the way, that he was resuming the march and would await his arrival at the fort. For this he could hardly be hung. Again the General lectured the troops, some of whom showed signs of wavering: "If there is any man under my command who lacks the patriotism to rush to the rescue, he, by paying back the money received from the Government, shall receive a discharge. I do not wish to command such." A militia-man who accepted this offer was ridden on a rail to the music of the "Rogue's March" and baptized in the river "in the name of King George, Aaron Burr, and the Devil."[30] It was a solution not resorted to under Hull.

The Ohio volunteer infantry—somewhat diminished in numbers—were overtaken near the site of the present city of St. Marys. Rude contempt was indicated by the Kentuckians. The opportunity for a brilliant counter attack at Fort Wayne had been lost to Ohio. As Harrison pushed on his combined forces—about 2600 men—for four days and nights the savages spattered rifle bullets against the walls of the fort, halting their fire only to prepare a trap for the army. But Harrison sent the mounted men ahead to reconnoiter, an onrushing force which was reckoned too strong for a successful ambuscade. "Kentuck too much," conceded the Indians as they retreated swiftly on horseback.[31] The mounted detachment pursued them as far as they should. Not far behind came the infantry which had marched twenty miles that day on half rations and very little water.

Harrison placed Captain James Rhea, "a second Hull," under arrest and moved two separate detachments against the Indians before relinquishing his present command. Learning from the friendly

Shawnees the identity of those chiefs, hitherto friendly, who had led the attack, Harrison struck a quick blow at their villages, leading a mounted detachment against the Miamis on the upper Wabash while another under Colonel Samuel Wells destroyed the Elk Hart Potawatomie towns sixty miles to the Northwest. Several hundred huts and much corn, which would have supplied other hostiles, were burned but the Indians had fled. Interested soldiers retrieved fragments of boxes bearing London and Amherstburg labels while a copy of a Cincinnati newspaper containing an account of the strength of Harrison's army was found in a Potawatomie town.[32] Some one, no doubt, had run who could read. Despite the lack of an enemy to subdue, Harrison expressed high satisfaction over the consistent performance of the men in accomplishing protracted marches on scant rations. "It is impossible to find language to convey my sense of the merits of the troops . . . from your state," he assured Governor Shelby of Kentucky. "I anticipated in this campaign a glorious triumph to our arms, and an equally glorious triumph to republicanism, since it will prove the falsity of the theory which proclaims the necessity of standing armies, or, in other words, that a man must become a slave before he can be made a warrior."[33]

This Northwestern Army comprised no slaves but an aggregation of some talent. Kentucky historians have called the roll. Now serving under Harrison were Major Richard M. Johnson, Major George Madison (later Governor of Kentucky), Captain John Simpson, Captain William Duval, Privates Samuel McKee and Thomas Montgomery, all members or members-elect of Congress. Also with Harrison were Colonel John Scott, his friend and physician, and Colonel John Allen, head of the Kentucky bar. These dignitaries naturally assumed that they should nominate their own commander or at least enter a protest against any undesired replacement. When General Winchester arrived on September 18 there was "very serious difficulty" in reconciling the troops to the change.[34] To quell an embarrassing disturbance Harrison made a public plea in behalf of his successor, extolling the Tennessean as a hero of the Revolution. Major Richard M. Johnson, however, confided his private thoughts in a letter to President Madison:

"Let me inform you that no event is now so important to the cause . . . as the giving Gov.r Harrison command of the forces from Ky . . . He has the confidence of the forces without a parrallel in our History except in the case of Genl Washington in the revolution. . . . The united exertions of us all cannot reconcile them to the transfer of the command. I speak what I know."[35]

Another Congressman, Private Samuel McKee, indulged in insubordinate and unmilitary conduct in circulating a petition urging Harrison's appointment as Commander-in-Chief.[36] Harrison took the paper with him as he returned with the mounted force to St. Marys and Piqua, his plans as yet undetermined, although mounted Ohio volunteers were being raised at his call for an expedition against the Indiana tribes. Of the fate of McKee's petition no word survives. Arriving at Piqua late on September 24, Harrison broke the seal of a War Office dispatch appointing him to the command of the Northwestern Army.

The hesitancy which preceded the order was born of administrative indecision. Although Madison respected Editor Duane of the Philadelphia *Aurora* none too highly, his editorial comment on Harrison probably had weight. When news of Harrison's militia commission reached the capital, Madison and Secretary of State Monroe discussed the known merits of that General and of Winchester. Rather than choose between the two westerners, Madison asked that Secretary Monroe, formerly a colonel in the Revolution, accept the command. For although conceding the "great superiority" of Harrison in respect to "qualifications," whatever the word may have meant, the President believed his military knowledge to be "limited" while "a more extensive weight of character," he added, "would be of material importance."[37] Certainly the publicity in the *Aurora* had aided Colonel Boyd, whose nomination as brigadier was to be confirmed by the Senate more promptly than was Harrison's.

However, new evidence appeared to indicate Kentucky's views concerning the question of character. Jonathan Monroe, citizen of Lexington, sent a candid letter to the Secretary of State: "If the Executive wishes to carry on a prosperous and efficient War . . . he must place the army under the command of Govr Harrison. He is the Idol of the People . . . certainly a military man with much experiance & fine talent, and why he should not be more popular at the city is astonishing to me. I fear that pettit maitre, Col Boyd, has prejudiced the President ags^t Harrison."[38] Winchester's talents were deprecated in a similar message to Doctor Thomas Monroe of the Navy Department: "The Militia is resolutely opposed to serving under his command. . . . The people of the Western country are less governable than in any section of the Union. . . . It will be wise policy to humour them. Harrison is now their Idol. Under his command they will fight."[39] Judge Thomas Todd of Kentucky was then writing Madison: "Harrison is now with the army making active preparations to retrieve our losses—the officers and soldiers in high spirit having the fullest confidence in the Gen¹. . . . Winchester's presence will damp this ardour."⁴⁰ Governor Shelby interpolated his concern in this wise: "This arrangement [the new assignments of rank] at once divides the army under governor Harrison, and renders either part unequal to any object of importance and ruins the fairest prospects of the expedition."⁴¹

Such letters as these, coupled with a recommendation by the citizens of Chillicothe that he appoint Harrison Commander-in-Chief, probably caused the President to modify his wish that James Monroe take the command in the West. Monroe put the matter very simply in a letter to Thomas Jefferson: "I had off⁴ to proceed . . . to take command and was on the point of setting out when it was thought best to decline."⁴²

The War Department order to Harrison under date of September 17, posted by fast express, clothed the western candidate with adequate authority. The General's prospective force, wrote Eustis, would include 3000 men from Pennsylvania and Virginia, the 17th Regiment under Colonel Wells, also volunteers and militia from Kentucky to the number of 6000 strong. A train of artillery was to advance from Pittsburgh and with authority to requisition funds and supplies of every kind, the General was ordered to provide for the protection of the entire northwestern frontier, to retake Detroit, "and with a view to the Conquest of Upper Canada, you will penetrate that country as far as the force under your Command will in your judgment justify."⁴³

Whether the conquest of Upper Canada was to be accomplished in conjunction with an adequate naval force on Lake Erie was not specified. Its attention fixed coastwise, the administration was dallying with that issue.

That Fort Harrison had been successfully defended relieved the General of anxiety and an immediate task. Surrounded by a mob of yelling savages during the night of September 3, that temporary outpost had been most gallantly defended by twenty-eight-year-old Captain Zachary Taylor and "not more than 10 or 15 men able to do a great deal." Taylor's report, which reached the General at Piqua, aroused gratification. Upon meeting that young officer at Vincennes some months before, Harrison had recommended him to the attention of the Secretary of War.

Taylor placed rifles in the hands of the "sick and indisposed" to beat off a frenzied attack. Then the savages had set fire to a corner blockhouse. "My presence of mind did not for a moment forsake me," assuringly wrote Taylor. "I saw, by throwing off part of the roof that joined the blockhouse that was on fire . . . the whole row of buildings might be saved."[44] The idea was effectively carried out, the enemy defeated. Harrison's project for a fort on the upper Wabash had proved sound. Never was the safety of Vincennes again threatened.

Although a subordinate rôle was not to Winchester's liking yet he had been rather fortunate. The immense problem of transportation and supply for the army was for Harrison to deal with. The contemplated dash into Indiana with a strong mounted force—and a surprise attack on Detroit had been in the back of Harrison's mind— was abandoned in view of the attendant risk. The General's first concern was for adequate clothing for the Kentuckians. Confident of a speedy victory when they mobilized in August, the men wore shirts of cotton or linen and carried no coats or blankets. "There is nothing that gives me more apprehension than the destitute condition of many of my men in the article of clothing," Harrison advised Eustis.[45] Early on the 25th, the morning after receiving his command, he dictated a statement to be printed on a thousand handbills and sent it away by fast riders in time for insertion in an extra edition of the *Kentucky Reporter*, printed late the next day at Lexington.

"FELLOW CITIZENS. . . . A contribution of articles . . . will enable your soldiers to withstand the keen northern blasts with as much fortitude as they will the assaults of the enemy. Can any patriot sleep easy on his bed of down when he reflects upon the situation of a centinel exposed to the cold . . . in a linen hunting shirt? Will the amiable fair sex suffer their brave defenders to be mutilated by the frost for the want of the mittens and socks which they can . . . procure for them?"[46]

With a view to the character of the country to be traversed and defended, Harrison outlined a plan to attack Detroit by means of a strong advance force carrying artillery while adequate mobile forces guarded communication lines in the rear. Preparatory to the final thrust by land, the advance forces were to unite at the Maumee (or Miami) Rapids opposite the scene of Fallen Timbers.

Harrison's plan incorporated more than the accommodation of supply trains. Within the State of Ohio were several Indian villages —Delawares, Shawnees, and Wyandots—and others within striking distance of Fort Wayne. For the protection of the exposed frontier, three lines of approach were mapped.[47] Winchester's main base of supply was to be a new outpost erected near old Fort Defiance, rendezvous of the army's left wing. The Ohio militia, assembled under General Edward Tupper at Urbana, on Hull's Road, were counted on to garrison the chain of forts erected during the march to Detroit in June. On the right wing, the Virginia and Pennsylvania volunteers, approaching from Pittsburgh, were to rendezvous with the eastern Ohio militia at outposts along the Sandusky River within striking distance of the Rapids. However, there were no lateral roads in northwest Ohio and a vast miry tract known as the Black Swamp would have to be causewayed, or frozen over, before the artillery could advance. Unless the fall would be dry, it was rather likely to be a winter campaign, and with this point in mind Harrison called on army contractors to supply a million and more rations to be deposited at outposts along the three routes. If Detroit and Malden town were to be taken, ample supplies would have to be deposited at the Rapids and a strong fort constructed to counter the threat of enemy warships. Such was the great project to be accomplished in addition to the defense of the Indian frontier. Furthermore, another defeat was not to be risked, according to James Madison's instructions.

Already it was late September; soon forage would be getting scarce and the streams too low to accommodate flatboats although Harrison foresaw a need for them if the fall proved unseasonably wet. Again moving up to St. Marys with newly arrived detachments of horse and foot, Harrison watched the construction of Fort Barbee. To insure transportation of adequate supplies to Winchester's army, then advancing northeasterly up the Maumee from Fort Wayne, he sent on a force to cut a road along the Auglaize Trail to Defiance, 60 miles in advance, and two intermediate outposts were to be erected. A drove of 300 cattle and 200 packhorses destined for Winchester were pushed forward by the road-builders as they labored in the Black Swamp.[48] The protection of this supply link became Harrison's primary concern and when two mounted officers brought word that British regulars and Indians were harrying the advancing left wing of the army he ordered a forced march to Defiance, hastening forward in the afternoon with a force of dragoons and infantry.

Rain which began to fall the next day, continuing throughout the night, mired the new road and drenched the bodies of tired soldiers. The men rested on their saddles beneath the shelter of great trees or sought the protection of logs. To revive flagging spirits amid rain, wind, and darkness, Harrison called for a song. A jovial Irish officer responded with some lively airs in which the men joined.[49] It was a strange setting for merriment.

On the morning of October 2, approaching the Maumee, Harrison sent a detail of scouts down that river to ascertain if the enemy had gone around Winchester to threaten Fort Wayne. It was discovered, however, that they had retreated from that direction a few days before. Hurrying on a supply train en route for the left wing, Harrison entered the camp at Fort Defiance that evening. Winchester, he learned, had failed to reach Defiance on time. His army too strong to be checked, the Indians had harassed the flanks while the British skillfully retreated and made their artillery safe. Harrison exchanged some sharp words with the General but Winchester, as his officers pointed out, was hardly to blame. Lack of supplies had prevented an effective pursuit and the army had done well to avoid an ambuscade. Harrison allowed his temper to cool as he dangled his wet socks before an open fire and ate a late supper.[50] Retiring early to bed he was aroused by Colonel John Allen and another Kentucky officer who expressed the fear that their regiment, ill-clothed and on short rations, was on the verge of mutiny.

Harrison declined to interfere at the moment but sent an aide to tell Winchester to beat the alarm in the morning instead of reveille. Neither Harrison's presence in camp nor his new rank was known to the rank and file. October 3, when the alarm was sounded at sunrise, the Kentuckians swarmed from their tents and formed a hollow square. Instead of an enemy, the plain, familiar figure of their leader appeared before them. Winchester introduced the Commander-in-Chief in complimentary terms:

"I have the honor of announcing to this army the arrival of General Harrison, who is duty authorized . . . to take command. . . . This officer enjoying the implicite confidence of the States from whose citizens this army is & will be collected, and possessing himself great military skill and reputation, The Gen¹ is confident in the belief that his presence, in this army in the character of its chief will be hailed with universal approbation."[51]

Shouts of greeting came from the ranks. Harrison waved for silence and delivered a speech reminiscent of those before malcontents on previous campaigns. Any men who wished to return home, he explained, were at liberty to do so; facilities for an immediate discharge would be provided. But what of their reception in Kentucky? If their fathers did not drive their degenerate sons back to the field of battle to recover their tarnished honor, then their mothers and sisters would hiss them from their presence. "But if my fellow soldiers from Kentucky, so famed for patriotism, refuse to bear the hardships incident to war . . . where shall I look for men who will go with me?"[52] Cheers and shouts "rent the air."

Harrison then announced some good news. Packhorses bearing supplies had arrived in camp only the previous evening; 200 wagons loaded with biscuits, flour, and bacon were en route from St. Marys. No longer was there talk of desertion. And as for discipline, a Kentuckian under Winchester opined: "In an army but one can rule. Harrison, *with a look,* can awe and convince, or persuade, where some would be refractory. He . . . makes all do their duty. . . . All are afraid and unwilling to meet with his censure."[53]

A short way down the River Auglaize, southeast of Defiance, Harrison selected a site for a new fort. A mounted detachment under General Edward Tupper was sent forward to sweep pillaging bands of savages from farms near the Rapids where much corn was stored. Winchester, who admitted himself willing to serve under Harrison, was requested to await at Defiance the arrival of adequate supplies. Turning back to St. Marys, Harrison surveyed a broad front. In the West, General Hopkins was leading a force of militia against the hostile tribes in Illinois. A battalion of Ohio infantry and 500 mounted riflemen, all new recruits, were ordered to reinforce Fort Wayne and pillage the Indian towns beyond. It was a task in which they miserably failed. Harrison returned to Piqua meantime to consult with army quartermasters. The situation was not encouraging. So much rain had fallen that the routes to the north were unseasonably wet. October 8 he admitted himself at a loss as to means for continuing the fall campaign. Kentucky would have to modify its views concerning a speedy conquest of Canada.

"I am straining every nerve to prepare & forward on the supplies," he wrote to Governor Shelby. "But for such an army & through a country so swampy it is really an Herculian task. . . . I have no other prospect than a winter campaign. From the latter end of this month until the ground entirely freezes the country . . . is absolutely not practicable for wagons."[54]

Most of the War Hawks were far from the front. During the normally dry month of October packhorses floundered for miles fetlock or full leg deep while axle trees "would drag on the ground for rods together."[55] These were long autumn days. Along roads cut through a wilderness where forage was scarce, horses would have to be fed from precious loadings, decreased upon arrival by full 50 per cent. Worn thin by careless drivers who were well recompensed for dead horses, the poor animals dropped in their tracks by the score; in the spring their bones could be traced by turkey-buzzards feeding. Flatboats were ordered for transportation along the Sandusky, Auglaize, and St. Marys rivers but before the craft could be launched swollen waters again became shallow.

From Piqua Harrison rode to Urbana and Franklinton to organize the right wing.

Franklinton, little frontier village where Harrison took up headquarters on October 13, was situated on a bend of the Scioto River about a mile from the present statehouse in Columbus. For a little more than a year the town was to enjoy a booming war prosperity. It was strategically situated as a main base of army supply, its citizens not adverse to profit.

Only with considerable effort were supplies accumulated and sent forward while the left wing of the army waited at Fort Winchester, the new outpost at Defiance. To spare the lives of horses and the consequent expense, Harrison requisitioned a hundred ox teams, which though slow in movement were calculated to consume less precious grain from their loadings. Droves of hogs, grown suddenly expensive, were marshalled along the Sandusky and Auglaize routes; at Fort Winchester the troops turned to cooperage, salting down half a million pork rations in barrels. As the winds of late autumn penetrated the outposts, clothing became more desperately needed than food. Thousands of shoes, jackets, trousers, and blankets had been ordered, yet articles expected from Philadelphia were unaccountably delayed and broken-down wagons retarded shipments from Kentucky. "It is painful to the feeling mind," observed General Winchester, "to see the situation of the Regulars on a frosty morning."[56] He was anxious to get on to the Rapids but the principal supply train and artillery had not yet started from Pittsburgh. To heap aggravation upon suffering, garments contributed by thrifty contractors were," from their size, only calculated for well-grown boys."[57] Soaring prices, shoddy materials and calculated delays provoked outbursts of frank statement from the General, the plight of Winchester's men bearing on his mind. "I am all out of patience with the rascally Contractors," he notified Quartermaster William Piatt and before his indignation had wholly subsided he addressed a letter to the Secretary of War:

"Notwithstanding my urgent demand the Contractors have done little or nothing towards Deposits I have required to be made. . . .

Major White has let out his contract . . . at so low a rate that the Sub-Contractors are unable to furnish the supplies and one at least . . . is as great a scoundrel as the World can produce. . . ."[58]

The people of Franklinton, observed an officer close to the General, "charge the most exorbitant prices for every article furnished either the public or soldiers. Every species of produce . . . have risen 50 per cent."[59] Fifteen hundred barrels of flour to be delivered at the Rapids would cost the War Department $15 a barrel. At this rate the sum of $200,000 originally advanced for the fall campaign would not last very long.

November, foretaste of winter, was not yet at hand. Tracing the northerly course of the Sandusky River, Harrison marked sites for outposts and storehouses and ordered roads built across Black Swamp to connect Upper and Lower Sandusky with the Rapids. Welcome stores of corn were discovered at Lower Sandusky where Fort Stephenson had been constructed. (From its position on the Sandusky River flowing north, the site of Upper Sandusky in 1812 was thirty-five miles south of Lower Sandusky, which was thirty miles southeast of the Rapids.) At the Sandusky, Harrison prepared to unite the right wing.

Continuing long hours in the saddle, the General rode east to Mansfield and Wooster and ordered on the Pennsylvania troops bringing a few pieces of artillery. To transport these guns to the Rapids, save over well-frozen ground, appeared a hopeless task. Cutting across the wilderness to the north he reached a lonely militia camp at Huron, on the shore of Lake Erie, where 800 Ohioans were encamped and directed them to proceed to Lower Sandusky. Flour, he ascertained, could be shipped down the Lake from Cleveland. When heedless individuals allowed the substance of certain letters to appear in the press, the public at large, including the enemy, was duly appraised of Harrison's present expectations: "That he had then under his command 4500 men well appointed; by the 10th he would be at Sandusky—by the 20th . . . at Miami—at this point which is only six days march from Detroit—General Winchester with 2000 or 3000 men it is expected will form a junction with Harrison," explained the Philadelphia *Aurora*.[60] The appearance of this and other useful intelligence concerning the strength and movements of the army caused an embarrassed War Office to order that no more such information be furnished unless under the direct supervision of the General.[61]

Returning by way of the Sanduskys, Harrison took up headquarters at Delaware, twenty-four miles north of Franklinton. Heavy rains which fell in early November inundated the whole country making the roads "desperate," the consequent destruction of horses "prodigious," and caused a revision of plans. Quartermasters resorted to flatboats but within a fortnight a sudden drop in temperature congealed every stream and "sanguine hopes were blasted." All along the Sandusky, Auglaize and St. Marys rivers the boats were frozen fast.[62]

Principal victims of the transportation problem, the Kentuckians and regulars under Winchester were mutinous again because of want and the weather. Many were sick, their beds the frozen ground. Only in meager quantities did clothing and flour reach this suffering left wing of the army. Harrison's present difficulties, water transportation failing, were greatly augmented from the want of drivers for the wagons and packhorses.[63] The line of communications was kept undisturbed by Indians, however. While engaged with the supply problem on the right wing, the General was still waging war. A second detachment of Ohioans sent against tribal villages in Indiana had largely failed through want of discipline and resolution in the men, nor had General Hopkins done any better in Illinois; Harrison therefore planned to organize a punitive expedition against the Mississinewa towns to clear the army's left flank.[64] War parties from the Wabash could easily intercept convoys en route to Defiance or even descend upon Winchester's own camp.

November 25, at Franklinton, the General reviewed a mixed force of 600 regulars and mounted riflemen and dragoons assembled under Lieutenant-Colonel John B. Campbell of the 19th U. S. Regiment. From the rank and file "a solemn pledge" was extracted that they would obey their officers and "support the character of American Soldiers." Harrison added another injunction of historical note. All Indian women and children, as well as "warriors who ceased to resist" were to be spared.[65] Campbell, "brave, sensible and judicious," moved forward with his command to Greenville from whence he set out for the Indian country on December 14. Each of his men carried ten days' rations and as much grain for his horse as he could stow away. The weather grew bitterly cold.

Riding rapidly to forestall the spread of information, the detachment covered eighty miles in three days and one night, destroyed four Indian towns, killed eight warriors and, according to instructions, took prisoners to the number of forty-two. Early next morning Campbell's fortified camp was furiously attacked. The troops stood firm behind their redoubts, "not an inch of ground was yielded," and marksmen took steady aim.[66] Victory, as Harrison pointed out following the Battle of Tippecanoe, lay with those who maintained discipline the longest. Following the battle thirty Indian dead were discovered on the field; the defenders had lost only eight killed but forty-eight were wounded, four of which later died, and the number of horses lost was "considerable." Carrying seventeen of the wounded on litters, the troops began a slow painful march back to Greenville, the task of fortification every night made difficult from the wretched quality of their axes which had become so few that most of the men were forced to await their turn in cutting wood for fires.[67]

The cold weather continued, toes and fingers were badly frost-bitten and many soldiers were unable to put on their shoes. They had been without food for two days when they began to gather up the grains of corn from where their horses had fed during the outward march.[68] Forty miles west of Greenville a mounted company bringing provisions rescued the army.

From one of the Indians taken prisoner, Campbell gleaned a rumor that Tecumseh and 600 warriors were patrolling the Wabash not a score of miles from the scene of action. Should this report be true, Harrison feared that a sudden thrust might intercept the supply convoys but decided against organizing for another raid. The detachment had done its work. Not only was the firm conduct of the troops gratifying but Harrison was highly pleased to commend "the most punctual obedience . . . paid to his orders." While the troops had been "vigorously attacked by the enemy," still "the claims of mercy prevailed." The commanding General, the statement went on, "believes that humanity and true bravery are inseparable," even, it was understood, in Indian warfare.[69]

Christmas Day found Harrison with the troops on the plains at Upper Sandusky debating with himself whether he would continue as Brigadier General of the regulars or send in his resignation as Governor of Indiana. Retainment of the Governorship, Senator Thomas Worthington advised him, had retarded the Senate's confirmation of his brigadier's commission.[70] Harrison had been frank, however, in expressing his preference for the rank of major general, an appointment seemingly justified by the extent of his command. Current rumors that he would resign from the army met with protests both public and private. The influence of Harrison alone was keeping the army together, an Ohioan wrote Senator Worthington, otherwise it would "brake up in confusion."[71] But by resigning as Governor of Indiana on December 28, Harrison served notice he would continue in the field.[72] Meanwhile, little good news had come from the Niagara frontier where the officer Harrison had rescued again at Fallen Timbers, Solomon Van Rensselaer, now a Colonel, had been seriously wounded in a disgraceful American defeat at Queenston. Generals Henry Dearborn, Stephen Van Rensselaer and Alexander Smyth having successively failed in that quarter, the war would not end, one might imagine, for another twelve-month.

MASSACRE AT THE RIVER RAISIN

WHILE the weather was brewing difficulties in the North-west, a statesman of an inquiring mind took command of the War Department. Secretary of State James Monroe, assuming the War portfolio upon the resignation of William Eustis in December, sought to discover why so little progress had been made in view of the fact that the war party had committed itself to the possession of Upper Canada ere snow fell, aye, ere the leaves fell.[1] The situation was the more serious inasmuch as the greater part of the six-months' service for which the Ohioans and Kentuckians had volunteered was now past, their terms due to expire in February, 1813.

Following a brief trip to Chillicothe, where Mrs. Harrison was visiting, the Commander-in-Chief returned to Franklinton early in January and perused an unusually long letter, crisply and concisely phrased, from Secretary James Monroe. "The object of your Expedition," Harrison was reminded, "was to retake Detroit, to take Malden, with the adjacent Country, and to hold them." The long delay and the great expense involved was giving the President "much concern." Yet the capture of Detroit and Malden was still considered "objects of the highest importance." Monroe went on and on, discussing matters which Harrison knew only too well, but at least he made acknowledgment of "all the hardships of the present season," and "the difficulty of procuring and transporting provisions," as well as the threatened exhaustion of the public treasury.

"The destruction of the Queen Charlotte [a 17-gun warship pro-tected by the guns of Fort Amherstburg] and of the whole of the naval force of the enemy frozen up," Monroe added, ". . . would be an important attainment." The President was also contemplating a mounted expedition of 1000 Kentuckians into Indiana and Illinois by way of Fort Wayne "for the purpose of . . . destroying the provisions collected in the Indian villages, scourging the Indians them-selves and disabling them."[2] But it was left to the General to decide whether the principal object of the campaign, the occupancy of De-troit and Malden, should not be postponed until spring.

A letter from Harrison reporting on the state of the army was already on its way to the War Office. Buffeted by the vagaries of climate, the perplexities of Black Swamp and galling criticism which began to resound, Harrison already had expressed his concern over the existing stalemate. Early in December, as he took stock of operation, boatloads of flour were frozen up in the streams. Forage, obtainable only "at an expense which can scarcely be conceived," constituted an immediate need and the lack of a single necessity was considered a tremendous handicap to winter operations in a wilderness. But Harrison would not admit of failure. "Should I be able to get one Million or even 800,000 Rations of Flour at the Rapids and the Weather is severe enough to freeze the Straight . . . I should be enabled to sit down before Malden (without going to Detroit) in six days from my leaving the Rapids." If the strait—the Detroit River—did not freeze, Detroit itself might be taken yet that was a post hardly tenable against bombardment from the opposite shore. One extraordinary phase of General Hull's conduct, Harrison observed, "was that he should choose to defend Detroit rather than to attack Malden."[3]

Harrison was free to admit—and Monroe, a veteran of a suffering Revolutionary army would understand—that he "did not make sufficient allowance for the imbecility and incompetence of the public agents and the Villainy of the Contractors." If "important political considerations" could be disregarded, Harrison added, touching the nerve center of the campaign, he would recommend that the government bend its efforts toward securing control of Lake Erie in the spring. Then, presumably, "Malden, Detroit and Mackinac would fall in rapid succession." Under the circumstances, all that the General could promise, if the strait did not freeze, was the retaking of Detroit with a possibility of occupying the opposite shore. "I am . . . very far from believing that the original Object is impracticable. . . . If it would be the determination to disregard expense . . . the President may rely upon the Exertions of the Troops . . ."[4]

But Monroe's letter of inquiry needed an answer. Harrison sat down and delivered it in two long dispatches, aggregating 4500 words. Boiled down they amount to a few footnotes to history plus a hint that the General would still prefer to co-operate with a naval force, capable of commanding Lake Erie, which would transport army baggage and artillery "to some point . . . below Malden."[5]

To build and equip war vessels for this purpose would cost no more than the transportation of army supplies for six weeks through the wilderness. On the whole, Harrison decided, the attempt against Detroit might as well be abandoned although taking advantage of rigorous weather, the artillery and baggage could be hauled over frozen roads and the ice on the lake to lay siege to Fort Amherstburg and Malden. "The principal object of the campaign could be accomplished sooner and consequently with less expense than by waiting untill spring," and since most of the Indians were then scattered about in their winter hunting camps there would be few of them to contend with. The contemplated mounted expedition into Indiana, which Harrison knew to be the project of Colonel Richard M. Johnson, then attending Congress, was dismissed as unwise. Until the month of April at least the Indian towns would be abandoned, the men hunting, the women and children "scattered about making sugar." And at that season "the corn is . . . universally hid in small parcells in the earth."[6] In view of the changeable weather—in early January it turned warm—Harrison asked to postpone his decision for a few days as to the advance upon Malden. Although he did not so state, he was then awaiting advices from General Winchester as to whether or not the Kentuckians could be persuaded to remain in service after the expiration of their term.[7] To Harrison's dispatches of January 3 and 6, 1813, Monroe replied:

"The President wishes you to attempt nothing in vain or at least without the fairest prospect of success. . . . Whatever ground is gained must be held, and he is content to gain it slowly, provided it be made secure, rather than to put the important interests of the Country to hazard by a rash enterprise . . ."[8]

Harrison, a devotee of precautionary measures, could be depended upon to obey this injunction. But the much beset left wing of the army was by this time out of his control and Monroe's doctrine came much too late for General Winchester to read.

The unhappy existence of the ill-clad Kentuckians and regulars in their lonely wintry camp on the Maumee deserves particular consideration, however. It did not seem possible that men could suffer more. When all the timber within reasonable distance had been used for firewood, a small garrison was left with the sick at Fort Winchester while the army, by successive stages, moved down the Maumee to Camp No. 3, otherwise styled "Fort Starvation."[9] Here the troops awaited a sufficiency of supplies before proceeding further. Many, lacking shoes, bound their feet in strips of cloth; successful hunters made moccasins from the skins of animals with the fur turned inside. The daily sick list ran to 300 victims of influenza and typhus, their beds exposed to the wintry ground, their principal nourishment

hickory roots and fresh pork. "Many times the dead march was heard
. . . and the solemn procession . . . carried our fellow sufferers to
the grave."[10] December 10 the restless and unshaven soldiers drew
their last ration of flour and when it was learned that flatboats with
supplies were frozen in the river a train of packhorses, bony and
shrunken from living on brush, was sent to bring on whatever food
was obtainable.

More weary days of waiting passed and one evening General
Winchester discovered among his belongings a pencilled note which
tersely avowed that unless flour arrived within the next two days the
Kentuckians would depart in a body to get it. Perhaps this would not
have been an unwise measure but "the officers used every argument
to suppress the appearance of mutiny."[11] All the beef and pork on
hand was issued to the men that evening. Next day, December 17,
Winchester was "gratified," according to the general order he issued,
to notify the troops that some 300 hogs had left Fort Jennings, thirty
miles below, and very fortunately this battalion of doomed porkers
arrived in camp before nightfall.[12] During weather "excessively cold"
the troops subsisted on fresh pork alone as they began the construction of sleds with which to haul their equipment to the Maumee
Rapids. Sixty pirogues built in anticipation of a voyage down the
river would have to be left behind.

On the 22nd, after twelve days of restricted meat diet, "a little
flour came to camp once more; quarter rations of that article were
issued." As the packhorse train at last straggled into camp on Christmas Eve the men rejoiced to have been "delivered from a state of
starvation."[13]

"Our sufferings at this place have been greater than if we had been
in a severe battle," a diarist conceded. The total number of dead at
Camp No. 3 was estimated at "more than one hundred," and the site
had become "a loathsome place."[14] A small supply of clothing and
shoes arriving, orders to march on the 29th were greeted with some
show of interest. A few decimated companies remained to guard the
sick. The men tossed harnesses of green hides onto the backs of
cavalry mounts, grown too weak and tame to resist draft horse service, but after only a few miles of travel they began to wear down
rapidly. Then the gaunt frames of soldiers bent to the task, trekking
through snow two feet deep, resting at night on beds of brush. "I
have seen six Kentuckians substituted instead of a horse, pulling
their plunder, drudging along through the snow, and keeping pace
with the foremost," recorded a soldier who appreciated the sight.[15]
Most of the snow melted during the warm spell in early January so

that the Kentuckians now plunged up to their middles in water, slush and mud. On the tenth, 1300 soldiers—the remains of three regiments —bivouacked at last on the far bank of the Rapids toward which Harrison had recently started 4648 expensive "large fat hogs."[16]

Harrison, meantime, had been preparing to push on to the Rapids as soon as Winchester arrived. Supplies were to be hauled on sleds. "Put all the work hitherto directed in train of execution," was the order to General Simon Perkins in command at Lower Sandusky. "The axes must be repaired. . . . Husband the forage. . . . Not a waggon must be kept idle. . . . Push on the sledmaking. . . ."[17] The snows of late December slowed contacts with the left wing of the army. Shortly before Winchester had decided to advance from Camp No. 3, Harrison entrusted a verbal message to Ensign Charles S. Todd (later Minister to Russia), two French guides and three friendly Wyandots. Harrison recommended that the left wing march on as soon as possible and, upon reaching the Rapids, construct a number of sleds for the main expedition against Malden. Todd was also to inquire concerning the disposition of the Kentuckians to serve over their time.[18]

Somewhere in the mazes of Black Swamp that officer passed two lonely marchers in Ensign Leslie Combs of Kentucky and a single guide. Combs and his comrade plodded some eighty miles through the snow, reaching Fort McArthur, on Hull's Road, late on the ninth day of their journey to taste their first food in forty-eight hours. Combs lay ill in bed for several days while Winchester's message, reporting his departure from Camp No. 3, was forwarded to Harrison.[19] January 11 it belatedly reached the General at Upper Sandusky but not for days did any word come concerning Winchester's safe arrival at the Rapids. Awaiting this intelligence "with great anxiety," meanwhile, Harrison cautioned General Perkins to hold his supply train in readiness until Winchester again had been heard from.[20]

Another important message from Winchester was on its way but by the same indirect route, Hull's Road and Fort McArthur. Word of his arrival which Harrison then awaited had been entrusted to a detail escorting the worn-out packhorses returning by easy stages to Fort McArthur, distant by forty miles from the right wing where Harrison was known to be. The situation became the more confusing when Harrison received a message which Winchester sent two days later by way of Lower Sandusky, stating that he could not rely upon retaining the Kentuckians in service but adding not a word concerning his arrival at the Rapids. The second message, of lesser importance, had reached Harrison before the first. The earliest intelligence received of Winchester's present position was gleamed from that officer's request of reinforcements from General Perkins, a dispatch very properly forwarded to Harrison at Upper Sandusky.[21]

It was the evening of January 16 as Harrison received the dispatch forwarded by General Perkins. He shot back a blunt note to Winchester at the Rapids, requesting "information as to your situation and designs," and ordered 300 Ohio and Virginia troops at Upper Sandusky to make ready for a forced march, with artillery, over a partially built road across Black Swamp.[22] Next morning he started for Lower Sandusky, setting a pace so furious that the horse of his aide dropped dead before the gates of Fort Stephenson. Winchester, meantime, was counselling with his officers and screwing up courage to take a step unauthorized by Harrison but urgently solicited by five settlers from Frenchtown on the River Raisin (now Monroe, Michigan), thirty-two miles to the north. Disturbed by the American advance, they warned a number of British in the town were arresting, "all suspected persons" and were about to seize 300 barrels of flour and all stores of beef, corn and wheat.[23] Save the stores, save your citizens, begged the settlers. The Kentuckians needed to hear no more. Winchester, however, and perhaps to his credit, took all the responsibility for the move. January 17, two regiments, numbering together 680 men led by Colonels William Lewis and John Allen, set out for the Raisin even though it was generally understood that any such premature move was "contrary to the instructions of Gen¹ Harrison," or, as a militia officer wrote, "without the consent or advise" of the General and "contrary to [his] wishes."[24]

More than that, it was contrary to the expressed wish and policy of the President of the United States whose one remaining hope for a victory on any front was the capture of Detroit or Malden. But as James Monroe that very day was writing the precautionary instructions by which the army was to be guided, General Winchester, it may be conceded, had no way of knowing that "important interests" should not be put to hazard "by a rash enterprise."

Marching along Hull's Road and the ice of Lake Erie, the detachment under Lewis and Allen approached Frenchtown at 3 P.M. on the second day out. The unshaven and ragged Kentuckians saluted the enemy with barks and cock-crows, driving a mixed force of British, Canadians and Indians—possibly 400 in all— from behind fences and houses. The men were careful with their fire so that no noncombatants were injured. "Both officers and soldiers supported the double character of Americans and Kentuckians," reported Colonel Lewis.[25]

His losses were twelve dead, fifty-five wounded. Most of the enemy stricken were carried off by Indians during the night although fifteen dead were picked up in a field the next morning. Joyously welcomed by the French villagers, the conquerors were regaled with apples, cider, butter, sugar-loaf and whiskey, a repast well deserved. It had been a long time since the men had tasted such luxuries. Yet heedless of peril in this remote spot, Allen and Lewis made their camp behind a fence of split logs on the far side of the river near a road wide open to approach from the north. The work of fortification was left to a later day, the customary roll-call forgotten. "All was joy and gladness with both Officers and Soldiers."[26]

Without first notifying Harrison, a good two-days' march in the rear, General Winchester now decided to reinforce Frenchtown by means of his own presence and the Seventeenth Regiment, now reduced to 300 men, under Colonel Samuel Wells. One company remaining at a safe distance to guard the baggage in the rear the number of effectives at Frenchtown was increased to nearly 900.[27] Not until after he reached the advance post did Winchester relay word— and by an officer sent on by Harrison—that he was in need of men and munitions. "The ground I am compelled to occupy is not very favorable for defence," admitted the General but he gave no sign of attempting to improve or fortify his position. Nor could he produce any evidence as to the movements of the enemy. He closed his remarkable diagnosis of the situation with a swift descent into the obvious:

"Axes are much wanted as well as fixed ammunition, the one for defensive, the other for offensive operations."[28]

Meanwhile the Kentuckians remained on level ground close to Hull's Road, along which an enemy might approach with cannon. The frozen river, the protection of its banks rejected, lay behind them. Oblivious to the degree of caution to be exercised in the Indian country, Winchester neglected also the shelter of a near-by orchard and hollow and permitted Wells' regulars to string out their line on the right of the militia, the traditional position which military rule dictated, and there they remained conspicuously posted in an open field.[29]

At Lower Sandusky on January 18, Harrison moved forward a battalion of some 200 Ohio militia under Major W. W. Cotgreave who was ordered to march all night, and a further reinforcement of 350 busied themselvs with preparations to follow. Arising early next morning the General took up his correspondence by candlelight.

A letter to General Tupper inquired if the Ohio militia under his command might be induced to remain in service "15 or 20 days" after their time was up.[30] His pen sped more rapidly over the page as he begged Governor Return J. Meigs of Ohio and Governor Shelby in particular to call out additional troops "with all expedition to join me."[31] At 4 A.M., in the midst of his writing, Harrison was interrupted by a mud-stained dispatch bearer from Winchester. Glancing over the message, which told of the first advance to the Raisin, Harrison expressed his reaction in a postscript to Shelby: "I greatly fear that Lewis and Allen will be overpowered."

The three letters completed, Harrison summoned General Perkins and an orderly on horseback and set out for the Rapids in a one-horse sleigh which pitched and jolted heavily over the Black Swamp trail. Harrison, who could hardly contain his impatience, finally mounted the orderly's horse and pushed on alone to join Cotgreave. Approaching darkness found him still in the swamp, his laboring mount sinking to his belly at every step; dismounting, the General leaped from sod to sod, leading the horse after him. A few stray hogs were encountered and then came one of Cotgreave's men who had dropped back in search of a lost bayonet. If he failed to find it, the soldier grumbled, the sum of one dollar would be stopped from his pay.[32]

Harrison promised to pardon him for the loss or obtain him another bayonet if he would only help him and his horse through the swamp. Rendering mutual assistance, the lonely pair pushed on to Cotgreave's camp where Harrison slept a few hours and arose by candlelight on the morning of the 20th. The difficulties of a wagon-master struggling with broken harness and damaged ox teams caused a vexatious delay; ultimately the men "hitched themselves to the drag ropes . . . and through mud to the waistband hawled their luggage four miles . . . with much cheerfulness."[33] Harrison plunged on ahead and was greeted with joyful surprise by the Kentuckians who remained at the Rapids. News of victory at the River Raisin verified, away went dispatches posthaste to Governor Meigs and to the Secretary of War. "It is absolutely necessary to maintain the position at the River Raisin," went his letter to Secretary Monroe on January 20, 1819. ". . . . I am happy . . . to inform you that our affairs . . . wear a flourishing aspect I fear nothing but that the enemy may overpower Gen¹ Winchester before I can send him a sufficient reinforcement."[34]

The time element, in the event of a counterattack, was of foremost concern. Delayed in Black Swamp, Cotgreave's men did not reach the Rapids until evening while the troops at Upper Sandusky, the artillery "being out of order and waiting repairs," were held up for some days.[35] On the 21st Cotgreave's men started over the ice

Scene of Harrison's Operations in the War of 1812.

toward the Raisin. En route from Lower Sandusky, meanwhile, were the 350 men under Colonel John Andrews who were to arrive at the Rapids late that day.

The problem of ascertaining General Winchester's immediate plans and prospects was not neglected. Harrison sent Henry Clay's brother-in-law, Captain Nathaniel Hart of Kentucky, to obtain information from the General concerning the strength and movements of the enemy. A cariole loaded with ammunition also moved forward.

Since the River Raisin lay but twenty-four miles from Amherstburg, it was expected that Winchester had scouts abroad. Winchester, however, had sent out no scouts. Accompanied by his young son, the General took up quarters at the of home of Colonel Francis Navarre, across the frozen river and some distance away from his troops. When two or three fleeing Frenchmen from Brownstown above brought in warnings of an oncoming enemy, one Jacques La Salle, a British sympathizer who was present, jovially assured the General that rumors of an attack were unfounded.[36] Yet the officers in the field must have expressed some difference of opinion as the unexpected appearance of Captain Hart on the 21st, just as Winchester was enjoying his dinner, "occasioned . . . consternation." Colonel Navarre later recalled a "considerable dissatisfaction" expressed at the meeting, the cause of which he was unable to understand.[37] But it was apparent that Winchester had done nothing in the way of fortifications, his right flank still entirely exposed. Hart remained with his fellow Kentuckians at Frenchtown, but sent back to the Rapids Colonel Wells who, General Harrison was advised—

"will give you the news we have received. The importance of holding this post I know you have fully weighed. In the event of its loss, the people having taken an active part against the British will be subjected to utter ruin. . . .

"The officers . . . are truly desirous of seeing you here, if it were even for a day. Many things ought to be done, which you only know how to do properly."[38]

Colonel Wells brought back "news" that a British and Indian force was reported advancing toward Frenchtown.

Colonel Henry Procter, commanding the Royal Newfoundland Regiment, the British 41st, and the 10th Veteran Battalion of militia, plus well-equipped Indian forces, emerged from Fort Amherstburg on the afternoon of January 19. His forces numbered 578 regulars and militia and about 500 Indians led by the Wyandot, Chief Roundhead, his path to the River Raisin leading over the frozen Detroit River and a well-travelled road. Seamen from naval vessels tied up at Amherstburg marched ahead with six small field pieces, including three howitzers. This equipage was described by a member of the British 41st:

"No sight could have been more beautiful than the departure of this little army. . . . It was the depth of winter, and the river . . . being four miles in breadth, the deep rumbling noise of the guns prolonging their reverberations like the roar of distant thunder . . . mingled with the wild cries of the Indians, seemed to threaten some convulsion of nature . . . the appearance of the troops winding along the road, now lost behind some cliff of rugged ice, now emerging into view, their polished arms glittering in the sunbeams, gave an air of romantic grandeur to the scene."[39]

Procter bivouacked the first night at Brownstown, eighteen miles above the Raisin, where he was joined by another Indian party. Late on the evening of the 21st General Winchester heard that the approaching enemy had reached Swan (also Stony) Creek, only five miles away; still he did nothing in respect to the placing of extra guards or erecting fortifications, for the news, he thought, was "only conjecture." But there was a stir among the men in the camp that night and the officers called in the foraging parties. If they looked to Winchester for special orders for the posting of guards they received none. The General had a good night's sleep in Colonel Navarre's best bed, only five and a half miles distant from the approaching foe.

Resuming his advance two hours before dawn on the 22nd, Procter needlessly gave the alarm by firing his cannon while still some distance away. Just as the five o'clock reveille was sounded the attack was launched against the dim forms of fences and sleeping men.[40] The noise of bombs reverberating sharply in the crisp morning air tumbled the soldiers from their beds. The Kentuckians quickly formed behind their split-log fence, but the regulars on the right were still in the clear. A charge by British regulars made little impression against the galling fire of sharpshooters with long rifles. The enemy artillerists suffered severely; wounded men seeking safety on their hands and knees were "tumbled over like so many hogs."[41] Finding a general assault unprofitable, the British began to concentrate on an obvious American weakness, the unprotected regulars in the open field. Here, once the line was breached, the savages could swarm in. At 5 A.M. General Winchester had been aroused from his sleep by his host. Throwing on his uniform over his nightshirt the General called for his horses but disregarding them when they were brought up he began pacing up and down in front of the house. The cariole of ammunition sent by Harrison stood near by but the General made no attempt to distribute it. Still he paced up and down and although the action became "very hot," he made no move "for a considerable time."[42] Fifteen or more minutes had passed when he finally mounted one of his horses, placed his son on the other, and rode across the frozen river. His first order was for Colonel Allen to bring the exposed regulars behind the puncheon fence but the movement was entirely unsupported and no effort was made to cover the men. Indians and Canadians posted in outhouses along the flank directed a destructive fire against the broken ranks. The unprotected regulars began to scatter toward the rear. Lewis and Allen detached two companies from the picketing in an attempt to rally the men while Winchester, "in a voice not loud," commanded them to form under the bank of the river.[43]

Mounted Indians with rifles were waiting along the rear and the flanks. Wanting discipline at this moment the rescuers were caught up in the backward current and swept across the river. The banks afforded no protection against Indians on horseback. From behind trees and houses came a deadly fire which sent the panic-stricken troops on a dead run down a narrow lane and into an adjacent wood. Indians thirsting for blood and for scalps closely followed, their war-hatchets cleaving the skulls of the hindmost. The slaughter, the screams of victors and vanquished, spread deep into the forest, warm blood staining the snow. Officers and men sank wearily to their rest crying: "Dam you—tomahawk me, it is all that you can do."[44]

"The men cannot be rallied, we must do the best we can," were the last words heard from Colonel Allen, distinguished head of the Kentucky bar.[45] A painful wound in the thigh brought him to a halt beside a tree-stump after retreating nearly two miles. An Indian chief rode up to claim the officer as his prisoner but Allen quickly covered him with his short rifle and used his sword on a warrior who recklessly rushed in. Then another redskin opened fire from the rear and Allen's career was ended. Winchester and Lewis, retreating slowly on horseback while endeavoring to reform the lines, fell into the hands of Chief Roundhead who stripped them of their uniforms, leaving the General in his nightshirt, and escorted them past the remains of their fallen comrades into the British line. It was a rich prize for the Chief. Accompanying the General was Major James Overton, his principal aide, and his son, "a handsome youth of sixteen."[46]

Few men can be heroic in a nightshirt. Blue with the cold and shaken by frightful scenes, Winchester made a pardonable effort to save the rest of the troops, sending Major Overton to Procter to report himself a prisoner and proposing, although with doubtful authority, a capitulation. Well pleased with this message, Procter ordered his men to hold their fire with the exception of two three-pounders which for a time continued active.

On the whole Winchester's proposition was most pleasing to the British leader. Thus far Procter had suffered 182 casualties, exclusive of Indian losses, and three howitzers and one three-pounder had been spiked in anticipation of defeat. Informed by an Indian runner of reinforcements approaching from the Rapids, Procter had posted an officer to keep a sharp lookout down the road and was prepared for an early retreat.[47]

With the opposing General a prisoner and hostage the British leader grew bold. Winchester was brought to the rear for a conference and the agreement was made that the surviving Kentuckians should be induced to surrender providing that "prisoners should be protected from the Indians, the wounded taken care of, the dead collected and buried, and private property respected."[48] Actually, as Procter must have known, these terms were impossible of execution in the presence of a force of blood-crazed Indians. But should the Kentuckians not accept, the British Colonel suggested, he was prepared to storm the works while the savages were to begin an indiscriminate massacre and burn the town. In the light of what had occurred in the rear of the American line it was a picture unpleasant to contemplate. Winchester readily agreed to the terms and Procter requested that he make his decision known in writing to his men.

While these negotiations were under way, 400 Kentuckians behind the split-log fence sat down and ate their breakfast while peering through loopholes to speculate upon the fortunes of war. None of them realized the fate of their General. The surviving detachments behind the fence had lost but five killed and some twenty wounded and although their ammunition was nearly exhausted they entertained no thought of surrender.

Placing Major James Overton conspicuously in front, Procter and his aides advanced under a flag and were met between the lines by Major George Madison, ranking surviving officer, and a single comrade. The message from Winchester which Madison now read was an embarrassing surprise in more than one respect. Their General a prisoner, yet still seeking to command them, and the command entirely at odds with their own sentiment! Asking to be convinced of Procter's good intentions, Madison returned for a conference with his men. The Kentuckians surged about in commotion as they heard the news, begging to be allowed to continue the fight. But the Indians were now coming up from their massacre, and the present ammunition supply, Madison realized, would not last very long. Again he went to Procter, pleading for time, then returned to his men. The flag passed back and forth several times between the lines. In the end, trusting in the solemn guarantee of safety to prisoners and wounded, Madison reluctantly agreed to yield. A tremor of rage and despair swept the lines. Was it for this that the Kentuckians had long suffered? As the surrender was announced they began shouting and cursing and their rifles were dashed to the ground. "There was scarcely a person that could refrain from shedding tears."[49]

And so the survivors of famine, sickness and two battles were escorted prisoners into the British camp, their spirit unsubdued. "You have taken the greatest set of gamecocks that ever came from Kentuck!" spoke one without exaggeration.[50] Ensign John Richardson of the British 41st recalled the external shabbiness of this fading remnant of an army, which, according to a Kentucky historian, was "composed of the most interesting and respectable citizens of the state."[51] Yet as Richardson saw them—

"They had the air of men to whom cleanliness was a virtue unknown and their squalid bodies were covered by habiliments that had evidently undergone every change of season, and were arrived at the last stage of repair. . . . It was the depth of winter; but scarcely an individual was in possession of a great coat or cloak, and few of them wore garments of wool of any description. They still retained their summer dress, consisting of cotton stuff of various colors shaped into frocks, and descending to the knee. Their trowsers were of the same material. They were covered with slouched hats, worn bare by constant use, beneath which their long hair fell matted and uncombed over their cheeks; and these, together with the dirty blankets wrapped round their loins to protect them against the inclemency of the season, and fastened by broad leathern belts, into which were thrust axes and knives of an enormous length, gave them an air of wildness and savageness which in Italy would have caused them to pass for brigands of the Apennines. The only distinction between the garb of an officer and that of the soldier was that the one, in addition to his sword, carried a short rifle instead of a long one, while a dagger, often curiously worked and of some value, supplied the place of the knife."[52]

Relief was not far away as the battle was fought. Had Procter delayed his attack five or six hours Cotgreave's battalion would have arrived to support the American rear. But the road from the Rapids was not so well travelled as that over which Procter had marched. Leaving the Rapids on the morning of the 21st, Cotgreave attempted a passage over the frozen Maumee but his oxen began to slip and those "poorly shod" threw themselves.[53] The Major abandoned the river and encamped that evening on Hull's Road. Only ten miles had been covered. Colonel John Andrews, bringing the second detachment from Lower Sandusky, had already reached the Rapids, but permitting these men to rest, Harrison sent away in the morning the remaining force of 300, mostly Kentuckians, under General John Payne.

At 3 A.M. on the 22nd Cotgreave's men struck their tents and were making good progress on the ice of Lake Erie when a strong wind came up and forced them to shore. The breeze bore indistinct sounds of cannonading and the sun was not far along when a company in advance met a Frenchman fleeing the scene of the battle.

The Frenchman "supposed" that the Americans were retreating. Cotgreave ordered his men to push ahead on the dead run. A mounted officer raced back to Harrison, who, with General Perkins and staff, started at once to overtake the Kentuckians under Payne. Cotgreave, meeting other fugitives, was shaken by their fearsome tale. "French Citizens were flying in considerable numbers upon the ice," the massacre was "overwhelming," the British victory "complete."[54] General Winchester, someone related, had been scalped and disemboweled, an arm slashed off and stuck in his body.[55] Fifteen miles from the Raisin, after loading his sleds with the wounded and other survivors "overcome with fatigue," Cotgreave wheeled about and joined Harrison and the Kentuckians at noon.

Just as affairs had appeared most promising, on the eve of realizing the original project of the campaign, the premature advance to the Raisin had ruined all. Harrison, thunderstruck, consulted with his officers. The victorious enemy was reported to be 1500 to 2000 strong and well provided with cannon; with good reason, therefore, it was decided to return to camp. The most vigorous of the troops were sent on to assist other survivors but only two officers and thirty privates all told were rescued. Shouts of rage and despair went up as the men learned the pitiful story. Those far behind the lines appeared as much affected. Grieved an Ohio officer:

"Our best Kentucky blood . . . officers and men sinking under the tomahawk without resistance. . . . Mourn, mourn, mourn, America your history does not furnish an equal. Arouse, unite and march to avenge your loss. . . . Harrison is now at our head—with men and means we shall yet succeed with the sanction of Heaven. . . ."[56]

A cloud of dejection enveloped the army as men strove in some way to reconcile their loss. Winchester's reinforcement of Lewis and Allen was only proper, Harrison conceded, but not the original advance. Still he did not seek to blame that officer and for the moment overlooked the dereliction of duty in respect to safeguarding his men. "In justice to Genl Winchester," Harrison reported to the War Office, ". . . I have understood that the detachment under Col^o Lewis was made at the earnest solicitations of his officers and perhaps contrary to his judgment. However deeply to be lamented . . . the destruction of the detachment . . . it has by no means destroyed my hopes of success with regard to . . . the principal object of the campaign."[57]

The British argument pertaining to the use of savages as allies appears a trifle specious considering the sequel to the unhappy affair at the Raisin. The British contention was hardly an argument, however, but a rather lame excuse. If the British did not employ the Indians, it was claimed, then the enemy would and while the Americans had only a few warriors in their service, "if they had not more, it was not owing to any want of exertion on their part."[58]

Yet the Madison administration still held to a faithful rendering of Jefferson's council that the Indians be kept "idle spectators" in time of war. The friendly Shawnees, Delawares, Wyandots, Senecas and a few Iroquois—Harrison's "pet Indians," as suspicious Ohioans termed them—were kept well guarded in their respective villages although Harrison was using a few of them as guides. The Ohio Shawnees under Chief Blackhoof were lodged at Wapakoneta on the Auglaize, the Delawares at Piqua. The Wyandots and Senecas of Sandusky, headed by Tarhe, the Crane, also remained peaceful. Another branch of the Wyandot nation living near Brownstown, however, had participated as British allies in the slaughter at the Raisin together with some ungovernable Creeks from Georgia, Chippewas and Ottawas from Michigan, Shawnees and Potawatomies from Indiana, a party of Saks and fierce Santees, the "Sioux of the Mississippi," led by the young chief Black Hawk. A Creek leader, present at the Raisin, later related that he "had got fat eating white people's flesh," and considering other similar testimony of the period this was no figurative expression.[59]

Attempts were made, according to a British apologist, "to soften the warlike habits of the natives,"[60] but their very numbers, so zealously recruited, rendered any such idea futile. "The Indians are necessary to his Majesty's service," counseled the British military leader in Canada, "and must be indulged."[61] Wrote Major (formerly

Ensign) John Richardson in describing a vicious circle for which he could offer no remedy:

"The most likely method of preventing the unnecessary effusion of blood [euphemism for massacre] was that of offering rewards for prisoners. This, however . . . was found to be ineffectual; for the character and disposition of the savage was not to be tamed by rewards, nor the impression of ages to be removed by such temptations. To have employed force would have been to have turned their weapons against ourselves. . . ."[62]

Yet the British persisted in fomenting such difficulties. The sequel to the affair at the Raisin indicated to what lengths official indulgence would go. More than 500 American prisoners had been taken; the killed and wounded, for which no separate figures are available, totaled at least 250 officers and men, most of whom had been slain during the retreat into the woods. In drawing up terms with Winchester, Colonel Procter had made promises which he knew he could not fulfill. Even as the Kentuckians laid down their arms the Indians began to plunder until "partially restrained."[63] The savages were permitted to retain many prisoners, stripping them of clothing, sidearms and cash, contrary to the terms of surrender. The prisoners were tied together in bunches preparatory for the march to Malden, and in a great hurry to be off, fearing Harrison's approach, Procter refused Winchester's final plea that an armed guard remain with the wounded, some of whom had lain in their beds since the battle on January 18. A promise was given to transport all the seriously wounded to safety next day but only two American surgeons, two interpreters and a single British officer remained with these unfortunates, "about 60 or 80 in number."[64] Procter took up the return march toward noonday, the Indians escorting all prisoners who could walk.

The Indians accompanied the army only as far as Swan Creek where they surrendered their prisoners in exchange for a liberal supply of whiskey. That night the savages held a drunken pow-wow and frolic. Their faces and bodies smeared with red and black paint they returned to Frenchtown early next morning to awaken the wounded with ear-splitting yells which boded no good. More whiskey was shared and the atrocities now performed were calculated, in their enormity, to avenge all Indian losses in battle. To lie wounded in bed and hear frenzied savages approaching was an experience which came only once. A dazed Kentuckian who managed to live through it all has left a word picture of this supreme culmination of suffering and horror:

"My feeble powers cannot describe the dismal scenes . . . exhibited. I saw my fellow soldiers naked and wounded, crawling out of the houses to avoid being consumed in the flames. Some that had not been able to turn themselves on their beds for four days, through fear of being burned to death, arose and walked out and about. . . . Some cried for help but there was none to help them. . . . Exclaimed numbers, in the anguish of their spirit, 'what shall we do?' A number, unable to get out, miserably perished in the unrelenting flames. . . . Now the scenes of cruelty and murder we had been anticipating with dread . . . commenced. The savages rushed on the wounded . . . shot, tomahawked, and scalped them, and cruelly mangled their naked bodies while they lay agonizing and weltering in their blood. A number were taken towards Malden, but being unable to march with speed were inhumanly massacred. The road was . . . strewed with the mangled bodies, and all of them were left for birds and beasts to tear in pieces and devour."[65]

A painted savage versed in the Anglo-Saxon vernacular carelessly kicked the ashes off the back of an expiring Kentuckian, the "damn'd son of a bitch."[66] Most of the houses were burned to the ground, the French inhabitants driven away. A hundred or more of the men lying dead were beheaded.

Carrying scalps, heads and booty, and escorting a few wounded prisoners, some of whom were dispatched along the route, the bloody scavengers rejoined their allies at Fort Amherstburg. The sight of these "handsomely painted" Indians carrying "an immense number of scalps," some with half a dozen or more fastened upon sticks, chilled the blood of the surviving Kentuckians who were pent up without tents or other covering in an open woodyard near the fort.[67] A few of the British officers privately expressed their indignation when they heard Procter congratulate the savages for their "bravery," but the Colonel, who later proved himself without a shadow of a doubt a poltroon, found it the easiest way. Even an attempt by Harrison to ascertain and assist the situation of the wounded proved utterly useless. An army physician escorted by a soldier and a guide advanced to Frenchtown under a flag, but one of these men was slain by Indians, the other badly wounded. The physician, whom Procter insulted and held as a spy, was robbed of his money and at length committed to a British prison at Montreal.[69]

The heads of the slain soldiers taken by Indians were stuck upon a picket fence at Detroit for the American inhabitants there to gaze upon. The British feared to remove them, naturally, and so they remained for days—

"their matted locks deeply stained with . . . gore—their eyes wide open, staring out . . . exhibiting every variety of feature; some with pleasant smiles, others, who had probably lingered long in agony, a scowl of defiance, despair or revenge; others wore the appearance of deep distress and sorrow—they may have died thinking of their far-off wives and children, and friends and pleasant homes which they should visit no more; the winter's frost had fixed their features as they died."[70]

XII

A FORT IS BUILT

GLANCING at the situation from a different time and place it becomes obvious that had Harrison continued his march to Frenchtown the village would have been retaken without a struggle and the wounded men saved. The hurried retreat of Colonel Procter was due to factors which the American leader could not comprehend. For Procter had seen enough fighting on his own account and his Indian allies were flushed with plunder. Moreover, he had many wounded men to care for and he dreaded the arrival of American reinforcements, then only a few hours in the rear.

But the fatal blow suffered by Winchester's army had paralyzed the American movement. Of the original force which had advanced to the Rapids, less than 300 fit and ready for duty now remained. Inasmuch as the savages had seized every horse in Frenchtown, no word of the British retreat could reach the camp at the Rapids that day. Harrison was still in the dark as to Procter's movements when he called a council of war at 9 P.M.[1]

In view of the reported numbers of the enemy a proposed retreat from the Rapids was debated. Winchester's choice of a camp ground, on the far side of the Maumee River, was obviously unwise. If rain and warm weather caused the ice to break up, the American line of communications would be broken. Should the ice continue to hold, an enemy flushed with victory could cross from above and, proceeding inland, destroy reinforcements then approaching from Upper Sandusky and capture the artillery train. Too, the fortified camp at the Rapids was ill-protected and insecure. Winchester had constructed his camp with the longest side facing the frozen river, the rear and the flanks exposed to attack from a near-by hillside.[2] And inasmuch as there was not a shovel or pickax in the camp, nor even enough axes to furnish a daily wood supply, it was unanimously decided to retrograde fifteen miles to the far side of the Portage River, a deep sluggish stream rising in Black Swamp. There the army would await the train of artillery and supplies from Upper Sandusky. Had Winchester not permitted Lewis and Allen to advance from the Rapids, a force overwhelming in numbers would have been assembled on the Maumee by early February, and bets of wine had been taken in Chillicothe that Harrison would "be in possession of Malden" by the sixth.[3]

At two o'clock in the morning of January 23, however, "cast down and dejected" soldiers arose to load the ox sleds and round up all the hogs in camp preparatory to retreat. Harrison ordered the supply sheds fired but no sooner was his army out of sight across the river than some Frenchmen quenched the flames and saved the provisions. The General would be glad to recover these stores upon his return.[4]

Rain poured down upon the retreating army, drenching also the Ohio and Virginia troops wading through Black Swamp on their march from Upper Sandusky. They paid the penalty for their tardiness: "It was with difficulty we could raise fires; we had no tents . . . nothing to cook with, and very little to eat. . . . When we went to sleep it was on two logs laid close to each other to keep our bodies from the damp ground. Good God! What a pliant being is man in adversity."[5] Harrison's encampment on the Portage River was flooded with water "three inches deep in some tents." The rain was followed by snow. As one weary militiaman philosophized: "It is the prospect of a soldier."[6] "Do not immagine that we beg much," added another—"though the Snow rests on our naked bosoms, the heart is not cold. . . . Gen¹ Harrison is with us, his eye Sees at once all and every part of the army . . . spedy relief . . . is already felt. . . ."[7] Additional reinforcements from Upper Sandusky arriving, on February 2 Harrison led an army of 2200 strong back to the Rapids and encamped on a smooth sloping ridge on the near bank directly opposite the scene of Fallen Timbers. The area was covered by a heavy stand of timber, "not a stick amiss." Here a fort would be built.

General Tupper's Ohio brigade at Fort McArthur and part of the force stationed along the Auglaize route were also ordered up, half a dozen companies remaining to garrison the forts in the rear. Faces brightened as an impressive train of artillery rolled into camp. All was anticipation again for the drive against Malden even though the terms of most of the men would soon expire. Provided the river and lake remained frozen, Harrison counted on action to keep the militia in the field. But following the rain and snow in late January the weather again turned warm. Frozen trails and roads were converted into bogs and soft ruts, and the ice on Lake Erie was slowly eaten away.[8]

Contemplating the threatened diminution of his force, Harrison set February 11 as the final date for the advance against Malden. First, however, in part to survey the ground, he led a detachment of 1100 men in pursuit of Indians who had been raiding a settlement on the far side of Maumee Bay. February 8, advancing quietly under cover of night, the men marched 26 miles before dawn but nearly lost a six-pounder through the rotten ice while several horses broke through and one soldier was nearly drowned. In the morning—Harrison's fortieth birthday—the General halted to rest his troops upon a small island. Then came word that the Indians had retreated past the River Raisin and so the pursuit was abandoned, "a monstrous disappointment." "Never," the General wrote, "was a Country so infatuated . . . never was an opportunity of destroying the Enemies of America was ever so well secured.[16]

This fruitless foray marked the final turning point in the campaign. "I have waited with an anxiety which I cannot describe for a change in the weather and untill this day I never abandoned . . . hope." Harrison advised the War Office in signifying the close of operations. "For the last twelve or fifteen days . . . it has been so warm that the roads have become entirely broken up."[10] Yet this was the season when as a rule "the most intense frosts prevail in this country giving the most perfect security and facility in passing the lakes and swamps with which it abounds." Moreover, the Kentucky and Ohio militia were clamoring to be discharged. As a final effort to win their stay Harrison assembled the troops and read them the text of laws recently passed by their state legislatures authorizing more liberal terms for new enlistments. "I . . . made to them such observations as I supposed the occasion called for . . . [and] dismissed them to give an opportunity for reflection."[11] Yet, despite appeals to "my own Kentuckians," only a few could be persuaded to remain.[12] Others expressed a willingness to serve after they had visited their distant families. The militia officers issued their encomiums: "On returning from service, Sir, we are happy in assuring you of our fullest confidence . . . in the measures you have taken. . . ."[13] and withdrew with their respective commands. The exuberance displayed by the Kentuckians as they turned homeward astonished a God-fearing Ohio recruit at Fort Amanda on the Auglaize: "All in high glee & Black & dirty as Indians [they] sang & danced in the most infamous manner & the most blasphemous swearing possible . . . to utter was made use of by those self-conceited Infidels."[14]

The camp at the Rapids left in a weakened condition, the arrival of General Richard Crooks with 600 Pennsylvania militia was timely. Present on the ground were a few regulars, some Virginia militia, the Pittsburgh Blues, a 12-months' volunteer troop, and a similar outfit from Petersburg, Virginia. Major Eleazer D. Wood, a respected and competent engineer, sketched plans for an immense fort to contain eight double-timbered blockhouses, a magazine and storehouses, elevations for four batteries, and covering eight acres of ground. Tools were distributed. Laboring with ax, mattock, and spade, "each brigade took up its assigned portion of the work with great vigor and spirit."[15] Hundreds of trees were cleared away. The men dug great ditches for drainage and tossed up thick embankments out of the frozen earth, the snow about one foot deep. Save for the space occupied by the batteries and blockhouses, the whole was to be picketed with timber fifteen feet long, about twelve inches thick, and set three feet into the ground. The amount of work accomplished in the next three weeks surprised even the men themselves and before the redoubts had been completed Harrison declared no camp in America was ever so well secured.[16]

One last thrust at the enemy was attempted following a brief spell of cold weather. The *Queen Charlotte,* the destruction of which Secretary James Monroe had advocated, was still tied up for the winter near Fort Amherstburg. Harrison selected Captain Angus Langham, a youth of recognized courage, to command a "forlorn hope" of some 200 regulars and militia with 30 Indian and French guides. According to the plan broached privately to Langham, the men were to cross Lake Erie on the ice, silently approach the vessel at three o'clock in the morning, set her on fire and hastily retreat. To cover their true design, the men were to march first to Lower Sandusky.[17]

Harrison lectured the troops upon their departure, representing their mission as one of peril and privation. The men retrograded to Lower Sandusky where suitable combustibles were prepared. Equipped with moccasins and cloth socks to deaden footsteps, and carrying spikes nine feet long, the detachment set out on sleds for Sandusky Bay. After proceeding a short distance Langham halted the men to reveal the true nature of the expedition and a score of militia and several Indians decided to withdraw.[18]

The undaunted continued their advance along Lake Erie, the wind driving snowflakes into their faces. But after reaching Middle Bass Island, some distance out, the guides discovered the ice to be weak and in the distance it appeared to be entirely broken up. Obviously the lives of the men would be endangered if the contemplated night march were attempted. Harrison, who had advanced to Maumee Bay to cover the retreat, had the "infinite mortification" to discover the detachment returning, its mission unperformed.[19] It was the last of a long series of disappointments. The *Queen Charlotte* was saved for the Battle of Lake Erie.

After reporting the campaign to the War Office, Harrison had confided additional details to Governor Isaac Shelby of Kentucky. There were still two modes of gaining the desired ground in the spring, he submitted, either with the help of the naval force then being prepared at Presque Isle (Erie, Pennsylvania), or by a land march "requiring a large force which principally must be drawn from Kentucky." The General's favorite recruiting ground lay south of the Ohio.

A few crumbs of comfort could be extracted from the late engagement at the River Raisin. "It is with great pleasure I inform you, my dear sir, that all the persons who have come in . . . agree in their account of the obstinate valor with which it [the action] was maintained. . . . But when shall I find words to express the horror and indignation which I feel at the circumstances. . . . All the ardent spirits among the men and . . . officers were sacrificed. . . ." Harrison requested that Shelby draft 1500 other such men and hold them in readiness to march. By this means opportunity would be provided "for preparing themselves with clothing."[20]

Several days later, however, Harrison reconsidered his problem. The term of the Virginia militia would expire late in March and the Pennsylvania brigade on April 2 leaving him with less than 1200 men "to garrison 10 or 12 forts and to maintain this important position."[21] Harrison asked the Kentucky governor to push on the militia as quickly as possible in detachments as they were made up. Apparently little was expected from Ohio. Journeying into the interior to supervise the recruiting, Harrison found the war spirit at a low ebb. Most of the best men had already served their tour, the militia officers of little use in recruiting.[22] March 10, reaching Franklinton, Harrison inspected a company of eighty recruits whose pretensions as fighters did not impress the General. Riding on to Chillicothe he gleaned from a letter from the War Office that prospects for a new army in the Northwest were far from bright. New policies were being formulated at Washington where a new political personality was endeavoring to dominate the scene.

As President James Madison delivered his second inaugural address on March 4, 1813, he faced a divided cabinet. Secretary of War John Armstrong of New York sat at the angle of division.

Petitioning elsewhere in vain, for refusals were many, Madison finally had called upon a member of the opposing Clintonian faction to take over the War portfolio, temporarily held by James Monroe. His choice could have been wiser. Armstrong had retired from a stormy Revolutionary service with the rank of major, and a reputation for intrigue. Originally a Federalist, he became a Republican upon marrying a sister of Chancellor Robert R. Livingston, ally of the Clintons of New York. When George Clinton became governor in 1800, Armstrong went to the United States Senate where he won little popularity in the South and the West. In 1807 President Jefferson nominated him as special minister to France and only the vote of Vice President George Clinton saved him from rejection by the Senate. Armstrong's ministry in Paris was marked by idleness and pique. Napoleon spoke of him as "a morose man with whom one cannot treat," and requested his recall.[23]

At the outbreak of the War of 1812, the perplexing Armstrong was commissioned a brigadier general in charge of New York City's defenses and was fast building up his own little bureaucracy, spending money a little too freely, when he was summoned to take charge of the War Office. It was not a popular choice. Armstrong had supported De Witt Clinton, Madison's opponent in the recent presidential campaign, and he had a friendly eye for the Federalist faction. The Senate confirmed his nomination as Secretary of War by a margin of only three votes, both Virginians absenting themselves and both Kentuckians voting to reject.[24] James Monroe once attempted to explain Madison's difficulties in filling the post, "several prominent citizens to whom the station had been offer^d having successfully declined it."[25] But as it was the appointment suited only "the malcontent junto of self-styled Republicans," or Clintonians openly opposed to Madison and Monroe. Armstrong had a propensity for active intrigue, used power and position to gain personal ends. "His disposition was eminently pugnacious," commented Martin Van Buren, a fellow New Yorker.[26] "Armstrong!—he was the devil from the beginning, is now, and ever will be," exploded Alexander J. Dallas, his successor as Secretary of War. Glancing at the situation three quarters of a century later, Henry Adams found Armstrong "an unusual character . . . a combination of keenness and will with absence of conventional morals . . . [and] avowed want of admiration for the Virginians themselves."[27]

Naturally the Secretary would seek to pit the Clintonians against Virginia in conducting the war. The existing cleavage in the Cabinet amounted to open dislike and distrust of Armstrong on the part of

James Monroe and Treasury Secretary Albert Gallatin. But Armstrong had the support of most Republicans in New York, a few in Pennsylvania, and of William Duane of the Philadelphia *Aurora*.

Duane, whom Madison found ready to make every sacrifice for liberty "but that of his passions," had waxed caustic over the affair at the Raisin. The story was circulated that Harrison had authorized the premature advance of Winchester who thus had been sacrificed and the General rid of a friendly rival for the command;[28] moreover, accomplishment in the Northwest had been nil even though "great sums" had been spent. "I . . . suspect the Secretary of W is not over friendly to you," Harrison was advised by Quartermaster General James Morrison who was in a position to know. "He is probably influenced by Duane, who condemns all your arrangements."[29] In March four senators who declined to confirm Harrison's promotion to the rank of major general were two Clintonians from New York, a Federalist from Boston, and a Duane partisan from Pennsylvania.

As Harrison strove to reorganize the army in Ohio he faced the harassing interference of Armstrong as well as Duane's open censure. Open criticism in the newspapers and knowledge of opposition to the General from within Madison's new Cabinet appeared to discourage the work of recruiting. The militia officers were sluggish and indifferent, their views of a political cast. A disquieting communication from Secretary Armstrong, which caught up with the General at Chillicothe, dictated modifications of future military operations in the Northwest. Disregarding the number of forts to be garrisoned and the menace of Indians emerging from their hunting camps, Armstrong proposed to limit Harrison's command to six regiments of regulars, of which the small remnants of two were already in the field, while another, also reduced in numbers, was to march from southern Illinois. Of the remainder, two were to be raised in Ohio and one in Kentucky. Employment of militia was authorized to make up any deficiency in the new regiments.

Harrison read on. The principal point of deposit in the Northwest was not to be Fort Meigs but the town of Cleveland, from which the approach to Malden would be made by water, Armstrong anticipated, about the middle of May. "What remains for us to do is to keep our present ground till the Lake opens, and then to approach our object . . . under convoy of the Vessels building at Presque Isle."[30] With this final point Harrison could agree but Cleveland, of all places, lay 85 miles east of Lower Sandusky, secondary point of deposit, and 120 miles from Fort Meigs and the town was then almost destitute of men, arms, and fortifications. And what of the number of regiments necessary to garrison the forts and protect the frontier while the recruiting was being conducted throughout the spring? By the time a regiment of 12-months' men could be recruited, Harrison well knew, half that number would be anticipating their discharge while sickness and desertion would account for a good many more.

"It is my decided opinion that the Rapids . . . should be the point of Rendezvous . . . as well as the principal depot," ventured Harrison in rebuttal—

"Indeed it must necessarily be the first deposit, the provisions for the army being so placed that they can be taken to the Lake in no other way. The Artillery and a considerable supply of ammunition are already there. Boats and perogues have been built in considerable numbers on the Auglaize and St. Marys, and every exertion is now making to increase them . . . for the double purpose of taking down the provisions to the Rapids and for coasting the Lake with the baggage of the army in advance. . . . With regard to the quantum of force, my opinion is that not only the regular Troops designated in your Letter but a large auxiliary corps of Militia should be employed."[31]

Armstrong had neglected to state that he had authorized Colonel Richard M. Johnson to raise the proposed company of Kentucky mounted volunteers and his response to Harrison's ready protest was characteristically indirect. Perhaps seeking to enroll a political agent in the State of Ohio, Armstrong left it to Governor Meigs to make known the "great expensiveness of a land movement . . . the increased number of army" involved in Harrison's plan. "Your Excellency," the Secretary concluded suavely, "will best know how and to whom to communicate these views."[32]

Events were to prove Armstrong's calculations of less than ordinary weight. The 24th Regiment of regulars, en route from Illinois, would not reach Fort Meigs until June when it would number only 314 men fit and ready for duty. The recruiting of regulars for two new regiments was to prove a failure in Ohio and the task of defending the frontier against two invasions by British and Indians would necessarily involve a considerable number of militia in the meantime. Nor could the advance by water toward Malden be started by the middle of May. The war fleet now under construction would not be properly manned or ready until the middle of July and the lake not cleared of hostile shipping, as it happened, until September 10.

By the time the new Secretary's instructions had been received, three militia companies had started their march from Kentucky. Harrison saw no reason for ordering them back. The militia embodied from Ohio "are not sufficient to garrison the small posts."[33] Late in March, Harrison arrived at Cincinnati to meet the Kentuckians and to visit a family stricken by illness. His stay was cut short by the news that the Virginia and Pennsylvania militia at Fort Meigs had served notice of leaving the moment their enlistments expired.

Harrison had added cause for concern at this juncture. Spring had arrived early and Indian depredations along the Ohio River had already begun. The ice on Lake Erie was disappearing and the waterways would soon be navigable for enemy gunboats. Should all the militia now elect to go home, only 500 men would be left to guard Fort Meigs. And discipline was growing lax at the post, work on the fortifications almost abandoned. Indeed some of the men were using the picketing as firewood, their conduct free and easy in the absence of the General. Indian parties had captured a few straying soldiers and from these Colonel Procter might soon discover the true situation at the fort.

Harrison collected packhorses for the use of the first detachment of Kentuckians then advancing and ordered them to march rapidly forward by way of Hull's Road. "You will be pleased . . . to push on the troops . . . with all possible expedition," he advised General Green Clay, commanding the rest of the Kentucky militia.[34] April 1, after a ten-day stay at Cincinnati, Harrison started for the Rapids by way of Piqua and St. Marys, gathering up fresh detachments along the route. Major James V. Ball and 200 Virginia dragoons who had been recuperating ever since the Mississinewa expedition, moved ahead promptly from Lebanon. At Fort Amanda Harrison found Colonel John Miller with a company of new regular recruits and about 150 militia who were building flatboats. There he surrendered his horses to an officer bearing dispatches to Fort Meigs and climbed into the boats with the men.

Swollen by spring rains, the Auglaize and Maumee rivers provided a rough passage. "We rushed on over rocks and sandbars, upsetting some of our craft and arrived . . . fearful lest this garrison might be attacked," wrote a soldier.[35] But the guns of Fort Meigs in saluting the General's arrival sufficed to scare away an Indian scouting party in the woods.

Two hundred Pennsylvania militia who had agreed to remain fifteen days past their time received the General's compliments. The first detachment of Kentuckians arriving, Harrison permitted the militia to leave after expressing his thanks. Their parting, however, proved a little premature. Frenchmen brought in by spies revealed that a huge Indian force was assembled about Fort Amherstburg.[36] Procter, advanced to the rank of major general following his victory at the Raisin, was contemplating attack.

Tecumseh and The Prophet had scoured the country for volunteers and a great stir in the Indian camp was reported. While the boys and squaws dressed deerskins the warriors engaged in their pow-wows and war dances. The British agents had promised them rich plunder and the ultimate seizure of General Harrison whom the savages hoped to torture and burn. Fort Meigs, it was argued, was badly constructed and weakly defended; a single day's cannonading would suffice to blast the Yankees out. Then the tribesmen could swarm in and regain the entire Northwest.[37]

In the American camps other scenes and other manners prevailed. "Ever since the General arrived . . . the greatest diligence and industry was displayed by officers and soldiers," according to one of the Tippecanoe boys. "Every moment of the General was occupied in carrying on the fortifications."[38] There was much sickness although by April 20 the four batteries, the blockhouses and all connecting pickets were "generally complete." Double tiers of staunch timbers with rawhides placed between protected the roof of the magazine from shellfire. A squad of recruits constructed barrels for salt beef and pork, drying the seasoned timbers in a kiln.

An invasion of the frontier at some point, Harrison knew not where, was daily expected. "My wishes," he emphasized, "are that they should attack us here."[39] Indications were that his wishes would be granted. May 25 a company of scouts discovered two enemy gunboats and a sloop on the margin of Lake Erie and next morning some British officers who surveyed the fort from the opposite side of the river rode away hastily as two 18-pounders were swung in their direction. When another enemy party came in sight the gunners were ready and "two elegant shots . . . covered them with dirt."[40]

From the increasing number of vessels in the river, Harrison's scouts estimated that an enemy force 2000 strong had landed on the opposite shore, making their camp near the ruins of old Fort Miami two miles below. Procter, in fact, was bringing up a force of nearly a thousand regulars and Canadian militia with 1200 Indians under Tecumseh and Round Head. Many of the warriors were well mounted and armed, with rifle, pistol, tomahawk and scalping knife. "To smoke the Yankees out," Procter ordered two batteries constructed on a high bank directly opposite Fort Meigs.[41]

The enemy's mode of attack thus revealed, Harrison ordered deep traverses dug and a main embankment, for the reception of cannonballs, twenty feet thick at the base and from ten to fifteen feet high to extend parallel to the river along the entire front of the camp. Tents were pitched directly in front to conceal operations. Mounting a rampart as the troops assembled on parade, Harrison reverted to a favorite theme:

"Can the citizens of a free country who have taken up arms to defend its rights think of submitting to an army . . . of mercenary soldiers, reluctant Canadians goaded to the field by the bayonet, and of wretched, naked savages? Can the breast of an American soldier when he casts his eyes to the opposite shore, the scene of his country's triumphs over the same foe, be influenced by any other feelings than the hope of glory? . . . To your posts then fellow citizens, and remember that the eyes of your country are upon you."[42]

The General's ready encouragement and the excitement of the occasion, wrote Major Eleazar D. Wood, caused the men to dig like terriers.[43] "Fortifications . . . were carried on with unparalelled exertions; every man inspired with zeal, courage and patriotism never surpassed," the Tippecanoe diarist recorded.[44] Extra half rations were issued to the troops. The traverses completed, the men excavated dirt lodgings covered with planks and loose earth.[45]

The troops appeared to be in fine spirits and the fortifications near perfection yet Harrison realized his man power—about 1200 effectives—to be quite insufficient. Where at this moment was General Green Clay, advancing with the rest of the Kentucky militia? Scout William Oliver, memorable for daring when Fort Wayne was besieged, rode out at night with a message for Clay who when last heard from was awaiting packhorses and a supply of ammunition at Piqua.[46]

THE SIEGE OF FORT MEIGS

O**N THE** morning of April 28 orders were issued for the men to dig all night but with such vigor were shovels swung even throughout a heavy fall of rain that at reveille time Harrison decided all should rest. The rain interfered more with the work of the British artillerists and engineers who were toiling night and day to plant two 24-pound guns and two howitzers on the opposite shore.[1] As dusk came on Tecumseh's warriors crossed over in their canoes and scattered about the fort. A troop of dragoons out reconnoitering was fired upon, the only casualty one shot in an arm. No longer could water be brought from the river, the fort was now in a state of siege.

Seeking to conserve the strength of his troops, Harrison kept only a third of the men on duty, relieving them every three hours. A squad was assigned to the task of digging a well.

It was a field day for snipers. Expectant and animated savages took advantage of every conceivable shelter: "There was not a stump, bush or log . . . but what shielded its man." From trees left standing some distance away they "poured down . . . prodigious showers of musketry."[2] A shot from a tree killed a man standing near Harrison on the main embankment and the General received a spent ball on the hip which caused considerable pain. Little other damage was effected by the enemy that day. As the Kentucky sharpshooters raised their long rifles, the brisk exchange of fire greatly stimulated the militia toiling in the ditch. The savages presented difficult targets but now and then a warrior would be toppled from his ambush among less than full-grown leaves. Amid the fusillades of rifles, the thud and clatter of shovels, came snatches of song:

"Freemen, no longer bear such slaughter,
Avenge your country's cruel woe.
Arouse and save your sons and daughters,
Arouse and expel the faithless foe."[3]

Harrison trained his field glasses on the enemy works and sighted four batteries then underway. He turned to his gunners. Orders to clear the 18-pounders for action brought a round of cheers. For the benefit of "very impudent" Indians a few shells and grapeshot were sent clattering through the trees; from Grand Battery facing the river some "first rate shots" impeded enemy progress and killed a few workers on the opposite shore. Thereafter the British carried on their engineering operations under cover of night. Having little ammunition to spare, Harrison withheld his fire. By the last day of April—

"The enemy had extended his batteries considerably . . . preparing them for cannon. . . . Boats were seen to pass from the old British garrison to this shore with many men; the General concluded that their intention was to draw our attention to their batteries, and to surprise and storm the camp in the rear. Orders were given for one-third of the men to be kept constantly on guard; the remaining two-thirds to sleep with their muskets in their arms. . . . The Indians annoyed us very considerable. . . . The General being constantly exposed, had several very narrow escapes."[4]

So passed the day. During the night the British towed a gunboat up the river and fired thirty shots only to retreat before daylight without registering a fatal hit. On the morning of May 1 Harrison had his grand surprise ready. As the enemy artillerists were seen loading their 24-pounders he ordered the tents in front of the main traverse, or embankment, to be struck and carried to the rear. "This was done in an instant," exulted Major Wood, who had devised the original plan, "and that beautiful prospect of beating up our quarters . . . had now entirely fled and in its place suddenly appeared an immense shield of earth, obscuring . . . every tent, every horse . . . and every creature belonging to our camp."[5] At 10 A.M. an enemy gunboat boomed. It was the signal for the opening attack.

Harrison summoned Colonel William Christy, acting quartermaster at the fort. "Sir, go nail a flag on every battery where they shall wave as long as an enemy is in view."[6]

Facing little to shoot at but staunch picketing and a high bank of soft earth in the rear, the British artillerists could only blast away and waste roundshot and for a time, their marksmanship unworthy, little damage was done. A few red-hot balls plunged through the picketing and tossed high the dirt. The excited yells of dusky spectators perched in treetops applauded every hit but as the days wore on the savages grew weary of waiting for plunder and scalps. Within the fort the militia, fairly inspired now, continued heaping up the dirt. Yet to burrow so deeply implied cowardice. During a lull a white flag fluttered past and Tecumseh flung out his challenge:

"General Harrison! I have with me 800 braves. You have an equal number in your hiding place. Come out with them and give me battle. You hide behind logs and in the earth like a ground hog."[7]

So much was true but Harrison himself was not outside the sphere of danger. An Indian bullet whacked a bench on which he was sitting and a red-hot cannonball plunged through the top of his marquee. The guns of the fort were used sparingly in reply. On May 1 the magazine keeper had but 360 18-pound shot and less for the 12- and 6-pounders. "With plenty of ammunition we should have . . . blown John Bull . . . from the Miami." A gill of whiskey was offered for every enemy cannonball that would fit the guns of the fort. Industrious soldiers dug into the embankment and searched outside the walls by night. The British had no 18-pound guns but their 12-pounders supplied the men with sufficient barter for a thousand gills of whiskey before the end of the siege.[8]

The British began the second day's cannonading at dawn. From a near-by height across the river they discovered the roof of Harrison's powder magazine barely visible over the dirt wall and began to concentrate their fire upon it. Bombs and red-hot cannonballs plunged into this target with a fearful hissing, sending forth great clouds of smoke and blasting loose dirt high into the air. The militiamen dropped their shovels to dig with their hands among shattered timbers and carry the wounded to safety. Part of the magazine roof was battered down but the inner layer of hide-covered timbers was never penetrated and the damage was sufficiently repaired that evening.

Harrison was still awaiting word from Captain William Oliver and General Green Clay. The daily routine within the fort went on. The men burrowed deeper into their dugout shelters and napped or played cards while off duty. Whenever the enemy slackened they mounted the walls to give three cheers for liberty. British marksmanship was freely criticized and after the first day or two the men paid little attention to the incessant cannonading. As enemy bombs came over the walls those nearest would shout a warning and throw themselves flat on the ground. One daring Kentuckian took his stand atop the main embankment to watch every approaching shot and after a little practice was able to predict the character and direction of the approaching missile almost as soon as the smoke issued from the enemy gun muzzles. "Shot" or "bomb," he would call, "Blockhouse

No. 1," "Main battery," "Lookout for the meat house." For a time he was eminently a lifesaver. Finally came a shot that seemed to defy all his calculations. The waiting sentinel stood transfixed as the ball sped directly toward him and swept him into the hereafter.[9]

Considering the number of shot and shell sent over by the enemy during the first thirty-six hours, casualties were few. According to those who kept tallies, 750 rounds had been fired but only three men killed, sixteen injured.[10] Rain again fell during the second day and evening and trickled into the muddy dugouts all night. With 300 sick men suffering from cold and exposure Harrison ordered tents pitched behind the dirt wall. At 10 o'clock on the morning of May 3, however, a burst of artillery fire about 250 yards in the rear revealed the particular purpose of the enemy force which had crossed the river a few days before. As bombs exploded among men and horses, excited Indians took positions so as to enfilade the main traverse.

The savages kept up their loud yells and a rattle of fire until a battery on the northeast wall of the fort silenced the guns for a time. Harrison was forced to strike his tents, however, the men were driven back into their shelters of sticky mud. An exceedingly heavy bombardment sustained on this day was otherwise unfruitful. Although 563 balls and shells were counted, only seven men within the fort were killed, one by an Indian bullet, and three wounded. The British still persisted. By night their sputtering shells and red-hot shot could be traced against the sky.

May 4—

"The enemy not on the alert this morning; did not commence firing until about 11 o'clock. A new battery was discovered erecting on this side . . . traverses were commenced to guard against them. . . ."[11]

But after endless digging, long night watches and sleep broken by shellfire the men were tired out and the sick list was mounting. Again in their mudholes, the soldiers were suffering from colds, fever and ague, ten thousand aches and pains. Lack of medical supplies added to the death toll while the judgment of army surgeons who prescribed amputations was openly distrusted. The doctors appealed to the General, a former medical student and a veteran of other wars, for final decision as the fate of injured limbs was debated.

Concerned as well over diminishing provisions and the tardiness of General Green Clay, Harrison realized that sheer want might induce a surrender if the siege were prolonged. Actual conditions within the fort may have become known to the enemy. During the afternoon the cannonading slackened and Major John Chambers of the British 41st, approaching under a flag, was shown into Harrison's marquee. Chambers bore a request for a capitulation from General Procter "to spare the effusion of blood." Harrison declared himself at a loss to understand the British conception of an American officer's duty. "The character of General Harrison, as an officer, is well known," replied Major Chambers. "General Proctor's force is very respectable and there is now with him a larger body of Indians than has ever before been embodied."[12]

Fresh detachments of warriors had been arriving every day in fact until some 1800 Indians were being rationed by the British. Harrison waved away the idea of overwhelming numbers. He believed he had a correct idea of the enemy force, which was not so great "as to create much apprehension." "Assure your general," Harrison continued, ". . . that he will never have the post surrendered on any terms. Should it fall into his hands it will be in a manner calculated to do him more honor . . . than any capitulation could possibly do." Major Chambers was ushered away.

The point was well taken. News of General Green Clay's approach arrived that night. Shortly before midnight, Captain William Oliver with another officer and fifteen Kentucky soldiers arrived from down the river and crept up to the fort. Clay and the rest of the Kentuckians, numbering 1200 men in eighteen large flatboats, were awaiting orders from the head of the Rapids only eight miles above, Captain Oliver reported and the boats were expected to arrive early next day. Fixing upon a means of taking the British guns across the river, Harrison sent back verbal orders by Captain John Hamilton and a subaltern who stole away bearing a canoe on their shoulders and spikes for the enemy cannon.[13]

The advancing Kentuckians under Clay had undergone their full share of hardship since the tap of the drum first sounded for volunteers. One pelting shower after another, "each seemingly colder than its predecessor," drenched the burdened men. Brush piles for beds kept the soldiers out of water by night but continual wading on the march caused the skin to peel from their legs "as high as the knee." A swarm of camp followers from Cincinnati, purveying food and drink, accompanied the army, each day's marching bringing higher prices for their goods. Finally, when only a few of the officers could afford to purchase the "cider oil" in stock—

"the prospect of another night, twin-sister to the rest, plays havoc with the hucksters; the cider oil wagons are upset, barrels . . . are rolled hither and thither . . . and without anyone seemingly to know who was doing these things or why . . . presto, the drinkables have disappeared and every soldier . . . suddenly forgets his weariness and becomes Lieutenant General commanding innumerable hosts of invincible veterans. Commands of officers in the heat of battle are being heard in every direction, innumerable game cocks are loudly crowing and all manner of songs . . . concord and discord all around. This last Jollification of our little command!"[14]

At St. Marys and Fort Amanda the Kentuckians embarked in flatboats stockaded with puncheons to provide cover against attack. As the boats entered the Maumee a rumble of cannonading to the northeast could be heard and Clay hardly needed to learn from Captain Oliver that the fort was in a state of siege. Awaiting further news from Harrison at the head of the Rapids, Clay received the General's midnight message early on the morning of May 5.

According to the verbal orders from Harrison, Clay was to land the greater part or all of his men some distance above the fort on the opposite shore and with Captain Hamilton acting as guide, storm and seize the enemy batteries. As soon as the Kentuckians had spiked the guns and cut down the carriages they were "instantly to return to their boats and recross the river." As a simultaneous movement in this well-devised plan, Harrison expected to launch a sortie from the fort and take the British guns in the rear.[15]

Darkness and high water delayed Clay's start for a few hours. As the boats approached the scene of action wind and a rapid current interfered with navigation and separated the craft. Colonel William Dudley was able to land twelve boats according to instructions but General Clay and two of the craft were carried further downstream while the remaining four, Colonel William Boswell commanding, went on to rescue their drifting leader. Clay and a third of his force ultimately landed on the American side of the river; Dudley, with 800 men, still had a sufficient force with which to carry the guns.

It was still raining that morning. Water poured from gun muzzles brought down from shoulders. Some Indians near the river opened fire as Dudley's soldiers tumbled from their boats but exhilarated at the prospect of immediate action the Kentuckians formed in good order and rushed toward the enemy works. Nearing the guns they set up "a most tremendous yell," and the surprised artillerymen put up little resistance. Soldiers watching from the walls of Fort Meigs re-echoed the cheers of the conquering Kentuckians as the British flag fell. Harrison, who had six guns placed so as to cover Dudley's retreat to the boats, now signaled in vain for that officer to return.[16]

But Dudley either lacked comprehension of the original order or failed to control his men. Instead of immediately spiking and dismantling the guns he allowed the troops to linger on the ground, inspecting every detail of the enemy position, gratifying "a vain curiosity." They learned nothing useful in the brief time afforded.

Beyond the bank of the river was a forest edged with high bushes where Indians might gather, the battleground of Fallen Timbers. Through his field glass Harrison could see Tecumseh summoning his forces to form an ambush in these woods. The General grew impatient, angry, alarmed. "Can I never get men to obey my orders?" His signals useless, he leaped down from the main embankment and offered a thousand dollars to any one who could get across the river and "raise the alarm."[17]

General Clay and Colonel Boswell, caught in a brief skirmish, had consented to be saved. Their six flatboats, separated four and two, were approaching the near bank of the Maumee several hundred yards away, when Harrison sent off two detachments of militia and regulars to cover their landing. A few well-directed round shot scattered Indians on the bank who were exchanging fire with the Kentuckians lodged behind their puncheons.

Taking advantage of a diversion created by Major Ball's dragoons and a battalion of infantry which raced down from the fort, General Clay's men hastened along the river bank and reached safety with but little loss. Negro servants carrying cannonballs rather than baggage raced after them. Fortunately, the Indians were busy plundering the boats.

Learning Boswell's position from Clay, Harrison sent out another rallying party and when the Kentuckians joined the detachment in good order the savages were driven nearly half a mile into the woods. But the men were in perilous territory. Through his glass Harrison caught sight of the enemy hurrying along the edge of the forest to cut off their retreat. He called for volunteers to warn Boswell and Ball, mounting Quartermaster James E. Eubank on one of his own fine horses.[18] Aide-de-camp James T. Johnson followed closely after Eubank but his mount was shot down. Another aide, Major Richard Graham, managed to get through. Eubank and Graham restrained the Kentuckians only with difficulty and the retreat was reluctantly commenced.[19] Some thirty casualties were suffered.

Colonel Dudley however was not to be reached. The officer who responded to Harrison's offer of a reward if he could restrain Dudley was halted by Indians near the river bank. From the edge of the woods on the opposite shore Tecumseh's warriors began a halting attack, giving no clue as to their real strength. The Kentuckians were maddened by their hesitant fire. Shouting their war-cry "Remember the Raisin!" the undisciplined but valorous militia raced into the thickly wooded ravines and skirmished about in every direction, their ranks in disorder. Harrison and the watching men saw a body of British regulars advance upon a single company left with the guns. "My God, what a moment!"[20] The lone company smartly repulsed the assault but instead of standing their ground the men rushed to aid Dudley.

But Dudley had been drawn into a skillfully laid trap. Posted behind trees and logs were Tecumseh's warriors with British regulars advancing from the rear. The Indians closed in, slaying and scalping. The Colonel, a heavy, fleshy man, was quickly singled out and tomahawked, his body atrociously mutilated.

Private Thomas Christian was an unhappy eye-witness of events:

"Our ranks scattered, our brave Colonel slain and most of the other officers mortally wounded seemed sufficient to have unnerved the bravest hero but even then I still heard the loud shrill cock-crowing of one brave spirit who seemed determined to die game . . . to the last. . . . Nearer and nearer came the . . . bloodthirsty foe . . . until . . . the deafening demoniac yells drowned all other sounds save the coarse, broad command, 'Ground your arms' . . . pronounced by British officers."[21]

The Kentuckians had no choice. The command was repeated: "Ground your arms or be slain." Rifles crashed to the ground, some surreptitiously pressed into the mud. Of Dudley's command of 800 men less than 200 had escaped, about 50 had been slain, and the remainder wounded or taken prisoners.

Indians bashed in the skulls of a few prisoners. The British on the ground were too few to control their bloodthirsty allies. A veteran soldier who tried to intervene was struck down. Aided by some Christian Wyandots the regulars hurried the survivors toward Fort Miami, their clothing and money seized along the way. Near the fort the savages prepared a gantlet for the prisoners. Knives, tomahawks and clubs descended upon the racing Kentuckians, the path grew slippery with human blood. Within the gates the warriors shoved the sentinels roughly aside and began shooting and scalping. Their half-naked victims were piled into a corner "like terror-stricken sheep hemmed in by dogs or a parcel of hogs in a butcher's pen . . . those at the top . . . being drenched with blood and brains [when] suddenly as the lightning's flash, the yelling ceased . . ."[22]

Chief Tecumseh, hastily summoned from the field, galloped up at full speed, "the maddest man I ever saw." The flat of his sword came down upon penitent shoulders. "Are there no men here?" he thundered. His own warriors, he cried, were behaving like squaws. When order was restored he galloped to Procter's tent. "Sir, your Indians cannot be commanded," protested the British leader. "Begone, you are unfit to command," was the retort from the savage.[23]

British colors again waving over the batteries across the river signalized Dudley's defeat. At ten o'clock that forenoon the cannonading was resumed. Although the loss of the detachment eliminated a vital part of his plan, Harrison still contemplated the capture of the enemy works in the rear. The arrival of Clay's militia meant nearly 500 more mouths to feed at the fort; somehow the British must be induced to retreat before the American supplies were exhausted.

Colonel John Miller of the 19th U. S. Regiment volunteered to undertake to capture the enemy guns and Harrison permitted him to select his own forces. About 350 men, most of them regulars with well disciplined volunteer corps from Pennsylvania and Virginia, and one company of Kentucky militia, were paraded in a small ravine flanking the fort. Harrison's instructions were for the troops to advance with trailed arms lest their ammunition be expended before their prime object was gained. A summary death penalty was directed should any man fire before the signal was given. Motives of duty and patriotism were stressed.[24]

Supporting the guns were 300 British regulars and infantry in addition to several hundred Indians, an enemy of uncertain strength. The advance from the fort was made in line. From the shape of a ravine which was crossed, the regulars on the left reached the summit in advance of their fellows to face a merciless fire. Miller halted his forces only to close the ranks, a movement executed with admirable "precision and coolness." The men advanced to within fifty yards of the guns before receiving the command to fire; then the entire line poured in a concerted volley and charged.

The British presented no further defense. Two officers and forty-one men who stuck to the guns were taken prisoners. Miller's regulars turned to rescue the volunteers and Kentucky militia who were fighting Indians. The savages were leading them into the woods while another body of redskins was about to cut off the American rear.

Harrison had to send another mounted officer to recall the troops, the victory maintained only after hard fighting. The guns had been spiked and the work well done although at a cost of thirty dead and ninety wounded.[25] In respect to the numbers engaged and the brief time involved in the action, Harrison considered the engagement the most bloody of the war.

The loss of the guns was the last straw for the Indians. For the past two days they had been expressing discontent, many of them deserting. Plunder seized from the captive Kentuckians and from Dudley's boats hardly sufficed for all. The savages complained they had been deceived by large promises. Never again would they be induced to fight the Americans. The Canadian militia, with whom Proctor was no favorite, were also abandoning the siege.[26]

His forces daily decreasing, Procter tried his last bluff. Again he sent Major Chambers to offer Harrison generous terms of surrender. Harrison replied in blunt phrases. Procter's proposal was an "insult" not to be repeated. Two days of comparative quiet ensued. During negotiations for the exchange of prisoners Procter broached terms which Harrison called "most extraordinary."[27] The British leader suggested that the Kentuckians in his possession be exchanged for friendly Indians within the American border. A rather insulting idea. Finally the regular troops taken by each side were exchanged and it was agreed that the British would take the Kentuckians down Lake Erie to the Huron River and there release them upon the condition that these men would no longer serve in the war. Harrison sent the prisoners several bundles of food and clothing from his diminishing store but it does not appear that the goods were distributed.

These negotiations over, on the afternoon of May 7 the guns across the river boomed a final salute which caught the Americans unawares and out of their trenches, killing ten men and wounding about twice that number. The British worked all night to dismantle their batteries and at daybreak were discovered loading their stores and cannon aboard a sloop. Harrison sent off a few parting shot as the enemy scurried off, "leaving a number of Cannon Ball . . . and other valuable articles."[28]

All told, according to the tally, nearly 1700 shot and shell had been discharged against Fort Meigs; casualties suffered within the walls and during sorties were placed at 77 killed and 196 wounded. Those who had died of camp fever, in three months, numbered nearly 200.[29]

XIV

"WE HAVE MET THE ENEMY . . ."

BEGRIMED and blackened for lack of water for bathing, the war-spent soldiers repaired blockhouse roofs and the powder magazine and recovered damaged stores. Detachments were permitted to go to the river and wash. The sick and wounded were in a pitiable condition. Many had been lying exposed to the damp ground and the rain. Hospital arrangements were reorganized and the militia took up a sorrowful duty in burying Colonel Dudley's men on the opposite shore. All had been scalped and "most dreadfully mangled." Joseph Hawkins, Speaker of the Kentucky House, who was with the burial party, was curiously affected: "God avert mine eyes from such another scene to the end of Time. Night after night did the horrid Spectacle of disembowelled bodies & raw sculls haunt my mind."[1]

Harrison vigorously directed every detail in progress. As soon as fortifications had been renewed he placed General Green Clay, "a man of Capacity," in charge of the fort and taking 200 dragoons as a guard he retraced the route across Black Swamp to Lower Sandusky. Governor Return J. Meigs and Brigadier-General Lewis Cass were awaiting him with warm congratulations and a force of several hundred volunteers. Possibly 3000 men had sprung to arms in Ohio during the siege, their march choking every road to the North. Harrison publicly expressed his "warmest gratitude" yet he was bound to order the greatest number to disband.[2] War Office orders were to remain on the defensive and the employment of volunteers and militia had been definitely limited. Uncertain as to where Procter's next attack might fall he ordered detachments to reinforce Cleveland, Fort Stephenson and Fort Winchester while the remainder were sent home. Naturally they were disgruntled. A few inquiries were made. Why did the General hesitate to pursue Procter? When was the long contemplated march to Detroit to begin? The situation did appear slightly perplexing but Harrison could not make public his orders to await the arrival of Commodore Oliver H. Perry's fleet from Erie.

The General broke open five letters from Secretary Armstrong which had been held up during the siege. According to a new plan of army organization he was to serve as Major General in charge of the Eighth Military District which included the states of Ohio and Kentucky, the territories of Indiana, Michigan, Illinois, and Missouri. Division commanders were Brigadiers Lewis Cass and Duncan McArthur; commanding at St. Louis was General Benjamin Howard who would find little to do. "Col° Procter is not in condition to carry on any distant or formidable Expedition," Secretary Armstrong had indicated under date of April 14.[3] Interesting news but currently true. Occasionally some such acute diagnosis of affairs in the West would emanate from the War Office. Armstrong now complained because Harrison had transferred two recruiting officers—General McArthur and Colonel Miller—from Franklinton and Chillicothe to more vital sectors as Procter menaced the frontier. "I do not consider I merit the rebuke," Harrison answered sharply.[4] Too few experienced officers there were in the Northwestern Army and Procter's intentions had been misinterpreted at Washington. When the frontier was endangered it was well to make the best use of all available talent.

"I have not yet been honored with your command upon the subject of the assembling of the Troops, the direction of their march &c," Harrison reminded the Secretary. Nowhere in Armstrong's instructions was there a hint that he had authorized Colonel Richard M. Johnson, for example, to bring on a mounted volunteer rifle regiment from Kentucky. Some confusion resulted from the oversight. Late in March, Johnson had written Harrison concerning his plans. In response he received a summons, properly transmitted through Governor Shelby, to march at once to the aid of Fort Meigs. But the regiment was not embodied in time for the purpose and having dismissed the greater part of the Ohio volunteers, Harrison also requested Colonel Johnson to disband.

Johnson, ruddy, stocky and untrammelled in garb, received the order soon after he had started out but he decided to ride on with a part of his regiment and consult with the General in Ohio. May 23, 1813, the two leaders met at Cincinnati and for the sake of the record Johnson presented his arguments in writing. The Colonel was confident that the service of his regiment would be of great value and if the men were now disappointed in their efforts to engage in the service it might be difficult to bring them again into the field. Johnson also produced a letter from Armstrong authorizing the employment of the volunteeer regiment.[5] Despite the element of surprise in the order, Harrison could not have wished for a more efficient and formidable corps, now that spring was well advanced, to guard the northern frontier. The regiment was made welcome. Colonel Johnson rested at Harrison's cabin at North Bend while his brother, Major James Johnson, hurried back to Kentucky with the news. As soon as the regiment had been raised to full strength it was to march past Fort Winchester to Fort Meigs and scour the woods for marauders.[6]

Early in June, Harrison returned to headquarters at Franklinton where problems pertaining to militia discipline and the status of the Ohio Indians awaited. Western freemen were not deemed amenable to regular army discipline and as a means of encouraging enlistments punishment by flogging had been officially banned in the United States Army just before the outbreak of war. "I was one of the officers who were consulted on that occasion who gave an opinion favorable to abolition of that disgraceful punishment," Harrison later recalled.[7] As a substitute, General Winchester once prescribed "ten or fifteen cobs on the bare posteriors well laid on with a paddle bored full of holes,"[8] a punitive measure ill-suited to the disposition of western soldiery. Still recurrent drunkenness, idling, thievery, and desertion would have to be curbed.

Harrison banned the sale of liquor at the various army posts and he also issued strict orders, in a public address, against duelling. However, a General who resembled "more . . . a father than a military commander" in the care of his troops was thought to possess "too much of the milk of human kindness for an efficient U. S. Commander-in-Chief."[9] Remarked a volunteer: "General Harrison's disposition was such a mixture of sympathy, kindness and humanity that he was like my Uncle Toby—he would not hurt even a fly."[10] The regular officers deemed these qualities incompatible with military sternness and bravery until it was discovered that tenderness of heart interfered in no wise with military efficiency.

For minor offenses Harrison ordered special parade duty in front of his marquee at an unusually early-morning hour. Deserters who would ordinarily be shot were confined in the guardhouse for two or three weeks and restored to their places after a public reprimand. Harrison was prone to take into consideration an offender's tender years and the disgrace which would devolve upon his family at home. Once a youth who had deserted three times was brought before the General. Harrison gazed at him sharply. "He regrets what he has done. . . . He will never be guilty again."[11] So it was, for the boy was killed in action at Fort Erie. When it was argued that pardons were obtained with too great a facility Harrison authorized the wooden-horse treatment, of physical and moral persuasion. The offender would be set astride a wooden horse with the saddle well sharpened, two ten-pound clogs of wood fastened to his legs and a label affixed to his cap: "Deserter returning to camp on horseback." So there the soldier would sit for half an hour three or four successive mornings during parade. At the end a bundle of straw was tied on his back and he was made to beg the *sergeant's* pardon in the presence of his regiment. Deserters might also be fined half their pay for six months and rations of whiskey for one whole week. But sometimes the punishment was light compared to the gravity of the crime. A militia private found sleeping on his post was plunged two successive mornings in the Scioto River and ordered to clear away brush two hours a day for three days.[12]

Perhaps the times were becoming sterner, old offenders less easy to forgive. Following a court-martial for four deserters at Franklinton, Harrison approved the death sentence for a man who had threatened the arresting officer's life. The troops were formed in a hollow square and drums rolled as the prisoner was led out. The sentence was read in solemn tones. The command: "Ready . . . aim . . . fire," was given and the guns of the guard carried out the death sentence. The local newspaper editor declared it a most horrible scene, the like of which he never wished to see again.[13] Nor was he required to. Harrison pardoned three other deserters, condemned by the same court-martial. Another pardon went down in army annals when a sleepy sentinel was led out to be shot. As the word "Ready" was spoken the General gave the command "As you were" and read the prisoner a pardon followed by a lecture for every one to hear "on the importance of a sentinel's keeping awake."[14]

Harrison's other problem, that of the so-called friendly Indian in Ohio, called for decisive measures in the face of public concern. The General had been criticized as much for his treatment of his "pet Indians" as for his pardons of army deserters. In the sad history of Indian affairs in this nation, this was a charge and a phrase applied to any army officer who sought to restrain blood-thirsty whites. Settlers on the lookout for new lands commonly believed that the friendly tribesmen, guarded to some extent within their villages, were serving the enemy as spies. Many were spies for one side or the other but it was advisable to make a distinction.

A bloody raid on Cold Creek settlement near Sandusky Bay had provoked the existing public anger which Harrison sought to allay. Some Indians from Malden took as prisoners one man and twelve women and children. One of the women, in an advanced state of pregnancy, was stripped naked and butchered in an extraordinary manner. Three or four small children unable to keep up with the party were successively slain.[15] When the news reached the interior it was only with difficulty that the settlers were restrained from taking revenge upon the peaceful tribes of Sandusky.

So Harrison called a council at Franklinton to determine openly the sentiments of representatives of four friendly tribes. June 21 some fifty chiefs and warriors of the Wyandot, Delaware, Shawnee, and Seneca nations assembled on the grounds of Lucas Sullivant, a leading citizen. An audience of townspeople, men, women and children, gathered to watch the proceedings. Harrison and his staff occupied chairs on the lawn. The recognized Indian leader was Tarhe, the Crane, a seventy-two-year-old Wyandot who had signed the Treaty of Greenville. Despite his years, Tarhe was a man of fine presence and physique whom Harrison called one of the best men he had ever known.[16]

The General opened the council. The Indians had been called together he said because some of their warriors were known to be in communication with the enemy. Had Procter taken Fort Meigs the disaffected warriors would have joined the British openly to further their conquest. This sort of situation could no longer be tolerated, Harrison went on at some length. To guarantee fully their friendliness the chiefs would be required to move their families within the white settlements and recruit their warriors as fighters for the Americans. A definite stand for one side or the other would have to be taken.

Chief Tarhe arose to respond. With an air of dignity he declared that the Ohio tribesmen still maintained their known attachment for the American government. For many moons his warriors had longed for an opportunity to fight against the British. They would gladly accompany the army under General Harrison. Tarhe's words were convincing. He terminated his speech with a few complimentary phrases and came forward to shake hands with the General. The spectators waved their hats and applauded. As Tarhe stood beside him Harrison delivered a warning that any warrior who joined his army must refrain from cruelty to women, children and prisoners. General Procter, he related, had promised to deliver him over to the Indians to be burned. But if the British General was ever taken Harrison promised to present his unworthy person to the Indians that they might "put a petticoat on him." The moral: "None but a squaw would ever kill a defenseless prisoner."[17]

Harrison accepted a "token" detachment of warriors under the command of Tarhe who further promised that other tribesmen would be summoned as soon as the army made ready to invade Upper Canada.

Affairs at Fort Meigs now demanded attention. General Green Clay relayed word that Procter and the Indians were about to renew the attack. Descent upon Fort Stephenson or Cleveland rather than Fort Meigs, Harrison suspected, was likely. He advanced a troop of horse to reconnoiter about Cleveland and placed Colonel Samuel Wells in command at Lower Sandusky with orders to destroy Fort Stephenson should the British "approach in force." Wells was then to retire to the more adequate protection of Fort Feree at Upper Sandusky, thirty-five miles south.[18]

Hastening then to Fort Meigs over roads "half a leg deep," Harrison was welcomed with "great joy and firing of cannon."[19] Colonel Johnson's mounted riflemen and the 24th Regiment of regulars from Illinois had recently arrived, the men at the fort much improved in health. Harrison sent Johnson to discover what was abroad. The Colonel buried the bones of his slain countrymen at the River Raisin and brought back five Frenchmen, two of them Canadians, who declared that Procter was not yet ready to march. Fresh forces of Indians were gathering, however. Satisfied with the strength of the fort Harrison decided that any further attempt against it would be in the nature of a feint to cover designs against Fort Stephenson, Cleveland, or Erie.

It was now nearly midsummer, long past the time set for the advance of the fleet. Harrison hurried back to Lower Sandusky and then rode to Cleveland to ascertain the strength of defenses there and also discover, if possible, the cause of Perry's delay. Should Perry bring out his fleet immediately his appearance would serve to ward off another British and Indian invasion. Harrison sent an officer to Erie to inquire into his present situation. The British, Harrison wrote Perry, had a new 19-gun vessel, the *Detroit,* built of green timber from the woods of Malden. Commodore Robert H. Barclay was training new seamen. "When will you sail? . . . We are waiting for your aid." Harrison also prodded the War Office: "Is it not indeed the intention . . . to bring to speedy issue the contest for the naval superiority upon this lake?"[20]

But the delay was not the fault of Perry. For weeks he had been waiting for crews. "As yet I hear nothing of the seamen destined for us," he advised Harrison in reply.[21] He wrote his superior, Commodore Isaac Chauncey, "Send me men, Sir," and again "For God's sake and yours . . . send me men and officers."[22] Chauncey, who was strengthening his Lake Ontario fleet at Sackett's Harbor, had few men to spare. To prepare for Procter's expected invasion, Harrison strengthened the fortifications at Cleveland and threw up log breastworks and earthen embankments at Camp Seneca, a new post located nine miles south of Lower Sandusky where recruits for the regular regiments were assembling. Camp Seneca was a training camp and supply center, the second line of defense on the Sandusky River.

Principal reason for Procter's delay was a precautionary order from Sir George Prevost, commander of the British forces in Canada. Fort George on the Niagara frontier had fallen to the Americans and for a time the British contemplated abandonment of every post west of Lake Ontario. Present policy bade Procter remain at Fort Amherstburg and Malden rather than risk the failure of another expedition. Procter would have remained if he could, but impatiently awaiting his bidding was a host of Indian warriors who were anxious to fight. British Agent Robert Dickson had recruited 600 warriors from the Northwest, many of whom had never engaged in battle against white men. They bore an air of pristine savagery and were eager for spoils. The Yankees were great cowards, they were reminded. A warrior could whip five Yankees single-handed and take all their possessions. Two hundred Potawatomies were led by the famous Chief Maipock wearing a girdle fringed with scalps, his ankles entwined with bear's claws and the bills of hawks and eagles.[23] With such forces as these Chief Tecumseh united 1400 Chippewas, Ottawas, Michigan Wyandots, Shawnees, Miamis, Winnebagoes, and a few Delawares.

Restive from inaction the tribesmen began to complain that Procter was putting them off. Tecumseh called a council. For eight years, declared the chieftain, he had been striving to bring about this war. Now he had everything ready, "all Nations from the North were standing at his word." As a climax to Tecumseh's defiant talk the issue was put. Against which side would Procter prefer to fight? "I have the mortification to find that my Indian Force is not a disposable one," the General notified Prevost. ". . . I am necessitated to yield to their unanimous Desire of going to the Miami."[24] A distressful compulsion.

Procter left his heavy artillery behind. July 21 two British gunboats and a hundred-odd small craft approached Fort Meigs. Many Indians passed around by land, their presence made known by an early morning attack on the picket guards. Six or seven men were killed, one taken prisoner. General Clay sent off three couriers in succession to Harrison at Lower Sandusky. At ten o'clock on the evening of the 22nd, Harrison received word that Fort Meigs was again besieged and within the hour a dispatch rider from Commodore Perry brought tidings of a British blockade of the harbor at Erie.[25]

General Procter was spared the trouble of erecting batteries. Watching the departure of Clay's dispatch-riders to Harrison, Tecumseh unfolded a plan to reduce the American fort. The Indians would stage a sham battle along the Lower Sandusky road leading the Americans to believe that Harrison, advancing a reinforcement, had been waylaid. A rescue party would sally out of the fort to be drawn into a trap and then the British regulars could take the work by storm.[26]

For the first few days the savages contented themselves with attacks by small arms. The defenders suffered a few minor casualties. "Never did I expect to see men grow so indifferent to the sound of bullets," explained Hawkins. "At home if a gun is fired at a man . . . it is a subject of great concern . . . but here that a man has his glass of grogg shattered as he passes it to his lips is but a subject of derision."[27] July 26 a message-bearer from Harrison outpaced pursuing Indians and entered the fort. If the General had sent word of approaching reinforcements it was time now to stage the sham battle.

Tecumseh posted several hundred warriors along the Lower Sandusky road in lines one mile long, rifles on the right, muskets on the left. Soon the men in the fort heard the firing of two distinct parties "accompanied by all the yells and screams of savage warfare."[28] So realistic was the skirmish that the British themselves were "half in doubt . . . whether the battle was sham or real."[29] And within the fort all was commotion. Officers and men demanded to be allowed to fly to the rescue. Clay restrained them only with difficulty. Although his message from Harrison was verbal it was none the less strictly obeyed. Satisfied that the strength of the fort was sufficiently adequate, with ammunition in plenty, Harrison had sent word that he was advancing no reinforcements.[30] At least such a defeat as Colonel Dudley's was not to be repeated with green troops.

Tecumseh's sham battle lasted nearly an hour; which side conquered was not ascertained.

At Lower Sandusky stood Fort Stephenson, the handiwork of a militia company which had erected it during the summer of 1812 before Harrison had reached the right wing. The lines of the fort had been extended about a government storehouse protecting 200 barrels of flour but it was poorly located and untenable against heavy artillery as a near-by hill commanded the work. During the second siege of Fort Meigs Harrison withdrew all but 150 regulars from Fort Stephenson and retrograded nine miles south to Camp Seneca. Indian alarms were becoming frequent and the troops lay on their arms every night.

Commanding at Fort Stephenson was one of Harrison's favorite officers, Major George Croghan, twenty-one year old nephew of Colonel George Rogers Clark of Revolutionary fame. Young Croghan had won laurels at Tippecanoe and Fort Meigs but Harrison apparently spoiled the Major's chances of winning additional honors by giving him instructions similar to those left with Colonel Samuel Wells in June. Should the British approach in force with cannon, Harrison ordered, Croghan was to burn the fort and retreat. If only Indians appeared he was to remain until relieved.[31]

Late on the afternoon of July 29, Harrison learned that the enemy was dispersing before Fort Meigs. Part of the Indians advanced through the woods toward Fort Winchester, to which Clay sent a mounted detachment; the rest were believed heading for Lower Sandusky or Camp Seneca. Procter and his fleet had sailed for Lake Erie.

Preparation was made for retreat to Upper Sandusky. In the morning—July 30—Harrison called a council of war to debate present prospects. Fort Stephenson, he announced, was to be immediately abandoned. Fresh troops, a mounted force in advance, were then advancing from Franklinton and Harrison favored consolidating the army at Upper Sandusky. Above all else, the General emphasized, defeat must not be risked. Perry's fleet was still bottled up in Presque Isle harbor and any disposable force which Harrison could immediately spare would not exceed 700 men. Generals Cass and McArthur, Major Eleazer D. Wood and other officers attending the council recommended that the army remain at Camp Seneca but concurred in the necessity of abandoning Fort Stephenson.[32]

Orders had already gone out for Croghan to burn the fort and retreat to Camp Seneca, but still the Major failed to appear. Interpreter John Connor and two friendly Indians, who took the message, contended that they lost their way in the dark; at any rate they failed to reach the fort until next morning, the day Harrison's council was held. Croghan, meantime, had been laboring heroically to strengthen the work. He dug a wide surrounding ditch, reinforced the picketing, cleared away near-by timber and brush. Reluctant to retreat from this labor of love the Major himself called a council of war to consider Harrison's message. Absenting himself from the council, Croghan learned that eight of his under officers had unanimously voted to remain. So back to Harrison went the Major's reply:

"Sir . . . Yours of yesterday [29th], 10 o'clock P.M. . . . was received too late to be carried into execution. We have determined to maintain this place and by heavens we can."[33]

This message was brought in by Connor at sundown on the 30th. Nettled at what he termed the young man's insolence, Harrison sent Colonel Wells under an escort of dragoons to relieve him. Croghan was arrested and brought before the General next day. As the young Major saluted, Harrison jumped to his feet. "Major Croghan, how come you to send me that insolent letter?"[34]

Croghan responded with befitting suavity. Enemy redskins were known to be about and it was possible that the message might fall into their hands. So he had sent "as bullying a one as possible," but Connor, "the damned rascal," had failed to explain. Coupled with the Major's recital of his incessant labors, his impromptu excuses sufficed. Harrison agreed to restore him to his post but gave him new orders. Should Croghan discover the approach of a British force by water in time to effect a retreat he should do so but if he could not retreat with safety he was to maintain his position until reinforcements arrived.[35] So Croghan went back to Fort Stephenson while Harrison's regulars and militia reinforced Camp Seneca against possible attack.

"Indescribable joy" greeted the young firebrand upon his return to his post.[36] His troops worked feverishly to prepare for the invader. Sandbags and barrels of flour were heaped up against outside walls and heavy logs placed on top of the picketing to repel a storming party.

Procter's red allies were still clamoring for spoils. Tecumseh prompted the General to bring his two gunboats up the Sandusky River while he led his warriors through Black Swamp. Early in the evening of August 1 the British gunboats stood off in the river and a light howitzer was planted on shore. Indians under Colonel Matthew Elliott and Robert Dickson were conspicuously present. Procter sent two officers under a flag to persuade Croghan to surrender and thereby "prevent the dreadful massacre . . . caused by your resistance."[37] An ensign advanced from the fort to decline Procter's offer and upon the return of the flag the General at once opened fire.

The light howitzer on shore and the two gunboats hurled missiles all night and for hours next day. Croghan had one iron six-pounder, "Good Bess," which he moved from place to place to give the impression that the fort was well armed. Tired men were buoyed up by high spirits and by the understanding that they alone stood between the enemy and a light line of frontier defense. Sand and flour were heaped up wherever the picketing suffered.[38] During the afternoon—August 2—Procter's gunners concentrated their fire against the northeast angle as if to prepare the way for a storming party.

Croghan made ready to meet the attack. He loaded "Good Bess" with slugs and grapeshot and concealed the gun behind a masked embrasure in a position to rake a storming party. Riflemen took positions aloft in the corner blockhouses, sighting their weapons through portholes. They had "positive instructions not to fire untill the enemy had advanced within 30 paces."[39]

An enemy bugler blew a charge and three columns of British infantry moved against the work. Two of the columns feinted an attack against the opposite side; the third approached the northeast angle where the masked six-pounder awaited. Sweating men in the ramparts delivered a concerted volley the noise of which split their ears. The advancing column leaped into a ditch and advanced obliquely ten paces. It was typical British blundering. Croghan kicked open the masked porthole. Scrap-iron and grapeshot raked the length of the ditch; rifle bullets heaped up the dead and the dying. The fortunate survivors raced back to the boats, the Indian spectators back to the woods. "A more than adequate Sacrifice having been made to Indian Opinion," wrote General Procter in his official report, "I drew off the brave Assailants."[40]

The British carried away a few of the stricken during the night but left fifty rank and file and two officers dead or wounded in and about the ditch. Croghan's loss was one man killed, seven wounded.

The sound of the cannonading had been plainly heard at Camp Seneca and Harrison's men were almost mutinous in their clamor to advance. The General was determined, however, to risk no infantry in the woods while Tecumseh was keeping watch but to await the arrival of a mounted detachment of 450 men then advancing from Upper Sandusky. The Indians still held the woods. Parties of scouts sent off in the direction of Fort Stephenson were unable to penetrate their lines. Harrison's uneasiness was dispelled in part by Major Wood's "decided opinion" that the enemy had only light artillery.[41] It was quite possible that the fort would hold out. "I know it will be defended to the last extremity for earth does not hold a set of finer fellows than Croghan & his officers," Harrison wrote in a hurry-up appeal to Governor Meigs who was gathering militia forces to repel the invader.[42] The mounted reinforcement from Upper Sandusky arrived late that afternoon. Scouts who managed a passage through the woods announced that the gunboats were retreating in the direction of Lake Erie. Harrison rode past Fort Stephenson in pursuit while General Cass advanced an infantry force behind him but Procter's boats and the Indians had vanished.[43]

The news of Croghan's sensational achievement reached a public satiated with the official policy of waiting. The Major was universally extolled, his General roundly condemned. A fort blindly ordred destroyed saved by a plucky young major! The British beaten back by only one gun! Harrison's detractors, including Secretary of War Armstrong, were greatly amused. Some patriotic young ladies of Chillicothe passed the hat and gave Croghan "an elegant sword," while President Madison made him a lieutenant colonel by brevet.[44]

The recruiting of regulars proceeding altogether too slowly, Secretary Armstrong had modified his order restricting the use of volunteers and militia in the army destined to invade Canada. In July, while Perry's fleet was making ready, Harrison was authorized to recruit such numbers as in his judgment would be necessary.[45] The six-months' terms of militia recruited in March and April would soon expire and the General turned to Governor Shelby of Kentucky for "as many good men as you . . . may deem proper . . . not less than *four hundred* nor more than *two thousand*" for a march into Canada. "The period has arrived when with a little exertion the task assigned to this section . . . may be finished," Harrison gave assurance. Shelby, the "Old Eagle of King's Mountain," hero of a battle with the British in North Carolina some thirty years ago, was invited to march at the head of his own troops:

"To make this last effort why not, my dear sir, come in person. . . . I have such confidence in your wisdom that you in fact should 'be the guiding Head and I the hand.' . . . Scipio the conqueror of Carthage did not disdain to act as a Lieutenant of his younger and less experienced brother Lucius. . . ."[46]

Powerful recruiting forces in Kentucky were promptly set in motion, the tap of the drum heard in every city and town. In Ohio, meantime, the greater part of 4000 militia recently called out by Governor Meigs to help repel the invader met with disappointment. Engaged only for a forty-day service, these Ohioans were not intended to form part of the army which was to cross the state line into Michigan and Canada.[47] Harrison asked if the men would fill up vacancies in the 26th regiment of regulars but few if any were willing to join. At "Grand Camp Ohio Militia" at Upper Sandusky the citizen army proved fractious and disorderly, consuming public stores at an alarming rate.[48] "No man who has once seen Militia in camp and has any respect for his own reputation or his countries interest would ever Risk an engagement or attempt an Attack where there was half the number of regular troops to oppose them," commented a citizen observer.[49] When Shelby wrote that he expected to recruit at least 2500 Kentucky mounted volunteers Harrison ordered most of the Ohio militia discharged. Again, as in May, a clamor arose. The General's intentions were declared to be highly mysterious so the militia officers passed resolutions condemning his known arrangements as they grumblingly went home.

What now of Commodore Perry? That worthy officer had learned of Procter's second appearance before Fort Meigs while the American fleet lay blockaded within Presque Isle harbor. The days passed slowly as Perry fumed. He received a few "blacks, soldiers, and boys," as reinforcements from Commodore Chauncey.[50] A sunken sand bar at the mouth of the harbor prevented any movement in the presence of Robert H. Barclay, the enemy commodore. Finally, on July 31, Barclay sailed out of sight perhaps to discover what Procter might be doing.

Immediately Perry moved his fleet as far as the harbor entrance. Guns were removed to lighten the ships and air-tight "camels" attached to the 480-ton brigs *Lawrence* and *Niagara,* largest of the fleet. After much exertion the ships were floated over the bar and the cannon hastily remounted with but little time to spare. Discovering Procter's hopes pretty well dashed, Barclay returned to Presque Isle a few hours too late. He exchanged a few shots at long range with Perry whose fortunes were beginning to turn. The Commodore was bound to have his chance. That evening he wrote Harrison: "The squadron is not more than half manned, but as I see no prospect of receiving reinforcements, I have determined to commence my operations. . . . My anxiety to join you is very great."[51]

August 12 the fleet sailed up the lake from Erie and dropped anchor five days later in Sandusky Bay. Perry courteously inquired whether he should come to Camp Seneca or wait for the General to visit the fleet. On the morning of August 19 it was raining but Harrison promptly set out with Generals Cass, McArthur, and staffs. Perry's guns boomed a salute as the army leaders climbed aboard the twenty-gun flagship *Lawrence.* The meeting between the General and the Commodore, not yet twenty-eight years old, was most cordial. There was no one whom Harrison could have been more delighted to greet. Chief Tarhe and a band of Wyandots who accompanied the General explored every part of the vessel and broke out in a war-dance on deck. Harrison had brought Tarhe for a purpose. The majesty of the fleet sufficed for the chief to send three runners to his tribesmen at Malden and persuade them to remove to a neutral spot.[52]

Harrison and Perry talked until late in the evening. The Commodore's leading problem was still want of men. He inquired if the army was ready to advance. "As soon as Shelby's Kentuckians arrived," replied Harrison. They were to rendezvous at Newport, across from Cincinnati, on August 31. Meantime Perry intended to bring Commodore Barclay to action. Harrison recommended Put-in-Bay at South Bass Island as an anchorage well sheltered from enemy observation. Resting that night on board the *Lawrence,* the General sailed up the lake to inspect the harbor next day.

Returning to Camp Seneca Harrison issued a call for volunteer seamen. Lake and river boatmen were culled from the ranks although any man who could handle an artillery piece or pull a rope would do. A few days later Perry was delighted to receive a detail of nearly 100 recruits, including some Kentucky sharpshooters, who arrived at Put-in-Bay in Mackinaw boats. The officers of the fleet watched the tall frontiersmen climb aboard and exchanged glances. Clad in blue linsey-woolsey hunting shirts, red belts and blue pantaloons fringed with red, and with long rifles on shoulders, these fresh-water marines from the Kentucky backwoods conducted themselves in the manner of youngsters, curious yet awestruck. Many of them had never seen a vessel before. They rambled through the flagship to inspect every part from hold to masthead, including the Commodore's cabin, and slapped their great palms on the big guns with rude exclamations of praise. Perry permitted the Kentuckians to run at large for an hour or so when they were mustered on deck and an officer broached the subject of naval discipline and etiquette.[53]

Tours in the direction of Malden revealed Commodore Barclay's fleet swinging idly from its moorings. Would the British ever come out? Again Perry dropped anchor in Sandusky Bay and invited Harrison to revisit the fleet. Harrison brought along forty more recruits for Perry but expressed scepticism of British intentions to fight. If Barclay persisted in his refusal to come out, however, the transportation of the army to Malden would furnish grave problems. Any considerable number of men on board would encumber the decks and interfere with the gunners. And should Barclay attack on the way a single broadside would likely kill scores. Perry agreed to move the army to Middle Sister Island, about twelve miles south of Malden, where a temporary camp would be set up. It was his belief, however, that Commodore Barclay would fight.[54]

Harrison again returned to Camp Seneca. Day after day Perry mounted a point of vantage on South Bass Island and raised his spyglass toward Malden. Would Barclay never come out? Another week of waiting passed. Meantime Shelby's Kentuckians, 3500 strong, swarmed about the Ohio River ferries for days, the flatboats almost sinking from the weight of horses and men.[55] Shelby, approaching his sixty-third birthday, was renewing his youth in taking the field. "Not a moment will be lost until I join you," he wrote Harrison from Newport.[56] Colonel Richard Johnson, who had returned to rest a few weeks in Kentucky, was again under way. Riding in advance, Johnson took the Auglaize route for Fort Meigs.

Detachments of friendly tribesmen arrived to join the army as Harrison prepared for an absence of indefinite duration. The General wrote a long letter to Governor Meigs warning against any harmful visitation upon the Delawares living near Piqua, whom settlers considered responsible for forays on livestock. Harrison was for placing the matter in the hands of the chiefs upon whose loyalty he could depend. "To attempt indiscriminately to murder these people, would inflict a blot upon the national honour that would never be effaced."[57] It would also compromise the friendly attitude of that nation. Little Beaver, a young Delaware warrior whom Harrison had known in Indiana as a boy, proved his personal devotion while at Seneca. Blue Jacket, a Shawnee chief, had swaggered into camp with the intention, indiscreetly conveyed, of murdering the General but was slain by the Delaware even while other members of his tribe looked on. Again, Captain Tommy, Shawnee war chief who had fought at Fort Meigs, asked and received permission to sleep at the door of the General's marquee every night.[58]

Harrison called upon Colonel Benjamin G. Orr, the army contractor, to deliver 300,000 rations to the army in Canada, a detail inadequately performed as it turned out.[59] Several hundred cattle were being driven toward Detroit by way of Fort Meigs. Major Wood of the Engineer Corps was ordered to take the ordnance to Portage peninsula, rendezvous for the embarkation with Perry. September 8 Harrison notified Secretary Armstrong: "I am now in complete readiness to embark the troops the moment Gov.r Shelby arrives,"

Nothing more, however, had been heard from Commodore Perry. On the morning of the tenth the sound of an "incessant and tremendous cannonading" reached the ears of troops marching from Fort Meigs on the Lower Sandusky road.[60] Miles away at Camp Seneca Harrison was waiting "all anxiety for the event."[61] Two days later the troops at Lower Sandusky sighted a boat coming up the river at a furious pace. An officer in a stained naval uniform leaped ashore and raced up to the fort. As the glad news from Perry winged through the encampment a great shouting went up. "Good Bess," the iron six-pounder, boomed out in celebration. The naval officer, Lieutenant Dulaney Forrest, chief signal officer of the *Lawrence,* mounted a horse and galloped to Camp Seneca with the Commodore's message scribbled in the back of an old letter: "We have met the enemy . . ."[62]

Harrison ordered a detachment to march to the shore of the lake to receive the British prisoners.

xv

VICTORY IN CANADA

ORDERS to General Procter, should he deem his situation "desperate," dictated the evacuation of Malden and Detroit and removal of his command to Burlington Heights at the head of Lake Ontario. The retrograde movement was to be carried out with dispatch, the troops to march unencumbered "with heavy or superfluous baggage."[1] Little concern was indicated over the fate of Tecumseh's Indians. The grand confederacy so diligently organized by the Shawnee chief might well disintegrate. Of what moment were Indian land squabbles compared with the fate of a British army? To a British general whose leadership was despised fell the difficult task of persuading the tribesmen that retreat was the only judicious course at present. Procter, incidentally, had anticipated the order to retreat while realizing full well his present dilemma. "It is my opinion that I should retire on the Thames, without Delay," he advised General De Rottenburg, September 12, 1813. ". . . I feel myself at a Loss with respect to the Indians."[2]

Tecumseh had his own idea of what should be done and not for a moment did he contemplate retreat. On the day of the naval battle he had paddled far out on Lake Erie toward the thunder of guns but was unable to learn a great deal inasmuch as enveloping smoke rendered indistinguishable the colors of the winning fleet. Procter endeavored to postpone his delicate task of enlightenment, explaining that the British fleet had gone to Put-in-Bay to refit. Insofar as it went, Procter's statement was indeed true. The British ships were now undergoing necessary repairs at Put-in-Bay although with Commodore Barclay, wounded in the fight, held a prisoner on board. Tecumseh seemed to miss him. As he hovered restlessly about Malden he could see "our father tying up everything and preparing to run away."[3] When Procter at length found it necessary to meet his Indian warriors in council, Tecumseh took the floor. He breathed contempt for "our father," the man in the red coat. Indignant and inflammatory phrases poured from his lips, "the vaulted roof . . . echoed back the wild yell of the Indians."[4] Tecumseh accused his British father of arrant cowardice and declared for making a stand "here" where there was still plenty of arms and ammunition. "We are determined to defend our lands . . . to leave our bones upon them."[5] As soon as quiet was restored among the Indians in the council chamber Procter promised to consider the situation further. His present intention, his interpreters explained, was to retreat only to Sandwich, opposite Detroit, or possibly to Chatham a few miles up the Thames River. The westerly course of the Thames roughly paralleled the northern shore of Lake Erie. To proceed eastward after leaving this river would bring Procter and his little army safely to Burlington but much was heard of a plan to make a stand at Chatham a short distance along the way. Tecumseh, however, was for making a stand in the thick woods and ravines near Malden.[6]

But Fort Amherstburg was ordered razed to the ground and Procter removed his headquarters to Sandwich where another week was consumed in making preparations for flight. "Our movements," confessed a British officer, "were extremely dilatory."[7] Procter commandeered all horses, wagons and grain in the neighborhood and invited all loyalist families who wished to depart to accompany him in the general exodus. On every hand were suspicious and watchful tribesmen who bore a menacing air. A letter dated Detroit, September 26, reveals the distasteful fruit of the seed sown by His Majesty's Indian agents:

"The Indians . . . have declared they will not budge one inch further and remind us of our general having promised to conquer. As we are now completely in the savages power, we are obliged in a great measure to act as they think proper. The celebrated chief Tecumseh . . . assured me his Indians were determined to give battle the moment the Americans approach. . . . These savages have no mercy. The tomahawk and scalping-knife decides immediately the wretch who falls into their hands, and many dread the war-whoop may sound in our ears, if we act contrary to their ideas. . . . We have spread a net which may catch us. *I hate these savage barbarians.* . . . Without a force sufficient to keep them in check, they are more plague than profit."[8]

Yet somehow Procter was enabled to complete his packing and leave. Contrary to official orders he encumbered himself with numerous wagons and much superfluous baggage. The idea that Harrison might pursue him up the River Thames was not seriously weighed by the General as he quit Sandwich early on September 27 and moved forward to Moraviantown on the Thames River leaving his army to follow him.

Harrison had lost little time. The day after learning of Commodore Perry's triumph he joined Major Wood at the mouth of Portage River. Entering the harbor in the 112-ton schooner *Ariel* Perry was greeted "with great congratulations and the booming of cannon." Next day, September 14, just as 300 British prisoners were being landed, Governor Shelby arrived.[9] A bluff and determined personality, capable of enduring great hardship, the Hero of King's Mountain had a distinguished record of frontier service dating back to the Battle of Point Pleasant fought in western Virginia the year after Harrison was born.

Harrison entrusted the British prisoners to a body of Pennsylvania militia who, with the exception of about 100, chose to stand on their constitutional rights, declining to enter Canada. "Thank God I have enough Kentuckians to go without you," Harrison reminded them.[10] General Cass brought up 800 regulars from Camp Seneca and General McArthur's brigade from Fort Meigs joined the army late on the 20th, after a march of three days through tall prairie grass. Colonel Johnson, arriving at the fort the day before McArthur departed, rested his horses and awaited orders to continue his march to Detroit.

For a mounted force, Harrison would depend upon Johnson. He ordered Shelby's mounted volunteers to leave their horses on the Portage peninsula and selected a guard by commanding every twentieth Kentuckian to fall out of line. A mile-and-a-half-long fence of brush and timber was to be extended across the neck of the peninsula and the horses turned out to graze. Major Wood and the ordnance embarked first for Edward's Island at Put-in-Bay, mounting his guns in six Mackinaw trading boats. Six vessels from Perry's fleet which were immediately available could accommodate only eight or nine hundred men at a time and even with the assistance of several score sailing craft and Mackinaw boats two return trips had to be made. Room was made for a young sow which had followed Governor Shelby all the way from Kentucky. Known as "the Governor's pig," she had become the pet of the army.[11]

The sight of Perry's stricken flagship, the *Lawrence,* and the captured enemy vessels swinging at anchor renewed the ardor of the men. The *Lawrence* had been bored through and through; the *Detroit,* largest of the British fleet, had not a spar left standing, her sides ragged with holes and heavy shot still encased in the wood.[12] The *Queen Charlotte,* 400 tons, also had suffered heavily. To the delight of the Kentuckians and a detachment of friendly Indians the men were permitted to go on board. General Harrison paid his respects to the wounded Commodore Barclay.

While awaiting the arrival of provisions the men swarmed over the little island and beat a muddy path into a cave where cool water flowed. Harrison ordered a third-time deserter shot, and sent marching orders to Colonel Johnson. Bad weather held up the flotilla until the 25th when the army re-embarked for Middle Sister Island, but when the Governor's pig declined to go further understanding soldiers observed that she was only standing upon her rights as a militia pig and was not to be forced over the line. All that day the sailing vessels and smaller craft shuttled back and forth between the islands. The rendezvous in the middle of the lake became "alive with men."[13] The presence of a kind of wild onion, the leek, was heralded; soldiers hungry for fresh vegetables began digging and scratching over acres of ground. Harrison, Perry, and the general staff sailed ahead in the *Ariel* next day to reconnoiter the Canadian shore and select a wide smooth beach for the debarkation. Traces of the enemy's recent departure were seen in smoke arising from the ruins of naval buildings and storehouses but in Malden harbor a dead silence prevailed.[14]

This did not mean that Tecumseh's warriors were not somewhere about. Harrison landed Captain Johnny, a Shawnee chief, in a secluded spot and bade him meet Colonel Johnson and guide him safely into Detroit. Johnson, as it happened, was then approaching the River Raisin where the bones of the Kentuckians interred the previous June had been dug up again by Indians. "The sight had a powerful effect upon the feelings of the men," recounted Captain Robert B. McAfee. "The bleaching bones still appealed to heaven. . . . The feelings they excited cannot be described by me—but they will never be forgotten."[15]

Harrison occupied himself during the return trip to Middle Sister by drawing up detailed plans for an order of march and battle when the troops debarked at Malden. A high wind sprang up and the landing was made in a violent surf. Waves swiftly dashing against the shore and rising water in the lake caused a fear that a large part of the island would be inundated; but a little after midnight, the gale subsiding, the soldiers slept at last and a bright clear morning greeted them on September 27.[16] Harrison issued copies of his debarkation orders and read a proclamation to the troops. Republican sentiment, humane feeling, was, as usual, uppermost:

"The general entreats his brave troops to remember that they are the sons of sires whose fame is immortal; that they are to fight for the rights of their insulted country, whilst their opponents combat for the unjust pretensions of a master. Kentuckians! remember the River Raisin! but remember it only whilst the victory is suspended. The revenge of a soldier cannot be gratified upon a fallen enemy."[17]

Precisely at 9 o'clock nine ships of war and eighty small craft took off from Middle Sister Island exhibiting, wrote Major Wood, "one of the grandest scenes mine eyes ever beheld."[18] The Major had six pieces of artillery mounted in the boats and the gunners approached the Canadian shore with matches lighted. From the deck of the *Ariel* Harrison and Perry saw a large eagle soaring overhead as if ushering the fleet into Malden harbor. Harrison was reminded of a similar eagle, if not the same bird, which had hovered over Fort Meigs on May 5, the most eventful day of the siege. An eagle, responded Perry, had followed the fleet far out in the lake as he advanced to battle on September 10. "It is an omen of victory!" exclaimed the General.[19] Early in the afternoon the vessels entered the mouth of the Detroit River. Every fife and drum was sounding "Yankee Doodle" as the boats almost simultaneously struck the beach at Hartley's Point three miles below Malden and out tumbled the men to form the order of battle. "In two minutes from the time the first boat struck the beach, the whole line was formed ready for action."[20]

Here was Canadian soil at last with no enemy anywhere in view. Harrison and his aides walked up to a near-by farmhouse and knocked. Assured that no harm was intended a woman opened the door and revealed that Procter's soldiers had burned the public buildings and retreated up the Detroit River only the day before. Harrison directed scouts to explore the woods. The army faced about and to the tune of "Yankee Doodle" marched by parallel roads into "England's scalp-market." Most of the loyalists had fled with Procter's army and those who remained appeared doubtful as to their fate. Harrison kept a sharp watch upon his Indian allies while Governor Shelby quieted the fears of a group of women who implored protection. According to the General's recollection of the scene:

"When I entered Canada and saw helpless women collected against the possibility of outrage, and innocent children playing before the doors of their cottage . . . I informed the Indians that if they offered the least violence to the . . . inhabitants, I would hang the perpetrator to the first tree. . . . The order was faithfully obeyed."[21]

The only instances of looting in fact were attributed to some hungry Kentuckians which caused Harrison to issue a sharply worded order promising "the utmost rigor of martial law" upon those guilty of any further violation of army amenities.[22] Scouts discovered stores of green corn and potatoes in a deserted Indian village nearby and the Kentuckians fished out a few small arms and cannon which had been dumped into the river. A detachment advanced four miles to save a bridge over the Rivière Aux Canards and found the rear guard of the enemy nursing a newly kindled blaze. A volley or two sufficed to disperse them and the bridge was saved. A regiment of regulars remained to guard Malden as the army set out on the 28th to cover Colonel Richard Johnson's advance. Other bridges over unfordable creeks had been destroyed and two whole days were occupied in reaching Sandwich, eighteen miles above.[23]

Sandwich was occupied on a fatiguing rainy day. Harrison dealt first with a swarm of enemy tribesmen who, deserting Procter, had been plundering the town of Detroit but now sought only peace. Headquarters at Sandwich were established at the Baby House, home of Colonel James Baby of the Canadian militia. It was with great satisfaction that Harrison drafted a proclamation re-establishing American rule over Detroit.[24] General McArthur with his brigade of 700 regulars was ordered to reoccupy the town. It was a joyful reunion of free-born Americans. As the boatloads of troops approached the American shore the daughter of Judge John May hoisted a cherished old flag which she had kept hidden in the attic.[25] A wave of grateful emotion swept the long-orphaned townspeople; many were weeping, glad shouts of joy and triumph were heard. Before the evacuation on the 28th the British had fired nearly 200 buildings while the savages quartered themselves in deserted houses, breaking out doors and windows. "But for our opportune arrival," Harrison notified Secretary Armstrong, "it is more than probable that there would have been a general massacre . . . and burning."[26] He kept his own savage allies occupied by bidding them round up detachments of enemy Indians.

However welcome the sight of McArthur's regulars Detroit was treated to a greater thrill next day. About noontime waiting ears caught the thunder of a thousand horses in swift motion as Colonel Johnson's mounted regiment emerged from the woods below the town. The citizens flocked to the street to cheer the motley-clad Kentuckians who galloped in perfect order down the wide road, boisterously responding to cheers. "Arrived at Detroit about 12 o'clock," Captain McAfee noted in his diary:

"Every heart beat High in the cause of his country. . . . Our

vessels . . . with American colors waving in the river . . . is truly
a flattering sight. . . . From this place you have a handsome view
of Sandwich on the Canadian shore now occupied by Gen[l] Harrison
& Gov[r] Shelby's troops."[27]

Hailing with delight the safe arrival of horses and men (the former a scarce article for miles around) Harrison ordered Johnson to
start crossing the river at once. The task occupied the best efforts of
the boatmen throughout the rest of that day and yet not every horse
and rider could be accommodated by nightfall. "I hope . . . they will
be all over early in the morning when we shall again take up the
line of march," Harrison wrote Armstrong, on September 30, his
letter giving notice of anticipated pursuit of the enemy, a significant
point in the light of later dispute. "Gen[l] Procter has with him four
hundred seventy five regulars of the 41 and Newfoundland Regiments sixty of the 10th Regiment of Vetrans 45 Dragoons and from
six hundred to a thousand Indians, some deserters that left him the
night before last give the latter as the number, the citizens of Detroit
supposed the former to be correct. . . . My great apprehension,
however arrises from a belief that he will make no halt. . . . The
Ottawas and Chippewas have withdrawn from the British . . . to
beg for peace. . . . I have agreed to receive them upon condition of
their giving hostages for their fidelity and immediately joining us
with all their warriors. The Wyandots, Miamis and the band of Delawares which had joined the enemy are also desirous to be received
upon the same terms. . . ."[28] Had General Procter chosen to make
a stand on the Canadian shore he would have been able to employ
three times his present Indian force against the Americans.

Harrison's forces numbered 4500 men, about one third of which
were guarding Malden and Detroit or engaged in forwarding army
baggage from Put-in-Bay and Middle Sister Island, while 500 Kentuckians had remained on Portage peninsula. Bad drinking water encountered on the swampy peninsula produced an epidemic of illness
which was making inroads upon Harrison's full strength. The problem of supplies also recurring it was necessary to fix the collective
volunteer mind upon the idea of pursuit. Scanning a British government map, Harrison decided that a sure means of cutting off Procter's retreat lay in landing an infantry force at Port Talbot on the
northern shore of Lake Erie, then marching quickly overland to the
River Thames but the lake route was vetoed by Perry and Shelby.
Perry pointed out that it would be difficult to navigate the lake in
open boats in October weather, while the larger vessels might en-

counter uncertain winds which would mean a fatal delay. Shelby damned the boats, for the Kentuckians were poor sailors, and declared in favor of the land route and a stern chase. Harrison agreed to favor the point at a council of war to be held in the morning, the pursuit to be made, it was understood, preferably by land.[29]

The council held on the morning of October 1 brought together a galaxy of Kentucky notables in Governor Shelby, General John Adair, his first aide, militia generals Joseph Desha, William Henry, John E. King, David Chiles, George Trotter, James Allen and Samuel Caldwell, and Quartermaster General David Walker. Harrison helped in selecting the route of pursuit by openly considering each factor involved. Against the feasibility of the land route were Procter's three-day start and the likelihood of his picking up reinforcements of Canadian militia if he found himself pursued. Too, provisions for the American army were scarce and it would be impossible to forward supplies by boat after the army reached a point where the River Thames ceased to be navigable. Stressed also were the precautions to be observed in pursuit of any body of Indians whose leader was Chief Tecumseh. But while the lake route might land the army well in advance of Procter's position, Harrison added, the uncertainty of the winds was a likely obstacle. He was interrupted by Major General Desha, a member of Congress, who expressed the view that even if Procter could not be overtaken by land the army could press him close enough to make him drop his heavy baggage. "The governor thinks, and so do I," Harrison observed, "that the pursuit up the Thames will be the most effectual."[30] So it was decided. A warm political dispute, which we will heed later, was to arise out of the proceedings of this council.

The remainder of Colonel Johnson's men, and the herd of beef cattle, were landed on the Canadian side during the day while the surrounding country was scoured for provisions paid for in cash. "It would be a hard march," Harrison remarked to the troops, "but no man must grumble or complain or even *think* of his wife or sweetheart until Procter and his army were overtaken and defeated."[31] The camp was closely guarded against any man leaving that night. The infantry brigades of McArthur and Cass remaining at Detroit and Sandwich, Harrison set out at sunrise on October 2 with a force of nearly 3000, including 200 friendly Indians and 150 regulars. A naval chase was already under way. Lieutenant Commander Jesse D. Elliott had taken four schooners and one brig followed by a flotilla of small boats carrying provisions and baggage, and heading into

Lake St. Clair along which the enemy vessels had retreated, entering the mouth of the River Thames on the second day out.[32] Commodore Perry's preference for the most active service won him a place as volunteer aide to the General. It was anticipated that the army would soon catch up with the fleet.

Paced by Johnson's mounted regiment, the army covered twenty-five miles the first day, the infantry continuing "often at a run" to keep up. Toward sunset as Harrison encamped at the River Ruscomb, nine miles from the Thames, mounted scouts brought in eight deserters from the British forces and the news which quickly spread through the army was greeted by jubilant cock-crows. According to the testimony of the deserters, Procter's main force, encumbered by loyalist civilians and baggage, was only a day's march away. Procter had no idea that a pursuit was intended, Harrison concluded, inasmuch as the bridge over the River Ruscomb was still entire. Promised an earlier start next morning the Kentuckians attempted to sleep. Captain McAfee recounted a "remarkable Dream" which he had. "I was annoyed by a Rattlesnake . . . an old offender . . . after a considerable struggle we Caught him and cut off his head."[33]

Soon after Perry's vessels had reached the Thames River the army caught up with the fleet. A sunken sand bar prevented vessels of more than one hundred tons from entering so the *Caledonia* and *Ariel* were anchored near by, the schooners *Scorpion, Tigress,* and *Porcupine* gliding over safely and continuing up the river. The pursuit was discovered by the enemy when Johnson's advance guard found a British lieutenant of dragoons and a dozen privates cutting down a bridge over the first tributary of the Thames. All were taken prisoners but a riderless horse dashed away to convey the troublesome news to the British main force. Bridge repairs essential to a safe crossing occupied only an hour. A short distance farther on another bridge was repaired and crossed as the advance guard engaged in a brief skirmish with a force of British and Indians who sought to delay the pursuit.[34]

Away went the army again over leaf-strewn roads and woodpaths, the maple and oak trees golden red and russet in the autumn sun. The barns of Canadian farmers were being filled with produce for the winter, their owners fearful of enemy raids. As the army encamped at Drake's Farm that evening Harrison received a tongue-lashing from the mistress of the place who blasted his soldiers as thieves and robbers and declared that not a single comb of honey would be left for her in the morning. "Madam," Harrison remonstrated politely, "I will put a guard over the bees." Provoked by the

woman's manner of speech when addressing the General, the Kentuckians one by one strolled past the sentinel who gazed at the moon,
the stars and the trees, methodically searching for Indians. Harrison had no choice but to order the army quartermaster to pay for the
honey in the morning.[35] A gentleman's war.

On the third day the trail grew warmer, the pursuit a little less
tame. The Kentuckians debated their chances of catching up with
old Simon Girty, reported fleeing with the British.[36] Although Girty
had scalped his last white man his long and bloody career had not been
forgotten. Procter's idea, however, was primarily to escape, his avowal
to make a stand near Chatham merely a blind to deceive Tecumseh.
The pursuit being discovered, the British General, who had returned
to his army, again rode ahead to devise a means of protection for his
family and baggage at Moraviantown, nearly thirty miles in advance.
Yet he left no definite orders with Colonel Warburton, his second
in command. Together with Colonel Matthew Elliott, Warburton
urged that the army stand and fight. The warriors unanimously declined. Had not their General again deceived them by leaving? But
the influence of Elliott finally prevailed and Tecumseh agreed to make
a stand at the cluster of cabins known as Chatham, bordering the
Thames River at McGregor's Creek.[37]

Less than a dozen miles from Drake's Farm was the farm of Matthew Dolsen where the enemy dragoons had rested on the night of
October 3. Here the river scenery became more rugged, high wooded
banks on either side affording sufficient cover for Indian snipers to
shoot down on the decks of vessels. Perry's schooners were anchored
and placed under the protection of a guard as Harrison drove stead-
ily on. Three or four miles ahead lay McGregor's Creek, spanned
by two bridges, right and left, about a mile apart. Johnson's regiment was riding merrily on in pursuit of the foe when a woman,
"our guardian angel," appeared to warn them that the main body
of Indians lay in ambush near the creek, the bridge on the left dismantled and set on fire. In accordance with well-emphasized instructions, Johnson sent a messenger back to Harrison who soon
came riding up and ordered the regiment to advance *cautiously* by
columns. A scattering inaccurate fire from the woods ahead was
designed, no doubt, to lead the Kentuckians on but Harrison immediately called a halt and sent back for two six-pounders.[38]

A few rounds of grape sent clattering through trees and bushes
sufficed to quiet the enemy. While an infantry company extinguished
the flaming bridge preparatory to repairs, Johnson took the bridge

on the right, a skirmish in which two of his men were killed and six wounded, but the Kentuckians brought back a few scalps and claimed thirteen enemy slain. The British made no further effort to bring matters to an issue that day. The return of General Procter to his army during the afternoon meant headlong flight so conducted, Colonel Elliott reported, "that the greater part of the provisions and stores fell into the enemy's hands."[39] Johnson's regiment found several barrels of flour as well as bear skins and brass kettles in an abandoned Indian camp and then saved a burning house in which a thousand muskets had been stored. An enemy schooner, carrying military stores "of an immense amount," was burned to the water's edge, bombs exploding savagely, and an hour later the Kentuckians salvaged some choice British ordnance from two other vessels abandoned in the river.[40] Altogether it was a busy afternoon. From a burning distillery two iron twenty-four-pounders, a quantity of fixed ammunition and several barrels of pork were taken. Gradually the army was retrieving the material losses suffered at Detroit, the River Raisin, and at Colonel Dudley's defeat. The enemy twenty-four-pounders had last been used to plough up the dirt in and about Fort Meigs.

Harrison encamped that evening at Bowles' Farm, his army depleted through sickness and the absence of several hundred men left to guard prisoners, ships, and stores. During the last three days the troops had traversed some sixty miles of broken country, had repaired three bridges and fought the enemy, yet when the order was circulated for the erection of breastworks "every part of the army seemed to vie with each other as to discipline and anxiety to outdo one another."[41] Observing no end of caution with Tecumseh somewhere about Harrison remained in the saddle inspecting arrangements until a late hour. It was to be another forced march in the morning. The troops were directed to supply themselves with strips of fresh beef from the drove of cattle which accompanied the army. All other provisions were to be left behind. The General himself was carrying his own equipment in a single valise, his only blanket fastened over his saddle.[42]

Warned to "remember discipline," Colonel Johnson again rode ahead in pursuit of General Procter. For weeks the ambitious Colonel had anticipated the day when his mounted regiment would catch up with Procter at last. Day after day while advancing through the Ohio forests he had trained his regiment to charge in line as hundreds of cartridges were fired to accustom the horses to the din of warfare. Foremost in the mounted ranks was a volunteer "Forlorn Hope" of twenty men "willing to doom themselves to certain death" by rushing in to draw the first fire of the enemy, leaving their comrades to follow swiftly before there was time to reload.[43] Years later, on the political hustings, Johnson recalled the urgency of the chase and the fervor of his band. "These men knew what they had to contend with. They did not go out to fight by the day but by the job. . . . O, how I did want to catch that fellow. I never thirsted for man's blood but Procter was a monster."[44] The regiment came up to two more gunboats and several small craft. Frightened loyalist women and children were quieted, a British sergeant and fourteen privates taken prisoners. At Arnold's Mills, a few miles farther on, Johnson caught up with a Canadian militia captain whom he threatened into revealing that Procter had crossed to the north side of the river.

The mounted regiment came to a halt near a shallow rapid, the fording place. Harrison brought up the infantry troops and formed them in order of battle preparatory to crossing the stream. Scouts were sent to reconnoiter the opposite bank, then a foot soldier was mounted behind every horseman while others crossed over in small boats or waded. No Indians were sighted. A burning bridge over a creek three miles ahead was repaired in short order and soon afterward the expectant Kentuckians marked the British encampment of the night before. "Being now certainly near the enemy," Harrison recorded, "I directed the advance of Johnson's Regiment . . . for the purpose of procuring intelligence."[45]

Perhaps the sting of Tecumseh's reproaches had penetrated Procter's hide but more likely did the harassed General devise a simple plan to thrust his army into the hands of the enemy in order to cover his own retreat. General Procter had halted in a wood of oak and beech trees, his left fringing the river road, his right on a narrow swamp where Indians were posted, their line curving around into a larger swamp where enemy horsemen could not enter. The British regulars, now reduced to 367 men, formed two thin lines strung out from the road where a single brass six-pounder, a trophy of the Revolution, was posted. Procter's subordinate officers roundly criticized his position, taken on level ground. Not far away lay a ravine easily defensible against enemy cavalry while less than two miles in the rear were the cabins and houses of Moraviantown where a mounted force would be entirely useless until the defenders were driven out. "It was downright murder if we attempted to make a stand where we were."[46] Still the position near the river would serve to check the

enemy for an hour or two while the General galloped off to Moraviantown and picked up his family and belongings. A crowning bit
of carelessness was the abandonment that morning of the ammunition for the only artillery piece and thus the sole function of the
British six-pounder was lodged in its threatening appearance.[47]

For nearly two hours the British and Indians awaited in silence
the approach of a vengeful, dreaded enemy. Tecumseh, plainly
dressed in deerskin, passed along the British line and spoke a few
brief words in Shawnee to each of the officers. "Father, have a big
heart!" was his final plea to Procter.[48] Whatever the fate of the regulars Tecumseh was determined to conquer or die, although a British officer considered him "seemingly sanguine of success."[49]

Colonel Johnson was advancing at a fast trot down the road when
his scouts overtook a British wagoner and learned that the British
and Indians were formed in the order of battle near a swamp not
300 yards away. When the wagoner stuck to his story despite the
threat of death if he lied scouts rode on to examine the ground ahead
and sure enough there was the six-pounder in the road and a swamp
on the enemy right. An officer galloped back to Harrison and in fifteen minutes, accompanied by Perry, General Cass, Major Wood,
and two aides, the General came riding up.[50]

Johnson at once went to Harrison and eagerly declared that his
regiment alone could whip the enemy and asked permission to charge.
Harrison, who had seen another Kentucky colonel drawn into Tecumseh's snare, was not so sure. He sent a favorite officer, Major
Wood, to take a look at the British line. The infantry coming up, he
conferred with Governor Shelby as to the best mode of attack under
present circumstances. Harrison had less than 2500 men on the
ground, his original force reduced to about 2100 Kentucky volunteers, 120 regulars, and perhaps 200 Indians.[51] He believed the
enemy force to be at least equal to his, although it was actually less
by about one third. One could see, however, that the British could
not be flanked while the concentration of Indians in the swamp
spelled danger for the American left and rear. So a direct frontal
attack by the infantry was determined upon. As soon as the infantry
had broken the lines Johnson's regiment was to charge the Indians on
the left.

But Major Wood returned to report that the British were formed
in open order. Harrison replied that was impossible, the British were
never known to form in open order even when fighting Indians.
They were formed in extreme open order, Wood persisted. The Gen-

eral reconsidered his plans.[52] Instead of the mounted regiment taking ground on the left, "I . . . determined to refuse my left to the Indians and to break the British lines . . . by a charge. The measure was not sanctioned by anything I had seen or heard of but I was fully convinced it would succeed. The American backwoodsmen ride better in the woods than any other people."[53] Harrison swung his horse

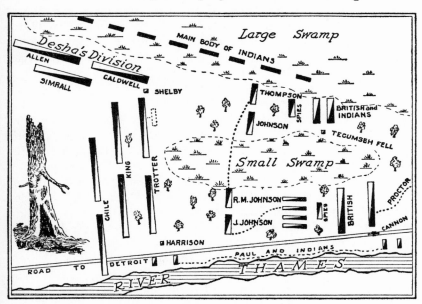

THE BATTLE OF THE THAMES

From a drawing made by Benson J. Lossing. This map and the one depicting the plan of the Battle of Tippecanoe (see page 100) were taken from Lossing's classic work, "Pictorial Field Book of the War of 1812."

about and called to Colonel Johnson who was forming his men. "We have decided to change the mode of attack. . . . You will now form your Regiment . . . to charge the enemy by heads of columns."[54]

The mounted regiment countermarched into position. The Colonel ordered his brother, Lieutenant Colonel James Johnson, to charge the British line with the first battalion while he rode with the second against the Indians in the swamp, a maneuver wholly unauthorized by Harrison although Johnson later excused himself on the ground that there was hardly room for both battalions on the right of the first swamp. Cass, Perry, and regular aides Colonel Charles S. Todd and Lieutenant John O'Fallon, assisted in forming the infantry. Two companies of regulars and the friendly Indians took ground between the road and the river, their assigned task to capture the enemy six-pounder. On the right of the road where the infantry lines began Harrison posted himself with his aides. Facing the British was Johnson's first battalion; the Colonel and his second battalion were gone from sight behind trees and bushes to face the most dangerous portion of the enemy line. Some of his men dismounted, their horses dangerously bogged in the swamp. Almost 500 yards from Harrison's position was Governor Shelby with the major portion of the infantry, formed at an angle, *"en potence,"* to counter the expected Indian thrust on the left.[55]

It was now 2:30 o'clock by the sun. Harrison rode up to a majestic Seneca chief and borrowed powder to reprime his pistols. He signaled to the mounted force that the infantry was ready. Colonel James Johnson passed the word along the line: "Charge through the enemy's first fire and follow it up close." Then the trumpet sounded. "Charge them, my brave Kentuckians," exclaimed Harrison.[56]

The Kentuckians raised a tremendous yell and made a brave start, but as they encountered the first enemy volley "nearly all" the riders dismounted to take cover. At once the order was given to remount. Before the British had time to reload, the tall, bronzed riders swept through their lines and wheeling to right and left gathered up prisoners by the score. The regulars and Indians posted along the river road had little difficulty in capturing the harmless six-pounder. From a safe position in the rear, General Procter and forty dragoons bolted for Moraviantown. The skirmish on the right was over in less than ten minutes.[57]

On the left, however, there was trouble. Johnson's second battalion encountered too much underbrush to render a swift charge possible and most of the men were fighting from behind trees. From well-sheltered positions the Indians poured in "a most severe and disastrous fire." Fifteen members of the Forlorn Hope were killed and four wounded at the very outset. The voice of Tecumseh could be heard loudly giving orders. His warriors advanced to new positions against the ragged line of dismounted Kentuckians. A portion of the second battalion was thrown back against the infantry and for some moments confusion disrupted the angle. Johnson was bleeding from five wounds; his white pony, also several times wounded, became entangled in the branches of a fallen tree. But the Colonel kept his nerve and as he extricated his mount he shot down an Indian who bore the appearance of a chief. His horse retained its strength barely long enough to carry its wounded master to safety.[58]

Harrison assigned to Major Wood the command of the chase after Procter, bidding him protect the British leader from the anger of his own Indian allies. A dozen Kentuckians were already hot on the trail. Stray enemy bullets were flicking the leaves from the trees near Harrison's position and a Kentucky youngster, wounded the day before at McGregor's Creek, called out: "Did you see that, General? They have shot me again!" An officer rode up to report danger on the left. Harrison sent instructions for Shelby to bring up his reserves and bidding an infantry brigade to follow galloped toward the threatened portion of the line. But Shelby had already anticipated the order, the voice of Chief Tecumseh was no longer heard and spasmodic exchanges of fire indicated that the battle was nearly won. A breathless soldier holding an Indian scalp in his hand caught the attention of his General: "Look here, General, I've got it! My father was an old Kentucky Indian fighter and . . . he made me promise to bring the scalp of a redskin killed by myself. . . . This is for the old man. Now I want one for myself."[59] Back he raced toward the swamp. "Never did more enthusiastic valor inspire men with more heroic courage . . . no dastardly fears or hanging back, every eye beamed with the fire of free men and each officer & soldier discharged his duty to the utmost."[60]

General Procter was given no time to pick up his baggage. Making a swift dash through Moraviantown he continued for a few more miles down the road then took to the woods and discovered safety in a swamp. His pursuers raced past dozens of wagons full of army supplies, personal effects and weeping women and children but after a run of seven miles admitted themselves outdistanced. The sudden appearance of the mounted Kentuckians so alarmed the Indian squaws that they threw their children into the river rather than permit them to be butchered, as they supposed they would be, by the enemy.[61]

The Kentuckians contented themselves by taking prisoners a body of Canadian militia who guarded the town and bore back in triumph General Procter's sword, carriage, and some interesting official and private papers, including several letters from his wife "written in the handsomest writing I ever saw."[62] Most of Procter's official papers may be found in the Library of Congress and War Department archives today, Harrison mailing to Secretary Armstrong all those containing military information. Save for deep and lasting regret over the escape of the British leader the aura of glory which enveloped the army as the sun went down was undimmed. From conflicting figures one may judge the American loss to have been 25 killed and some 50 wounded; the British had suffered possibly 35 casualties, while the bodies of 33 dead warriors were counted on the field. Harrison reported a total of 601 prisoners taken during the three-day campaign. Other esteemed prizes were a number of field pieces "taken at Saratoga and York [in the Revolution] and surrendered [at Detroit] by General Hull," while the number of small arms recovered was placed at upwards of 5000.[63]

Harrison fed the British officers strips of roast meat from his own scanty mess and gave his only blanket to a wounded colonel. Ruminating upon the disgraceful flight of their General and the supposed death of Chief Tecumseh the prisoners were a subdued lot that evening. After the Kentuckians had stripped the skin from the back and thighs of a chief whom they believed to be the dead Tecumseh, two Canadian militia officers who viewed the body "there . . . identified in the mangled corpse . . . all that remained of the late powerful and intelligent chieftain."[64] Was it truly Tecumseh? When Harrison examined the swollen features next day he was unable to determine whether the body was Tecumseh's or that of a Potawatomie chief who always accompanied him on his travels.[65] A half-breed Shawnee who examined the remains could only say it was "about Tecumseh's size and some like him but . . . could not say it was truly his body."[66] An Indian interpreter with the British, wounded in the fight, informed a Kentucky officer that the body had been carried from the field, testimony which tallies with the account of Chief Black Hawk who was present:

". . . I saw Tecumseh stagger forward over a fallen tree . . . letting his rifle drop at his feet. As soon as the Indians discovered he was killed, a sudden fear came over them, and thinking the Great Spirit was angry, they fought no longer. . . . That night we returned to bury our dead, and search for the body of Tecumseh.—He was found lying where he had first fallen, a bullet had struck him above the hip, and his skull had been broken by the butt end of the gun of some soldier. . . . With the exception of these wounds his body was untouched; lying near him, however, was a large fine-looking Potawattimie who had been killed decked off in his plumes and warpaint, for he was scalped, and every particle of skin flayed from his body. Tecumseh himself had no ornaments about his person, save a British medal. During the night we buried our dead and brought off the body of Tecumseh, altho we were within sight of the fires of the American camp."[67]

The rumor that Tecumseh was dead could not be accepted as fact.

Extra guards were posted about the encampment, precautions taken against their falling asleep. The drum tattoo for reveille dispersed Kentuckians wrestling before camp-fires and the men slept on their rifles ready to repel an attack. At midnight the sentinels heard a cry: "O Lord! O Lord! Indians, Indians!" The entire camp aroused, men sprang to arms. A restless Kentuckian, far from home, was asleep and dreaming.[68]

THE HERO OF THE THAMES

THE hungry Kentuckians pounced upon the little village of Moraviantown, raiding missionary homes for stores and devouring raw vegetables in the gardens. Procter had made the town his principal headquarters during the retreat and although the Moravian missionaries protested, late in the afternoon of October 6 it was burned. The post would have afforded convenient shelter for the British and their allies during the winter.[1]

Harrison left Governor Shelby in charge of the prisoners and infantry. Taking Johnson's mounted regiment he retraced the route to Sandwich and Detroit. A day or two in the rear the foot-soldiers were making forced marches to ward off starvation. October 10, Shelby's men arrived at Sandwich in the midst of a gale which brought snow; as soon as the storm had subsided they were ferried across the river to an encampment south of Detroit.

The Kentuckians were nearly exhausted and many were ill. Protests in volume greeted an announcement that Perry's ships would not be available to take them across Lake Erie. Harrison was called upon to appeal to the troops. Again he urged that their sense of patriotism sustain them on the long march to the peninsula where their horses awaited. With the exception of Johnson's regiment which was rounding up enemy Indians the volunteers took their leave on the 13th, halting at the River Raisin to rebury the bones of their slain countrymen.[2] They had gained partial revenge.

Capture of Malden, Sandwich, and Detroit still left in British hands Fort Mackinac, commanding the strait between Lakes Huron and Michigan. Harrison planned to embark General McArthur's troops in the fleet and recapture the post. October gales delayed the embarkation, however, and two schooners bringing army baggage failed to arrive. When some of the baggage was found washed up on the shore near Malden it was feared the vessels had been lost, although as it happened the cargo had been tossed overboard to lighten the belabored craft, driven nearly as far East as Buffalo. Harrison conferred with Commodore Perry and Generals Cass and McArthur who agreed that in view of lack of supplies and equipment the season was too far advanced for a successful expedition against Mackinac. The post had no immediate strategic value, cut off as it was from the British army, yet the Americans were not to recapture it during the war.

Hungry and ill-clothed Indian families were swarming into Detroit. Harrison ordered supplies distributed. By means of a little management, he advised Secretary Armstrong, the Indian aggression could be terminated without further bloodshed.[3] He required enemy chiefs to deliver up hostages. While any white prisoners in their possession were to be surrendered to the Indian Agent at Fort Wayne. The warriors would be permitted to enter their hunting camps and remain there unmolested "provided they behave themselves peaceably."[4] When thirty-seven chiefs placed their signs upon a preliminary truce Harrison issued a proclamation calling upon "all citizens" to keep the peace and "neither to engage in nor countenance any expedition."[5] The command at Detroit was placed with General Cass, a bold and vigilant young officer and a man of Harrison's own mind in respect to fair treatment of peaceful savages. Although instructions from Armstrong were lacking Harrison determined to sail with McArthur's brigade to the Niagara frontier.

Armstrong himself was somewhere in northern New York. Early in September the Secretary had removed the War Office, incorporate in his person, to Sackett's Harbor, principal center of American shipping on Lake Ontario. Armstrong's actual purpose in leaving Washington to interfere with his generals has been a puzzle to historians but at any rate he was able to prevent any officer he personally disliked from gaining any stated objective. For a time he amused himself by issuing contradictory orders to Generals James Wilkinson and Wade Hampton who were marching and countermarching through upper New York, their assigned destination first Kingston on the St. Lawrence and then Montreal. Confusion and ill-feeling were such that neither post was in any wise threatened by the American army. Finally Hampton was moved to express his doubt that Armstrong actually intended any serious movement against Montreal.[6]

Writing Harrison from Sackett's Harbor on September 22 Armstrong had suggested that after recapturing Malden, the General could take his main force down Lake Erie to Fort George, a stroke "much more important . . . than to pursue the Indians into the woody and distant recesses."[7] This letter however never reached Harrison as the bearer was washed overboard from his ship during the late storm. October 30, after learning that Harrison had decided for himself to pursue Procter, Armstrong again wrote:

"The dispatch . . . lost in Lake Erie, suggested as an *ulterior* movement, the coming down to the Niagara & the putting yourself on the right and rear of De Rottenburg's position before Fort George while Gen¹ McClure with his brigade should approach them in front. . . . The capture of this would be a glorious finale for your campaign. . . . I beg you, General, to accept the assurances of my great respect & most cordial good wishes."[8]

On the day that this letter was written Harrison arrived at Fort George. The voyage down the lake with Commodore Perry was not uneventful. The schooner *Ariel* arrived at Erie, its home port, on the morning of October 22. Citizens swarmed to the shore as the vessel was sighted. "It was with no ordinary feelings two heroes were received. . . . The rejoicing . . . was warm and universal."[9] A Federal salute welcomed the ship's boat bringing Perry, Harrison, Adjutant General Edmund P. Gaines, and Commodore Barclay of the British fleet.

Between lines of cheering citizens Harrison and Perry assisted the wounded Barclay up a hilly street to the McConkey House. The borough council declared a grand holiday of celebration. That night the town was "brilliantly illuminated" and a torchlight procession bore transparencies emblazoned with patriotic emblems and the words, "WE HAVE MET THE ENEMY," "TENTH OF SEPTEMBER," "HARRISON—VICTORY," "FIFTH OF OCTOBER." At three-minute intervals an artillery piece was discharged, "the whole being prepared and conducted in the most perfect order," according to the local gazette.[10]

The rest of the fleet with General McArthur and 1300 men on board sailed past the harbor next day. Perry parted with Harrison at Buffalo and took the stage for his native Rhode Island. "You know what has been my opinion as to the future Commander-in-chief of the army," wrote the Commodore during his tour of triumph homeward. "Yes, my dear friend, I expect to hail you as the chief who is to redeem the honor of our arms in the North."[11] Perry's sentiment was indeed generous but events of the next few weeks were to give no furtherance to the prediction.

Harrison left General McArthur and 400 men at Buffalo. Taking 900 troops, he crossed the Niagara River to the Canadian side and marched for Fort George situated near the southern shore of Lake

Ontario. On the 30th, General George McClure and a smartly dressed regiment advanced to greet the western hero and a salute of fifteen guns welcomed his arrival. "Gen¹ Harrison's troops look much fatigued," one of the greeters denoted. "I am somewhat disappointed in his appearance. . . . He is an extremely plain looking man . . . *very ordinary clad* . . . [although] very sociable and a man in whose company we cannot but be perfectly at ease."[12]

Irrespective of the Westerner's appearance, General McClure was elated at the prospect. He had high hopes of dislodging a force of 2000 British and Indians from Burlington Heights on the opposite shore where General Procter had fled. Present forces at Fort George numbered less than 2000 effectives, however, and the terms of the New York state militia would soon expire. Inasmuch as Fort George and Fort Niagara on the American side required garrisons of several hundred men Harrison urged that fresh detachments of militia be summoned and within the next ten days 300 recruits eager to serve under the western commander showed up.

Harrison expected a start could be made by November 15 provided that adequate equipment was forthcoming. Officers and men hopefully anticipated a successful campaign and affairs were progressing quite favorably when on November 9 the General received another letter from Armstrong. Finding Harrison of the same mind as himself in respect to Fort George the itinerant Secretary, on November 3, ordered him to transport his force to Sackett's Harbor. Commodore Isaac Chauncey's fleet, Armstrong wrote, was sailing to meet him. The Secretary pointedly added another suggestion. "It is not intended by these instructions to prevent either you or General McArthur from visiting your families or from going to them, if you so desire, from Fort George."[14] Armstrong himself, after ordering General Wilkinson into winter quarters, was turning his back on the campaign and preparing to return to Washington. Any victory thereafter on the northern frontier would be wholly unauthorized.

November 14 a fleet hove in sight before Fort George. The long roll was beaten and the troops prepared to meet an attack. The ships proved to be those of Commodore Chauncey who served notice that he wished to sail at once for Sackett's Harbor. Secretary Armstrong's instructions on that point had been definite. Chauncey could neither await nor take part in the contemplated attack against Burlington. Yet Armstrong on that same day was writing President James Madison:

"Harrison has found his old enemy in a new position, at the head of Burlington Bay, and is preparing to attack. . . ."[15]

It had been the stormiest autumn in years. Commodore Chauncey was "extremely pressing" for the troops to embark. General McClure hotly protested, his troops voluble with wrath. Disappointment was the order of the day. Harrison's departure would mean not only abandonment of the expedition against Burlington but Forts George and Niagara would be left insufficiently guarded. "If not incompatible with your instructions and your better judgment," McClure remonstrated, "you will not abandon our projected expedition. . . . Such is the anxious wish of the Militia."[16] The orders I have received from the Secretary of War leaves me no alternative," replied Harrison. "Will you be so obliging at the proper time as to explain . . . to the Patriots who have left their homes with the intention of assisting me to drive the Enemy far from our borders. . . ."[17] McClure's own explanation to the public some months later was a demonstration of injured feelings and wrath: "The arrival of Chauncey's fleet at the moment when we had matured our plans of marching against the enemy threw the militia & volunteers into such a rage, that, had Armstrong appeared amongst them . . . he would have felt the force of their indignation."[18] Harrison, however, put the best possible face upon the matter by pleading that the troops were needed at Sackett's Harbor toward which British forces at Burlington were understood to be moving.

With General McArthur and 1100 troops enjoying sound health Harrison sailed up the Niagara River and into Lake Ontario on the 16th. The voyage was not favored by good weather. A biting east wind increased to gale strength, bringing a hard rain followed by snow. For two days the scattered fleet was driven backward almost to the head of the lake. Some of the ships lost masts and sails, one drifted about helplessly without a rudder. The storm-tossed crew and the troops suffered severely from icy waves and flying spray. Several men were washed overboard. But with the exception of the rudderless vessel which was driven ashore at the mouth of the Niagara the fleet arrived safely at Sackett's Harbor on the fourth day out.[19]

The voyage gave Harrison a little time for reflection. Many tasks were awaiting him in his own district. A stray letter or two from the West revealed the outposts were inadequately supplied for the winter and that some of the militia were continuing to serve without pay.[20] The Indian situation was likewise precarious. Uneasiness was felt in the outlying settlements and it was possible on the other hand that peaceful Indians in hunting camps would be attacked by the whites. At Cincinnati, meantime, Anna Harrison had been in confinement. The General had not yet learned of the arrival, on October 26, of his ninth child which was to be christened Anna Tuthill. Mails carried between Cleveland and Buffalo had been greatly delayed.[21] Incidentally the lake shore road was regarded in post-office circles as the worst in the land.[22]

At Sackett's Harbor Harrison boarded the stage for Albany where he hoped to have an interview with Secretary Armstrong. He met the Secretary for the first time at the breakfast table of Governor Daniel D. Tompkins who was also entertaining Colonel Joseph G. Swift, head of the army Engineer Corps. When the Governor jocosely remarked that John Bull was not occasioned to bring over veterans "as he would do if the war was pressed to the east," the Secretary turned the subject.[23] Following breakfast on the morning of November 27 the party took a steamboat, the *Car of Neptune,* for West Point and then embarked for New York. It was Harrison's first trip on a steamboat. The party reached the metropolis seasonably next day.[24]

New York, outstripping Philadelphia in size, was a city of 100,000 souls, "the greatest commercial emporium in the nation." Sixteen hundred houses in town extended the streets nearly two miles above the Battery. On the east side of Broadway, the leading thoroughfare, the house numbers went as high as 415. Many of the cross streets were still narrow and crooked, with paved sidewalks of brick.[25] Two theatres, the Park and the Commonwealth, were playing three evenings a week. Mayor of the city was De Witt Clinton, political ally of Armstrong.

The Clintonians were alive to the exploits of naval heroes, Federalists almost without an exception.[26] Recently the city council had passed resolutions of thanks to Commodore Perry voting him also a sword. A resolution asking recognition of Harrison's victory on the Thames failed of passage, 12 to 5. Had it not been for the protests of the republican minority there would have been no public illuminations, as in other cities, to celebrate the triumph. At a celebration tardily held on October 23 Perry's victory was again stressed and the incident brought chiding comment from a Madison organ:

"General Harrison, though not considered in New York as coming quite up to the rank of 'the Washington of the West' [currently a popular phrase west of Broadway] is, nevertheless, deemed too respectable and meritorious in his station to be passed over in total silence, as was almost the case on Saturday evening. . . . Republics should be as just as they are grateful to their servants and benefactors."[27]

A few minor honors, at least, were to befall the General. Monday evening, the 29th, Harrison and Governor Tompkins witnessed a performance of "The Virgin of the Sun," a Peruvian drama, at the Park Theatre. The house was brilliantly illuminated for the occasion, the General greeted with cheers and applause. With Secretary Armstrong, General Henry Dearborn, and Colonel Swift next day, Harrison made a tour of inspection about the forts in the district and that evening attended a special performance at the Commonwealth Theatre where a "grand transparency" depicted him receiving Indian hostages in token of surrender.[28]

The Clintonians still remaining aloof, the administration faction planned its own celebration to honor the General. On Wednesday evening, Harrison, Governor Tompkins, and General Wade Hampton, a recent arrival, sat down at a dinner at Tammany Hall. Judge Brockholst Livingston, brother of Judge Symmes' wife, was prominent in the gathering and a score of army and navy officers were seated. A long series of set toasts eulogized the nation, its government and its foremost officials. The guest of honor was accorded "The plaudits of a grateful people—the patriot hero's best reward. (9 cheers, Harrison's March)," and after the General had retired the company drank to "The deliverer of our western frontier. (17 Cheers)."[29] With Tompkins and Hampton, two agreeable companions, Harrison again went to the theatre to witness a comedy followed by Shakespeare's "Macbeth."

While Secretary Armstrong still lingered in New York, Harrison continued on to Washington stopping for several days in Philadelphia where Republican sentiment was undimmed. For a Thames victory celebration held on October 22 one wealthy individual spent $1500 in illuminating his house and for the "transparent paintings prepared for the occasion."[30]

At a public dinner held in his honor Harrison touched upon an idea which Secretary Armstrong had recently broached, conscription, in short. Anathema to Republicans, conscription clearly stemmed from Federalism. "With much impressiveness of manner," the General asked leave to offer a volunteer toast and "briefly to state the motive which prompts me." The company was all ears as the General continued:

"Believing as I do that a sentiment is gaining ground unfriendly to republicanism and injurious to the nation . . . I will give you—

"THE MILITIA OF THE UNITED STATES. They possess the Roman spirit and when our Government shall think proper to give them that organization and discipline of which they are susceptible they will perform deeds that will emulate those of legions led by Marcellus and Scipio."[31]

After having his portrait painted, Harrison hurried on to Washington, declining an invitation to a public dinner at Baltimore. Congress was now in session. Among interesting developments forecast was the appointment of a Lieutenant General of the army, a post to which Harrison might well aspire if the tone of certain public and private remarks was any indication. A friendly letter from General Joseph Desha, Congressman from Kentucky, declared that "if you, my dear sir," and the Kentucky volunteers, had served in the place of Wilkinson, Hampton and their armies, then Montreal, by this time, "would have been ours."[32] Desha had fought on the Thames.

Trailing Harrison into Washington and running the rounds of the press was an editorial paragraph from a New York paper:

"A legion of 5000 mounted riflemen, commanded by such an officer as general Harrison, would be a most formidable corps for offensive operations against Canada, and could be raised in a much shorter period of time than any other equally effective force."[33]

The Richmond *Compiler* sustained prevailing republican sentiment in this wise:

"GENERAL HARRISON. This estimable officer is at Washington reaping the rewards of his patriotic zeal & military achievements. His character is now the object of general attention and the point on which consolation seems to rest. His cautious & cool deliberate valor inspire universal confidence and point him out to be the *safe* as well as able conductor of our armies. . . . The public opinion is very much in his favor and . . . will designate him for the *conqueror of Canada.*"[34]

General Harrison was hailed in the halls of Congress and at the President's House according to a correspondent of the *Freeman's Journal* of Philadelphia:

"General Harrison made his appearance at the drawing room last night. His deportment was very correct. He is apparently idolized by the war-hawks here. . . . I foresee that he is destined to be the commander-in-chief of our armies in Canada."[35]

Secretary Armstrong and Editor William Duane of the Philadelphia *Aurora* would get around to this in time. A great lack of optimism concerning Harrison's chances was felt in the West. A disgusted young ensign with the Northwestern Army at Lower Sandusky expressed the view that no western general would be allowed to remain in the forefront. "We understand the whole matter out here. The people at Washington have got scared at Harrison's victories. They are afraid a few more might make him President! Therefore they have determined to put him out of the way. Mark my words: You will not see them give Harrison another command in the field during this war. They will simply leave him here where he can gain no more victories for the reason that there are no enemies left to whip. So far as the folks at Washington are concerned . . . this struggle from the start has been about three parts politics to one part war."[36] Ensign David Buell had witnessed the recent disappointment at Fort George on the Niagara frontier.

Harrison lingered at Washington six days, seven days, and then addressed a letter to Secretary Armstrong, still absent. President Madison, he wrote, was apprehensive that the enemy would attempt to regain Detroit and Malden during the winter. Since General Cass had been called east to attend a court-martial for General William Hull could Benjamin Howard of St. Louis be spared to take his place? Immediate attention should be given to a suggestion of the Secretary's that the tribes recently hostile be recruited in force to fight the British. The chiefs were desirous of learning whether the existing land boundaries were to continue, Harrison went on; the Westerners in Congress as well as the President were in general agreement with his view that the Indians should be left in possesion of their lands. Would the Secretary give particular directions as to the number of frontier outposts to be retained? "Upon the subject of Indian affairs I should be glad to receive your directions in detail," Harrison concluded. "Permit me to request that your answer to this letter may be immediately forwarded to Cincinnati to meet me upon my arrival there."[37]

With Aides Todd, O'Fallon, and Major John Chambers, Harrison took the western Maryland stage on December 23, embarked at Pittsburgh on New Year's Day and reached Cincinnati on January 9, 1814. A citizens' committee awaited him with an invitation to a public dinner but as the General's father-in-law, Judge Symmes, was suffering from cancer, his end not far off, Harrison declined.[38]

Symmes, one-time proprietor of all the Miami country, was now living at the General's rented home in Cincinnati, a victim of circumstances as well as disease. Possibly his greatest disappointment lay in the development of Cincinnati as the Queen City of the West rather than the settlement he had founded at North Bend. The site of Cincinnati had been bartered for seven land warrants valued at $35 but when an army officer stationed at North Bend pursued the wife of a settler who moved a few miles up the river, Fort Washington was erected near the beloved one's cabin and here a new settlement flourished.[39]

Symmes had never been popular in the Northwest. In 1811 a personal enemy set fire to his North Bend mansion; all his precious papers and account books were lost and the victim accounted as ruined. Collections of monies due, which usually had been poor, soon ceased altogether.

The end of Judge Symmes, an embittered old man, came on February 26, 1814. The funeral was held at Harrison's home, the body taken by flatboat to North Bend and interred on high ground overlooking the river.[40]

HARRISON RESIGNS

EDITORIAL rejoinders to the acclaim for Harrison began to appear in the Philadelphia *Aurora* shortly after Secretary Armstrong's passage through that city. Harrison had "sacrificed" General Winchester, had blundered in his orders to Croghan, and had failed to catch General Procter. A single concession was made. "Bravery, that ordinary quality of American character, cannot be denied him." Otherwise, the argument went on, he was no competent general.[1]

Armstrong arrived in Washington a day or two after Harrison had left. He brought with him his idea of conscription and a few other plans. Secretary of State James Monroe, Armstrong's chief antagonist in the Cabinet, promptly warned Madison that the War Secretary was urging congressmen to embrace the conscription idea without any reference to the President's wishes. On the score of army promotion, declared Monroe, Armstrong was determining the future lot of officers in relation to his own personal ambition and prospects. Armstrong had been refurbishing his political machine in New York, handing out promises of advancement, and teaching "young men of talents . . . to look to him . . . for preferment."[2]

Monroe discountenanced a plan on foot to censure Armstrong in Congress as any such move would further embarrass the administration. But since the northern campaign had been a total failure under Armstrong's own eye, Monroe suggested that the President get rid of the Secretary altogether. Madison was prone to move slowly, however, and he had no desire to risk another change now. Secure in his post, the self-assured Armstrong held to a course which involved no shilly-shallying. In conferences with Federalist senators the issues were lumped together under "legislative matters" and co-operation "ag* Virginia." Colonel Swift, who represented the Secretary's views to Senator Jeremiah Mason of New Hampshire, declared he was "to have his just weight in the Cabinet or throw up his office." Senator Rufus King of New York was also approached. It was agreed that the Virginia dynasty should be broken and a Northerner elected the next President.[3] The progress of the war was becoming wholly subordinate to politics.

The subject of army promotions naturally brought out sectionalist views. Armstrong had two important posts to fill in New York as General James Wilkinson was skidding into a court-martial and Wade Hampton wished to resign. Nomination of a Commander-in-Chief or a Lieutenant General was in order.

The process of elimination occupied the Secretary for some days. Criticism was lodged against Harrison on the ground that he had wasted the public funds. And a curious tale was circulated by Congressman Joseph Desha who swerved from the friendly view expressed in his recent letter to Harrison. "Had not Governor Shelby persisted in pursuing Procter," the story went, "General Harrison would have gathered no laurels."[4] Just what was Desha's idea now that Harrison had left Washington and Armstrong arrived?

Two years later, when the "calumny" was hauled out into the daylight, Governor Shelby declared it was Harrison's "determination" and "exertions" which prevailed,[5] but the disparagement served its particular purpose. After Generals Hampton, Wilkinson, Harrison, and Henry Dearborn, an admitted incompetent, had been passed over, no active veteran remained for the post of Commander-in-Chief. Armstrong earmarked for promotion two young brigadiers from the East, George Izard and Jacob Brown, promising army leaders still under forty. Harrison was the senior of both in point of service and grade for Brown's commission as brigadier had been issued as recently as July, 1813, Izard's in March. On January 21, 1814, Izard was nominated a major general to succeed Wade Hampton while Brown replaced James Wilkinson in February.[6] Nothing was done concerning a Commander-in-Chief, but here at least were two new eligibles and it was Brown who ultimately was favored.

Meantime Armstrong had neglected to reinforce the posts on the Niagara frontier. The British attack, he expected, was to be made against Sackett's Harbor, his stated reason for ordering Harrison there. But following his withdrawal of Harrison's forces from the vicinity of Forts George and Niagara, an enlightened enemy swept down upon these outposts to sack and burn the neighboring villages of Lewiston, Buffalo, and Black Rock.

The calculated movements of army chess pieces at Washington gave Harrison no hint as to what he might expect in the way of an active command. At headquarters at Cincinnati the General was wrestling with the renewed problem of army supply, as dutiful and humane a task as one could imagine when an aggravated militia general confessed himself ready "to hang half the quartermasters and all the contractors, if I was to remain in service much longer."[7] While the victory on the Thames had lightened the burden of frontier defense, there was need to exercise vigilance. Still tied up at Put-in-Bay were two British vessels which an alert enemy might strive to capture. A British detachment was reported recruiting Indian forces at Delaware on the Thames River. Harrison ordered detachments of regulars northward from the interior posts to reinforce Detroit and Sandwich. A thousand Ohio militia were called out to replace deminishing forces at Forts Stephenson and Meigs.

General Howard of St. Louis, Armstrong wrote, would be instructed to receive Harrison's orders; after reporting at Cincinnati he was to "lose no time in pressing forward" to Detroit.[8] Pending other assignments in rank, this was favorable news. A competent handling of affairs at Detroit would leave Harrison free for transfer back to the northeastern frontier. Newspaper opinion in the West continued to urge that he receive the command.[9] General McArthur, detailed at Albany for the pending court-martial of William Hull, forwarded another view of the situation: "You, Sir, stand the highest with the militia of this state of any general in the service . . . and I think their extreme solicitude may be the means of calling you to this frontier."[10] Shortly after promoting Izard, however, Armstrong quietly ordered General Howard to suspend his march to Cincinnati and Detroit. Merely a copy of the order was sent Harrison.

Unaware of a previous understanding between Armstrong and Howard that the latter was to receive orders direct from the War Office and not from the Commanding Officer of the Eighth Military District, Harrison based his complaint upon tangible ground. "I think, Sir, I have a right to complain of that order, both as to its matter and manner. However important I might have deemed the service of Gen¹ Howard upon the frontier, an order from you directing me to permit him to remain . . . would have been instantly obeyed . . . [and] would have been more consonant to . . . rules of Military Etiquette. . . . Apart from considerations of duty to my country, I have no earthly inducement to remain in the army and if the prerogatives of my rank and situation . . . be taken from me . . . I should much rather . . . retire to private life."[11]

Harrison's closing sentiment gave the Secretary his cue. Armstrong was perfectly willing that the General retire. Presently he began making moves which were calculated to aggravate. Although his initial excuse for the countermand to Howard was that the latter's health was bad, he now replied by declaring that officer had been selected to fill a vacancy at New Orleans and any delay in the transmission of the order would have been hazardous.[12] But the New Orleans climate, as every one knew, was notoriously fatal to army men; moreover an order to any officer stationed west of Cincinnati would have been delayed little if transmitted through Harrison's hands. General Howard, it may be added, was to remain at St. Louis.

The Secretary was not at loss for means of further interference. Just as Harrison's orders transferring troops to the North went out, Armstrong began to order western officers to take up recruiting service at various points. Men who received conflicting commands from Washington and Cincinnati appealed to Harrison, to their senator and to high heaven for decision as to what should be done.[13] While admitting himself "embarrassed," Harrison discovered himself to be bound by a new set of rules for army recruiting forwarded from Washington on February 16. According to these blanket instructions, all officers "not otherwise employed under special orders" were to report to the recruiting rendezvous of their respective regiments in accordance with a specified list.[14] Harrison ironed out the difficulty by deferring to Armstrong. Officers ordered north returned to take up recruiting duties.

The familiar routine of frontier service went on. Harrison met Tarhe, Blackhoof and other friendly chiefs at Dayton and urged that they summon their followers for a grand council at Greenville in June. Militia called out to reinforce Lower Sandusky and other exterior posts were held up by unseasonable rains, high water and bad roads. A scouting detachment of American regulars scored brilliantly over a company of Royal Scots and some Canadian militia near Delaware on the Thames.[15] Lieutenant Colonel George Croghan received the command at Detroit and Colonel John B. Campbell took over at Put-in-Bay. Citizens of Fleming County, Kentucky, sent their congressman an ardent disclaimer of a statement reported made at Washington to the effect "that 'Gen¹ Harrison is at present so unpopular in the Western Country that the people will not again enter the public service under his command.' " Not so, read the memorial, adding three hundred or more words of acclaim—"Resolved that it is our opinion and belief that Gen¹ Harrison was never more popular among the Western people than he is at this time . . . our fellow Citizens, if again called . . . will serve under him as cheerfully as . . . heretofore . . . [tell the President]."[16]

"I am not yet informed what is to be my destination," Harrison wrote Governor Shelby on March 20, 1814. "I believe the Sec^y of War is not my friend."[17] Armstrong, in fact, had recently indicated that the transfer of General McArthur to the Ohio frontier might soon be expected.[18] McArthur still remained at Albany for the court-martial of Hull. Charges advanced by army contractor Benjamin G. Orr were considered as one means to get rid of Harrison. Orr, a Washington politician and merchant, stated formally that Harrison's unbounded "interference" in the purchase and distribution of army supplies tended to "jeopardize the public interest" and went on to show why. The firm of Orr & Greeley, appointed by Armstrong to supply the Northwestern Army, was calculated to render recourse to special commissaries unnecessary yet Harrison had continued to employ special purchasing agents from time to time, particularly since his return from the East. Orr's complaint took the form of a double-barrelled attack against Harrison and John H. Piatt, a wealthy merchant of Cincinnati, whose charges for army supplies had been represented as exorbitant.[19]

The gossip concerning Piatt had arisen before. Flour supplied the Northwestern Army had not cost $50 to $60 a barrel, Piatt advised a Washington newspaper during the previous November. His charges had been $6 a barrel at Cincinnati, $10.50 at St. Marys, $14 at Fort Defiance, and $15 at Fort Meigs. Hogs averaging 170 pounds each had been delivered at St. Marys for $4 per hundred-weight.[20] Aware of the criticism lodged against Piatt, Harrison wrote an open letter defending him from charges of exorbitance and mismanagement,[21] but before the General's testimony reached Washington a special committee of inquiry named by the House reported its findings on April 9.

As far as one can ascertain, the committee considered only evidence submitted by Armstrong and Orr. Certainly Harrison was unaware of the action, and the report, which was laid on the table, was not generally circulated. "Sundry instances in which general officers have interfered with contracts for supplying the army, in a manner and to an extent, highly prejudicial to the public interest and injurious to the rights of individuals," were the basis for an unfavorable report in which no specific "instances" and no names were mentioned.[22] The inference was that certain officers had shown special interest and favoritism in respect to army commissaries and had profited through their transactions. Without reference to the one-sided investigation, Armstrong forwarded to Harrison a blunt order requiring him to submit a full accounting of all purchases by commissaries. Further employment of special commissaries was forbidden.[23]

If the Secretary of War was attempting to force General Harrison out of the service he was perhaps now in a position to choose between securing his dismissal or his voluntary resignation. Harrison's hint that any further orders sent over his head would cause him to resign probably sufficed for the Secretary. On April 25 he sent an order directly to Major A. H. Holmes at Detroit bidding him lead an infantry force against Mackinac in co-operation with a fleet commanded by Captain Arthur Sinclair.[24] The fleet was not ready, however, and Armstrong's order backfired when Colonel Croghan, commanding at Detroit, declined to allow the Major to leave. Croghan dispatched an unreserved remonstrance to Captain Sinclair and sent a copy, with some further explanation, to Harrison. "Major Holmes it is true," blazed the hero of Sandusky, "has been notified . . . that he is selected to command the land troops on the expedition . . . yet this notification *to the Maj*[r] is by no means an *order* to me nor can I own it in itself sufficient to justify me in weakening the present *reduced* strength of my Command." And in explanation to Harrison, whose position he well understood: "The Sec[y] of War, nor no other authority, is justified (aggreably to *strict* Military Etiquette) in thus interfering with the *internal* Police of an Officer comd[g] a District. At least such is the principle *I* contend for. . . . "[25]

Harrison, meantime, was contending for the same principle in his own way. May 9, when a mere copy of the order to Holmes reached the Commanding Officer of the District, Assistant Inspector General Charles S. Todd indicated forebodings to Governor Shelby. "Such frequent interferences . . . by the Secretary" now led to the belief that the General would remain active little longer. Todd urged that the Governor write at once to President Madison lest "the services of the only *Regular* General, who has done anything, will be lost." This request was being made without Harrison's knowledge, Todd added, "and no doubt would be without his consent—but Sir, I fear the result of the present state of things."[26]

Shelby had little time to act. Harrison's resignation, dated May 11, went out by the next post. Inasmuch as he had already made himself clear on the subject of War Office orders to subordinates, the General confined himself to another issue currently in the wind:

"Cincinnati, 11th May, 1814.
"Sir: I have the honour through you to request the President to

accept my resignation of the appointment of Major General in the army. . . .

"Lest the public service should suffer before a Successor can be nominated, I shall continue to act untill the 31st inst. by which time I hope to be relieved.

"Having some reasons to believe that the most malicious insinuations had been made against me at Washington, it was my intention to have requested an Enquiry into my conduct from the commencement of my command. Further reflection has, however, determined me to decline the application because from the proud consciousness I have palpably done my duty, I can not believe that it is necessary either for the satisfaction of the government or the people that I should pay so much respect to the suggestions of Malice & Envy. It is necessary however that I should assure you, Sir, that I subscribe implicitly to the opinion that military officers are responsible for their conduct and amenable to the decision of a Court Martial after they have left the Service for any improper act committed in it.

"The principle was established in England in the case of Lord George Sackville, after the Battle of Minden. It was known and recognized by the ancient Republics and I think particularly applicable to a Government like ours. I therefore pledge myself to answer before a court martial at any future period to any charge that may be brought against me.

"I have the Honour to
"be Very Respectfully
"Sir Yr Humble Sevt.
"William Henry Harrison."[27]

"The Hon. J. Armstrong, &c."

A letter to President Madison who was visiting his Virginia home, Montpellier, was dispatched side by side with Armstrong's. In it Harrison reasserted his belief in this "just and necessary" war. "The crisis requires the sacrifice of every private consideration, which could stand in opposition to the public good." Nevertheless, the General was convinced that his retirement was "as compatible with the claims of patriotism, as . . . with . . . a proper regard for my own feelings and honour." He could render the government no further important service in his present position, be it understood.[28]

Of interest in this connection, also, is the letter which Governor Shelby wrote Madison, at the suggestion of Colonel Todd. Shelby, veteran of the field and of councils, was of the belief that united effort only would win the war. A non-politician, the Kentucky Governor avowed an interest in the "prosperity" of the country, not an intention to eulogize a general of "conspicuous" merits. Wrote Shelby to Madison, May 15, 1814:

". . . Having served a campaign with general Harrison, by which I have been enabled to form some opinion of his military talents, and capacity to command, I feel no hesitation to declare to you, that I believe him to be one of the first military characters I ever knew; and, in addition to this, he is capable of making greater personal exertions than any officer with whom I have ever served. I doubt not . . . that the command of the Northwestern army . . . has been one of the most arduous and difficult tasks ever assigned to any officer in the United States yet he surmounted all.

"Impressed with the conviction, that general Harrison is fully adequate to the command of the northern army, should a change take place in that division, I have ventured thus freely to state my opinion of him, that he is a consummate general, and would fill that station with ability and honor; . . . if, on the other hand any arrangement should take place . . . which may produce the resignation of general Harrison, it will be a misfortune which our country will have cause to lament. . . ."[29]

This letter was forwarded to the President at Montpellier. Had it been more promptly received, its unreserved sentiment would have sufficed to retain Harrison in service, Madison later conceded. But inasmuch as Armstrong acted promptly to accept the resignation, a decision which actually lay with the President, Shelby's considered opinion went for naught. Armstrong clinched the matter by appointing Andrew Jackson of Tennessee to the existing vacancy. Respecting this latter move another irregularity was noted, and later made much of, by Secretary of State Monroe. Notified by Armstrong under date of May 20 that Harrison's resignation had been received at Washington, Madison had recommended that a Major General's commission by brevet, which had been pending for Jackson, he held in abeyance "till I see you . . . two or three days after the arrival of this." But Armstrong did not choose to wait. May 28, two days before Madison's return to Washington, the Secretary notified Jackson of the existing vacancy "which I hasten to fill in with your name." Whether or not Jackson knew that Armstrong wished to appear as the official source of favor, he correctly replied by acknowledging the receipt of the new commission as coming from the President, not the bureaucratic head.[30]

Another sequel to the affair plainly showed Armstrong's hand.

Colonel Croghan's hot letter to Captain Sinclair of the Navy, complaining of the order to Holmes, ran the course of official channels until it reached Madison and then Armstrong who sarcastically counter-attacked. Were War Department commands to be sent every colonel in the army before their co-operation could be obtained? "The order," the Secretary quibbled, "was sent to General *Harrison.*"[31]

Any inquiry from Washington concerning the status of the Indian tribes was sure to receive fulsome responses from Harrison's pen. Two letters penned shortly before the occasion of his resignation provide rich source material for historians. Pending was the summer council at Greenville. Whether or not the Indians could be induced to cede lands, a point suggested by western congressmen, was what the War Department required to know. Stimulated by pressure from their home districts, representatives from Ohio suggested the removal of the friendly tribes to a portion of the Illinois country which had been ceded by the Saks and Foxes in 1804.[32] It was to be a sort of exchange of Indian lands.

In view of the fact that present boundaries had been guaranteed the Ohio tribes in return for their war service, Harrison could provide no encouragement on this score for the present. If more Indian territory was to be gained in the future, the way could be cleared by discouraging any attempt, such as that of Tecumseh's, to unite every tribe and hold fast to every acre in common. It would be useless to discourage the progress of settlers. A rushing Land Office business at Cincinnati provided an argument for "further extinguishment of Title . . . at no distant day." Harrison's land treaties of 1803–09, in respect to monies brought in, were helping to win the war. "The land office at this place is doing more business . . . than it ever has done before. In one day of this week they received $3,000. The tract . . . of 50 miles by 12 [ceded at Fort Wayne] is nearly all sold and has already paid into the Treasury at least $200,000."[33]

But to show further the impracticability of attempting to remove Indians living east of the Wabash to the Illinois River, Harrison followed up his preliminary remarks with a long dissertation on the status of the surviving Northwest tribes and a history of their movements and possessions of land since the Revolutionary War. Tribal claims to land had been definitely fixed by treaty and existing jealousy of prerogative would allow no deviation. There was, however, one practical means of removal: permit the tribesmen to resume their own mode of warfare among themselves. Harrison did not agree with Jefferson's doctrine in keeping the tribesmen pacific. "But for the humane policy . . . pursued by our government the Delawares, Kickapoos and Shawanoese would long since have been out of the way."[34] In other words, if the tribesmen were allowed to hunt and to fight according to custom a sufficient outlet for white immigration would be the natural result.

President Madison reasserted his faith in the General by appointing him a commissioner to treat with the tribesmen at Greenville. Shelby and Colonel Richard M. Johnson of Kentucky also were named as commissioners but when they declined this somewhat disagreeable parliamentary duty General Cass, recently appointed Governor of Michigan Territory, was obtained. Armstrong's instructions to Harrison stipulated a treaty of peace and the further allegiance of all the western tribes in the war plus a cession of lands in Ohio. But President Madison, who read Armstrong's letter before it was sent, caused a postscript to be added which sustained Harrison's view concerning any immediate cession. The stipulation of Indian alliance in the war was then modified to be viewed as an obligation of assistance in effect, "if so required."[35]

The usual difficulties in assembling the tribesmen were encountered. The Indians were never known to be hurried. Toward the last of June, Harrison received word from Indian Agent John Johnston that delegations from five tribes had arrived at Greenville.[36] Entering the encampment on July 3, Harrison was pursued into the council house by several hundred tribesmen who exchanged felicitations with their white father. "Many of the chiefs," wrote Colonel James Dill, secretary of the council, "delivered . . . [their sentiments] with great cordiality and friendship."[37] Harrison ordered the council house moved about thirty-five feet onto historic ground—the exact site of General Wayne's councils with the tribesmen at Greenville in 1795. The structure was a temporary bark-roofed affair, open at the sides for purposes of ventilation and egress.

Fitting ceremonies hailed the Fourth of July. On the sixth arrived General Cass, then the Shawnee delegation entered and saluted officials and troops. Harrison visited the Indian encampments and greeted many chiefs and warriors by name. He was informed that some of the Indians had brought up their rifles to shoot him during the war but had refrained from pulling the trigger.[38] On Friday, July 8, the council assembled. Some 4000 Indian men, women and children from eight tribes were present. The warriors formed a great circle as Harrison lighted the peace pipe and passed it about. His commission was then read and explained. A special message from President Madison acknowledged the faithful war services of the Ohio

Wyandots, Senecas, Delawares and Shawnees. Four large silver pipes, "elegantly ornamented," were held up for the tribesmen to admire; Harrison impressively explained the devices thereon and presented these peace-time trophies to the four leading chiefs.

The council fire thus lighted, the commissioner made his opening address. Figures of speech and hyperbole were the natural embellishments of council proceedings. Just as in the other world evil spirits were working to counteract the good, Harrison explained, so on this earth a nation was "sowing dissensions and kindling war and discord." But here on that venerated spot where the original chain of friendship had been woven, the broken links were to be rejoined as new. Harrison reviewed the history of events leading up to Tecumseh's confederacy. The Treaty of Fort Wayne was defended as an open and just dealing; the bloody climax of the Tippecanoe campaign after a peace council had been scorned, was detailed as provoked. "The Great Spirit, who always punishes perfidy, specially interposed in our favor." A great battle had been won. Our next enemy—the British.

"My children, the Seventeen Fires love peace, but they are not afraid of war. Look . . . the bird . . . chosen as their emblem . . . holds in his right talon an olive branch, in his left a bunch of arrows."

The Seventeen Fires, though usually peaceable, were able and willing to fight. And while President Madison had warned the Indians to remain aloof from the quarrel Great Britain had adopted the opposite course. At last, when it was discovered that the warriors were determined to fight on one side or the other, those who had been solicitous to join the American army were received into the ranks. Harrison continued:

"There are many of you present, my children, who recollect me . . . [as] a boy sitting on this spot, alongside of General Wayne; most of you know me, however, only as Governor of the Indiana Territory; and if, in all my transactions . . . you can say I have ever deceived you, or told you a falsehood, come now forward and boldly declare it; it shall be put on this paper . . ."[39]

The object of the council was to bury the hatchet of those tribes who had been fighting for the British, Harrison reiterated. A peace treaty, however, was conditional upon receiving the tribal aid in further conducting the war. Great Britain would never conquer the Seventeen Fires.

A recital of grievances was solicited from the dissenting chiefs next day. When the claim was made that Harrison, as well as the

British, had deceived them the General inquired when and how so and the charge was withdrawn as erroneous. Charley, a Miami spokesman and commissioned British officer, pictured the tribal dilemma. The influence of the Munsees, ancient British allies, had swayed "our young men . . . we were no longer at liberty to choose . . . the Great Author of Nature had placed us in this situation, and not we ourselves." Nothing was said of the influence of Tecumseh. Charley added that the Americans had drawn the first blood, a charge quickly refuted by John Johnston whose brother had been slain when enemy savages lay siege to Fort Wayne. Johnston identified as Miamis certain chiefs and warriors who had conducted the siege. What "astonishment" had been his, Harrison now declared, at finding "my own children, the Miamis," among the besiegers of that same outpost from which they had drawn their supplies for years. Governor Cass interposed, stressing Indian partiality for the British. Last fall the Miamis had appeared at Detroit "in a deplorable situation . . . [yet] the Seventeen Fires had generously taken them by the hand and relieved their wants." It was not the Seventeen Fires which had "used deception."[40]

Harrison encouraged free discussion among the tribesmen but as the days of palaver went by it was clear that following Charley's speech nothing more, unless repetitious, could be said in rebuttal. Five Medals, a Potawatomie, was the first to declare he would take hold of the American war hatchet. "I speak plain . . . hide nothing." A chief of the enemy Wyandot faction made his excuses. His warriors, he pleaded, had been forced to join the British against their will. He offered a string of wampum in atonement. On the eighth day of the council Tarhe, the Crane, held up two shining gold medals, gifts from the British. "I will now cut . . . [them] to pieces," he said striking them with a large knife. His weather-beaten features indicated "every mark of contempt" for the medals as he surrendered them to Harrison and Cass. A medal bearing the American coat of arms was conspicuous on Tarhe's breast. Peccon of the Miamis and Lapoussier, the Wea chief, came forward next to declare their allegiance. Two Ottawas, also a Kickapoo, a former neighbor, spoke. "Father Harrison listen . . . I often thought of the words you had spoken to me at Vincennes but now it was too late. . . . I salute you all and . . . bow with reverence to the Great Spirit."

The great war belt, prepared with much care, was presented to the principal chiefs of each tribe who sang their war songs in turn and flourished the tomahawk menacingly. Only Charley and one other Miami chief, with a few followers, stood aloof from the ceremony.

The Indians asked and received rations of whiskey "to whet their hatchets." After a two-day recess the council house was cleared and a war-post erected. The painted warriors bellowed and whooped in a great war dance and flourished their tomahawks and scalping knives within an inch or two of the spectators. Next day the Crane invited the commissioners to attend a "religious dance" held by the Wyandots.[41] Such were scenes which took place in western Ohio a century and a quarter ago from this writing.

July 22 the treaty was drawn up and submitted. Sworn interpreters explained it sentence by sentence. By its terms Indian neutrality was outlawed, the protection of the United States acknowledged, existing boundary lines confirmed.[42] The warriors were to fight with the American army if and when called for, a promise later discovered to be of no consequence. After 112 chiefs and headmen had placed their signs on the document Harrison turned homeward.

Once again the pulse of war was renewed in the West as post-riders galloped through the towns with news of the sacking of Washington. August 24 a British army had dispersed ineffectively led American forces at Bladensburg, seven miles away on the Baltimore road. The presence on the battlefield of President Madison, Secretary of State James Monroe, Secretary of War John Armstrong, and Major General William H. Winder did little to mitigate the fact that the American army had no leader. Next day the enemy entered a defenseless city and burned the President's House and the Capitol. The news of war which reached Cincinnati two weeks later created widespread excitement. Harrison addressed letters to the Governors of Ohio and Kentucky suggesting "the propriety" of sending a mounted volunteer force to aid the stricken seaboard; a few mounted detachments had been set in motion when word came that the British had been repulsed before Baltimore.[43] The resignation of Secretary of War Armstrong, who had been publicly denounced as he undertook to command certain outspoken Baltimore militia, was the ripe fruit of the thorns.

HARRISON ASKS CONGRESS TO JUDGE

Since Harrison had shared in none of the war profits which made many Westerners rich he was relatively poorer in 1814 than when he built Grouseland for a family of five at Vincennes. In 1814 Harrison had a family of ten children, including the daughter of Thomas Randolph, victim of an Indian bullet at Tippecanoe, and he was helping Captain Spier Spencer's son James through West Point. Harrison's army pay of $2400 a year had not sufficed to pay ordinary expenses during the war nor had it stayed the necessity of recourse to loans.[1] In stocking a large farm at North Bend, as a matter of fact, Harrison found it necessary to borrow additional funds. Judge Symmes had bequeathed him most of the land.

To build a brick mansion then befitted neither the chosen situation nor the condition of the retired General's purse. Sixteen miles down the Ohio River from Cincinnati stood the log cabin which Harrison had purchased in 1796 from Judge Symmes. Interesting construction operations centered about this old cabin, the original home of Lieutenant Harrison and his bride.

Externally the logs were covered with clapboards, within by wainscoting, and two spacious wings were added on either side. A wide ell which ran back from the center made the whole a commodious dwelling of sixteen rooms. The original log cabin became a large living room and adjoining it in the west wing was a dining room of unusual size.[2] Within a short time the General's home, the "Log Cabin," became a famed rendezvous for "emigrants, tourists, travelers, and gentlemen from the east, many of whom came regularly consigned."[3] It was added that 365 hams and other considerable portions of farm produce were consumed yearly at Harrison's table.

Throughout most of his life the General lived by a river. The mansion at North Bend, facing south, stood about 300 yards back of the Ohio. A spring arising in the hill above watered an extensive lawn; eastward were grass-covered knolls and a deep valley. The grounds were shaded by locust, catalpa and evergreen trees and a formal garden of fruits and flowers was planted.[4] Harrison's 3000 acres covered several miles of undulating country back of the river running

westerly to the fertile delta, "Point Farm," formed by the juncture
of the Great Miami with the Ohio. Timothy Flint, itinerant Con-
gregationalist missionary and an occasional lodger at the North Bend
home, has left his impressions concerning the setting and the man:

"Of his urbanity and general hospitality and kindness, I entertain
the most grateful recollections. I could desire no attentions, no facilities for discharging my duty, which he did not constantly proffer
me. His house was opened for public worship. He kept an open table,
to which every visitor was welcomed. The table was loaded with
abundance, and with substantial good cheer, especially with the different kinds of game. In these respects his house strongly reminded
me of the pictures, which my reading had presented me, of old English hospitality. He is a small, and rather sallow-looking man, who
does not exactly meet the associations that connect themselves with
the name of general. But he grows upon the eye, and upon more intimate acquaintance. There is something imposing in the dignified
simplicity of his manners. In the utter want of any show, and in-
signia, and trappings, there is something which finely comports with
the severe plainness of republicanism. On a fine farm, in the midst
of the woods, his house was open to all the neighbours, who entered
without ceremony, and were admitted to assume a footing of entire
equality. His eye is brilliant. There is a great deal of ardour and
vivacity in his manner. He has a copious fund of that eloquence
which is fitted for the camp and for gaining partisans. As a commander, you know in what different lights he has been viewed. Having no capacity to form an adequate judgment upon this point, I can
only say that my impression was, that his merits in this respect had
not been sufficiently appreciated."[5]

During frequent visits to Cincinnati, Harrison made his headquarters with his old friend, General James Findlay, an honest warm-
hearted pioneer who had become rich. A fairly large interest in the
capital resources of the country assured Harrison membership on the
Miami Exporting Company Board of Trustees and he had sold land
jointly held with Findlay and Judge Jacob Burnet to purchase $5000
worth of stock in the company, a banking as well as an exporting
house.[6] This little hegemony of financiers and producers linked the
interest of the merchant and farmer by shipping flour, pork and
whiskey to New Orleans. Community growth during the war years
had been rapid and the flatboat business out of Cincinnati became
truly enormous by 1817.[7] The future, in fact, was most promising.

The last of a fourteen-year series of Indian councils interrupted

Harrison's farm work at North Bend. Although the British successfully defended Fort Mackinac they made no decided effort to regain control of the West. The war in Upper Canada closed auspiciously in November, 1814, when General McArthur with a force of 800, including seventy-odd Indians, skirmished his way from Sandwich almost as far east as Lake Ontario, with a total loss of only one man killed and six wounded.[8] Outbreaks which followed ratification of the peace treaty of Ghent were generally the work of the whites. The son of a friendly Ottawa chief and his squaw were reported slain near Detroit; another Indian, Popping Dick, was shot at Vincennes.[9] "Several Delawares, Miamis & Wyandots," recorded Harrison, who kept account of these matters, "have been murdered in the same way." Writing Secretary of War Dallas to acknowledge a new appointment as peace treaty commissioner, Harrison reminded official Washington that just as long as the memory of injuries was kept fresh among the Indians attempts to conciliate them would be quite in vain. Still the western settler and his congressman wished to expand the frontier.

If new land must be attained for the settlers there were two courses to choose from in respect to Indian relations, Harrison notified Secretary Dallas:

"We must fall upon them & murder them all or we must still pursue the course which has hitherto been followed so successfully, viz, that of obtaining their Confidence & Attachment by treating them with Justice and Humanity and convincing them that their only resource against want and misery is in the annuities they receive from us. A few violent and unprincipled men upon the frontiers and some misinformed ones in the interior are very solicitous to adopt the former of these plans. . . . It cannot but happen that the Indains are often in the wrong, but . . . they are generally misrepresented and a spirit of hostility kept up against them."[10]

His good offices were desired, nevertheless, in the transaction of a final peace treaty to mark the close of the war. General Duncan McArthur and Chief Clerk John Graham of the State Department were appointed assisting commissioners.[11] Harrison fixed upon Detroit as a likely point of vantage to gain the attention of tribesmen recently hostile; the date, August 25, 1815. The reason that the Indians assembled more tardily than usual, Harrison discovered upon his arrival, lay in prolonged British councils at Malden. Correspondence polite in form but edged with acrimony was exchanged with Lieutenant Colonel William James, commander at Fort Amherstburg. Harrison suggested that the British must not be considered as acting in violation of the ninth article of the Treaty of Ghent which had bound the two nations to transact a separate peace with the Indians. James replied that the tribesmen were considered to be "their own free agents . . . not to be forced to act beyond their own pleasure," which begged the question.[12] The Treaty of Ghent was being fully explained to the tribesmen at Malden, the British leader asserted. Harrison could quite understand. The difficulty arose from the fact that the British considered their own explanations as wholly sufficient and made no move to let the Indians go.

Within six days, however, a representative assemblage gathered in the woods at Spring Wells just south of Detroit. Chief Tarhe performed the solemn ceremonies by which a state of peace and concord was arrived at. "One bunch of wampum was to clear the eyes, unstop the ears, cleanse the throat, and amend the heart; another was to collect the bones, to bury them, to smooth the graves, and to secure them by a board, which the sun could not warm, nor the rain moisten." By means of peace presents of wampum, Harrison now manifested that the tomahawk was buried "under this great house." Then "hands were received," the council fire lighted. The one-eyed Shawnee Prophet appeared one day to speak for the Indians. He represented the nine hostile nations, he said, as well as the four who had stood by the Americans in the war. "The British had told them of the treaty with the Americans & taken the tomahawk from their hands; coming over to the American side, here also the tomahawk was taken out of their hands so that they were now so completely deprived of tomahawks he was apprehensive that their old women could hardly cut wood enough to make a fire." The Prophet and all the other chiefs were willing to make a peace which should be "solid and permanent." The Treaty of Spring Wells, signed on September 8 by nine tribes, was liberal in view. In accordance with Harrison's idea the government required no cession of tribal lands and agreed to restore all previous possessions and rights. Previous treaties were renewed and confirmed, hostilities on every frontier considered at an end.[13]

Gossip picked up in the halls of Congress, especially if of an unfavorable nature, has been known to go a long way. Delegate Jonathan Jennings of Indiana Territory continued to deal in slander reckoned to harm his one-time political detractor. In a recent communication of Jennings to an Indiana constituent there appeared a statement ascribed to the chairman of the committee which had investigated the Northwestern Army supply system: "This bundle of papers con-

tains matters to produce the political damnation of Gen¹ Harrison."¹⁴
Harrison got wind of the remark from Colonel James Dill of Indiana. When Jennings, brought to account, denied that the statement
was "intended in the least to impeach the integrity" of the General,
Harrison confessed himself at a loss to understand the divorce of personal integrity and public honesty in his case. From the Congressman
who was quoted, Harrison received a disclaimer that no "decided
opinion" or intemperance of expression" had ever been employed.¹⁵
But not content with pursuing shadows, he sent to a former army associate, Congressman Joseph Hawkins of Kentucky, all the information deemed necessary to rebut the charges and insinuations of army
contractor Orr.

Concerning the real nature and extent of Orr's charges Harrison
declared himself ignorant but at least he knew what might have been
represented to Secretary Armstrong and to the Congressional committee. In reply to Hawkins's request for information, Harrison
wrote out a summary of Orr's services to the Northwestern Army
and of his dealings with that worthy. In June, 1813, Orr had arrived
at Franklinton, Ohio, where he proposed to issue for two and a half
cents per ration all army supplies already purchased and on hand.
Harrison declined this proposal but referred the contractor to Secretary Armstrong for a final decision. Orr went to Washington and
was not heard from again until late in August when he wrote the
General from Cleveland. Orr was then seeking "salted provisions"
to comply with a requisition for 300,000 rations for the army destined to invade Canada. Since Orr's profits would have been excessive
if permitted to issue the stored rations, army commissaries continued
to function, and when Orr's report of rations which he had secured
showed a deficiency of salt pork and other meats, Harrison engaged
John H. Piatt of Cincinnati to make up the lack and a drove of beef
cattle was herded into Detroit. Still no ill-feeling appeared to exist
between Harrison and the contractor until Orr insisted that he should
be reimbursed for the expense of transporting the supplies from
point to point until the army reached Canada. His contract provided
that when the provisions had been deposited for the use of a post,
the government should pay the cost of removal. Harrison did not
consider this clause to apply to provisions which he had required
stored on the shore of the lake for convenient removal. "The astonishment and indignation which I expressed . . . [when he offered] this
[clause] as an excuse for making no exertions to procure vessels to
transport the provisions . . . gave him, I believe, great offense, and
his making the demand was not calculated to raise him in my esteem."

Orr tardily moved the provisions and put in a claim for extra compensation, for which Harrison again referred him to Armstrong. But Orr failed to supply the troops at Detroit during the winter making it necessary for General Cass to resort to special commissaries. When Harrison returned to Ohio he discovered that Orr had placed everything in the hands of subcontractors, some of whom refused to perform their duty, and in consequence the garrisons were "frequently in a state of starvation." Piatt had concluded his duties with the army so Harrison engaged Captain William Oliver of Cincinnati to purchase needed supplies.

Concluding his detailed account of Orr's services, Harrison left it to his friend Hawkins "to ascertain whether anything had been really said or written which impeaches my honour."

"If such has been the case I pledge myself to meet it in the most direct way. I will immediately address a letter to the House of Representatives requiring an investigation, and will forward to you documents. . . . "[16]

The substance of the gossip reported by Hawkins and other friends in Congress determined Harrison's course. The "tongue of defamation" in Washington openly insinuated he had shared in the profits of commissaries. Harrison collected a number of sworn depositions from leading men in the West who could testify as to methods used in combating difficulties of army transportation and supply and who could give reasons why employment of special commissaries had been necessary upon the failure of contractors. Three individuals recollected furthermore that Orr had stated in their presence "he should have made $300,000 had it not been for the conduct of Gen¹ Harrison."[17] Orr's profits had been only one-third of that sum.

Over a course of some weeks, Harrison carefully drafted a letter to the Speaker of the House calling for an investigation of his official conduct.[18] The final draft of the letter, dated December 20, 1815, was forwarded with the other documents, to Congressman John McLean of his district. McLean showed the letter to Speaker Henry Clay who suggested that it be laid before the House in the form of a resolution or motion which was done. The House agreed to investigate. A select committee headed by Colonel Richard M. Johnson took up the subject and called upon the War Office to submit evidence.[19]

Harrison, meantime, had been visiting Kentucky and Vincennes, "everywhere received with the warmest demonstrations of respect and attachment."[20] An advertisement in western newspapers, however, indicated an effort to raise cash: "200 building lots and a number of out lots adjoining the town of Vincennes for sale on June 6."[21] That this land may have been purchased by ill-gotten gains was perhaps in the back of Delegate Jennings's head when he recommended that Congress secure a detailed statement of Harrison's accounts as Superintendent of Indian Affairs in Indiana from 1801 to 1803.[22] The action was ill-advised. As Governor of Indiana, Harrison had handled little cash. Bills presented for any purchases of Indian goods were satisfied by drafts drawn upon the War Office and a copy of the draft and the receipt for payment forwarded to Washington in the same mail.[23] The request of Jennings, agreed to by Congress, was satisfied without difficulty and the matter finally put to rest.

The Johnson committee was not to report until during the second session of the Congress. Meantime, another detractor was still active. Congressman Desha's tale that Harrison had been forced to pursue Procter left a black mark alongside Orr's smutch. For two years this story had been going the rounds *sub rosa* in the capital. For one reason or another, therefore, the United States Senate moved on April 13 to strike Harrison's name from a resolution offering the thanks of Congress and two gold medals to him and Governor Shelby.

The resolution linking Harrison and Shelby as proper subjects for public reward was being considered by the Committee of the Whole when Senator Abner Lacock of Pennsylvania moved to expunge the General's name. The motion was carried by a vote of 13 to 11, seven Federalists taking the affirmative side. A week later when the question to concur in the amendment arose the Senate supported the original resolution by 14 to 13 and the question was then recommitted.[24] Governor Shelby, as soon as he heard the news, wrote Henry Clay declining to allow Congress to consider his name alone. "How mortified I should feel," the Kentuckian assured Harrison, "to be noticed if you were not—who had rendered ten times more service to the nation than I had. . . . You must spare no pains to get into Congress."[25] Harrison's former aide, Colonel Todd, a young lawyer of Frankfort, had already made this suggestion. "[By entering Congress]," wrote Todd on April 23, "you can then meet the insinuations made by your enemies upon an equal footing and by confronting them, establish for yourself a fame which cannot be effected by their base slander."[26]

Harrison quite agreed. After Congressman John McLean resigned his seat to become a judge of the State Supreme Court "a respectable meeting" at the Sign of the Green Tree in Cincinnati advanced Harrison's name for the vacancy.[27] The General was announced as a candidate for McLean's unexpired term in the Fourteenth Congress and for a full term in the Fifteenth, ending March 3, 1819.

Any one unaware that Congressman Desha hailed from another state might have deduced that Harrison was running against the Kentuckian in the campaign for Congress. The political campaign was not exactly under way, however, during the several weeks that summer in which Harrison pursued his detractor. "You have been given up to me as the author of a calumny, which was the principal, if not the sole cause of that vote of the Senate . . . which expunged my name from the resolution of thanks," Harrison wrote Desha. ". . . Major Chambers will receive your answer."[28]

Chambers, a volunteer aide on the Thames campaign, bore no duelling challenge but a request for a satisfactory explanation. Desha gave ground here and there although his net retraction was small. He discussed principally the council of war held at Sandwich on the morning before the army set out.

"I spurn the expression of calumny. . . . In the council of general officers . . . you stated the policy of pursuing was doubtful, that the scent was cold, the enemy having a great start of us; that provisions were getting scarce; that the enemy could move their troops with great facility. . . . This was certainly all rational. To which I replied that . . . I thought it our duty to make the attempt . . . [and] when it was decided unanimously in favor of a speedy pursuit . . . you cheerfully acquiesced."[29]

This was as far as Desha would go but Harrison had received a detailed account of the incident from Shelby who was better acquainted with what took place during private councils at Sandwich. "You were as anxious," wrote Shelby, "to pursue Proctor as I was but might not have been entirely satisfied as to the route. . . . You observed that there were two ways by which he might be overtaken. . . . I assembled . . . [the officers] to whom you stated your determination to pursue Proctor . . . and after explaining the two routes . . . you observed, 'that the governor thinks, and so do I, that the pursuit by land up the Thames will be most effectual.' . . . During the whole of this long and arduous pursuit, no man could make greater exertions or use more vigilance than you did to overtake Proctor. . . ."[30]

Desha, as it happened, was running for re-election that fall. To be opposed by Harrison on the Thames campaign issue might cause him some inconvenience in his district. Harrison was not unaware that the point of honor was a political stumbling block for the Kentuckian as well as himself. The sequel to Desha's "all rational" rejoinder was a public appeal to "officers, non-coms, & privates of the army that fought on the Thames." It was for them, Harrison suggested, to determine the merits of an officer who had been "censured" by the negative vote of the Senate.[31] This shot found its mark. Desha began to labor under a slight handicap in his campaign for re-election. Among the testimonials which Harrison received was one from a total stranger: "Desha in his election speeches . . . denies that he was your enemy, or that he ever said you was opposed to pursuing . . . the evidence of his having lied came too late to prevent his being elected, which I regret."[32] The sum of the evidence was reserved for perusal by interested friends in the Senate.

To gain the good will of voting constituents in Ohio called for something more than a defense of military conduct. Late in August Harrison got around to discussing his motives in standing for election. His first wish, his statement affirmed, was to discover a proper system for the organization and discipline of the militia. Second, he would obtain proper relief for needy war veterans; third, he had a private object—a seat in Congress would give him an advantage in replying to calumny. But Harrison also had to deny that he had been favorable to the Kentucky militia during the war.[33]

The pure and simple military point of view hardly sufficed to satisfy the electors in respect to an issue discussed at every crossroads and corner. This was the matter of repeal of the Compensation Law, the first session of the Fourteenth Congress having raised its own pay from six dollars a day (about $900 annually), to $1500 a year, taking care to make the provision retroactive. There were few homes or public places west of the Alleghanies that this unauthorized pay-grab was not resentfully denounced. A salary reckoned on an annual basis was all the more objctionable since Congress sat for only an average of five months a year. In Kentucky that popular Westerner, Henry Clay, found himself facing his hardest fight for re-election because he had supported the measure.[34] Richard M. Johnson, its sponsor, was likewise considerably embarrassed. In Ohio Harrison's constituents nudged him with a set of resolutions declaring the law "not only a grievance, but unconstitutional," to which the General agreed.[35] The essential dignity of Congress, Harrison submitted, had been compromised by an over-hasty move to increase its own pay without first consulting the people.

Five other candidates presented themselves in the Congressional district which comprised Hamilton, Warren and Butler counties. James Heaton of the Ohio state legislature "guessed" Harrison's chief rival was T. R. Ross, a lawyer of Lebanon, who would be "supported pretty strongly on account of his supposed interest in having a great turnpike through this country and on account of his supposed eloquence." The General, Heaton added, "will be supported by a number of the leading Federalists . . . by a detachment from all parties & Religions whatsoever and . . . many of the army folks. I defy . . . any politician to augur the result."[36] While the reference to Federalists was a little unusual, Harrison was linked to party leaders in Cincinnati by ties of finance.

The October election gave him a satisfactory majority both for the balance of McLean's term and for the Fifteenth Congress. Harrison led his nearest opponent, Ross, by a plurality ratio of two to one with four minority candidates trailing far in the rear.[37] The news that the Virginia dynasty at Washington remained unbroken surprised very few as the national election returns came in a month later. In his first campaign for the presidency, Secretary of State James Monroe took all but three states from Federalist Rufus King of New York. The home state of Armstrong and the Clintonians had supported the Virginian whose carefully selected running mate was another New Yorker, Governor Daniel D. Tompkins.

The flame-swept President's House and the war-scarred Capitol at Washington offered reminders of enemy invasion in 1814. The Fourteenth Congress was meeting in a structure known as the "Brick Capitol," erected by public subscription on the site of the present Supreme Court Building. The National Capitol had not yet been repaired nor completed and between its two detached wings were two wells of drinking water.[38] Harrison engaged living quarters at Mrs. Clarke's on F Street, one of the numerous boarding houses in the city. Here Congressmen William Burwell of Virginia and Stephen Ormsby of Kentucky resided; also Senator James Noble of Indiana, a new state.[39] One of Harrison's Virginia cousins, Burwell Bassett, resumed his seat in the House. A distant relative, John Randolph of Roanoke, again appeared, also James Pleasants of Goochland, an old friend. Two stern-visaged members were young Daniel Webster and John C. Calhoun; neither in fact had yet reached his thirty-fifth year. Another in a series of fateful coincidences joining the names of Harrison and Tyler was the entrance into the House of the son of Colonel Ben Harrison's old rival, John Tyler of Charles City, who was chosen to fill a seat recently vacated by death.

Henry Clay again took up the Speaker's gavel as the Lame Duck session convened on December 2, 1816. Because of their vote favoring the Compensation Law, seven Kentucky congressmen had been defeated; in Ohio, McLean's seat excepted, five out of five.

Harrison lost no time in redeeming his pledges. December 6 the House agreed to consider his resolution providing for the relief of "distressed" soldiers. Together with other war members of Congress, Harrison protested a move to eliminate indemnity for houses destroyed by the enemy and the motion was lost. January 27, 1817, the House also agreed to consider the subject of remuneration to private citizens who had redeemed prisoners during the war. Harrison further advocated relief of sufferers on the Niagara frontier, but turning now to the pressing subject of its own compensation Congress considered it had done enough.[40] Final passage of pending relief measures went over until the next session.

Revision of the militia system, which had been recommended in President Madison's message, was a task assigned Harrison by a Congress satiated with details of war. Chairman of the Militia Committee, Harrison labored long over a report and bill which would make "every citizen a soldier." The idea was approved by two Southerners in the cabinet, Secretary of State Monroe and William H. Crawford of the Treasury, the latter drawing up a constitutional amendment to embrace it.[41]

Harrison's argument for universal military training was much the same as that advanced some years ago to Governor Scott of Kentucky. The "ancient Republics," whose example had proved useful in founding our civil institutions, would furnish "a most perfect model for our system of national defence." Prime examples of military education were the Campus Martius and the Gymnasia. Harrison advocated the training of every American youth in the schools and the colleges, and in two age groups in civil life thereafter. "The whole secret of ancient military glory—the foundation of that wonderful combination of military skill and exalted valor which enabled the petty Republic of Athens to resist the mighty torrent of Persian invasion; which formed the walls of Sparta, and conducted the Roman legions . . . to the conquest of the world, will be found in the military education of youth."[42]

A block or two away stood the damaged National Capitol yet the war had been won and another invasion was deemed unlikely. Congress failed to respond to the idealistic urgings of the gentleman from Ohio and the plan was laid on the table. Still pending was Compensation Law repeal and a showdown over internal improvements. Harrison made a short speech against the extra compensation and voted whenever the bill came up to restore the old pay of six dollars a day to take effect immediately but the Lame Duck members would not so agree. The final vote on the measure yielded nothing from the $1,500 salary asked by the Fourteenth Congress but restored the old scale to take effect at the close of the session.[43] A scheme advanced by Henry Clay and John C. Calhoun to appropriate a permanent Federal fund for internal improvements—post-roads and canals—won the assent of the Ohio member on a day when every vote was needed but following passage by a majority of two the bill was vetoed by Madison.[44]

Harrison had been waiting meantime for a report of the committee considering his case. On the last day of the year, Acting Secretary of War George Graham laid a collection of military and financial documents before the House.[45] Amounts paid out for the supply of the Northwestern Army from September, 1812, to the following June had totaled $1,160,000. "No part of this sum has been advanced to General Harrison." Upon this basic testimony and that given by witnesses at private hearings the committee was to base its report. Three weeks later, January 23, 1817, Johnson arose to declare the committee "unanimously of opinion that General Harrison stands above suspicion as to . . . any pecuniary or improper connection with the officers of the commissariat." The General did not "wantonly or improperly interfere with the rights of the contractors," on the contrary his policies had been inspired by a "laudable zeal . . . and devotion." To dissipate any taint of whitewash from the proceedings, Congressman John W. Hurlburt of Massachusetts detailed the full scope and adequacy of the investigation. Not once but several times had the committee questioned witnesses, including Benjamin G. Orr, Washington's new mayor. Although he had once "entertained impressions very unfavorable to the general," Hurlburt added, it now "gave him pleasure . . . [to declare] the insinuations and complaints . . . unmerited, groundless and unjust. . . . The General, in the exercise of his official duties, had neglected his private concerns to his material detriment."[46]

At Mrs. Clarke's boarding house that evening Harrison reviewed the leading events of the day for James Findlay. A paragraph covered the repeal of the "cursed compensation law." The Johnson committee had reported and "Mr. Hurlburt's observations were received with great approbation by the House." It was possible now that Harrison's friends in the Senate might reintroduce the resolution of thanks. James Morrison and James Taylor (of Cincinnati),

Harrison continued, "are on the wing for Philadelphia to attend to the final arrangements for our Bank." The Bank of the United States, rechartered by the previous session of Congress, was about to establish a branch in Cincinnati. Harrison had recommended Judge Jacob Burnet to the Philadelphia officials as branch president but since Burnet was a Federalist he submitted the names of several Republicans, including Findlay and John Piatt, for membership on the Board of Directors.[47]

Another item. John Quincy Adams had been selected as Monroe's Secretary of State. Since Henry Clay had been passed over, this choice was bound to be unpopular in the West. "I have heard that many of the candidates will not serve with Adams at all," Harrison went on. "It is said he is a disgusting man to do business. Coarse, *Dirty* and clownish in his address and stiff and abstracted in his opinions, which are drawn from books exclusively. You ask will the W[ar] D[epartmen]t be offer[d] to me; I answer—I cannot tell. I *know* the *wishes* of the P[residen]t Elect are in my favor, but . . . other circumstances are to be considered. . . . If it is offer[d] shall I accept it?"

Harrison's remarks concerning John Quincy Adams bore a little hard on the greatest Secretary of State since Thomas Jefferson, but this was probably also the opinion of Henry Clay, confidant and friend of the General. Pending appointment of a Secretary of War, James Monroe received suggestions from Isaac Shelby and Judge Thomas Todd of Kentucky.[48] The choice of General Harrison would meet with the approbation of the people of Kentucky, Tennessee and Ohio, Judge Todd pointed out. Shelby again declared Harrison "amongst the very first military men I have ever known." Other circumstances, however, prevailed. Monroe offered the post first to Henry Clay, who emphatically declined, then to Shelby who declined also. Nor did General Andrew Jackson of Tennessee wish to be named, nor William Lowndes of South Carolina. Eventually John C. Calhoun accepted.[49]

The Fourteenth Congress drew swiftly to a close. Contests over appropriation bills and internal duties left no suitable occasion to bring up the resolution of thanks to Harrison and Shelby. A motion by Harrison asking that the War Department investigate contracts for the supply of arms was carried, his proposal for a constitutional amendment to provide training and discipline for the militia was lost.[50] But with the exception of postponed action on his militia bill, Harrison could count his pledges fulfilled, his detractors rebuked. In court circles he won favor with society arbitress Margaret

Bayard Smith, who met our "Western Hero" at a party given by M. de Neuville, the French minister.[51] Again, "at an intollerable squeeze," Mrs. Smith "talk'd a little to a hundred people but had conversation only with Gen¹ Harrison and Abbe Correa." The former was "the most agreeable."[52] Harrison at any rate was the only man in Congress who could describe early social life in Cincinnati, Detroit, Vincennes, Cahokia and St. Louis. After witnessing the inauguration of President Monroe on March 4 the General departed on a long-deferred visit to his native Virginia.

POLITICAL FORTUNES

HARRISON'S two brothers, Benjamin and Carter, were no longer living and the Berkeley plantation was in the hands of a nephew, Benjamin Harrison VII. The General remained nearly three weeks in Virginia. Honors of the usual sort were paid him by the Petersburg Volunteers who had fought at Fort Meigs. Another native Virginian, Colonel Waller Taylor, Indiana Senator and comrade-at-arms at Tippecanoe, accompanied the General to a public dinner at Poplar Spring.

While Petersburg was no Athens, the guest of honor admitted, "to be feasted in the prytaneum of their native city was the greatest reward which an Athenian general could receive." Toasts were offered to the town of Petersburg, the seed-bed of patriotism, to the State of Virginia, to "the fair daughters of America—May their sons be as attentive to their posts as Harrison."[1]

An invitation to a public dinner at Richmond was declined as the General departed homeward two days before the date set. Arriving at Pittsburgh he was approached by a party of five gentlemen who wished to engage the services of a pilot for their private craft. Harrison agreed to the request of Gorham A. Worth, a representative of the United States Bank who was on his way West to set up the branch at Cincinnati. An inspection of the boat took him immediately into the pantry where sufficient provisions were discovered to supply a voyage to New Orleans. So the party was encouraged to toss our supplies to immigrant families coasting down the Ohio on flatboats and rafts. "That tea and coffee . . . are luxuries that many of them may not taste for years," explained Harrison.[2]

Spring came early that year and the river was broad and full. Immigrants "bound they knew not exactly where" frequently drew alongside for an hour's conversation while Harrison asked questions and gave needed advice. The voyage proved an enjoyable one for the party and the little "ark" reached port safely on April 10, 1817. Worth had an old travel-stained trunk filled with hard money which was landed and taken to the home of General James Findlay.

A cannon was heard to boom in honor of his coming, or rather, as Worth claimed, to salute the arrival of the trunk. The branch bank was set up with Judge Burnet president, Worth cashier, Harrison, Findlay and Piatt among thirteen directors representing prominent financial interests of the community.[3] Correlative to the organization of this mundane affair was the founding of Christ Church (Episcopal), on May 18. As one of its sponsors Harrison was named vestryman.[4]

The publication of a *History of the Late War* by Captain Robert McAfee of Kentucky stimulated fresh argument over the conduct of the more inglorious campaigns. That the history be written was Colonel Richard M. Johnson's suggestion and the manuscript had passed through Harrison's hands. Its treatment of certain controversial points was quite favorable to Harrison, Shelby, Johnson, Perry, Cass and McArthur while rather less appreciative of Winchester and Hull. Criticism of Winchester, in fact, was laid on so well that the Tennessean was moved to reply in a series of articles published in the *National Intelligencer* of Washington. Harrison's promotion to the command of the Northwestern Army and the unauthorized advance of Winchester to the River Raisin were sore points. Winchester complained of jealousy, lack of co-operation, and active intrigue.[5] Invited to respond, Harrison, nearly two years later, published his own version of events and thus the campaign of 1812-13 was laboriously argued up and down columns of type.[6] Still certain other military figures were finding it necessary to refurbish their name and repute. Commodore Perry was having his quarrel with Commander Jesse D. Elliott, a jealous subordinate at the Battle of Lake Erie.[7] General Andrew Jackson was moved to reply to McAfee's criticism concerning his disposition of Kentucky troops on the west bank at New Orleans.[8] General James Wilkinson labored long over his "Memoirs"; General William Hull, court-martialed and pardoned, took to his bed.

While the General Winchester articles still blazed in the press Harrison journeyed again to Washington and renewed his efforts to aid the war victims. Many individual claims had been pressed upon him with power of attorney to collect pay bounties. A bill to commute bounty lands of soldiers for cash got nowhere but Congress agreed that the Military Committee should consider an extension of the five-year pensions allowed war widows and orphans. This was a subject of interest to a retired general whose pocketbook was usually open to the needs of the bereaved. "I have seen," declared Harrison, " . . . the wounded and expiring warrior in that awful moment . . . when the sacrifice being made . . . the thoughts of his family would fill him with the greatest solicitude."[9] When another compensation measure was brought up, Harrison urged that the House do justice first "to others whose claims are stronger and of longer standing . . . the sufferers in the war of the Revolution." He voted first to continue the old compensation of six dollars a day instead of a suggested increase to nine but the measure was lost. Harrison then moved to amend the bill to read six dollars a day for the present Congress and eight dollars for the ensuing. The members considered themselves justified, however, by a vote of 109 to 60, to grant themselves a modest raise of two dollars.[10]

January 20, 1818, Harrison rose to announce the death of General Kosciusko, Polish Revolutionary patriot and adjutant to General Washington. Congress was asked to consider "proper measures of public respect . . . not, Sir, to perpetuate his fame—but our gratitude." An oratorical appeal traced the tumultuous career of the "martyr of liberty . . . the devoted soldier of liberty" but the motion was strongly opposed. Harrison withdrew it finally and donned a mourning band of crape.[11] He gave way to pessimism in a letter to an advocate of the claims of Robert Morris's widow. "There seems to be apathy in Congress on every subject of that sort. . . . I shall, however, make the attempt."[12] He proposed a pension of $1000 a year for Arthur St. Clair and pressed an old claim of the General's for monies advanced. Both motions were lost, the sum of $60 a month finally granted.[13] However, Harrison's bill to provide for the relief of "distressed" officers and soldiers, introduced during the previous session, became law on March 15, 1818.

"If you knew the number of letters I receive, you would pity me," Harrison wrote George P. Torrence of Cincinnati. "The reading of them is intolerable labour."[14] Individual war claims for back pay and other compensation arrived in numbers, also "reiterated complaints" concerning the transportation of western mails.[15] The Committee on Claims and the Postmaster General saw Harrison often. Work in the House went on. That body tabled another detailed plan for the reorganization of the militia, a measure favored however by President Monroe, and rejected a Military Committee bill to extend pensions of war widows and orphans. Thereupon the persistent Ohio member asked leave to work out another relief measure and was named chairman of a special committee to do so.[16] A personal issue was won on March 30 when both Houses of Congress voted thanks and gold medals to Harrison and Shelby. The resolution, unanimously passed by the Senate, went through three readings in the House that same day with only one member dissenting.[17] As the session drew to a close Harrison begged that the House would not adjourn before extending aid to General John Stark, destitute Revolutionary hero of New Hampshire. Congress was asked to sit on the following Sunday, if necessary, in order to consider the measure. The Sunday idea was not agreed to nor was Harrison's motion to postpone adjournment to Wednesday, April 22, instead of on Monday as was planned. Harrison then renewed the motion for a Sunday session in order to obtain action on his bill benefiting war widows and orphans.[18] A member from Connecticut objected. "For my part," Harrison remonstrated, "I cannot conceive that a more acceptable sacrifice can be offered to Heaven on the Sabbath." The Committee of the Whole approved a $60 a month pension for Stark but the House would take no further action. On the final day of the session the House considered briefly a report on African colonization for slaves and took up a grist of Senate bills, adjourning by candlelight. Possibly as a tribute to his zealousness, Harrison was appointed on a committee of two members sent to inform President Monroe of the approaching recess of Congress.[19]

The General returned home by way of Philadelphia to attend a public dinner in his honor. Responding to a toast, Harrison advanced the merits of the Pittsburgh Blues, a volunteer corps, and the loyalty of the Pennsylvania militia who stood by at Fort Meigs in April, 1813. Then he added a few words concerning the defense of Fort Stephenson and an unfriendly report of his speech was transmitted to Colonel George Croghan who had resigned from the service. Croghan happened to be visiting at Red Hook, New York, home of former Secretary of War Armstrong, who probably gave him his cue. Writing Harrison on July 1, Croghan particularly complained of an inference that the victory at Fort Stephenson was due not so much to a gallant defense as to the enemy's "blindness & folly." Moreover, the account of the battle given in McAfee's "Late War" was "devoid of the truth . . . as you very well know."[20] Harrison suggested in reply that the Colonel should have confined himself to a "friendly remonstrance . . . more consistent with the friendship which has existed between us," and added: "How could I have been so inconsistent as to disparage the defence of Sandusky . . . when I had spoken of it in such exalted terms in my public dispatch."[21] Still this did not exactly follow and Harrison went on to reiterate his belief that Sandusky "could have been taken, and that the Enemy acted most stupidly," all of which did little to allay the rising indignation of an officer from whom Congress had withheld a vote of thanks. Croghan replied in bitter terms and some years later, following publication of a laudatory biography of the General, the correspondence was fulsomely renewed.[22]

A three-year-old child, Findlay, was ill as Harrison arrived home and had not much longer to live. However, the General had suffered his first family bereavement as a grandfather. Eighteen years and some months separated the births of his first-born, Betsey Bassett, and Findlay; in June, 1814, Betsey had married a cousin, John Cleves Short, and their only child, a baby girl, had died in 1816.

Economic problems loomed large during the summer and fall. The farm was yielding little profit from surplus over and above the requirements for feeding numerous guests and a large family, which included nine children of school age. Nor was the Miami Exporting Company prospering just now. Although the arrival of the steamboat on the Ohio had been expected to encourage business the year 1818 witnessed the acceleration of war boom decline. Using his land holdings as a basis for credit, Harrison was "very reluctantly" drawn into a partnership with Burnet, Findlay and Piatt to extend the works of the Cincinnati Bell, Brass and Iron Foundry established the previous year.[23] The business was managed by one William Green, and quite unsuccessfully as it turned out. To add to the reverses now commonly experienced the United States branch bank at Cincinnati, after indulging in a heedless over-inflation of note issues, refused to extend state banks any further credit unless all balances due were collected before October 30. But the banks were impoverished, their notes almost driven from circulation, and suspension of specie payments soon followed.[24] A similar situation prevailed in Kentucky. Harrison determined to withdraw from Congress at the end of the next session in order to devote his attention to local affairs.

The second session of the Fifteenth Congress, which met November 16, was the stormiest that Harrison had witnessed. By a majority of three he secured passage of his bill extending for five years the pensions of war widows and orphans. Opposition developed on the ground that the government had gone far enough in relieving distresses. "We had a long and pretty warm debate on the subject."[25] General Stark was then granted his pension, "an imperious duty."[26] Of greater political portent was Harrison's stand on the admission of Illinois and Missouri to statehood and his vote to censure General

Andrew Jackson, who, in chasing Seminole Indians into Spanish Florida, had hung two British subjects.

The slavery issue overshadowed the admission of any new state. In 1818 the states numbered ten free and ten slave. When the question of admitting Illinois and accepting its own constitution arose James Tallmadge of New York, a prominent abolitionist, urged that the Ordinance of 1787 forever bound Congress to outlaw slavery from any state carved out of the original Northwest Territory. Harrison disagreed. The clause in the Illinois state constitution: "Slavery shall not hereafter be introduced," he said was sufficient. Harrison went further. He wished "to see that State and all the Territory, disenthralled from the effect of articles to which they never gave their consent, and to which they were not properly subject." It was purely a question of state sovereignty. Harrison added that he was opposed to slavery and "should lament its introduction into any part of that Territory," a remark which left his stand open to misinterpretation.[27]

Illinois was admitted, making eleven free states and ten slave. The question of the admission of Missouri found abolitionist and slavery members of Congress greatly aroused. A Tallmadge amendment outlawing slavery in the state of Missouri was adopted and the admission bill passed on February 17, 1819, Harrison voting against and he reiterated his stand during debates over the organization of the new Territory of Arkansas. When Congressman John Taylor of New York sought to prohibit the further introduction of slavery and to free all negroes in the Territory as soon as they reached the age of twenty-five years, Harrison lined up with the southern contingent and both proposals were negatived by a close vote. Taylor then introduced the "thirty-six thirty" line, Missouri's southern boundary, as the northern limit of slave soil. Harrison countered with an amendment placing the line farther up, at the mouth of the Des Moines River in northern Missouri, but the House declined to act on this motion and voted down Taylor's amendment.[28] Arkansas was thus left open to slavery and so was Missouri when the amended admission bill failed in the Senate. Respecting his own vote Harrison was to have some explaining to do in the "Yankee State" of Ohio.

Harrison's censure of Jackson for the hanging of both, rather than only one of the Britishers, was maintained with a shade of punctiliousness. Unconcerned with any political issue involved, Harrison based his plea upon the law of court-martial. The orginal argument, advanced by Henry Clay, denied Jackson's right to execute Robert C. Ambrister and Alexander Arbuthnot, British traders with the

Seminole Indians. Yet British traders, as everyone knew, were more than likely to be active against the American settlers. Jackson's action was based upon knowledge that Arbuthnot "and other foreigners" were "exciting the Seminoles to . . . hostility."[29] Following a court-martial which recommended hanging for Arbuthnot but only a year's confinement for Ambrister, Jackson had hanged both.

Clay forces in the House took up a great deal of time at eight dollars a day in forcing the issue. The debate in a hushed chamber lasted almost a month. Its importance to Andrew Jackson's personal honor brought him to Washington to direct his own fight. Harrison saw little of the General, but he heard him all right, "for I was in an adjacent room and I thought . . . that if all his supposed enemies had been in his power and had but one neck they would have lost their heads in a twinkling."[30] Harrison spoke twice on the resolution to censure. In brief he granted the right of the United States and of the military authority to punish both Ambrister and Arbuthnot. The sentence of the court-martial, however, specified only the hanging of Arbuthnot—"the execution of Ambrister was wrong, because it was not in accord with . . . the court."[31] Satisfied that this stand was the only correct one, Harrison moved for a division of the question.[32] The House so agreed but Harrison's vote against censure in the case of Arbuthnot and his yea on Ambrister was the only one so recorded. Insofar as the entire contest was concerned it was a Jackson victory and a Clay defeat. March 3, 1819, the Fifteenth Congress adjourned.

Visitation of hard times upon the western country engendered some sacrifice in sending William Henry, Jr. to Transylvania University at Lexington. Although a trustee of Cincinnati College, Harrison did not believe it could "compare" with Transylvania. Of course money was scarce but still he hoped to give his son the best education obtainable west of the Alleghanies. "There is no exertion that I would not make & scarcely any sacrifice I would not incur to give you a Good education," he wrote his son and namesake. William Henry was a youth of great popularity but occasionally erratic. There followed sundry warnings against the perils of fast living "[To become a drunkard] would be Destruction. . . . The very desire to indulge . . . [in gaming] Springs from a base principle i.e. that of getting the property of another without an equivolent."[33] Harrison mentioned a carefree son of Colonel Winthrop Sargent, one-time Secretary of Northwest Territory, as an example to be avoided. The embarrassing escapades of Henry Clay's son Thomas and of

Martin Van Buren's John also were to become noted in history. Harrison requested William, Jr. to help him locate a reliable negro woman for a house servant. It had been his custom to purchase negro slaves from Kentucky masters and bind them by indenture upon promise of their freedom.

"I want one more than ever as Priscilla's former master has much to my satisfaction come on for her and repaid her the money I gave him. Ask Mr. Wilkins to look out for one for me & buy her & tell him that I will send him a check on the U. S. Bank . . . as soon as he informs me he has made the purchase. . . . The woman should be of such a character as will promise fidelity in the performance of her engagements. I will agree that she shall be free at from 6 to 8 years in proportion to the price she may cost. . . ."[34]

Such was one narrow road from slave to free soil, an arrangement dependent upon a master's integrity. While living in Vincennes Harrison had purchased a runaway slave from his Kentucky master who caught up with him; the price, $400, being paid upon agreement to serve twelve years. The arrangement turned out well. After release as a free man Jack Butler and his family lived for years on a small farm of Harrison's on the east bank of the Wabash.[35]

Two weddings in the Harrison family took place early in the fall. September 29, Clarissa Pike, daughter of the late General Zebulon M. Pike, the explorer, was wedded to John Cleves Symmes Harrison. At the North Bend mansion next day Lucy Singleton Harrison married David K. Este, rising young Cincinnati lawyer and financier.[36] Symmes, as Harrison's oldest son was called, had been appointed by President Monroe as Receiver of the Vincennes Land Office, taking up his residence at Grouseland.

Business was poor at the iron foundry that summer and fall and Harrison contemplated his finances with concern. "I am already *up to the Hub* as deeply as I can go . . . our debts are very large & extremely pressing."[37] A candidate for the Ohio State Senate, he was called upon to explain his position as a director of an unpopular bank. Branches of the Philadelphia institution established in Cincinnati and Chillicothe had taken over much western real estate at low valuations in liquidating debts. The slump in western fortunes added to the feeling against the bank. Men once considered rich and a host of small entrepreneurs had been ruined.

Concerning his own ventures, Harrison could show that he held only fifty shares in the Miami Exporting Company, that he had less than $500 in the Bank of Cincinnati and owned not a share in the

United States Bank. That he happened to be a director of the local branch, Harrison argued, was no issue. He derived greater revenue from the produce of his dairies alone than from the bank stock he possessed. Was not his true interest therefore identified with that of the farmer and of the mechanic? During the recent session of Congress, he emphasized, he had supported a move to repeal the bank act and had even suggested to the Treasury Department that the government deposits be removed to another institution.

"In the . . . [Bank of the United States]," affirmed Harrison, "I view an institution which may be converted into an immense political engine to strengthen the arm of the general government, and which may at some future day be used to oppress and break down the state governments."[38] In other words the director of a United States Bank was an enemy of bank principles, not an uncommon situation along the fringes of western finance. Policies were not determined at Cincinnati but at the home office at Philadelphia, a long distance away. Cashier Gorham A. Worth criticised the institution from an intimate vantage-point. "Conceit, vanity, and a withering sort of tyranny," he wrote, forecast the doom of the bank.[39]

The local campaign was infused with excitement anti-bank partisans raiding one Harrison meeting. The General and his opponent, William Gazley, a Cincinnati lawyer, each polled the same number of votes in the city but the rural districts gave Harrison a majority of 348.[40]

Since 1816 the Ohio legislature had been meeting in the borough of Columbus, near Franklinton, the new and permanent capital. As the legislators convened opinions were exchanged concerning the United States Bank situation which had developed at Chillicothe. In February a law had been passed taxing each United States branch bank in Ohio the exorbitant sum of $50,000 provided the banks continued in business after September 1. When the bank declined to pay, the sum of $100,000 was removed with the aid of a crowbar from the branch at Chillicothe, and loaded onto a sheriff's wagon for deposit by the state auditor.[41]

But in the famous case of McCulloch vs. Maryland the United States Supreme Court at this juncture declared that a state had no right to levy a tax upon a bank chartered by Congress. The Ohio Senate appointed a committee to consider the matter, and a report was formulated which justified the "crow-bar law" by declaring the bank charter unconstitutional although the state had a "conclusive right" to tax. But this failed to clarify the muddle and Harrison disagreed with the latter conclusion in part. The state had a right to tax, he concurred, but since the Supreme Court had nullified that procedure there the matter should rest. The only possible solution would be to abolish the bank entirely, taking care to avoid any un-constitutional or violent means.[42]

Such was the gist of a substitute report which Harrison offered. Although this report was defeated, only a modified version of the original, its tones of defiance struck out, finally passed. Harrison had lost no credit meanwhile and further action was lodged in his hands. Chairman of a joint bank committee which reported during the next session, Harrison argued that the state was a sovereign with jurisdiction, for the purposes of taxation, over all property within its limits. The state could not be haled into court in a suit to recover, therefore, but since the highest legal tribunal had overridden this argument, right or wrong, an "independent and superior" bank was actually alien and entitled to no recognition by the sovereignty whose inherent jurisdiction it defied. Was the bank bigger than the state? The next result of new legislation which deprived the bank of legal protection in Ohio was the withdrawal of that institution from inhospitable soil.[43]

Again the Missouri question. The plan submitted by Senator Jesse B. Thomas of Illinois to Congress provided that Missouri Territory might frame a state constitution without restriction as to slavery while Maine was admitted as free. Taking into account the admission of Alabama as a state in December, 1819, the slave and free states would then number twelve each. But that Missouri might permanently become slave soil aroused a storm in the North. Legislative bodies in every state rushed through resolutions declaring their representatives should act at once to maintain Missouri as free. That reported by the Ohio State Senate asked "our senators and representatives in Congress . . . to use their zealous endeavors to prevent the adoption of so odious and dangerous a measure."

Harrison, who had opposed every attempt in Congress to limit the spread of slavery, suggested another phrase. To conciliate the southern element he asked that Ohio's representatives be instructed to prevent the extension of slavery by every means "which the con-stitution . . . will allow."[44]

But the Ohio Senate was largely made up of men from New England and it did not care to search the Constitution for a means by which ready indignation could make itself felt. Harrison's motion was promptly voted down, the forthright original adopted. Harrison thereupon lost the ensuing election of a United States Senator, the winner in January, 1821, being Benjamin Ruggles, a Connecticut man.[45] Another political test further humiliated the once masterful southern contingent. In December of that year Senator William Trimble of Ohio died at Washington. Harrison was late in entering the contest for the vacancy, his purpose being probably to capture votes from Governor Ethan Allen Brown for the benefit of Thomas Worthington. The legislature took nine ballots to elect Brown, another native of Connecticut, over Worthington, Virginia.[46]

Symbols of public regard during the middle years took the form of public dinners during trips to Vincennes where a son, John Cleves Symmnes, took charge of the Land Office as Receiver. In 1820 Harrison cast his presidential vote as an elector for Monroe and Tompkins, re-elected with no opposition. Although not a candidate for the governorship that fall, he received 4330 complimentary votes.[47] His interest in the development of a common-schools system in Ohio, for which he brought out several bills in the Senate, and a trusteeship of Cincinnati College won him an honorary degree from that institution.[48]

Harrison was also named a trustee of Ohio Medical. His third son, John Scott, a large-framed youth, studied medicine for a time but was graduated from Cincinnati College in 1824. Harrison encouraged William Jr. to keep up his studies at Transylvania. "An indulgent parent is willing to furnish the means. . . . I will certainly keep you at school." William's mother added a precaution: "Money is very scarce and hard to be got."[49] Financial burdens, the foundry going under, made necessary the mortgage of lands for $8372.17; public notices in western newspapers offered a reward for the recovery of eighty-one sheep stolen from the North Bend farm.[50] Ending his work in the Ohio Senate, Harrison saw fit to answer publicly "a few of the calumnies . . . in circulation against me." For one thing he had been accused of being "friendly to slavery."[51]

Harrison's public letter explained in detail his stand, distinguishing between his championship of "human liberty" and his votes against restricting the spread of slavery. Seemingly his course had not been consistent. Harrison went all the way back to his membership in the Humane Society of Richmond, "the object of which was to ameliorate the condition of the slaves and procure their freedom." He had lately secured a certificate of this membership and considered himself still loyal to its principles. However, it took a long letter to convince his Yankee constituents that his vote on Missouri and Arkansas was incompatible with abolitionist principles. Harrison showed himself a supporter of state sovereignty and the property rights of individuals inherent in the Constitution, and on his final point he was both sound and prophetic:

"Congress had no more legal or constitutional right to emancipate the negroes in those sections of Louisiana [Territory] without consent of their owners than they have to free those of Kentucky. These people are secured in their property by a solemn covenant with France when the country was purchased from that power. To prohibit the emigration of citizens of the southern states [slaveholders] to the part of the country, the situation and climate of which was peculiarly suited to them, would have been highly unjust, as it had been purchased out of the common fund. . . . We cannot emancipate the slaves of the other states without their consent, but by producing a convulsion which would undo us all. . . . We must wait the slow but certain progress of those good principles which are everywhere gaining ground, and which assuredly will ultimately prevail."[52]

Although sentiment appeared to be running strongly against him, Harrison was induced once more to run for Congress. The favored conservative leader, Bellamy Storer, declining to run, it was only "to make a show of fight," explained William Henry Harrison, Jr., that the General consented to enter his name.[53]

Harrison was to have cause to regret it. The campaign of 1822 was bitter and virulent and long remembered in Cincinnati. The opposing candidate, young William Gazley, dipped into the Winchester letters and held up Harrison's war record to scorn. A new newspaper, *The Independent Press,* dealt in scurrility and personal abuse, all of which was quite a shock to the General. Anti-bank and anti-slavery slogans were smeared on a thousand handbills and caricatures of Harrison appeared. Gazley posed as a reform candidate. "Gigantic corruptions" were laid to the government at Washington and had not Harrison prevailed upon President Monroe to place his son Symmes in the Vincennes Land Office? This had been as much the work of General James Findlay as Harrison; the General had previously employed Symmes in the Cincinnati Land Office from which promotion finally came. Quite without basis was a charge that the General held title to some land which Judge Symmes was supposed to have granted for a college township.[54] As administrator of the Judge's tangled estate, Harrison had retained no disputed claim.

The result of the election, which Gazley won by 542 votes,[55] left

Harrison with the feeling that the slavery issue was the real cause of his defeat. Altogether it was an ill-tasting brew for the son of a Signer from the Virginia Tidewater district. Gazley made little impression in Congress and two years later General Findlay handily defeated him for re-election.

So disturbed was a Cincinnati newspaper friend over the election outcome that he proposed to publish a biography of Harrison with the idea of re-establishing his fame. "His character as a Soldier and a citizen has been impugned."[56] Editor Moses Dawson soon set to work and brought out his book in 1824. This early treatise contains much interesting Indian lore but its eulogy of the General was a little fulsome, particularly at the instance of a partisan who later swung over to Andrew Jackson and Martin Van Buren.

On the heels of his latest political defeat, Harrison was also facing financial collapse. He no longer had any hope of retrieving any part of his business investments. The Miami Exporting Company had been swallowed up by the United States branch bank and the foundry enterprise had left him some $20,000 in debt. Almost as a last resort, basing his claim upon the present needs of his family, Harrison petitioned President James Monroe for appointment as Minister to Mexico.[57]

Monroe, however, had recently made Judge John McLean his Postmaster General and no other major post was likely so soon to go to Ohio. But Ninian Edwards of Illinois, selected for the Mexican ministry, became involved in a controversy with Secretary of the Treasury Crawford and got no farther than Washington. Supported by "a very strong recommendation" from Henry Clay and other westerners, Harrison's name was again advanced in the summer of 1824 but ultimately Monroe left the appointment to his successor in office.

Another presidential campaign was at hand, the contestants Adams, Clay, Crawford and Jackson. Nominated an elector on the Henry Clay or "Agricultural, Manufacturing and Internal Improvements" ticket, Harrison circulated his views. From a letter signed "Shelby" we have: "The popularity of Gen. Jackson is confined to a few counties along the river. In the middle and northern parts of the state we hear nothing of it."[58] "If we cannot elect Clay," declared a *Liberty Hall* editorial, "it will be impossible to elect any Western candidate. . . . Jackson is said to be a Western man and has the best chance. He is not a Western man but is completely identified with the South." Over his own name Harrison published as "a malicious falsehood" the report of a coalition between Clay and Crawford in favor of the latter. "Mr. Clay . . . will not withdraw from the contest but by the fiat of his Maker."[59]

In November, Clay emerged the winner in Ohio by a plurality of less than a thousand votes, while trailing the other three candidates in the country-wide returns. On the strength of Clay's showing in Ohio, however, Harrison posted himself to Columbus, where the legislature was to elect another United States senator in place of Senator E. A. Brown, recently chosen governor. Wyllis Silliman, a veteran lawyer of Marietta, was a foremost contender and the name of Thomas Worthington was also advanced. Harrison engaged in a busy statehouse campaign.[60] After pledging the votes of some forty members he returned to North Bend in time for the Christmas holiday. Then the opposition really got to work.

"Some reports and certificates . . . lately come on from Cincinnati . . . I think will put him in the background," a legislator notified Governor Brown shortly before the election.[61] "The Cincinnati people, enemys of H. have started some ugly reports of the Gen¹ and . . . it is doubtful whether he could be elected," corroborated another.[62] The reports alleged seduction of a "respectable member of her sex," and although no time remained for an investigation of the slander, Harrison achieved a majority of the Ohio Assembly votes on the fourth ballot after leading all the way. The pastor of the lady in question, the Rev. J. L. Wilson, was called upon to dispel the cloud of scarlet which temporarily hovered over the General's marquee.[63]

The popular upswing for Andrew Jackson did not suffice to overcome the combined strength of Adams, Crawford and Clay and the Tennessean fell short of an electoral majority by thirty-five votes. February 9, 1825, the House decided for Adams, second in the national poll. President Monroe's call for an extra session of the new Senate to confirm treaties and the new cabinet brought Harrison to Washington about the last of the month. News that Adams had selected Henry Clay for his Secretary of State met the steamboat at Wheeling; arriving at the capital Harrison learned that Clay had accepted. Then the cry of "bargain" went up. Clay had thrown his influence to Adams in the House election. On the day before Senate confirmation of Clay's appointment, Harrison reviewed the gossip for a supporter back home. Talk concerning Clay's "compromise" occupied the major part of the latter but it was evident that the Mexican ministry was still open.

"You will have heard of the intention of Mr. Clay to make one of

Mr. Adams cabinet. I was at first opposed to his taking the situation. But I have become convinced that it was not only proper but that no other course was left to him. . . . If he had not formed part of it the Western interest would have had no Representative in the cabinet capable of sustaining them. Refusing the post . . . would not have shielded him from the charge of having bargained for it. It would have been said that the development of the plot as it was called had prevented his accepting it. . . . The Inauguration Address of Mr. Adams has given general satisfaction. You will see that he is *up to the Hub* for internal improvements. . . . The Mexican mission is not yet filled. I do not know whether it will be offer^d to me or not. Indeed I do not care for I had positively rather hold the appointment of Senator. But I am determined to try the strength of the Western Interests . . . in my favor. . . . Accept the best wishes dr sir Yr friend

"W. H. Harrison"[64]

President Adams, surveying the several recommendations in Harrison's behalf, adjudged him to be "exceedingly anxious to obtain the appointment." Secretary of State Clay expressed himself in favor of the General but had "no particular objections" to Congressman Joel Poinsett of South Carolina.[65] Poinsett had been recommended by James Monroe and he was a political opponent of Vice-President John C. Calhoun, whom Adams disliked. So it was Poinsett who was sent to troubled Mexico there to become involved in a partisan feud.

In December Harrison returned for the opening of the regular session, his garb as a Senator a black fustian frock-coat, Kentucky jeans, woolen hat, cowhide boots. Observers spied in Congress "a tall, spare gray-haired gentleman who had gone from his Virginia home into the western wilderness." A lady journalist denoted: "His face is thin and oval, his complexion fair . . . his countenance serene and engaging."[66] There remain stray glimpses of Harrison as dinner guest at the British and the Dutch embassies and at Navy Secretary Samuel Southard's in company with Henry Clay, Publisher Joseph Gales of the *National Intelligencer,* and Editor Thurlow Weed of the Rochester (N.Y.) *Telegraph.*[67] Guest of Sir Charles Vaughn, the British minister, Harrison advanced, as once did Wellington, the possibility of a successful invasion of England. It is unlikely that Sir Charles ever invited him again. Mrs. Huygiens, wife of the Dutch minister, gave Harrison "some pretty comfits" for his grandchildren who were six in number at present. Three daughters had been born to Symmes, a daughter to Lucy Harrison Este; in

1824, Harrison's sons John Scott, a farmer, and William Jr., a lawyer, had both married, producing a boy and a girl, respectively, the very next year. Harrison continued to enjoy a close intimacy with Clay, an occasional visitor at North Bend. The Kentuckian left with Harrison the one letter he wrote before engaging in a "high-toned" but bloodless duel with John Randolph of Roanoke.[68]

As chairman of the military and militia committees, Harrison had occasion to make several speeches which, in effect, encompassed an early history of the American army. For the prevention of desertions he favored an increase in soldiers' pay rather than increasing disciplinary measures.[69] Punishment, in itself, Harrison could show by citing instances, had proved insufficient. Although the bill failed to pass, the Senate decided to improve the officers' lot. Harrison countered a move to abolish the office of major general; too, the army should be retained at its full present strength in order to maintain national defense. Also favored were an increase in the naval force and the establishment of a naval academy. "Decatur did not enter the navy until he was grown to manhood and had received a good education. . . . Perry also was an educated man. . . . A liberal course of instruction would serve to attach . . . [our officers] to the country. . . . It is too late in the day to endeavour to depreciate the benefits of education in any class of the community. . . ."[70] But the "Naval School" was not founded until 1845.

"I am obliged to devote a part of the morning to exercise . . . & the rest to official business," Harrison informed his wife Anna. "Directly after breakfast I have to attend on Committees or to some business at the Public offices. We generally sit now from 12 to 5 o'clock last evening until half past five—fasting so long gives a great appetite & it is not for some time after dinner that I can begin to answer some of my numerous correspondence which really worry me to death."[71]

Individual claims for bounties and back pay still demanded attention; reports recommending new arsenals and forts also consumed a great deal of time. Harrison attempted to obtain a return on a claim of his own for services rendered as commander of regulars and militia on the Tippecanoe campaign. Although his plea was based on similar allowances made to Governor Edwards of Illinois and Governor Tompkins of New York as militia commanders, President Adams, to whom the claim was referred, based his refusal on the precedent of a claim withheld from General William Hull who, indeed, had been court-martialed for cowardice.[72]

Harrison actively supported the President on questions of internal improvements, the Cumberland Road and a Florida canal project. His vote to increase the tariff on certain manufactured imports placed him in opposition to Vice President Calhoun, who had reversed himself on this issue. Nor was the southern contingent interested in sending two envoys to a Panama Congress of South American republics, a measure steered through by the Adams-Clay forces with which Harrison was aligned.[73] The General had improved so fast in his speeches, and his popularity was such in the West, that he had strong hopes of being nominated as vice president. The *Literary Cadet* of Providence, R. I., urged his selection. "He is a statesman of admitted talents and superiority, and if, as the Jacksonians contend, it is necessary that the statesman should also combine the qualities of the soldier, then is General Harrison decidedly the man for the people."[74] Harrison sent a copy of the article to an editor at Columbus. "The whole of the New England states," he wrote his son William, "seem to be determined to support me if they can."[75] But, as Harrison also discovered, Henry Clay's object was "to prevent any Western man from being elected." In the February preceding Clay had privately urged Harrison's nomination upon Adams as Minister to Colombia. Arriving for the opening of the Twentieth Congress in December, Harrison marked Clay's attitude as openly cordial and yet the Kentuckian would say "not a word on the subject of the election."

January 4, 1828, the Clay forces in Pennsylvania nominated Treasury Secretary Richard Rush of that state for vice president. Harrison expressed his disappointment as the Clay men in Virginia formally supported this nomination. In Ohio the "Central Committee" deferred action until the proceedings in Virginia and Pennsylvania had provided some clue as to which way the band-wagon was moving.

Soliciting support in Ohio, Harrison unwittingly chose a Clay man, Bellamy Storer, as one of his correspondents and word of the maneuver got around. Harrison discovered a change in Clay's attitude. Mr. Clay . . . returned my salute so coldly at a party . . . that I did not know but what it would lead to breaking off the common civilities," he wrote William, Jr. ". . . J. Johnston says that I was never more popular in Ohio than at this moment."[76]

The nomination still clung to Richard Rush, a man little known to the West. From Cincinnati came mutterings that the Clay men had treated Harrison "unfairly for they universally ridicule his pretensions." Harrison would have been able to capture a "powerful Jackson influence" in the forthcoming election, it was argued; Clay's men had sacrificed "everything" to "preserve the influence of their

Idol."[77] But Henry Clay had not risked his reputation and honor in putting down one military hero only to have another emerge.

What was left to Harrison perhaps was appointment as major general of the army to succeed the late General Jacob Brown, or as minister to the new Republic of Colombia. Certain newspaper correspondents in Washington predicted his early appointment to the army post[78] but at a cabinet meeting held on April 14, the claims of other nominees were considered. Four cabinet members, Clay, Barbour, Southard and Wirt, united in favor of General Winfield Scott of Virginia; Adams and Rush preferred Alexander Macomb of New York. Both these officers had conducted themselves commendably on the northern frontier during the war and both were still active. Scott, however, had defied army regulations by sending a dueling challenge to General Edmund P. Gaines, an officer of equal standing and, incidentally, another native of Virginia. Macomb, on the other hand, had made a name for himself as head of the Engineer Corps at the capital. "I attributed the preference of Scott to a feeling of which these gentlemen were probably themselves not conscious— the Virginia sympathy," Adams noted in his diary.[79] Macomb, a non-Virginian, was the New Englander's final selection. Both Clay and Daniel Webster, a new Senator, were quite willing that Harrison should go to Colombia and although holding to a preference for Congressman George Robertson of Kentucky, Adams reluctantly yielded "the right . . . to the expedient."[80] On May 22 the nomination was sent to the Senate to be promptly confirmed.

XX

SOUTH AMERICAN ADVENTURE

THE second campaign to elect Andrew Jackson found Harrison silent on one of the day's leading issues. In the administration press Jackson was being smeared as an adulterer, a biased charge based on the fact that Rachel Donelson Robards had not been freed by divorce, as she had been led to expect, at the time the General married her for the first time. So Harrison issued a cautioning warning for his son William, friend of an Adams-Clay editor in Cincinnati. The editor was Charles Hammond, a "sinewy, solid man," who still wore his hair in a cue.[1] With the Cincinnati *Daily Gazette,* a conservative family sheet on his hands, Hammond brought out an anti-Jackson monthly, *Truth's Advocate,* in which the scandal was spread. "If you have anything to do with the new paper for heavens sake do not mention Jackson's family affairs," Harrison wrote his son from Washington. It has done too much mischief already. . . . I would not have one of my family concerned in such an affair."[2] Harrison returned to North Bend early in June to put his affairs in order and on July 3, 1828, he notified Secretary of State Henry Clay that he was ready to start for Colombia.[3] But since the summer and early autumn season in Colombia was accounted harmful to northern constitutions, the General was permitted a stay of two more months on his farm.

The *Daily Gazette,* which came regularly to North Bend, was devoting a fair amount of space to South American affairs. The new Republic of Colombia, welded out of the Spanish provinces of Ecuador, Venezuela and New Granada, had been cherished as a liberal hope by the Adams administration. This sort of benevolent attitude, however, naturally became a party affair with Vice President Calhoun and the southern contingent strictly on the hands-off side. At the head of the Colombian government was Simon Antonio de la Santisma Trinidad Bolivar, liberator of South America from the despotic power of Spain. The tall fiery General had let loose a torrent of rebellion which he was unable to stem and internal peace was not realized. Early in 1828 a convention of statesmen and generals quarreled over proposed constitutional reforms and republican government, if ever attained, was peremptorily shelved. So Bolivar assumed dictatorial powers as the "first step to the lofty station of an Emperor."[4] According to the *Daily Gazette's* correspondent Bolivar's dictatorship was believed wise and essential "until the passions of the Factious shall be reduced." The Liberator had no competent cabinet, it was argued, certainly no Hamilton or Jefferson as Washington had when the American republic was formed, and a change from an absolute monarchy to a libertarian state could not take place without "violent convulsions." An "Aristocratic Republic" would have to answer the purpose until a "Federal Republic" could be safely attained.[5]

The South American correspondent might have added that Bolivar, after a dozen or more years of fighting and a more comprehensive term of love-making on three continents, was ill and worn out at forty-five years. The dominant mood of the great Venezuelan could prevail but little longer in the field and he had less than three years to live. Bolivar desired most of all a means of security and rest but the anti-monarchists would not readily yield their newly won independence. In September the ruse of his mistress Manuela saved the Liberator from an assassination conspiracy.[6] Insurrection in the South and war with the neighboring Republic of Peru followed; meanwhile the United States Minister Plenipotentiary set out from the farm at North Bend, receiving his instructions at Washington from Secretary Clay.

Clay's letter clearly gave Harrison the right to proselyte in behalf of republicanism but not to interfere openly in Colombia's internal affairs. "The distracted condition of that Republic," wrote Clay on October 13—

"the uncertainty whether a constitutional Government or a military despotism is existing there, and the disorders . . . likely to arise in the contest . . . for supreme power, render the mission one of great delicacy. . . . It is hardly necessary to say to you that . . . you will cautiously abstain from identifying yourself with either of the contending parties. Our policy has been long and firmly fixed, to avoid all interference in the internal concerns of any country. . . . It is not, however, inconsistent with it for you to avail yourself of proper occasions to express . . . sincere regret on account of the dissensions which unhappily prevail in Colombia, and . . . ardent hope that they may terminate in the establishment of a constitutional Government, so as to secure her liberty and advance her happiness and prosperity, nor that you should, on proper application, communicate freely and frankly the nature of our institutions and their practical operations. . . . You should collect and transmit . . . any information relative to the view of the Colombian Government. . . . A war is threatened . . . between Colombia and Peru. This government has been requested by Peru to assume the friendly office of mediator. No answer has yet been returned to the application. . . . The President feels an anxious wish that the war may be averted . . . you will embrace some suitable occasion to communicate this sentiment to the Colombian Government."[7]

Clay listed the outstanding claims pending against Colombia which Harrison was expected to settle. A number of American merchant vessels had been seized and large sums in duties illegally exacted.

Insofar as current American politics went, the presidential election had been conceded to Jackson and so Clay had the threat of military usurpation pretty much on his mind. He followed up his instructions to Harrison by writing a long letter to Bolivar urging him to abandon his plan of dictatorial rule in favor of a moderate republican regime but this purposeful action on Clay's part was decidedly inconsistent with an avowed policy of non-interference.[8]

The blunder of nominating a northerner and easterner for vice president had killed Adams's chances in the presidential election. Even Pennsylvania, home state of Rush, would cast its full strength for Jackson; also Kentucky, Clay's state, and his native Virginia. The coming triumph of Jackson was noticeably in the air as Harrison arrived in New York to take passage on the sloop-of-war *Erie*. "I calculate upon returning in two years at farthest and perhaps gen¹ Jackson may shorten that period," he wrote a friend on November 3. "My great object is to save a little money."[9] His salary as minister would be $9000 yearly and $9000 for an "outfit," but Harrison was many thousands of dollars in debt while the affairs of William, Jr., were such as to give concern. Reputed more for conviviality than for success as a lawyer, William had solemnly promised his father that he would reform. Yet "doubts and apprehensions" still clouded the outlook. Harrison suggested that William sell his farm at North Bend, a marriage gift from the General, explaining:

"If I could possibly spare the money you should not be driven to this measure but the alternative of continuing embarrassed and involved in debt & the certain consequences of loss of Happiness & Reputation are not to be thought of without horror. . . . I would not say anything now upon the subject of your habits if I did not know how difficult it was to change . . . but I must again exhort you to abandon the lounging & procrastinating mode of life which for sometime you have followed. In the morning go to your office & stay there until dinner & if you have no other business read professional books & never open any other book in those hours devoted to business."[10]

Carter Bassett Harrison, a youth of seventeen, accompanied his father as attaché while the son of General Solomon Van Rensselaer of Albany was to join the American mission in June at Bogota. "You must fit him out, and *frank him* to me, after his arrival I will pay all his expenses."[11] Harrison's secretary, Edward Tayloe, was the son of Colonel John Tayloe, one of Virginia's wealthiest men. Outside of some linguistic ability, Tayloe was an unfortunate choice. He had accompanied Ambassador Joel Poinsett on his ill-fated mission to Mexico where the minister's open sympathy for the *federalistas,* the republicans of that country, helped to bring about a civil war which led to his recall.[12]

November 10, the party embarked on the sloop *Erie.* The dreaded equinoctial gales of autumn tossed the ship about in the Caribbean Sea, the voyage "most boisterous and protracted."[13] About the middle of December the vessel touched at the Dutch island of Curaçao off present-day Venezuela. Harrison's first impressions of the existing government bore out what he had read of dictatorship. The late constitutional convention had ended ill for the republican faction. At Curaçao the minister was visited by "several gentlemen" banished "by arbitrary edict." Entering the Bay of Venezuela, Harrison transferred to a smaller vessel and landed at Maracaibo, a sleepy port town, on December 21.

Harrison remained for a week at Maracaibo. A. B. Nones, the American consul, placed in his hands sundry evidence of the "illegal confiscation of monies" in the form of excessive levies on American cargoes. More was heard of arbitrary banishment of "respectable men"; military service was forced. Children of the poorer classes customarily ran about the streets naked, their parents indolent and ragged. "The affairs of this country are not only in a most unsettled state," Harrison reported in this first letter, "but the prospect . . . is still more gloomy and ominous. . . . I have found it extremely difficult to obtain a knowledge of facts . . . I run no risk . . . when I say that the government appears to be a complete military despotism; agriculture and commerce appear to be . . . most wretched . . . "[14] Still the patrician ladies, of an olive complexion, their eyes black, their teeth very white, were generally handsome and of limited conversational powers. Mantillas of lace, elaborate tortoise-shell combs, figured silk stockings and slippers of satin set off their complexions and figures. To light a cigar and offer it to a stranger was considered a great mark of civility.[15] Christmas at Maracaibo was given over to a routine of dancing, gambling, and drunkenness among the natives.

The General and his entourage sailed down Lake Maracaibo to the interior. Mule trains traversed the land route to Bogota, a journey of 750 miles south by southwest. The party skirted snow-capped mountain ranges and threaded fertile valleys. Harrison found the natural scenery varied and striking, evidences of man's tyranny most disturbing. "I beheld long strings of manacled wretches, goaded on by the bayonet, to be victims of a distant war in which the People . . . could see no single advantage from its most successful termination."[16] Many had fled to the mountains. In his own country, Harrison was reminded, the ranks were filled by free voluntary enlistments. The party followed the Caracas road through Mérida, Cucuta, and Pamplona. In the town of Saota Harrison learned that a local physician, to whom he had a letter of introduction from America, had been arrested and spirited away. "Through the whole course of my journey, indeed, I met with evidences of a Government which was anything but by which it was called. . . . I was visited in one of the towns . . . by a venerable old man who . . . told me I would find the Government in much confusion and that he hoped I would set them all to rights. Upon my telling him that it was not possible for me to interfere . . . he said that I might do it by speaking to Bolivar, that he believed him to be a good man who intended well to his country, but . . . was surrounded by bad advisers, who were constantly leading him astray. . . . Upon my objecting that I was myself a soldier and very little skilled in such matters . . . he repeated that my countrymen all understood them better than any people in the world."[17]

His introduction to Colombia rounded out by similar scenes and reflections Harrison reached the mountain-perched capital, remote and inaccessible, on the evening of February 5, 1829. He was received by Vergara, Minister of State and Secretary of Foreign Affairs, in a cordial and flattering manner. Vergara reported his impressions of Harrison to Bolivar, who was putting down rebellion in Ecuador. "He is a man who inspires confidence . . . and . . . seems very mild."[18] Vergara added a detail or two five weeks later: "The Minister seems to be a simple and good man . . . more a countryman than a diplomat, not military. But his secretary merits the indictment of being a petty intriguer."[19]

The General Jackson government, recognized as being "a breeze,"[20] was about to take over at Washington. First on the docket, after a Cabinet had been selected, was the subject of spoils for western supporters. Congressman Thomas Patrick Moore of Kentucky, a Crawford man who had switched to Jackson in the House election of 1825, coveted the Colombian post and in return for past favors the General was disposed to grant him his wish. Moore declared it was his intention to serve as minister for about eighteen months and then return to Kentucky as candidate for governor.[21]

A less familiar figure in quest of favors was General Solomon Van Rensselaer whose son had sailed to join Harrison. Although an Adams man, Van Rensselaer had hopes of retaining his own office, that of Albany postmaster. Calling at the White House he breezily pulled off his coat and showed Jackson the wounds suffered at Fallen Timbers in 1794 and at Queenston.[22] Reinstatement followed with little further ado and Van Rensselaer then advocated the retention of Harrison. "From the kind and friendly manner in which General Jackson treated me and the subject," he wrote his son, Major Rensselaer Van Rensselaer, "I was really in hopes I had succeeded. He observed, '*I like this, I like this,* 'tis an amiable feeling we soldiers have for each other, I will think of it, I must see you tomorrow.' " But the President had a consultation with his inner circle that night which decided Harrison's recall. "I . . . would have succeeded," Van Rensselaer was confident, "had it depended solely upon *him* and *me,* but there was interference."[23]

Moore's appointment followed on March 11, one week after Jackson took office. Jackson based his action upon party disapproval of the instructions to the American ministers assigned to the Panama Congress of 1826. The Congress adjourned before the ministers arrived but their instructions had barred any action tending to compromise our relations with Spain, Bolivar's enemy, and they were warned also against encouraging the Liberator's monarchical designs. "It was urged," Jackson explained, "that the recol of the Minister was necessary to show to Boliva & the world my disapprobation of the insulting expressions contained in the instructions which had been imprudently published."[24]

As matters then stood the appointment of Moore was regarded as no reflection upon General Harrison nor did the President wish to hurry the new minister away. "Nothing has occurred to the necessity of his early departure," Jackson wrote Secretary of State Martin Van Buren on May 23. Harrison was instructed to continue in office until the arrival of Moore who was to bring the letter of recall, dated June 2. Van Buren arranged for the sloop-of-war *Natchez* to take Moore to Colombia and to pick up Harrison and his party at Curaçao sometime in the fall.[25]

Bogota lay only 340 miles north of the equator but its location 8660 feet high in the mountains brought perennially cool breezes with two rainy seasons each year. The streets were narrow, the better houses massive. The city was well supplied with churches. Facing the principal square, the Plaza de Bolivar, were the government buildings and a large Corinthian cathedral. Harrison engaged a sizable mansion, the Garden of James, and spent much time in cultivating rows of vegetables new to that country, the seed imported from North Bend. His garden flourished abundantly in a moist soil at some 60 degrees F. The produce, freely dispensed, was in great demand at legation dinners.[26]

An early riser, Harrison cultivated his garden and did his own marketing, and was frequently seen in the handsome coach of James Henderson, British consul-general, who had three charming daughters. A young general in the garrison at Bogota, the antimonarchist Cordova, was a suitor of one. Sigismond Leidersdorf, Danish agent of a British banking house who had personally espoused the cause of Santander, a late revolutionist, became Harrison's chief informer concerning "the secret political history of this government." Colonel Torrens, the Mexican envoy; Albert Gooding, a jeweler from Boston; Count Szeliski, an expatriate from Poland; Doctor N. R. Cheyne, an Englishman, and an American lady suspected as accessory to the attempted assassination of Bolivar rounded out the republican ranks. The presence of two royalists, Colonel Campbell, British chargé d'affaires, and De Bresson, special commissioner from France, further defined the anti-republican breach. A decided coolness was noted between Campbell and Henderson.[27]

That much criticism of Bolivar had appeared recently in American newspapers helped not to smooth the new minister's path. Harrison early discovered that the monarchist and government sentiment yielded little encouragement in the way of refunding excessive levies on ships. The Liberator's defenders protested that the only object of his dictatorship was to restore peace and tranquillity. As soon as all this was achieved, Bolivar would resume a free government.[28]

Harrison's first official letter from Bogota expressed disbelief. The dictatorship was no temporary affair. Bolivar had turned squarely about in his tracks. Although the late constitutional government had provided for a gradual abolition of monasteries and appropriation of their wealth, the church had received back all its privileges. New churches and convents were being erected "even in wretched villages," and "an enormous tax" limited distribution of the "necessaries of life." The press had been muzzled, arms forbidden the people, and a ban placed on patriotic societies which were likely to hatch plots.[29]

That Colombia, its treasury empty, declined to favor restitution of import duties illegally exacted possibly lent vigor to Harrison's pen. The war was not popular, he continued. Colombia was expecting the United States to mediate. Abiding closely by his instructions, Harrison sent Bolivar a reminder of his government's wish to see all differences settled, but by the time his letter arrived the war had been won and in March the rebellion in Ecuador was temporarily quashed. During the greater part of the crisis Bolivar lay seriously ill and as he again took to his bed at Lima that summer Harrison was not to meet him before leaving the country. It is quite possible that misunderstanding would have occurred nevertheless. Harrison had won his first diplomatic victory, the Council of Ministers conceding postponement of a 5 per cent levy on American imports, when he learned that Bolivar was planning to abolish the republic in favor of a constitutional monarchy.[30]

Although Bolivar had asked the United States to guarantee a definite treaty between Peru and Colombia he approached France and England on an issue incompatible with American interests. Bolivar contemplated no successor among his generals and statesmen. After assuming the crown, or a dictatorship for life, as the plan was advanced, he wished either England or France (preferably the latter) to designate a prince, house or dynasty to succeed him upon retirement or death. Should any American republic become alarmed over this measure, he wished these two countries to guarantee their effective intervention in behalf of Colombia's rights.[31]

Although the plan won the favor of Colonel Campbell and De Bresson in the end it was turned down by both England and France. The powers wished to avoid offending Spain, and again no prince in his right mind could be drafted to accept a principality infested with rebellion and anarchy. Another factor perhaps quite as important was the Monroe Doctrine of 1823. "We could not view any interposition . . . by any European power in any light than as a manifestation of an unfriendly disposition toward the United States," read this famous message.

Harrison reported with scorn a city election in which each voter was required to endorse his name on the back of his ticket. In June a new conspiracy against Bolivar was reported and a number of secret arrests disturbed antimonarchical sympathizers.[32]

The American minister continued to cultivate his garden. Harrison's status as a military lion helped to gain him much information. Confidential reports of affairs in Colombia went out to Secretary Van Buren in cipher, while letters of a personal nature, couched in the usual longhand, were risked passage out of the country. "I have made the acquaintance of . . . the Professor of Botany . . . here and he has promised to get a collection of the rare and beautiful plants which may be likely to succeed with us," Harrison wrote his son-in-law, John Cleves Short. "I have two very beautiful small trees growing in my garden that I think will thrive in our climate, one a species of bloom with a yellow flower; the other covered with blossoms of purple." News of the spoils system in operation at Washington and of an actual dictatorship set up had created a stir at Bogota. "It is impossible to conceive the injury to the National Character which the conduct pursued by Andrew Jackson has . . . [wrought here]. Is this the pure Government of the United States? is the question asked by all . . . [Bolivar] and his friends are now using every exertion to get him proclaimed Emperor and I think it highly probable that there will be an explosion even before I get out of this country."[33]

Harrison sharply contradicted a report that Jackson proposed to crown himself King of the United States. Major Rensselaer Van Rensselaer joined the American legation in time to leave a description of a civic event. On the Fourth of July a large party including "all the beauty of the metropolis" celebrated the day at the American legation. Government officers and the foreign diplomatic corps turned out in court costume; the National Band, which had practised for the occasion, played "Hail Columbia" and "Washington's March." By mid-afternoon the dance program was started and dinner, commencing at four, was served to 150-odd guests. Then the company retired to the large parlor decorated with the Stars and Stripes, a framed copy of the Declaration of Independence, and a bust of George Washington. In the evening the floor was again filled with dancers and a collation was served. "The utmost hilarity and good feeling pervaded throughout the whole . . . till midnight when the guests retired . . . well delighted with Yankee hospitality and the urbanity of their Host. Among the toasts many were given in favor of Liberty; but many ambiguous ones were likewise given, by the officers of Government and their friends."[34]

The toasts, it is true, were of significance. Affairs had reached a pass where Harrison's presence at a public function, and his own words, no doubt, provided stimulus for the expression of monarchist sentiments. One afternoon the Bishop of Carthagena, professor of Theology at the Colegio de San Bartolomé, called to invite Harrison to attend a public examination of his pupils. Harrison poured him a glass of wine and heard the good Bishop offer a toast: "The United States of North America: May Colombia follow the course which they have pursued with so much glory and establish a Government that like theirs will secure its happiness and . . . establish universal toleration in religion."[35] Harrison applauded this sentiment and consented to attend the exercises at the college next day. A large company of ecclesiastics, civil and army officers partook of a collation. The Bishop offered first the health of the Liberator, then a toast to the King of France, adding a wish that existing friendship with that country might be fulfilled by a treaty. Harrison, who felt his spleen rising because the King of France had been noticed ahead of the United States government, was put in a more responsive mood when the prelate offered next the very same toast given before the American minister. "The toast appeared to be received by the greatest applause." Harrison arose to acknowledge his great satisfaction at the high compliment. His own people were anxious to see the Colombian government established on a basis which would secure universal liberty and happiness. Still the United States, he continued, did not propose to interfere. He was confident that the political institutions of his own country "provided a sum of human happiness . . . nowhere else to be found," and the people of America would take great pleasure in seeing their example followed. . . .[36]

Two ministers of state who were present sedulously distinguished between a proper degree of freedom and a government too weak to protect itself from the factious and unruly. One of Bolivar's generals then spoke. He too wished for liberty but he knew that liberty could only be secured by a strong ruler. He for one was in favor of putting the scepter in Bolivar's hands. This was the first time, Harrison reported, that the proposal for a monarchy had been publicly advocated. The words of the monarchist created something of a sensation but they went down.[37]

Harrison's statements had been misquoted before and now he was reported as saying that the Colombians were unfit to sustain a free government. Other compromising events stimulated official suspicion and he began to be watched. While chatting with Secretary Vergara at the legation he received an untimely visit from the American lady, accompanied by her son, who was suspected of connivance in the attempted assassination of Bolivar. The lady's son had come to bid Harrison good-by before leaving on a trip to America, but the circumstances were a little awkward. Tayloe, Van Rensselaer, and Harrison's son, moreover, were known as frequent visitors at the home of another lady, charming, no doubt, but "avowedly disaffected" and slated for exile. A week or two later occurred a diplomatic quarrel over the arbitrary imprisonment of an American citizen at Mompos in the North. When Vergara pleaded lack of jurisdiction, Harrison's indignant and extra-diplomatic language led to the return of one of his notes. A final scorching rejoinder failed to heal the widening breach.[38]

Meantime the threat of the monarchists inspired the smuggling of 1500 stand of arms from the Bogota arsenal which gossips got around to Harrison somehow. Civil war was expected to break out momentarily, he wrote Secretary Van Buren on September 7. "Cordova has seduced the battalion at Popáyan and has now gone to Cauca and Antioquia both of which are ripe for revolt."[39]

Major Thomas P. Moore of Kentucky, "an active little man . . . full of anecdote," arrived a week later in the midst of a rapidly brewing storm.[40] September 25, on the evening of his formal presentation to the Colombian government, word reached the city that Cordova was leading a revolt in Antioquia, one of the richest provinces of the republic. The loyalist army at Bogota, commanded by General Daniel F. O'Leary, prepared to march to oppose him.

Perhaps all would have gone well with the American minister at this juncture if Harrison could have gone straightway home; but the sloop-of-war *Natchez* had sailed on to Rio de Janeiro. A letter from Captain Claxton brought by Moore offered Harrison passage home from Curaçao about the first of November to which Harrison replied that he would more conveniently await the vessel at Carthagena, about thirty-six hours' sail from Curaçao and only a journey of twelve days from Bogota down the Magdalena River. To pass the time in the interval Harrison planned an excursion or two into the neighboring country.

Complimented in the grand manner by Secretary Vergara upon

taking leave of the ministry, Harrison took his words to mean that the recent diplomatic quarrel had left no lasting ill will. During the past week the General had been writing a long letter (4400 words) to Bolivar warning him against monarchical advisers and praying for the return of republicanism.[41] He dated and dispatched the letter on September 27, the day after leaving office, and together with Tayloe and Doctor Cheyne rode 72 miles to visit Consul General Henderson in the town of Anolaima. Harrison's son Carter was visiting a Spanish colonel at Guaduas, a neighboring village, where he was presumably safe.

Harrison's stay at Anolaima was interrupted by the arrival of Major Van Rensselaer who had ridden at a breakneck pace from Bogota with startling news. A young Virginian in the loyalist army, Lieutenant Dabney O. Carr, Van Rensselaer reported, had turned renegade and informer against Harrison, Tayloe, Henderson, Colonel Torrens of Mexico, Leidersdorf the banker, and Harrison's son Carter. Presumably all these gentlemen had been fomenting Cordova's rebellion. Carr's tale was readily believed and the youth was rewarded by the appointment of aide-de-camp to General O'Leary. Van Rensselaer wished to warn the General against what seemed to him to be actual intrigue on Moore's part but Harrison declined to listen further.[42]

Harrison sent Tayloe to escort his son to Bogota lest he be subjected to insult. Returning to the capital he at once went to Moore, intending, as he put it, "to demand of the Colombian Government a specification of the charges . . . against me."[43] Moore demurred. Carr's statement, he said, had implicated neither Harrison nor any member of his official family and although the Colombian ministry had expressed alarm over a suspected plot he did not believe any further charge would be made. Actually this was not quite the fact. Harrison had been allowed to return only on Moore's personal guarantee of his deportment. For several days Harrison remained at the legation as Moore's guest but he declined to attend a state dinner arranged in the minister's honor, dining instead with Albert Gooding the jeweler. But Gooding was a man of republican principles as well as a creditor for large sums. On October 13, after Harrison had gone on a trip to the salt mountain of Zipaquira, thirty-six miles away, word was brought that Gooding had been arrested and jailed.[44]

A message from Moore warning that Gooding would not be released until Harrison left the country was couched in matter-of-fact terms. Harrison replied warmly that notice of his intended departure on October 19 had already been given. Was it not the instant duty of the minister, he suggested, to order Gooding's release? But when Harrison returned to Bogota another assassination plot was in the air. According to whispered confidences from Moore, Harrison and Gooding were concerned in a plot to kill Colonel Campbell, De Bresson, and Secretary Vergara. A report had been circulated also that Cordova had beaten the loyalist army which had marched to attack him.[45]

Harrison took command at the American legation. If reports of Cordova's victory were true warm work might be expected. Moore darted out ostensibly to obtain information but returned with no further news. He was, however, known to be in the confidence of Vergara's chief clerk. Twelve men were then mustered and a watch kept up during the night. Finally it was discovered that the loyalist army could not have advanced two-thirds as far as the assigned place of disaster. The story, traced to a government minion, had been a ruse to enable Vergara to discover his enemies had there been any demonstration of joy.[46]

Harrison occupied himself in securing Gooding's release and was accompanied wherever he went by a volunteer bodyguard comprising Carter, Van Rensselaer and Tayloe. October 19, four days after Gooding was let out of jail, the party took leave of Bogota. Harrison bore away in the shape of a farewell souvenir a note "pregnant with charges" from Secretary Vergara. It was plain that he had been suspect for weeks.

The Magdalena River provided a swift passage coastward and after stopping at Guaduas and Mompos on the way, Harrison reached the walled city of Carthagena on November 13. Cordova's revolt had been crushed, the General slain, and the Colombian government remained a dictatorship. Three new exiles, Count Szeliski, Sigismond Leidersdorf and Colonel Torrens, arrived and consorted with the rest of the proscribed.[47] It was a long weary wait. The *Natchez* failed to appear and so, early in January, passage homeward was secured at the General's expense in the packet brig *Montilla*. The presumption is that Harrison's letter had been delayed in reaching the *Natchez,* which had proceeded under orders to Norfolk.

A rough homeward passage brought the party into New York on February 5, 1830, one year to the day following the arrival at Bogota. Harrison had an interesting story to tell when he dined with the editor of the New York *American,* scholarly Charles King. The publicity spotlight trailed the deposed minister as he rode to Washington to make a personal report. For weeks the press of the city debated

Bolivar's policies and career, the propriety of Harrison's removal, the extra expense involved in appointing a new minister. It was the New York *American* and the *Commercial Advertiser* vs. the *Morning Courier* and *Enquirer,* a vigorous Jackson sheet, and the items were widely reprinted. Letters from Bogota dubbed Moore a panderer, a reputation already won in his own country, and he had made himself unpopular with Harrison's friends.[48]

Moore's dispatches to Secretary Van Buren apparently were not calculated to absolve Harrison in any way. Suspicions of revolutionary and assassination plots were coldly exhibited while the new minister showed he had done his best through it all. Vergara's formal charges against Harrison contended that by the minister's acts, his conduct, and in his official notes, he had always shown himself an enemy of Bolivar and the Colombian administration.[49]

Harrison defended himself in a pamphlet covering some seventy pages and reprinted his letter to Bolivar. Naturally there was much to be said in the minister's behalf yet Harrison revealed that he had barred few friendships, a catholicity of taste somewhat dangerous in an arbitrary state. And he had consistently praised the merits of liberty and republicanism in a country heading the other way. It is unlikely that Harrison had exceeded his instructions but, nevertheless, his words and actions had been sadly misconstrued. One does not pause to wonder why.

The pamphlet won an appreciative word from former President James Madison and restrained criticism from John Quincy Adams, now living in retirement at Washington. Madison wrote from Montpellier: "Whatever may have been the different views taken of the letter to Bolivar, none can contest the intellectual literary merit stamped upon it, or be insensible to the Republican feelings which prompted it."[50] Harrison paid a morning call on John Quincy Adams who summed up the situation in his diary:

"The conduct of Bolivar has for many years been equivocal. As a military leader, his course has been despotic and singular. His principles of government have been always monarchical. . . . Harrison was but a short time there, but long enough to get involved in some of their party divisions. It was perhaps impossible to avoid it. . . . [His letter] must have nettled the Liberator beyond measure. . . ."[51]

Harrison also called on President Jackson and was "very graciously" received.[52] The Tennessean was the seventh chief executive with whom Harrison had enjoyed personal acquaintance, although in this case no substantial favor. Jackson had also removed Harrison's son, Symmes, from the Vincennes Land Office. A charge of defalcation was lodged against Symmes.

Party lines stiffened in Congress as Harrison asked for a redress in salary to make up for time lost at Carthagena and the application was denied. The old financial problem was harrying the General again as he started home on March 31 to unravel the tangled affairs of his sons, William Jr., and Symmes.

DEPRESSION YEARS

ILLIAM JR. had failed to keep his pledge to be diligent and sober. His law practice almost abandoned, he had moved his family from Cincinnati to the North Bend "Cabin." In March, 1830, he arose from a sickbed "a sadder and wiser man" and resolved to do better but mounting debt unsteadied him.[1] Harrison's third son, John Scott, a local magistrate and justice of the peace, had fared well in comparison. To Scott, as a business partner, Harrison had entrusted the management of his farm during the ministry to Colombia. Scott's own farm of 800 acres, deeded him by his father, bordered the Indiana line on one side and William Jr.'s farm on the other, the family property ranging about five miles west from the Cabin. Son John Cleves Symmes, removed from the Vincennes Land Office, was living with his wife and her widowed mother on the Kentucky side of the river, two miles from North Bend.

Symmes had been highly respected and popular in Vincennes. In addition to his Land Office duties he served as chairman of the Borough Board of Trustees and supervisor of the library which was installed at Grouseland, Harrison's former home. He encountered financial difficulties after cashing a $5000 draft on the United States Treasury for Captain William Prince, a local lawyer and former associate of the General. The draft was protested as unauthorized, Prince proved insolvent, and Symmes was held liable for the amount plus interest and certain disputed Land Office claims, a total of $12,-000.[2]

Of Harrison's other six children, Benjamin had studied medicine and obtained his degree; Carter Bassett was about to enter Miami University to prepare for the law. Betsey and her husband, John Cleves Short, were living on a near-by farm, a wedding present from the General; Lucy Singleton Este, the second daughter, had died some years ago; Mary Symmes had recently married Doctor John H. Fitzhugh Thornton of a Virginia family and was living in the near-by village of Cleves; Anna Tuthill, the youngest, was a maid of sixteen.

"My Maxim through life," Harrison wrote William Jr., "has been

'Nil Desperandum.' I will set myself to work to renovate your Fortunes."² The sidewheeler *Telegraph* landed the General at Cincinnati on April 15, 1830, whereupon steamboat captains began to acquaint themselves with his personal schedule. Whenever Harrison was in the city, the late afternoon boat awaited his arrival on board before putting out.⁴ Arriving home after an absence of nineteen months, the General exhibited a bright-plumed macaw and some exotic plants for Anna's flower garden.

After a talk with his son, who had decided for himself to work on his farm, Harrison returned to Cincinnati for a stay of three days. "The object of the General's visit," a friend explained, "was to make arrangements with his creditors, and as far as possible to relieve himself from embarrassment, and also to satisfy William's creditors. The latter object seems to interest him much more than the former. . . . The General himself is highly flattered with his prospect of accomplishing both objects, without great difficulty. He is, however, of a sanguine temperament and what would, to most men, seem insurmountable difficulties . . . would to the General be disposed of very easily. It may be considered a happy circumstance that he is possessed of this disposition. Were it the reverse, he could not be otherwise than miserably unhappy."⁵

The outlook was rather serious. While the amount owed by William is not revealed Harrison himself was still involved for at least $20,000 largely on account of the failure of the iron foundry. After satisfying interest charges the General secured postponement of the principal, in order to satisfy his son's debts first. His friends in the city, including a number of Jackson men, made him the guest of honor at a public dinner, the non-partisan nature of which was acknowledged by a toast to Minister Thomas P. Moore.⁷ Harrison came to regret this conciliatory gesture. Letters received from Colombia declared that one of Bolivar's generals had "publicly denounced Mr. Moore as the informer of your participation in Cordova's conspiracy and in the assassination plot." The book closed slowly. Correspondence continued for months. In August, finally, Harrison assured young Van Rensselaer of his belief in the chicanery of Moore who in fact had been shown "as being the sole Author of all the Violent Conduct of the Gov^t of Colombia against Mr. Henderson and myself. . . . I must confess too, that I was so far deceived by his professions as to come under mutual obligations of friendship with him. . . ."⁸

The principal means by which Harrison could raise money to pay off William's debts and his own was to sell land. First he offered at auction some tracts located east of Cincinnati, in addition to sundry holdings in Vincennes, and finally some highly prized land in eastern Indiana, including that part of the Great Miami delta which lay just across the Ohio state line.[9] Despite his present financial difficulties, citizens everywhere turned out to welcome him home. His appearance at Madison, Indiana, while on a trip to Kentucky to witness a court hearing on Symmes's tangled affairs, was the signal for another public dinner in his honor. With Jacksonians less conspicuous at this gathering, Harrison advocated continuance of Henry Clay's "American System," which had set up a protective tariff to pay for Federal improvements of roads and waterways, and the construction of canals. Although farmers in Colombia could not complain of inadequate tariff protection, Harrison pointed out, flour shipped from America met with little competition in seaport towns because of a lack of good roads connecting mills at Bogota and Mérida with navigable waters. "Would it be believed that in all Colombia, there is not a road upon which a carriage can travel for a single mile but in a circuit round the walls of their principal cities? Nothing can prove more clearly . . . that an adherence to our system of internal duties is necessary to give its proper effect to the tariff."[10] Harrison went on to criticize Jackson's spoils system to the tune of hearty applause. "Nothing could exceed the enthusiasm with which the speech and toast [to the town of Madison] were received."

Invited to attend a public ceremony at the Tippecanoe battleground, Harrison declined by reason of an attack of ague and fever. October 21, the remains of the dead heroes were collected and interred in one large coffin bearing the inscription "Rest, warriors, rest."[11] Speakers on this occasion referred to the General in "warmest terms of admiration" but had he attended he could not have returned home in time to find his son Symmes still alive. Aroused by a message bearer during the night, Harrison reached his son's deathbed only in time to witness the end. The disease was diagnosed as typhoid fever.[12] "It almost broke my heart," Harrison wrote General James Findlay, then sitting in Congress. "And never did a house exhibit a scene of greater distress. Never was a man taken away whose life was more necessary to his family. Mother and Daughter both in bad health and the six orphan children, four ill."[13] The widow and children were taken into the Cabin at North Bend where medical attention and solicitous care soon brought restored health. To Major Van Rensselaer Harrison declared Symmes's death "the most severe affliction I have ever experienced."[14]

Party opinion was sensitive to every turn of phrase and the anti-Jackson press would make the most of the death of Harrison's son. Friends of Symmes in Vincennes passed resolutions of regret and voted to wear armbands of crape for thirty days. The *Indiana Gazette* left nothing unsaid in emphasizing the high standing of Symmes in the community. "His integrity, honesty and capability was frequently exercised in the several offices he sustained. . . . His friendly attachments and the general esteem of his fellow citizens, furnish proofs of the goodness, simplicity and honesty of his heart." Editor Charles Hammond of the Cincinnati *Daily Gazette* took pleasure in reprinting these remarks, adding his condemnation of the "spirit of proscription that removes such a man from public employment." His editorial was interpreted by a local Jackson sheet as a malignant thrust at the President and for days the point was warmly debated.[15]

To satisfy Symmes's debt the government had sued for Mrs. Pike's property, consisting of a modest home and some farmland on the Kentucky side of the Ohio. Harrison anticipated that the decision might be adverse in which case the care of the family would devolve upon himself. "It is however not the trouble and expense which I fear," the General admitted, "but . . . that my utmost exertions to provide . . . will be ineffectual."[16] He advised that his son's widow, Clarissa, petition Congress for allowance on the disputed items charged against Symmes and "for relief generally." After taking a fling at the Senate race, won by the Clay candidate, Thomas Ewing, Harrison departed for Washington to confer with Colonel Richard M. Johnson, Congressman from Symmes's district. Johnson, a large-hearted sponsor of relief legislation for veterans, willingly undertook to mediate. Politics was laid aside for the moment. The widow of Symmes was not only the daughter of the late General Zebulon Pike but the daughter-in-law of General Harrison whom the Kentuckian now eulogized before the House. "Who is General Harrison? . . . The son of one of the signers . . . the history of the West is his history. . . . Universally beloved in walks of peace . . . he has been yet more illustriously distinguished in the field."[17] Congress agreed to allow a substantial credit on the disputed Land Office items and set a period of eighteen years for payment of the debt without interest.[18] The action was rather the more gratifying from the fact that a Jackson partisan had been its principal sponsor.

Returning home in good spirits, Harrison rented out William's farm to a tenant. There was no longer any hope of his son's permanent reformation. Always a temperate man, Harrison had become something of a prohibitionist, abandoning the corn distillery common to every large western farm. As president of the Hamilton County Agricultural Society he made his stand known in an address before the annual meeting. "Dark, unsightly manufactories of a certain poison" established on farms ill-suited the "heart cheering prospect of . . . fields of grain exhibiting the spiritual proof that the seed has been cast on good ground. . . . I have sinned myself ; *but in that way. I shall sin no more.*"[19] Sweet cider only was served at Harrison's table.[20]

After a moderately successful harvest season, profits realized by the firm of Harrison & Harrison were wiped out early in the spring. The year 1832 was most troublesome financially. The General had two families besides his own to support, he entertained innumerable visitors, many for periods of weeks, and he was now approaching sixty. During February and March he lay "dangerously ill" from ague and fever.[21] Then a great flood carried away buildings and fences along the Miami and Ohio Rivers, desolating farm lands and the lower portions of Cincinnati. His strength not wholly recovered, Harrison rode out to direct the rebuilding of fences but suffered a relapse and again took to his bed. Toward the last of April he felt well enough to accept appointment on the Board of Visitors attending the June examinations at West Point. Lewis Cass, Jackson's Secretary of War, had extended the invitation.[22]

Money was exceedingly scarce but the General decided to make the trip, having some personal business to transact with a creditor, the United States Bank at Philadelphia. To pay his traveling expenses he borrowed $220 at interest of 3 per cent a month.[23] The ceremonies at West Point were enjoyable but while visiting the Van Rensselaers at Albany the General was again stricken ill. At home, he learned, the weather had been cold, the crops backward. Scott and William replanted most of the fields and then came a disheartening drought. "With one exception I have not seen a single field of corn higher than a man's knee," William wrote General Findlay on July 4. "You know at this time it is generally high as a man's head. We have a parched earth and a brazen sky. What is to become of us, God only knows."[24]

The combined efforts of the General and his sons resulted in a fair hay and wheat crop but the corn was light and interest charges on debts left barely enough money for taxes. Admittedly despondent, Harrison lay awake nights endeavoring to plan some sure means of extending the farm income without further recourse to loans. By converting the stone distillery into a steam mill, he decided, it might be possible to manufacture kiln dried Indian meal as soon as there was enough money to purchase a small engine. Monies received from land sales had satisfied all of William's creditors and most of his own yet he still owed $12,000. Two thirds of this liability lay in a note signed by a Cincinnati iron merchant for whom the General had stood security. Although Thompson Neave, Harrison was confident, was "doing a most profitable business," apparently the cosigner of the note would have to pay, his creditor the United States Bank.[25]

Politics and the state of the nation were not entirely abandoned. Ohio swung back into the Jackson column in the state election of 1832 and helped to build up the President's majority over Henry Clay in November. An avowed friend of the United States Bank and the monied interests of the country, Clay carried only Massachusetts, Rhode Island, Connecticut, Delaware, and his own state of Kentucky. The new Vice-President was Martin Van Buren of New York.

Harrison again had cast his vote for Clay, but he could hardly do otherwise than support the administration in respect to an issue which threatened the bonds of the Union. The state of South Carolina, declaring against a high tariff obnoxious to the cotton planter, had threatened "nullification" of Federal revenue laws. John C. Calhoun argued that since the Constitution was a mere compact between sovereign states, a state therefore possessed the natural power to nullify any Federal law which it considered unconstitutional. While New England cotton manufacturers tried to conciliate Calhoun, the cry of nullification was taken up by Senator Robert Y. Hayne and Governor James Hamilton of South Carolina. Declining to collect tariff revenues at the customs houses South Carolina called upon her sons to defend her. Daniel Webster and Jackson united in resisting Hayne and Calhoun. In 1830, Webster's famous reply to the Senator had breached the southern defenses; in December, 1832, reassured of support by the electorate, Jackson issued a proclamation which branded nullification as an "impractical absurdity." He went further: "Disunion by armed force is treason."[26] South Carolina temporized while Representative Gulian C. Verplanck of New York offered a tariff measure cutting duties as much as 20 per cent in two years. The bill was still an administration measure however. It was making little headway in Congress when Jackson insisted upon the enactment of a so-called "Force Bill" which would permit the use of armed forces, if necessary, in collecting the public revenues in South Carolina.

Although a states' rights man, Harrison regarded himself also as a representative of a family which had sacrificed much to secure and maintain a united government. Nullification, he argued, was a states' rights doctrine carried to such an extreme as to injure the Union, an incomprehensible stand. Supporting therefore Jackson, who would maintain the law first and then reduce tariffs, he made his attitude clear in a letter to Secretary of War Cass:

"I have never been more astonished at anything in my life than at the opposition in the senate to the [Force] bill reported by the Judiciary committee . . . I can come to no other conclusion than that many of them have lost their senses.

"In relation to the tariff I think that the course is so obvious that it is . . . [strange] it has not been adopted at once by those amongst the enemies of the [American] system who are the friends of the Union as well by the moderate tariff men. I mean a gradual reduction of the duties to commence after one year and to bring them down to the rate that is proposed by the anti-tariff men in the course of five or six years more.

"I hope to Heaven that the President will adhere to the principle of his Proclamation. He . . . will be supported by the great majority of the American people. I can answer for Indiana & if need be I will abandon my farm & take the rounds amongst the *boys*. . . . It has been for my country that I have endeavoured to . . . fix these Principles, and in that cause I would spend my last breath. . . .

"Do not, my dear friend, suffer the sarcasms of fools to induce the Executive to decline the support of those who were his political enemies. . . . There are those of us little folks who will support him to the death . . . altho we disapproved of some of his former acts. . . ."[27]

Harrison could answer for Indiana rather than Ohio as he had recently visited Indianapolis, the new capital, and there declared his sentiments. Since the statehouse was then under construction, the legislature met in the courthouse where Harrison was greeted as a friend home from the wars. Resolutions of gratitude for his past services were placed on the record. At a public dinner in his honor the General was extolled in a speech "extensively circulated & . . . very kindly received."[28]

Harrison's suggestion that tariffs be lowered over a period of five years occupied middle ground between the Verplanck bill and a compromise measure to be introduced by Henry Clay. While the former bill, an administration measure, would lower the tariff by 20 per cent in two years, Clay's required ten years to bring down duties by about the same amount yet it won the favor of the states' rights men in Congress on the ground that it was an actual compromise and so was enacted.[29]

Clay was still powerful in the Senate, his principal rival Daniel Webster who had not only opposed disunion but any tariff concession whatsoever. No one yet knew whether the Kentuckian would again run for the presidency. The field being more or less open on both fronts, an early bird in Colonel Richard M. Johnson was advanced as successor to Andrew Jackson and following the adjournment of Congress in March, 1833, both Clay and Webster planned trips.

Clay contemplated a journey, starting in July, to Buffalo, Niagara Falls, Canada and Boston; Webster got away some weeks earlier and toured the West. Webster's Federalist politics of two decades ago had been almost forgiven during the recent nullification crisis. As he sat between Generals Harrison and Findlay at a public dinner in Cincinnati he (the guest of honor) and the Constitution "were lauded to the skies."[30]

Webster was accepted as a favorite candidate by many regular Clay men in Ohio, although, as Senator Thomas Ewing acknowledged: "It is not thought best to make any public demonstrations in his favor at present lest it arouse the old distinctions of party, which are not yet fully at rest."[31] Webster's chief rival in Ohio was in fact not Clay but Judge John McLean of that state. McLean, a former Adams man, had been elevated by Jackson to the United States Supreme Court. Nominated at a public meeting in Baltimore, McLean was taken up in Ohio by a coalition of National Republicans—the Clay party—and regular Jackson men who were unwilling to transfer their allegiance to Martin Van Buren or Colonel Richard M. Johnson, heirs apparent on the Democratic side.[32] Daniel Webster, however, had been cordially received in the West.

For the past thirty-five years Harrison, the son of a Signer, had been prominent at Fourth of July celebrations at Cincinnati and Vincennes. July 4, 1833, the General spoke at Cheviot, east of North Bend. The nullification question settled, the Constitution itself and a growing abolitionist problem were of primary concern. The city of Cincinnati had attracted several prominent Easterners—Doctor Lyman Beecher of Boston was one—who were wont to disparage the assumed moral right of man's rule over slaves.

Urging the cultivation of amity between the sections, Harrison declared there should be no "insulting interference with the domestic concerns of the South." Although the principles of secession and nullification were "equally dangerous and repugnant to the Constitution," yet neither the national government nor the free-soil state governments could legally interfere with the right of the South to possess property in slaves. By constitutional principles, Harrison went on, "the slave population is under the exclusive control of the States which possess them." If the national government wished to aid the cause of emancipation, then the existing Treasury surplus should be appropriated for the purpose of slave colonization and the purchase of freedom. "With the sanction of the States holding the slaves, there appears to me to be no constitutional objection to its being thus applied. . . . By a zealous prosecution of a plan formed upon that basis, we might look forward to a day . . . when a North American sun would not look down upon a slave."

In view of recent slavery outbreaks, how would it be possible to allow negroes equal social rights and privileges in a community in which they composed the majority? Harrison expressed both the pride and the fears of the South:

"Is there a man vain enough to go to the land of Madison, of Macon, and of Crawford, and tell them that they either do not understand the principles of the moral and political rights of man; or that, understanding they disregard them? . . . To whom, then, are they to address themselves but to the slaves? And what can be said to them that will not lead to an indiscriminate slaughter? . . . I support my assertion that the discussion of emancipation in the non-slaveholding States is equally injurious to the slaves and their masters, and that it has no sanction in the principles of the constitution. . . . The principles upon which our glorious Union was formed, and by which alone it can be maintained . . . [are] those feelings of regard and affection . . . manifested in the first dawn of our Revolution, which induced every American to think that an injury inflicted upon his fellow-citizens, however distant his location, was an injury to himself, which made us, in effect, one people. . . ."[33]

A printed pamphlet, which set forth the speech, plainly showed Harrison to be an enemy of secession and nullification, a protector of property rights in slaves, and, differing from Clay, an advocate of emancipation through colonization. Although historians have denoted Harrison's political beliefs as cloudy and undiscernible, his anti-abolitionist sentiments were to be reiterated many times.

A son was born to John Scott and his second wife, Elizabeth Irwin Harrison, that summer. Inasmuch as Scott's house at Point

Farm was then under construction the mother was made comfortable at the General's home, the "Cabin," which thereupon became the birthplace of a United States President.[34] Harrison's sons customarily gave each other's names to their children; Scott named his fifth child for Doctor Benjamin Harrison, who was then absent on a trapping expedition in the Rocky Mountains.[35] The doctor was of a lively and adventurous disposition, his namesake a scholarly youth who became a lawyer and Indiana Supreme Court reporter, a Civil War general, United States Senator, and twenty-third President.

Viewing an early scramble to make Colonel Richard M. Johnson, now a Senator, the leading candidate for the Democratic presidential nomination, one ponders the reason for so much activity. It was explained, however, that the Colonel was being advanced to rally the working men to the cause of Martin Van Buren, a non-hero from New York.[36] Johnson, sponsor of a bill abolishing imprisonment for debt, was presented as the foremost western military figure who might step into President Jackson's shoes. If there existed any hero fit for the White House, in fact, Colonel Johnson and none other had to be it.

Early in 1833, therefore, military history in the West began to be rewritten to suit the demands of the moment. A new version of the Battle of Tippecanoe, for example, appeared and although Colonel Johnson had not fought in that battle it was pointed out, nevertheless, that another Kentuckian, the late Colonel Joseph Hamilton Daveiss, had been the real hero of that conflict. "The army was completely surprised, dismay and despair seized upon the commander and his men—all was given up as lost when a Kentucky field officer [Daveiss] called upon his own command of mounted rangers to follow him, rushed upon the enemy and with the loss of his own life gained a complete victory and saved the army." It was indicated as a fact known to every one that Daveiss was the real hero of Tippecanoe.[37]

The story appeared in the administration press of at least four States in the West. A Jackson man, Senator John Tipton of Indiana, replied for Harrison under the signature of "Volunteer." Harrison's comment, in a letter to Tipton, pointed out that Daveiss had fallen early in the action while leading only a few men and that no Kentucky mounted rangers, so-called, had taken part in the campaign.[38]

With the wind blowing strongly from Kentucky, Harrison declined an invitation to attend a celebration of the Battle of the Thames held in October near Frankfort. The actual object of the affair was to celebrate Colonel Johnson and it might, a partisan noted, "lead to his candidacy for President." The same idea was in the minds of New York Democrats who assembled at Tammany Hall to celebrate "the victory achieved by col. Johnson at the river Thames."[39] No notice was taken of any general or of Governor Isaac Shelby, actual leader of the Kentuckians. Shelby was no longer living and Harrison, seemingly, was a political corpse.

Heroes could come and go. Harrison's present scheming centered about a means to earn his numerous family a living. He went to great lengths in preparing for the manufacture of kiln-dried corn at his farm, but contemplated an alternative should the plan fail. It was the General's idea to conduct an expedition of volunteer followers up the Missouri River and south to the "frontiers of Mexico," in other words Texas. Harrison confided the plan to Senator Tipton, his friend and defender. My principal object, Harrison wrote after thanking the Senator for the "Volunteer" article—

"is to enquire whether you know any thing of a Delaware chief called Nicoming who was with me at the battle of the Thames & an other called Little Beaver of the same tribe. The latter . . . saved my life by killing the Indian . . . sent . . . to assassinate me when I was with the army at Seneca. . . . Two Indians such as I know Nicoming & the Beaver to be may be of great service . . . on an expedition of the kind I contemplate. You will say perhaps that such an enterprise is not suitable to my advanced age. If my health should continue until the Spring as good as it is now I would have no hesitation in undertaking it. My constitution seems suited to exposure & hardship. But at any rate if my corn drying scheme fails I shall have no alternative. The Bank U. S. which is my creditor for all of the Neave debt must soon wind up its concerns. I have sold so much of my property that should I be obliged to sell as much as would clear me of debt I should be left without the means of supporting the large family or properly families which are dependent upon me. . . ."[40]

Harrison's good health did not continue. In February, 1834, as he was preparing to go to New Orleans to obtain finances from an interested backer he was again stricken by ague and fever. In swift succession followed several other strokes of misfortune. The General was not exactly pleased to greet his son Benjamin, who returned unexpectedly from his trapping expedition after getting rid of "at least $1000 in a maner totally unaccountable." In April, a cargo of farm produce en route to New Orleans was lost when trees uprooted by high water crashed on the boats. Benjamin and Scott, who accompanied the cargo, fortunately escaped, but the net loss was estimated to be $700. Finally "a most vilanous attack" upon his military reputation found Harrison admittedly "in bad health, in bad spirit & feeling more like a misanthrope than . . . ever . . . in my life before."[41] The derogatory article came this time from Washington. Combined loss of money, health and military repute after thirty-odd years spent in the service of his country the calumny now instituted for quite another purpose made Harrison feel miserable indeed.

EVOLUTION OF A CANDIDATE

APPARENTLY the royal road to popular favor lay over the body of the retired General, ill and despondent, at North Bend. The periodical which sought to elevate Colonel Johnson at Harrison's expense was the *American Mechanic,* of which no issue survives. The article in question occurs however in a campaign biography of Colonel Johnson. Through jealousy or malice, the complaint ran, Harrison had failed to mention in his official report of October 9, 1813, that Johnson had killed the great Chief Tecumseh at the Battle of the Thames.[1]

The article reminded Harrison of the style of another which had appeared in a New York paper some years ago. A visitor from the East happened to fall in with a Kentuckian from whom he learned that when Johnson's regiment finally located the enemy the General was nowhere to be found and so it fell to the Colonel to arrange all the troops and charge the enemy lines.[2]

After perusing the *American Mechanic,* which Senator Tipton sent, Harrison left his sick-bed to write his former aides-de-camp, John O'Fallon, Charles S. Todd, and John Chambers. The replies of these gentlemen indicated unanimity in the belief that not until several months after the battle was anything heard of the Johnson-Tecumseh story. Most of the Kentuckians in the fight had assigned the "honour" of the slaying to a private, David King. After the war, however, at a time when Johnson was running for Congress, O'Fallon was asked whether if the Colonel "did kill an Indian there was not more probability that it was T——e than any other."[3] O'Fallon thought it rather likely and insofar as probabilities went, Harrison confessed that he was of the same mind although the story came much too late for him to include it in his official letter to the Secretary of War.

Colonel Todd volunteered to answer the article in the *Mechanic.* Realizing that Colonel Johnson probably had no hand in it, Harrison declined to be quoted. Relief legislation then pending in Congress interested him to the extent of a three-column long letter to a Kentucky Congressman urging the claims of the veterans of 1791–95 to pensions. The enforced hardships suffered were recounted in detail and some personal experiences of a young ensign were mentioned.[4]

The Chilton letter helped place the General's hat in the ring for the Congressional race in his district but the younger members of the party took matters into their own hands by nominating Bellamy Storer. Harrison's friends were in the minority and could do little to check the movement. Storer, they charged, was the great opportunist. He had declined to run for Congress in 1822 when the outlook was dark; only when party meetings showed signs of strength did "our young aspirants" press for his support.[5] And as Jackson sentiment had slumped in the district Storer was easily elected.[6]

Harrison did not realize it but actually he was the protagonist in a much broader picture. If Colonel Johnson was to be up, the General had to be down and the Democrats strove to assign due credit to each. Nevertheless every seesaw has a tendency to go into reverse. Present accounts of the General's military career were at such marked variance with what army veterans had seen and known in their own day that reaction soon set in. It was at the height of the Johnson-for-President boom that certain western "Whigs" began collecting funds "for the purpose of disseminating political knowledge favorable to the election of the people's candidate for the presidency—William Henry Harrison."[7] The Whig party was the successor of the National Republican and an attempt was being made to affix the label "Tory" upon the Jackson-Van Buren men.

Lest any doubt exist concerning the General's availability, Democratic supporters of Colonel Johnson were helpful in supplying an opportunity for him to emerge. Early in the fall Harrison received an innocently worded letter inviting him to attend a Battle of the Thames celebration at Indianapolis on October 5. But Harrison had read in the paper that the Indiana legislature had moved to "celebrate the victory . . . [obtained] by the American forces under gen. Harrison and col. Johnson on the 5th Oct. 1813." The plum which dropped into the General's lap was sufficiently ripe. Here was an invitation to divide hard-won glory with a one-time Kentucky militia colonel whose partisans were more aggressive than wise. In 2500 words, more or less, Harrison respectfully declined the invitation, mailing a copy of his letter to an influential Whig editor, the friendly and sagacious Hezekiah Niles of Baltimore. Harrison's sentiments received wide circulation in *Niles' Register*.

". . . If it was found necessary to associate any one with me in the command of the army, why were the general officers passed over, and why, particularly, was the venerable, the magnanimous and patriotic Shelby omitted? . . . If I had an associate in the command of the forces, it was unquestionably gov. Shelby and not col. Johnson. But gentlemen, I had no associate in the command of the army. I was as completely clothed with the character of 'commander of the forces' as was gen. Brown or gen. Jackson in their respective districts, to each of whom I was the senior in rank. . . . Have you ever seen a reference to . . . [the Battle of Niagara] as having been gained by 'the forces under gen. Brown and col. Miller?' . . . Would it have been tolerated by any company of the army which achieved that glorious victory [New Orleans] to have it said that the command of the army . . . was a copartnership affair between gen. Jackson and one of his colonels."

Harrison mentioned a few other versions of historical events in which he was supposed to have had a part. Recently an "Epic Poem" had appeared, "purporting to give the history of the war." In this freely rendered account of the late conflict a Kentucky poet had assigned Governor Shelby the role of commander-in-chief of the Northwestern Army throughout the campaigns of 1813. Shelby became the "Agamemnon," Colonel Johnson the "Ajax Telemon" of the poem. The tale that he had been absent during the Battle of the Thames was also examined.

Harrison begged to be excused from the charge of envy or jealousy as he expounded the soldierly principle:

"I pray you to recollect that I was a soldier from my earliest youth; that there are principles recognized in that profession which every one belonging to it is bound to defend, which he may not on any occasion surrender or abandon without dishonor. For his friend a true soldier will willingly part with his wealth; in his defence shed his blood or loose his life, but his right to command he will give up to no one. On such an issue 'he will cavil for the ninth part of a hair.' "[8]

Harrison's letter, declared Hezekiah Niles in his editorial column, "will come home to the feelings of every reflecting man." Lacking the semblance of a popular issue not dominated by Jackson, Webster or Clay, Harrison had been brought out in those quarters where Democratic glory-hunting aroused resentment. However, the General was not considered particularly good political timber in his own district, which was one reason perhaps why he had recently received an appointment destined to relieve his financial burdens. The appointment was based upon public sentiment rather than a strict application of the law. Four judges of the County Court of Common Pleas were evenly divided over accepting a Jackson man for clerk when 1300 signatures were attached to a petition asking that Harrison be appointed Clerk of the Court. The four judges would have split likewise over Harrison's appointment had not illness prevented Judge John M. Goodenow, Democrat, from attending the session which elected the General.[9] Harrison received two votes, one judge dissenting, and although confirmation by three of the four officials was necessary to give the appointment validity it was deemed too popular to be contested with any success.

Harrison took up his duties immediately, receiving some assistance from his son Carter who was attending law lectures in the city. Father and son boarded at Main Street Hotel, where a French traveler in America caught a glimpse of the General. The comment of Michel Chevalier set forth the man:

"I met with one incident in Cincinnati which I shall long remember. I had observed at the hotel table a man of about medium height, stout and muscular, and of about the age of sixty years yet with the active step and lively air of youth. I had been struck with his open and cheerful expression, the amenity of his manners, and a certain air of command which appeared thru his plain dress. 'That,' said my friend, 'is General Harrison, clerk of the Cincinnati court of common pleas. . . . He is now poor, with a numerous family, neglected by the federal government, although yet vigorous, because he has the independence to think for himself.' "[10]

The General had received his present position, Chevalier added, "as a sort of retiring pension." *Niles' Register* with its pointed paragraphs was then crossing a hundred or more editorial desks, East and West. One scant month following the appearance of Harrison's letter, the *Pennsylvania Intelligencer* of Harrisburg recommended "Old Buckeye" as a match for "Old Hickory" Jackson. Although the nickname failed to catch on, "sundry correspondents" of the paper fell in with the idea that Harrison was the man to run against Martin Van Buren.[11] Colonel Johnson had lately taken on the status of vice presidential candidate.

Democrats favoring Van Buren began to take shots at the General. A letter published in a Harrisburg paper signed "No Swiss" Harrison considered "a favorable omen," writing William Ayres of the Pennsylvania legislature:

"The well trained Mercenaries . . . who serve under the Van Buren Banner, fire no useless shots. They select for their victims those only whom they fear. The same writer . . . probably a month ago, if he had spoken of me at all, would have done it with some complacency. . . . You were in no danger of wounding my feelings about anything you could say against the Masonic institution. Neither myself or any member of my family . . . have ever been members. . . ."[12]

Mention of the "Masonic institution" provides a clue to the nature of political activity centering about Harrison's name in Pennsylvania. The "Anti-Masons" of that state were a strong crusading unit. This party received its start some years ago when William Morgan, an itinerant stone-setter, was spirited away in western New York for divulging, so it was claimed, secrets of Freemasonry. Prominent men backed the movement. The excitement which followed Morgan's disappearance was converted to political purposes by opponents of Jackson and Van Buren in up-state New York. In 1832 Henry Clay disclaimed Anti-Masonic support and the group set up a national ticket with William Wirt of Virginia as its nominee for the presidency. Wirt, however, carried only the state of Vermont and although the Anti-Masonic party failed to gain any considerable further power the agitation continued in many rural districts in the North and Northwest. Without doubt the party would strive again to select a national candidate with Webster and possibly Harrison as converts.

In his letter to Ayres, Harrison had disclaimed any partiality for Masonry. Quite likely this sentiment was a keynote of a county convention of Whigs and Anti-Masons held at Harrisburg on January 9, 1835. At any rate the General was recommended as their outstanding choice for the presidency.[13] The news had not yet reached North Bend when the candidate revealed his emergence to a staunch Whig friend in New York, General Solomon Van Rensselaer:

"The last correspondence between us was a letter from you dated about 18 months ago. I did not answer it—for at the time and long after I was greatly afflicted in mind and frequently so in person. I could not write to you without telling you all the tale of my woes. . . . In the midst of my difficulties, however, I . . . resolutely resolved to apply every remedy within my reach to overcome what I could overcome and palliate what I could not. My efforts . . . have so far approached success as to give me every encouragement to persevere. . . . I am greatly aided by the support of an office humble indeed, but still honourable and lucrative. . . . But I have news still more strange to tell you. . . . Some folks are silly enough to have formed a plan to make a President of the United States out of this *Clerk* and Clodhopper!"[14]

The national election was still twenty-two months away, yet with Judge McLean of Ohio already in the field the General's partisans would never win the state if they moved slowly. Early in January, anti-Jackson men of the Ohio legislature joined with a few leading Whigs had nominated McLean at Columbus. The news from Harrisburg was very coolly received by the Cincinnati press. By way of experiment, therefore, Harrison's supporters promulgated two meetings in the near-by towns of Delhi and Miami at which the "Pennsylvania Nomination" was seconded. Then a circular signed by about 250 persons summoned Whig partisans to a meeting in the Cincinnati courthouse. January 31 was a cold windy day yet the report was: "Well attended, better than we expected."[15]

The individuals in charge of the meeting were minor in character but still they did their job by setting an example for the rest of the nation to follow. The proceedings of the Harrisburg meeting were read, a formal report advocated the nomination of Harrison as the "People's Candidate," and a committee was named to bring his candidacy to the attention of every voter. The *Pennsylvania Intelligencer* hailed the news in bold-faced type, giving the attendance in the little courthouse as "SEVERAL THOUSAND" instead of possibly two hundred.[16] Then came word that the Massachusetts legislature had nominated Daniel Webster, who had friends in Ohio, while Alabama designated Congressman Hugh Lawson White of Tennessee as its choice. Judge White was no Whig but a states' rights Democrat who recently had seceded from the Jackson banner. A veteran Indian fighter and statesman, White was regarded as one who could best concentrate the opposition strength in the South.[17]

In the West the people's movement for Harrison became evident alongside names in hotel registers. A custom of the day was to signify one's choice in a column set aside for that purpose. During January the names of Clay, McLean, Van Buren and Daniel Webster were listed in the register of the Union Inn at Indianapolis; February entries were "Whole Hog for Harrison," and "Harrison up to the Shoulders."[18] Another sign of the times was the organization, by sons of veteran soldiers, of "Tippecanoe Clubs" which celebrated every Harrison victory in the field, on its anniversary date, with great éclat.

Van Buren and Johnson were united by Democratic Congressmen on a proposed national ticket that spring while the party's first national convention was to meet at Baltimore to ratify this choice. As running-mate of Van Buren, Johnson faced difficulties. However well he had fought at the Thames he was handicapped politically because of years of association with a colored mistress. During a recent cholera epidemic his faithful mistress had died leaving him two octoroon daughters who were brought up as whites. The South could hardly stomach this. Only strenuous and fraudulent organization work at the Baltimore convention gave Johnson winning majority over Senator William C. Rives of Virginia.[19] As the choice was announced the New York delegation, supporting the Colonel, "set up a tremendous shout!" But "the friends of Rives hissed! All was confusion. All uproar!"[20] Such was the outcome of the first Democratic national convention.

The Baltimore ticket was promptly dubbed the "black ticket." As Editor Duff Green of the *United States' Telegraph* commented:

"It may be a matter of no importance to mere political automatons whether Richard M. Johnson is a *white* or a *black* man—whether he is *free* or a *slave*—or whether he is married to, or has been in connection with a jet-black, thick-lipped, odoriferous negro wench, by whom he has reared a family of children whom he has endeavoured to force upon society as . . . equals. . . . But thank God, to the great majority of the people of the United States we may with safety address ourselves on this subject, with a full conviction that in their breast we shall find a response to . . . patriotic feelings . . ."[21]

Editorial wits went to great lengths in making plays upon the word "color." Still the Democrats were effectively united while the Whigs, coalescing fragments of opposition, had yet four candidates to consider. Henry Clay fumed over the plural party nominations. Scarcely anyone was looking his way. Favoring Webster over any other candidate yet named, Clay well realized the Yankee Senator could never carry the West. Daniel himself was growing a little restless. "They might, at least," he wrote his friend and patron, Nicholas Biddle of the United States Bank, "preach the necessity of supporting *a* Whig Candidate—*some* Whig Candidate. We are in danger of breaking up, & dividing. . . ." Another close friend of the Senator's, Congressman Edward Everett of Massachusetts, advanced the suggestion that the Whigs of the Ohio legislature should nominate Webster, with Harrison occupying second place on the ticket.[22]

Webster, in a letter dated July 2, had the same idea: "It would be very well, if on the 4th in various places, Gen¹ Harrison should be toasted as the Whig candidate for the Vice Presidency."[23]
There was hardly time, however, to arrange this.

Certain historians, in dealing with Harrison's career, have described him as a Governor of Indiana Territory who assembled a few Indians together and cheated them out of their lands (apparently on his own initiative); the tribesmen resentful, he marched up the Wabash and "provoked" a fight with Tecumseh at Tippecanoe.[24] Largely because of military glory won in the Black Hawk war, the Whigs nominated him for the presidency (the learned gentleman who wrote this was confusing Harrison with Lincoln),[25] but he was also available on the ground that, as a respectable retired soldier, he had no record whatsoever on any outstanding issue.

Concerning this last point (the others are obviously out of focus), Harrison did have the advantage of absence from Congress and the Senate during the past seven years. Since newspapers of the day customarily devoted one-half or two-thirds of their editorial space to proceedings in the state and national legislatures a member's speech or his vote on any issue was brought home quite readily. Harrison's lack of support in recent political contests may have been a valuable asset at a time when slavery and tariff and pro-bank men, such as Henry Clay, were cultivating enmities in both the North and the South. At the same time, newspaper files of the period will show that Harrison had been doing some talking and writing on these issues. Although Nicholas Biddle of the United States Bank suggested that the General be permitted to say "not one single word about his principles or his creed"[26] (compare Mark Hanna on William McKinley), Harrison did manage to have his say out on several matters of interest.

First the Anti-Masons asked him a question or two. Was he or was he not, in principle, an Anti-Mason as recognized by them?

For a budding presidential hope, the General's reply was rather stiff. Of course he was no Mason, he reiterated, but he had no knowledge of Anti-Masonic principles other than what was implied in the name. Should it be his fortune to be elected to high office he would not suffer his opinions of Freemasonry to influence him against a group containing "a full proportion of the talent and private virtues of the nation." If Freemasonry was actually an evil, then the remedy lay in public opinion, in the people themselves and in their agents, rather than with the administrators of the national government. The Chief Executive could admit "no qualification of a citizen . . . not declared by the Constitution itself."

Harrison shot an arrow at the spoils system. He would have nothing to do with the spirit of party proscription. Should his friends be successful in placing him in office they might expect in return "every thing that could be required of one possessing a grateful heart" but any debts of gratitude could not and would not be discharged "by the violation of any public obligation." Executive power was vested in the president for the advancement of the public interest "and not to requite personal favors or gratify personal animosities."[27]

In other words, no comfort was assured the crusading Anti-Masons even though they had yet to nominate their presidential choice. Harrison realized he had made himself clear. "I have . . . expressed my sentiments without disguise and whether it be for good or for evil I could not do otherwise," he wrote William Ayres. "I am persuaded too that a general declaration for me by the Whigs & Anti-masons of your state would at once put Webster *hors de combat*."[28] East and West the Whig party was looking to Pennsylvania for the most available candidate. The Keystone State was considered the true testing ground.

It was not too late for Harrison to reaffirm his natural distaste for abolitionism. On May 25, honored at a public dinner in Vincennes, he spoke in the same vein as at Cheviot in 1833. "Am I wrong, fellow-citizens, in applying the terms weak, presumptuous and unconstitutional, to the measures of the emancipators?" Their schemes of "mischief" were deemed highly dangerous to the safety of the white population in the South. Harrison declared even the right of petition unjustifiable as utilized by abolitionists.[29]

The season was late spring, an excursion through familiar woods and valleys inviting. When a long-postponed visit to the Tippecanoe battleground was suggested the General sailed up the Wabash and surveyed the new towns of Terre Haute, Rockville, Crawfordsville, and Lafayette. A round of public dinners and balls served to introduce him to hundreds of settlers in that Indian wilderness he had known some twenty years ago.[30] Harrison declined dinner invitations at Indianapolis and Rushville but was feted at Brookville in the southeastern part of the state. A toast which was offered struck his fancy:

"General Harrison—Like Cato, his countrymen are about to call him from the usual pursuits which have occupied his attention in latter years, to preside as Chief Magistrate, over the destines of . . . [this] Nation. . . ."[31]

The General was very well pleased with his reception. "Everywhere on his journey," read a comment, "the *people,* not partizans, came forth en masse to tender him respect."[32] He felt fairly justified when two Ohio editors placed Webster at the head of a tentative Whig ticket, in authorizing the statement that he would not run for the vice presidency on *any* ticket, a statement which dropped into one editorial column after another. Harrison spent a festive Fourth of July at Lawrenceburg, Indiana, and following other social and military gatherings in his honor at Madison, Louisville, and New Albany two prominent Kentucky newspapers "hoisted the Harrison flag" for President, followed by the Indianapolis *Journal* and the Richmond *Whig.*[33] What now was the sentiment in the General's own district?

When the boat on which Harrison was returning was a little late in reaching Cincinnati several hundred waiting partisans boarded the *Portsmouth* and met the *General Pike* near North Bend. The two boats were lashed together with ropes. Cannon on both sides of the river roared in greeting, steamboat captains tied down their whistles. Harrison was escorted to the Commercial Exchange on the public landing where he gratefully acknowledged the public acclaim. The hat of the Clerk of Court was in the ring.

Public enthusiasm for "Old Tippecanoe," as Harrison began to be called, was still limited to three states in the West when an influential group of citizens fell in with a plan to build a railroad to Charleston, South Carolina. The local sponsors, men interested in Harrison's presidential candidacy, were Doctor Daniel Drake, Cincinnati's best-known physician; E. D. Mansfield, George H. Dunn, president of the Lawrenceburg & Indianapolis Railroad, and Judge James Hall, editor of a pro-Harrison newspaper, the Cincinnati *Courier,* and publisher, in his *Western Monthly Magazine,* of the first campaign biography of the General. In South Carolina, Governor Robert Y. Hayne and Joel Poinsett, antagonists in the recent nullification battle, united in favoring the project. The railroad was expected to link the Ohio Valley with the Southeast, the West supplying its manufactures and farm products, the South its cotton, tobacco and anti-abolitionist ideas.[34]

In August the General was named chairman of a committee representing three states, Ohio, Indiana, and Kentucky. His supporters at once made it clear that his attitude on the bank question, on the tariff and on slavery would be wholly satisfactory to South Carolina. This was stretching one or two points yet it could be said that Harrison had favored Clay's compromise tariff bill of 1833 which the South had supported. The plan for the railroad was deserving of a better fate than the failure which awaited it. Senator John C. Calhoun opposed it on the ground that it would interfere with a united South; administration Democrats in Kentucky and Ohio were outraged because a Harrison group was behind it.[35]

To some extent the movement served to promote Harrison's candidacy. Significantly, also, it coincided with the withdrawal of Judge McLean from the presidential race. Even Henry Clay found himself admitting that Harrison had the best chance. Early in September Harrison and Clay attended an agricultural fair at Carthage, twelve miles up the Dayton Canal. "Very little passed between us on the subject of the Presidency," Clay wrote of the meeting. "He was very respectful and cordial . . . appeared to be in good spirits and I thought seemed confident. I adhere to the opinion . . . that if Pennsylvania will give satisfactory demonstrations of an intention to support him, it will be expedient . . . to run him as the most available candidate against Mr. Van Buren. . . . I fear that it is in vain to look even to New England for the support of Mr. Webster."[36]

Very little may have been *multum in parvo*. Whig newspapers began to quote Harrison as saying that under no conditions would he, if elected, be a candidate for a second term.[37] One Clay paper after another began to come out for the General in Ohio and Pennsylvania while no further doubt remained of Kentucky. And in respect to the important state of New York, a Whig and Anti-Masonic mass meeting in Albany announced a preference for Harrison as President with Congressman Francis Granger of that state occupying second place on the ticket.

Returning home from the county fair, Harrison was thrown from his horse and a "severe contusion" confined him at home for a few days.[38] The wound proved not serious. Excusing himself on the ground that he had to attend the fall meeting of court he declined invitations to attend Battle of the Thames celebrations at Lexington and New York City. The celebration at Lexington was crowded with old soldiers.[39] In New York 300 Whig partisans gathered at Niblo's Garden and applauded a reading of Harrison's official report of the battle. A rival Thames celebration was staged at Tammany Hall where a message from the local Debtors' Jail was produced:

"Sir: Persons confined in the Debtors' Jail beg leave to offer the following . . . [toast]. May the sentiments of Col. R. M. Johnson, which forbid *imprisonment for debt,* become universal. P. S. We shall drink it in cold water, if allowed."

A committee of seven loyal Tammany men was appointed to convey "evidence of sympathy and felicitation."[40]

The election in Ohio that fall was a Jackson triumph in eight districts out of fifteen, the Whigs losing much ground. Harrison sought to explain the defeat in his own district. "Our house was divided against itself." No organization, no "committee of vigilance" existed and the ticket had been named by a clique which the General disowned.[41] As a result, less than 1500 Whigs had turned out to vote in Cincinnati, a city of 31,000 people.

So an effort had to be made to show Pennsylvania, which had elected a Whig and Anti-Masonic governor, that Harrison was still strong in his own district. Handbills announced a big courthouse meeting which, in Whig oratory and enthusiasm, was a real success. The Pennsylvania Anti-Masons were preparing to hold their convention, mailing pointed inquiries to Harrison and Webster. An appeal to join them "in the use of all constitutional, fair and honorable means" for the suppression of Freemasonry elicited a discomforting reply from the General: "Although . . . far from asserting that evils arising from Masonry do not form a proper subject for the deliberation and actions of some constituted authorities of the country," yet he "was certain that there exists no such power, either in the whole government of the United States or in any of its Departments, and that the attempt to exercise it would constitute an usurpation of power, pregnant . . . with mischiefs. . . ."[42]

Under the circumstances the response was unsatisfactory. Daniel Webster answered rather more agreeably. In three different letters to Pennsylvania Anti-Masonic officials Webster denounced secret associations as dangerous to civil liberty and good government, condemned secret societies bound by secret oaths, and announced himself "altogether incapable of disappointing . . . any natural and just expectation which friends may form."[43] Thaddeus Stevens, young Anti-Masonic firebrand, resolved to go for Webster and swing his party with him.

If the Harrison cause in Pennsylvania appeared dark at this moment a split in the Anti-Masonic ranks let in the light. Two conventions, the one heralded as "Democratic-Whig," the other as Anti-Masonic, met in Harrisburg on the second Monday in December. The

Democratic-Whig convention defiantly elected a Masonic president and one or two Masons vice presidents, adjourning then from day to day to await action by the other convention. Thaddeus Stevens, the extremist of his party, advocated calling a national Anti-Masonic convention at which the nomination should be made. It became apparent however that Anti-Masonry might give way to expediency. Following a session of bristling speeches Stevens and eight of his partisans condemned the threatened amalgamation with "Masonic Whiggery" and left the hall. Next day the convention nominated Harrison for president by 89 votes to 29 for Webster. Granger, a leading Anti-Mason of New York, received 102 for vice president.[44]

The other convention at once adopted this same electoral ticket and resolved also against calling a National Whig convention. Although the first choice of many, it was admitted, Webster had been passed over because "we cannot carry him."[45] A Federalist in Congress in 1813, Daniel Webster had opposed the war.

HARRISON VERSUS VAN BUREN

G RANGER for vice president won sanction in Indiana but Maryland nominated Harrison and John Tyler. The South had no particular interest in Anti-Masonry. Granger represented a political trend which was merging with abolitionism.

The nomination of Tyler, a states' rights man who had supported South Carolina's nullification idea, showed clearly the divergence in Whig ranks. A Richmond paper, remarking upon the Harrisburg nomination, rejoiced that the "ultra federalists . . . and a half score disappointed anti-masons" had seceded from the Harrison ticket but paid no attention to Granger.[1] Friends of John Tyler, the ruling choice in the South, hopefully turned to Ohio where state Whigs were to meet on Washington's birthday. Should Tyler be successful in breaking into the Granger phalanx in the Northwest the New Yorker might be induced to withdraw.

Such at least was the hope of Tyler's supporters. Others regarded as unfeasible a national ticket containing the names of two men, two native Virginians, of states' rights and slavery principles. And of course Henry Clay's wishes had to be taken into account. Clay preferred Granger to Tyler, or so the word was passed in Ohio where the Kentuckian's influence was still strong. With Harrison committed to a single term, supporters of Tyler believed that Clay was working to prevent the emergence of any rival Whig who might become eligible for the presidency four years hence.[2] In this one particular Granger was considered no threat.

February 22, 1836, the largest political convention ever held in the western country met in the public square at Columbus. A great ox, weighing 3375 pounds, was divided among delegates numbering 1064 strong.[3] After considerable fanfare and oratory outdoors the delegates hired a theater and settled down to business. Clay men argued that should Ohio fail to sustain the Pennsylvania nomination the Whig cause would be injured, perhaps lost. The financial measures of Jackson's administration were attacked, General Harrison's career duly eulogized. It took a great deal of back-stage argument, however, to bring around the friends of John Tyler.[4] The resolutions finally presented lauded Henry Clay and Daniel Webster as "godlike men" but all the votes went for Harrison and Granger.[5] New York and Vermont also nominated Harrison and Granger in separate Anti-Masonic and Whig conventions. Whatever his views on Freemasonry, Harrison was believed the one candidate who could concentrate the greatest number of votes against Martin Van Buren. Since the vice presidential candidates were voted upon separately, Harrison, if elected, might go into office with Colonel Johnson; Van Buren with Granger or Tyler. So here was one more reason for Clay's efforts to eliminate Tyler from the Whig ticket inasmuch as Johnson was weak in the South.

An attack on Harrison's military career on the floor of the House was replied to by Congressman Bellamy Storer. Once the despair of Andrew Jackson's opponents, the "admiration for *military glory*," a Whig partisan observed, seemed to be working well.[6] Occupied with court duties and the planting of crops, Harrison remained at Cincinnati and North Bend throughout the winter and spring. In a letter to the Maryland Whigs he expressed his thanks for nomination by a group to whom he was little known personally. Well aware of the "partiality" for military fame the General hoped he was otherwise worthy:

"With thousands of those of some other States, I have been associated in scenes where the difficulties and dangers to which we were in common exposed have created a feeling of partiality, which is often found to warp the judgments of good men, and induce them to bestow their confidence and suffrages on those possessing qualifications. Having no advantages of this kind to boast of in relation to my fellow-citizens of Maryland, I am gratified, considering the pre-eminent talents . . . [of others] that I am indebted for the distinction with which they have honored me, to the greater length of my public service, and the belief that, in the discharge of the various trusts which have been committed to me, the confidence of my country has never been betrayed, nor its interests sacrificed. This is precisely the ground which I wish to occupy. . . ."[7]

A letter of thanks to the New York Whigs expressed the belief that he would carry into office, if elected, "a mind uninfluenced by the passions and prejudices which the heat and violence of the late contests have unfortunately produced."[8] Delaware Whigs, who nominated Harrison in April, received an acknowledgment somewhat delayed by illness. Meantime "melancholy news," had come from Texas. Benjamin, the adventurous man of the family, was reported slain and his body mangled by Mexicans.[9] This temporary spell of adversity interrupted a long letter to Congressman Sherrod Williams, a little-known Whig from Kentucky, who was employed, if that is the word, to quiz Harrison, Van Buren and White on issues of paramount interest to most voters.

Most of the questions dealt with Clay measures, pro or con. If the candidate should be elected would he approve of the distribution of surplus revenues and the proceeds of public lands among the states? Would he approve of Federal improvement of navigable streams above ports of entry? How would the candidate dispose of a bill chartering a Bank of the United States? Finally, what was his view of the constitutional power of Congress to expunge from the journal records of a previous session? The last point dealt with the efforts of Senator Thomas Hart Benton of Missouri to expunge from the record a Clay resolution censuring the President for his disposition of the public revenue. Clay had been particularly nettled when Jackson ordered the removal of government funds from the Bank of the United States to various "pet" banks, a measure which all Whigs disapproved.

In one of his unabridged trends of thought which was calculated to leave no doubt in the minds of his readers, Harrison replied in effect that if the first three proposals were approved by the Senate and House he would not veto them. In regard to the fourth question he replied that his previous opposition to the United States Bank had arisen from the fact that its charter had been "clearly violated." Although no enemy of banks in general, he would sign an act to charter another United States bank only "if it were clearly ascertained that the public interest would materially suffer without it." For the present he believed it was feasible to proceed under the existing arrangement in order to discover if government finances could not be carried on without the aid of the bank. Concerning the expunging issue, which was still being argued in Congress, Harrison let it be known that he was definitely against any alteration of the record.[10] Incidentally Judge White of Tennessee had broken with the President as expurging was debated in Congress.

With the exception of pragmatism applied to the bank issue, Harrison's answers can be interpreted as current Whig doctrine. The reply of Martin Van Buren, delayed several months, was orthodox anti-Whig. To the first four questions Van Buren gave negative answers although when he wrote there should be no Bank of the

United States "until the people give to Congress the right to establish one," he occupied common ground with Harrison. The question of the power of Congress to expunge its own records, Van Buren added, was one in which the President had no concern. However, the action was probably commendable in this particular instance, he stated.[11]

Disregarding the final issue, which was petty politics, the processes of historical change indicate the superiority of the Democratic platform over the Whig. Distribution of the surplus revenue did the states little or no good; Clay's land bill, of questionable merit, failed; and the country had outgrown any need for a privately controlled United States Bank. There remained for the Whigs the credit of furthering internal improvements wherever, as Harrison argued, constructive projects were found "of greater advantage to the Union generally" than to the state within which the work happened to be done.[12]

Benjamin Harrison, the volunteer soldier of fortune, had not been killed but only slightly wounded as he escaped a "massacre" of a detachment of Texans. After hiding out for three or four days, hunger and an undressed wound forced him to surrender. He explained who he was to a Mexican general, and in consideration of his father's reputation was supplied with a horse, money, arms and a guide, and turned loose. When the well-equipped ex-prisoner finally showed up the Texans concluded he had turned spy, a theory supported by the Mexican guide. Benjamin was confined for a few days but after a hearing was allowed to go home.[13]

The rejoicing over Benjamin's safety culminated in a double wedding at North Bend. June 16, 1836, Carter Bassett Harrison married Mary Sutherland of Hamilton, Ohio, and Anna Tuthill, the youngest in the family, wed Colonel William Henry Harrison Taylor of Berkeley, the Virginia homestead. Taylor was a grandson of Lucy Harrison Singleton, the General's sister, and therefore a second cousin of his bride. The couple resided at Berkeley until early fall, when Harrison secured Taylor's services as substitute Clerk of the Court. His son Carter had opened a law office in the city. "Your prospects in New York are certainly very flattering," Carter wrote his father upon entertaining a visitor from that state.[14]

Harrison declined with regrets an invitation to attend a Fourth of July celebration in Philadelphia, but wrote a letter in praise of the Pennsylvania militia which had stood by at Fort Meigs.[15] A Virginia Whig convention which met on the holiday endorsed the nomination of Judge White and John Tyler but labeled the choice the "Union

Anti-Van Buren Harrison Ticket." Harrison was most popular in that section which later became West Virginia but even he, a native son, could not offset the claims of "a plain, unassuming Southern Gentleman," in other words, White.[16] Edward Tayloe added a footnote to the convention proceedings, a sad disappointment to Harrison men: "With us there is more virtue than intelligence, at the North the reverse is the case. . . . The banner of State Rights . . . must be our flag."[17] This ruled out a candidate known to favor a high tariff and internal improvements. Moreover, Harrison's early affiliation with the Humane Society of Richmond had not been forgotten.

Harrison still received numerous visitors at North Bend. The situation in Virginia, however, as well as circulated reports that he was feeble and sickly, called for something more than a front-porch campaign. Believing his position to be "one of dignity at least," the General did not intend to enter upon any protracted tour. Still he had relatives in Virginia he had not seen for years.

Early in August Harrison left North Bend and visited the medicinal springs in western Virginia. At White Sulphur Springs he discussed the object of his trip in a letter to General Solomon Van Rensselaer, who had invited him to visit New York. Harrison gave no assurance that he would do so. "I should by no means place myself in an attitude which would give my opponents an opportunity to say with truth, that I was traveling for the purpose of Electioneering." There was only one reason connected with the campaign which had authorized the journey, he added, "and that is to counteract the opinion, which has been industriously circulated, that *I was an old broken down feeble man.* Upon this subject it gives me pleasure to say . . . that I was never in better health in my life."[18]

Invitations to public dinners along the route were declined. A correspondent of a New Jersey paper noted Harrison's appearance at White Sulphur: "He is the object of general attention . . . and is very affable and agreeable. He does not look in very firm health but says he is well. . . . Politics . . . are seldom alluded to."[19] Traveling in the public stage through a wild and mountainous country, Harrison visited Sweet Springs, then Hot and Warm Springs, where the curative waters varied some sixty degrees in temperature. Favorable newspaper comment trailed in his wake. When he declined an invitation to a public dinner at Staunton, the local editor remarked upon his "old fashioned modesty," and "republican simplicity." The Staunton *Spectator* then railed against "the impudence of those hireling editors and letter-writers who . . . have pronounced him an 'imbecile and dotard.' The vigor of his body and mind seem entirely unimpaired—his information on all practical subjects profound and accurate."[20] On September 14 Harrison reached Richmond to find some Whig cohorts awaiting him. Inasmuch as considerable comment concerning his health was still going the rounds his steering committee, represented by Major David Gwynne of Cincinnati, had decided to make something of the trip.

With the national election less than two months away and state elections even closer, the Whigs were on the defensive. They had made some use of the religious issue, condemning Van Buren as a friend of the Pope, "the fawning sycophantic flatterer of a foreign tyrant." In Virginia Van Buren was hailed as an advocate of free negro suffrage," his running mate Johnson pinked for his "marriage" to a "negress of unredeemed blackness."[21] Yet the persistent attacks on Harrison's military record, the cry that the Battle of the Thames was planned and fought by Johnson, and the canard that Harrison, while a member of the Ohio Senate, had voted to sell debtors into slavery, called for explanations which were tedious, perhaps, but necessary. An old friend, John Pleasants of Richmond, obliged the General and his committee by inquiring into the charge concerning maltreatment of debtors,[22] a class of men for whom Colonel Johnson had labored.

Harrison had explained his vote in the Ohio legislature some years before. To offset a growing deficit in the penitentiary budget, this earlier letter shows, the state legislature considered the idea that petty offenders, instead of being whipped, should be "sold out to any person who would pay their fine and costs."[23] The proposed law applied to criminal offenders rather than debtors but after passing the Ohio House was turned back by the Senate. While cheerfully admitting that he had supported the measure, Harrison further observed to Pleasants that he had been a member of the United States Senate committee which brought out the bill to abolish imprisonment for debt. "When the bill was before the Senate, I advocated its adoption and on its passage voted in its favor."[24]

Opportunity was allowed for only a brief visit to Berkeley.[25] Declining an invitation to a public dinner at Charles City, his home town, Harrison returned to the Powhatan House at Richmond and gave himself over to his steering committee which outlined a thorough-going campaign tour.

A steamboat boarded at Fredericksburg took Harrison and his party up the Potomac to Washington. Strong winds and a heavy thunderstorm drove the craft aground some miles below Alexandria and a safe landing was not accomplished until about 2:30 o'clock in the morning. Nevertheless a reception committee and a Whig orator were on hand for the scheduled greeting. After resting at Gadsby's Hotel, Harrison greeted "upwards of 1,500 persons," and received the public acclaim. "The General looks remarkably well, as vigorous and hearty as he was a dozen years ago, and as if he could go a-campaigning for twenty years more." At a public dinner that evening Harrison remarked that increasing facilities for travel tended to remove the possibility of a shift in the seat of government "so long as we continue a united people." A toast was offered to internal improvements, "the bond of our Union."[26]

Harrison and his escort rode to Baltimore in a barouche drawn by four gray horses, a mounted cavalcade awaiting him about a mile outside the town. Crowds gathered before the Eutaw House to hear the oration of welcome.[27] After resting a day and a night Harrison sailed for Philadelphia in the steamboat *Ohio*.

The General was accorded an imposing reception in Philadelphia. Cheers and salutes from boats in the river greeted the *Ohio* as it approached the Chestnut Street wharf. A salute of thirteen guns and a blaring brass band so frightened the horses attached to a waiting barouche that they became unmanageable. Whigs called for ropes and "more rope," and a hundred men hauled the coach through the streets. At Independence Square a brief halt was made while Harrison addressed the crowd, pointing to the "noble structure" in which his father and other patriots had signed the Declaration of Independence.[28] There, too, the Constitution of the United States had been written. The moral was plain. Old-fashioned constitutional principles would ever be upheld by the candidate.

Harrison put up at the Marshall House, attended church and the theater, and addressed a gathering at Commissioners' Hall. Whig delegations from neighboring towns urged that he pay them a visit. The General retrograded to Chester and Wilmington, and proceeded to Trenton by railroad. At Princeton Harrison spoke from the library steps[29] and was welcomed by cheering crowds at Rahway and Newark. "His appearance," reported the Rahway *Advocate,* "is that of a hale, hearty Ohio Farmer, of about fifty years of age, wearing a face so honest that numbers . . . were struck with it as remarkable."[30] September 29 the General arrived at the Battery in New York and a procession of horse and foot escorted him up Broadway as he stood erect in his carriage waving his hat to the throng.

A two-day stay in New York was crowded with dinners and

speeches at the American House, visits to City Hall, to the Brooklyn Navy Yard, and to the Park and National Theatres amid "rapturous plaudits." The Whig press considered his stay productive of much good. "Tens of thousands" had looked upon a man "of plain farmer-like appearance, of quick and intelligent eye, and altogether as little like decrepitude as can well be imagined." His impromptu speeches had "evinced tact, knowledge, instruction, and principles well settled in his own mind."[31] It was a day when a Whig candidate, even though he were not a Clay or a Webster, was supposed to know something, while physical appearance, under the circumstances, seemed to count a great deal.

The trip homeward occupied five weeks of splendid receptions in New Jersey, Pennsylvania, Maryland, and Ohio. Every town had its Harrison committee, everywhere were welcoming citizens on horseback, carriage processions, brass bands, bonfires, torchlights, clanging church bells, booming cannon, young ladies with flowers, enthusiasm "unprecedented."[32] Old soldiers with tears in their eyes crowded forward. "Hurrah for Harrison!" "Hail Columbia" was played in every village and town. At Harrisburg, where the Second Continental Congress had met, the General visited the State House and was shown the chair to which his father had carried little John Hancock whom he had nominated president of the Congress in 1775. The relic "called forth . . . the most lofty and animated expressions of patriotic feeling."[33] In powerful well-sustained tones, Harrison would roll off sonorous phrases bringing back to a plain people memories of hard-won glories in historic councils and on the battlefield. There was such a thing as public nostalgia in an era of bewildering change. The appearance of the gray-haired farmer and General served as a reminder of heroic and difficult years.

Public discourtesy, the only untoward incident of the tour, was encountered at Lancaster, home of Democratic Senator James Buchanan and a hotbed of Anti-Masonry. Hecklers prevented the General from addressing his admirers in front of his hotel and a crowd followed him on the street "with fiendish and savage yells."[34] Harrison went on to Columbia, an old army post, to deliver an address "amid loud cheers." At a celebration that night citizens set up a tar barrel and lit it with candles; out popped a snake which was pursued with shouts of "Van Buren! Van Buren! There he goes! Put it to him"[35] amidst an uproar of mirth and applause. The General dipped into Maryland as far south as Frederick. At Middletown along the way the ladies offered him a basket of peaches tied with a handsome bouquet. Stops were made at Hagerstown, Pittsburgh,

and Wheeling in three different states.[36] Passing overland through
Zanesville and Lancaster, Ohio, home of Senator Ewing, the General reached home well convinced that Virginia and possibly Pennsylvania were won. "As it is the contest will be a hard one."[37] The
grand tour had occupied three months, quite a sufficient test of endurance.

Harrison supporters were cheering themselves with high hopes of
victory if only the election were thrown into the Whig-controlled
House. President Jackson contributed to Whig optimism by a move
to check currency inflation and a breezy speculation in lands. A flood
of paper currency issued by government deposit banks had fostered
the land boom with sales mounting altogether too fast. Little specie,
incidentally, could be found in the West.

And so in July the National Treasury was directed to accept only
gold and silver in payment for public lands. Jackson's "Specie Circular," which tightened an inflated money market, was doubtless a wise
measure but it touched pocketbook nerves throughout the West and
Southwest where hopes of becoming rich rested upon paper currency
values. The move hurt the Democrats politically. A financial depression was almost in sight.[38]

Although the administration won the early fall elections in Maine
and Pennsylvania, their margin of victory was a narrow one while a
Whig triumph in Ohio pointed the way for a Harrison sweep west
of the Alleghanies. For the November election a huge vote was forecast.[39]

Compared with Clay's showing in 1832, the foremost Whig candidate did make handsome gains. Harrison carried Ohio, Indiana,
and New Jersey, which Clay had lost, while in Maryland and Delaware, narrowly won by Clay, he received substantial majorities.
Vermont and Kentucky also supported the General; Illinois, where
the Whigs were unorganized, was lost by some 3000 votes. Of fourteen states in which Harrison opposed Van Buren (excluding Michigan, not yet admitted), the General carried seven and a shift of
2200 votes in Pennsylvania would have thrown the election into the
National House. The difference in Rhode Island and Connecticut
(Van Buren vs. Harrison), and in North Carolina, Mississippi and
Louisiana (Van Buren vs. White) was in each case less than 600
votes. Webster carried Massachusetts, White captured Georgia and
Andrew Jackson's own state of Tennessee. South Carolina threw
away her vote on a nullifier, former Senator Willie P. Mangum. In
the electoral college, Van Buren's 167 to 73 for Harrison, 26 for

White, Webster's 14 and Mangum's 11 constituted a plurality of only 43 for the Democrats with less than 27,000 in the popular vote. Virginia's stand for Tyler instead of Johnson forced the vice-presidential election into the Democratic Senate, the result: Johnson, 33; Granger, 16.[40]

Harrison blamed the defeat on "want of confidence" on the part of his friends. A rather light vote was cast in New York and in Virginia while Anti-Masonic conflict in Pennsylvania diluted Whig strength. Victory in Indiana by nearly 9000 was gratifying. In respect to 1840 the General was content to allow party leaders to "pursue their own Course."[41]

The promptness with which Harrison's candidacy was renewed was an index to a ruling suspicion that Webster or Clay or even Calhoun would seek to carry the Whig banner next time. Two months after the national election a New York City meeting felicitated the General as a citizen "of great natural powers, of high attainments, and unblemished reputation."[42] Whigs everywhere, cheered in some measure by the Democratic depression, were anticipating better success. As the result of Jackson's Specie Circular, labor and living costs soared. Van Buren, upon taking office, declined to repeal the measure and within a few weeks came a crash precipitated by the failure of a large cotton house in New Orleans. On May 10, as candidate Daniel Webster set out on his second tour of the West, the banks of New York suspended payment.

The year 1837 was one of maneuvering. Webster visited Harrison at North Bend and received a cordial reception wherever he went, although his movements, Clay argued, were "to be regretted as premature."[43] While disclaiming his own candidacy Clay expected, as soon as the Harrison bubble should vanish, to rally considerable strength in New York and the South. Another observer pointed out nevertheless that while few Jackson men would cross party lines for the Kentuckian, they had and would vote for Harrison in droves.[44]

The General's own neighbors were among the first to renew the impetus his name had received. In January, 1838, a Hamilton County meeting held at Cincinnati reopened the campaign. A laudatory preamble introduced a brace of resolutions nominating the "FARMER OF NORTH BEND," and declaring against a Whig national convention.[45] Indiana spoke up again for Harrison but Clay was nominated at Whig meetings in Kentucky, Rhode Island, and Maryland. Still there was much opposition and Clay editors began to decry the claims of

the General, to complain of the "obstinate and continued presentation" of his name.[46] The presentation persisted. Harrison was set
forth as a stronger candidate than either Webster or Clay inasmuch
as few prejudices existed against him. Harrison was also "best calculated to concentrate geographical strength and . . . [he] stands
foremost in the hearts of the people."

A disgraceful and bloody duel between Congressmen Cilley of
Maine and Graves of Kentucky precipitated that spring a flood of
debate in which Harrison and his partisans had the last word. When
an inquiring Whig in New Jersey wrote the General for his own
opinion of duelling a long letter from North Bend detailed sorrowful
scenes in the Northwestern Army of 1791–95.[47]

The letter was reprinted by few Clay editors whose favorite was a
noted duellist in his own right. One exception was Charles Hammond
of the Cincinnati *Daily Gazette* who appraised the letter as "worthy
of a high-souled patriot and Christian philosopher." Hammond
added a rebuke for party prints which had failed to republish it.
Long a friend of Clay, he declared he was all for "fair play" in this
case.[48] It naturally followed that a convention of Ohio Whigs should
present the General as their first choice for the presidency with a
pledge of cordial support to Clay or Webster should either be nominated.[49]

During the past twenty years many large towns not as yet visited
by Harrison had sprung up in Ohio. July 4 found the General at
Massillon in the northeastern sector. Delegations from a dozen
counties swarmed in to honor the day. Reported the *Scioto Gazette:*
"They had speeches from Harrison, Ewing, and many others. They
had letters from Webster, Clay, Burnet, &c. . . . they had processions, music, banners, cannon-firings, shoutings and a dinner for
3000, all of the *ad captandum* kind—in short, they had great doings
at Massillon."[50] Harrison's speech belittled the "senseless cry against
the banks" and he singled out Clay and Webster for praise. Few invitations pressed upon him by delegations from other towns were
declined. Harrison continued his tour as far north as Ravenna and
east as far as Steubenville. "The old general . . . has done more
for the North-West and seen more service in it than any other man
living," applauded the Circleville *Herald* as the "veteran *Father of
the West"* passed through the town on his way homeward.[51]

Harrison's tour had won over many Clay men in a district where
the Kentuckian had been strong. Too, "the good Whig cause has
been advanced."[52] A Young Men's Whig Convention held at Mount

Vernon nominated Harrison for President without reservations, but by now the Clay blood was up. The Whig banner trailed in the fall gubernatorial election while the loss in Congressmen was eight, for the splitting up of Harrison and Clay strength did seriously handicap those candidates committed to either faction. Had General Harrison been the only prominent national candidate, the Democrats would have suffered an overwhelming defeat, opined the Cincinnati *Republican.*

The election showed too that the Jackson–Van Buren organization would not easily be overthrown. Democratic gains in Maryland, Pennsylvania, and New York City taught both the Whigs and Anti-Masons a lesson. November 13, a national Anti-Masonic convention representing six northern states unanimously nominated Harrison and Webster on motion of Thaddeus Stevens.

Harrison accepted the honor in a letter to Harmar Denny, close friend of Stevens. What were the principles he would apply to the office of chief executive if elected? Determined to give himself a free hand, the General entirely passed over the Anti-Masonic issue, but his letter outlined the party platform for 1840. If elected, Harrison declared he would:

1. Confine his service to a single term.

2. Disclaim all right of control over the public treasury.

3. Eschew any attempt to influence the elections.

4. Exercise due regard for laws passed by representatives of the people and, within specified limitations, limit his exercise of the veto power.

5. Never suffer the influence of his office to be used for partisan purposes.

6. If requested, he would furnish to the Senate his reasons for removals from office.

7. Never suffer the executive "to become the source of legislation" (expunging resolution).[53]

In respect to slavery and Anti-Masonry, the General's idea was to "conciliate" opposing forces within the states. With a Whig party made up of Federalists, Anti-Federalists, Masons, Anti-Masons, states' rights men, free constructionists, slavery men and abolitionists, 1840 was to prove the year of the great straddle. Although Harrison classed himself as a states' rights republican of the old Jeffersonian school which would leave the slavery issue to the states, to him fell the responsibility of reconciling an abolitionist faction to his leadership. Could he conciliate as well the several other opposing groups including the bank men? No one could yet tell but that the campaign might well be conducted on the issue of personal popularity with Harrison's name the talisman of Whig fortunes. As the General wrote an abolitionist friend in New York: "We have also many recruits in our ranks from the pressure of the times."[54]

TIPPECANOE AND TYLER TOO

HARRISON's triumphal tour of 1836 set the pattern for one made by President Martin Van Buren three years later. In June, 1839, Van Buren set out from Washington on a journey to his birthplace at Kinderhook, below Albany, New York. Like Harrison he traveled modestly in an open barouche, delivering speeches along the way, and his welcome in New York was tremendous. The President spent a full week in the city, everywhere engaged in receptions and hand-shaking. An extension of his tour up the Hudson, however, aroused none of the enthusiasm with which Harrison had been received by the people.[1] The villagers and the small city men cared little for the White House nabob represented by the Whig press partaking of the traits and manners of British aristocracy.

The gentleman responsible in large part for sentiment so molded was Thurlow Weed, tall, dark-bearded editor of the Albany *Evening Journal*. As an influential legislator and newspaper publisher in two cities, Weed long since had taken the inside track as pilot of up-state political forces. Weed did as much as any man to elect John Quincy Adams President in 1824. It was Weed who united the Anti-Masons with the abolitionist forces in New York. In 1836 Weed guided the proceedings of the New York Whig convention which nominated Harrison and Granger. In 1838, passing over Granger, an undependable vote-getter, Weed set up young William H. Seward of Utica for the governorship and helped to elect him over the Democratic incumbent.

Thurlow Weed had met Harrison a dozen years ago at the dinner table of Joseph Gales, the publisher of the *National Intelligencer* of Washington. He had not forgotten the General's ability to make friends, a valuable political asset at a time when national hatreds were ripening. Early in 1839 Weed had gone to Washington to suggest that Webster accept the support of New York for the vice presidency. Webster declined, an unfortunate decision, and Weed began to look elsewhere. "Question is who will poll the most votes," he reminded the great orator when doubt was expressed that Harrison should again be the leading Whig candidate.[2]

Weed made no move in the direction of Henry Clay who was attempting now to consolidate his strength. Whigs in Pennsylvania divided, one group nominating Clay, another, three months later, naming Harrison. Clay, who had made light of the Anti-Masonic "pretended convention," wrote an Indiana Senator to inquire concerning the probable course of that state and received a disquieting response. "I greatly fear that your name would not be sufficiently potent to stem the current that has set, and is still running against us," replied Oliver H. Smith. ". . . On that class who joined us under the Harrison flag we cannot rely, should you be the candidate. They have not forgotten the old contest when their idol Gen. Jackson and yourself were in the field. They still retain a deep-rooted prejudice against you. . . ."[3]

In New York the famous "Triangular Correspondence" served to dissipate Clay strength. Under a plan sponsored by Thurlow Weed, three men in as many key cities were to swap letters expressing doubt of Clay's strength in their own districts and exaggerating sentiment in favor of General Winfield Scott, who had acquired recent prominence during a Canadian border uprising. From Millard Fillmore of Buffalo, a Whig ally, Weed was probably not surprised to learn: "There is a strong feeling pervading all the western part of the State for Scott. The impression is that . . . there is no hope of being able to elect Clay."[4] On the other hand a Niagara Falls man, who apparently was not acting with Weed, wrote a New Yorker: "What can . . . professed Whigs in your city mean by pushing forward Genl Scott at this time? . . . The attempt . . . to create an impression that Genl Scott is the most popular candidate in the *western* part of our state is altogether deceptive. Mr. Clay will command ten votes to Genl Scott's one."[5] Clay, welcomed with a parade and garlands of roses at fashionable Saratoga that summer, was nevertheless instructed by Weed that he could never carry New York and there is a possibility that he was shown Fillmore's letter.

Another helpful communication signed by former Governor James T. Morehead and other "prominent gentlemen" in Kentucky also played some part in shaping affairs in New York. Harrison's good friend Colonel Charles S. Todd had arrived a little in advance of Clay's visit. Todd produced for Seward and Weed a consensus of weighty opinion, from Clay's own state, that "General Harrison is the most available candidate as he alone can secure Pennsylvania, Ohio, Illinois & probably Indiana."[6] It is rather unlikely that Clay saw this letter.

Daniel Webster was touring England. As the result of some management on the part of his advisers, who were acting with Weed, he wrote on June 12 withdrawing his name from the contest. Since Judge White of Tennessee had not re-entered his name the race was confined to Clay, Harrison and Weed's stalking horse, General Scott. Clay toured Ohio on his return from New York. Arriving home he renewed a correspondence, long broken off, with the General. Clay courteously apologized for rallying Whig partisans during his trip through Ohio. "No one who knows you would suspect you of poaching," Harrison replied, "but at any rate, Ohio is a free Manor and you particularly ought to have as great privileges within her borders as any other person. . . . Knowing your great admiration for female beauty, you must have been highly gratified by your reception at Saratoga." One gathers that Henry Clay had been kissed.

Harrison could not well avoid mention of politics:

"I can only say that my present position as regards yourself is to me distressing and embarrasing. . . . A few years ago I could not have believed in the possibility of . . . apparent rivalry to you. Particularly in relation to the Presidency, an office I had never dreamed of attaining. . . .

"I confess that I did covet the *second* [in 1828] but never the first office in the gift of my fellow citizens."[7]

Harrison sincerely admired Clay, if other remarks of this kind are to be believed, and considered him a disinterested patriot. He was happy to remain in his good graces. On the day the above letter was posted, he received another from Clay and responded: "I could not have failed to answer your letter because I have not received one for a long time more gratifying to my feelings, as it once relieved me from all apprehension of any existing coolness on your part towards me from the position which my destiny rather than my will has placed me."[8] Harrison went on to ask Clay's advice concerning an imported Spanish jackass which had become prematurely impotent. Clay was famous for his handsome blooded jackasses and bulls. A picture of his prize donkey, Magnum Bonum, has a place in the Library of Congress today.

The Democratic press trained its fire on the General some months before the meeting of the first national Whig convention, set for the first Monday in December, 1839. Harrison was pronounced a "superannuated and pitiable dotard," and critical pen-wielders again questioned his honesty in the handling of public funds. Originating in the

Van Buren press in Ohio, the attacks were reprinted throughout the East and South.

The *Ohio Confederate,* a states' rights paper which a Virginian had established at Columbus, replied in such terms as to bring a grateful response from North Bend. "Candor obliges me to say," Harrison wrote the editor, "that you have done me more than justice in attributing to me uncommon merit in my disinterested management of the public funds submitted to my control. . . . How could I act otherwise, considering the tutorage I received in my youth, and which is common to all brought up in the part of the country from which we both came. . . . Great confidence [was] reposed in me by the great statesmen and patriots under whom it was my good fortune to act."[9] Virginia for virtue, and New York? Well, smartness perhaps. Thurlow Weed, the practical politician, was drilling his cohorts along the lines of expediency.

Harrison was confident of the support of most of the 20,000 soldiers who had served with or under him at one time or another and the loyalty of veterans was dearer to him than anything else. "There is something strange in the fact," he confided to his friend General Van Rensselaer, "that the sons and grandsons of my soldiers are, if possible, more attached to me than the soldiers themselves. 'They have heard,' they say, 'their Fathers talk about me.' " And thus they would suppose that an insult offered their General was an insult offered to them.[10] But Harrison was not to be elected on the basis of army fraternalism alone. The old and young soldier element which Harrison knew was largely confined to the states of Ohio, Indiana, and Kentucky, which together had only 45 votes in the electoral college. New York alone had 42 votes, Pennsylvania 30. So Thurlow Weed and his Websterite friends strove to convince delegates en route to the Whig convention that Harrison or perhaps Scott was their man. Certain members from New England, where a high tariff was favored, agreed to act with the New Yorker.[11]

Early in December some 250 men from 22 states assembled in the Harrisburg Lutheran Church. Colonel John Johnston, Indian Agent at Fort Wayne years ago, moved that the deliberations be opened with prayer, the one spiritual note of a convention guided by practical men. An informal poll of the delegates had given a majority to Clay, so Weed and his friends put a unit rule into effect. Each delegation was asked to determine its views in regard to Clay's chances of carrying their states and then report through a committee of three.

The Ohio, Indiana, and Pennsylvania delegations unanimously

decided that Harrison could carry these states but they could not answer for Clay. The Virginia delegates chose Harrison rather than Scott, another native son, after Thaddeus Stevens carefully dropped a letter which Scott had written Granger in the hope of conciliating the abolitionist sentiment in New York.[12]

Thurlow Weed succinctly recorded the maneuvering under the unit rule. "In the opinion of a large majority of the delegates from Pennsylvania and New York, Clay could not carry either of those States, and without them he could not be elected. After full and free discussion and deliberation between the delegates friendly to Generals Harrison and Scott it was deemed best to unite in favor of the former."[13] The first ballot read: Clay 103, Harrison 91, and Scott 57 votes, but Weed controlled most of the Scott delegates, of whom twenty were from New York. On the final ballot, delayed twenty-four hours in an attempt to conciliate the Clay men, New York, Michigan, and Vermont shifted from Scott to Harrison while Illinois shifted from Clay, the result: Harrison 148, Clay 90, Scott 16. Clay's friends were violently angry.

Weed attempted to put up a Clay man as vice-president but Senator B. Watkins Leigh of Virginia declined the honor, also Senator John M. Clayton of Delaware. John Tyler of Virginia, courteous and tactful in address, was chosen near the close of the session. The split between the Clay and Harrison forces drenched party enthusiasm for the ticket. The Clay men were "disappointed and grieved even to tears."[14] As one loyal Southerner wrote: "Just think of a man such as Mr. Clay after 30 years of such services as no man has rendered to the Republic except Washington . . . cast aside."[15] Word reached Congressman John Quincy Adams at Washington that Harrison's nomination was the work of the Anti-Masons and of Governor Seward of New York.[16] Somehow Thurlow Weed had kept himself out of the pictures.

Elsewhere the nomination was received according to various lights. Clay, recovering from a drunken paroxysm of anger, prophesied in sober spirit that Harrison would beat Van Buren "tremendously." A Kentucky Congressman declared himself "astonished and surprised," but promised to work for the Harrison ticket.[17] General Van Rensselaer was crowing over what he claimed to be a personal victory. He alone, he wrote Harrison, had swung the New York delegation from Scott. Abraham Lincoln of Illinois announced that the nomination was taking "first-rate" among "a great many of the grocery sort of Van Buren men, as formerly."[18] Horace Greeley of New York felt that the convention had set up "the strongest possible ticket."[19] In Harrison's own district, the "bone and sinew of the land" rallied on New Year's Day, 1840. Numerous gray-haired and weather-beaten farmers came to the city, many of them old supporters of Jefferson and Jackson. As Martin Van Buren's financial policies were denounced, the proceedings at Harrisburg recounted, "indignation, sorrow and gladness were alternately depicted in their sunburned countenances." The people were convinced that fundamental principles had been violated, the government arbitrarily mismanaged. They adjourned with a common determination to support their honest old neighbor, the Farmer of North Bend.[20]

What were the issues? The Whig convention had adopted no platform. In his letter of acceptance, Harrison referred to his correspondence with Sherrod Williams and Harmar Denny, which had been widely republished, as the chief sources of his views. John Tyler alluded to Harrison's "long and faithful services . . . his early republican creed and . . . devoted . . . [advocacy] of the free principles and of popular rights."[21] A leading Virginia Whig placed the General on the record in a manner deemed most satisfactory to slave states. This was Senator William C. Rives, Colonel Johnson's rival for the Democratic vice-presidential nomination in 1835. Inasmuch as Harrison was on record as favoring a Federal appropriation to purchase emancipation through colonization, his views on the slavery issue were distrusted by many Southerners. Yet a lengthy defense could be made out of the General's anti-abolitionist speeches at Cheviot and Vincennes. "Where is the man . . . who in the practical assertion of the rights of the south, and in energetic and decisive reprobation of the designs of the abolitionists, has gone farther than General Harrison!"[22] So much was true but Senator Rives then went to to deny that Harrison favored a high tariff, internal improvements, and a national bank.

A letter which the General had written Congressman J. M. Berrien of Georgia in 1836 was uncovered. Curious but not unnatural was its publication by Whig editors in the South and by the Democratic press in abolitionist territory. In response to Berrien's friendly inquiries, Harrison had expressed the view that Congress could not abolish or interfere with slavery in the states except upon the application of the states, nor abolish slavery in the District of Columbia without the consent of the residents therein. Clay's compromise tariff bill should be carried out, he added, and the presidential power of appointment should be used only for the public advantage, not to promote the interests of party.[23] Eastern Whigs by now were proclaiming Harrison as a champion of Clay's public land distribution bill, which was popular in that section; west of the Alleghanies the General was described as the man to whom the settler owed the division of the public lands into small lots. "He was the first to introduce the pre-emption law into Congress."[24]

A casebook for the Northwest was developed at the traditional Whig convention held at Columbus on Washington's Birthday. The crisp atmosphere tingled with holiday rejoicing; numerous fife and drum corps and Tippecanoe Clubs with floats of log cabins, a great ship and a faithful replica of Fort Meigs with every porthole and battery in place, passed through the streets. A huge canoe drawn by six horses displayed the banner: "Old Tippecanoe Forever." Some 2000 farmers and townspeople sang campaign songs to the tunes of "Highland Laddie" and "Rosin the Bow." Banners announced "Harrison and Reform," "We'll Cleanse the Augean Stables." Transparencies depicted scenes in Harrison's life. The convention keynoter, a former soldier under Harrison, defended his fame against the assaults of an ungrateful people. The policies of "Matty Van" were derided until "the emotion in the throng seemed to arise from a sense of shame for public debasement, of sorrow for the wounded character of the country and degradation of liberal government."

Another Whig orator expressed abhorrence at the tendency of the Democratic executive to attain "absolute power." Van Buren's appointments and removals and his financial decrees were attacked. Resolutions urged that the general and state governments strive to secure a safe and uniform currency. Young Whigs from eight states, including western Pennsylvania and New York, were formally invited to celebrate the anniversary of Fort Meigs on that battleground in June. It was resolved to use "every fair and honorable means" to secure the election of Harrison and Tyler.[25]

Thus the issues were formulated, the abolitionist Whigs foremost in attacking Van Buren's financial policies, the old Northwest reviving the old frontier spirit with festivals and parades, the South immersed in argument in attempting to decide which was the more friendly to abolitionism, Harrison or Van Buren, the Democratic press in a desperate effort to expose the conflicting phases of Whigism, North, South, East, and West. The log-cabin motif, incidentally, had originated in the remark of a Clay partisan at Harrisburg. Why not, the Clay man suggested, allow the General to enjoy his log cabin and hard cider in peace? The remark was taken up by a Baltimore paper: "Give him a barrel of hard cider and a pension of two thousand a year . . . he will sit the remainder of his days in a log

"The Times," a Whig cartoon satirizing tight money and the depression of 1837.

THE

HARRISON ALMANAC

1841.

PUBLISHED BY J. P. GIFFING.

NEW-YORK

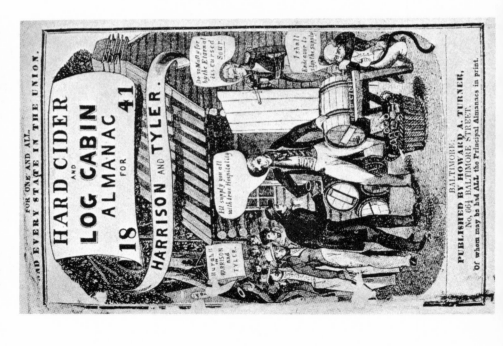

FOR ONE AND ALL,
AND EVERY STATE IN THE UNION.

HARD CIDER
AND
LOG CABIN
ALMANAC
FOR
1841

HARRISON AND TYLER.

BALTIMORE.
PUBLISHED BY HOWARD & A. TURNER,
No. 66½ BALTIMORE STREET.
Or whom may be had ALL the Principal Almanacs in print.

cabin . . . and study moral philosophy."[26] But the West was proud of its early struggles and its log cabins. What was the first qualification of a candidate opposing the "aristocratic" Van Buren? Nothing more than a humble beginning and an honest career as a man of the people. Under the circumstances the "Eagle of the West" had a wealth of natural advantages to be deprecated only at some risk.

But like the election campaigns of John Quincy Adams and Andrew Jackson this was one of calumny and hooting. A Whig military candidate say you? Compelled to decry military merit and not militarism *per se*, Democratic congressmen and writers proclaimed Harrison's "federalism," his tariff advocacy, a war record of no consequence. What of his economic ability, if he is now reduced to a log cabin? But General Harrison "is not a poor man, he does not live in a log cabin. . . . He is a rich man, he lives in a magnificent frame house, is surrounded with a princely estate. . . . So, sir, all this story about the log cabin is a falsehood. It is a mean fraud. . . ."[27] As mean and malicious was the tale that a Winnebago squaw represented her three half-breed children as Harrison's sons and therefore deserving of substantial annuities. So the offspring drew "about $1,000 apiece."[28]

February 9, 1840, at the start of a wearisome campaign, Harrison entered upon his sixty-eighth year. For nearly fifty years of his life he had been active in the West. That country had no better known patriarch; citizens from everywhere still flocked to visit him at the famous Cabin at North Bend. Harrison received them all cordially except for a delegation who wished to discuss politics on a Sunday. "I have too much respect for the religion of my wife to encourage the violation of the Sabbath." Visitors were much impressed by Mrs. Harrison's appearance, "one of the handsomest old ladies I ever saw . . . a perfect beauty and such a *good* person."[29] She ruled the General apparently. The brilliantly plumed macaw which Harrison had brought from Colombia still flew among the trees in front of the house, its cry "a most unearthly croaking noise or scream so shrill." Horace Mann, the Massachusetts abolitionist and educator, observed the family's humble surroundings. "The furniture of the parlor could not have drawn very largely upon any one's resources. The walls were ornamented with a few portraits, some in frames, some disembodied from a frame. The drawing-room was fitted up in more modern style; but the whole furniture and ornaments in these rooms might have cost $200 or $250."[30]

A Whig editor from New York, James Brooks, encountered the

General in Cincinnati and was invited to visit the Cabin. The two men were to meet on the levee where the steamboat was awaiting the General as he appeared toting saddlebags on one arm and a tin pail full of groceries on the other. He stopped to talk with a friend and a group of men gathered about "becoming unpleasantly large." Some teamsters from Indiana who called themselves his "Hoosier Boys" followed Harrison onto the boat. At North Bend, Brooks saw "a large ditch," the Cincinnati and Whitewater Canal, which was being dug through Harrison's farm. The Irish and German laborers, he wrote, "are all very fond of the General." Cattle and sheep were grazing outside a fence enclosing a lawn on two sides of the house; there was an "aspect of economy, simplicity, and neatness over all." Entering, Brooks took note of an antique sideboard, a plain home-made carpet, the Lord's Prayer and the Declaration of Independence in "time-worn" frames. Harrison kindled and tended a blaze in the spacious fireplace and showed his visitor the telescope which Commodore Perry had used at the Battle of Lake Erie. Mrs. Harrison superintended the housework. Following supper served at six, the two men discussed western affairs and the contrasting accounts of the Battle of Tippecanoe, which was still being discussed in the papers. As the clock struck nine the General said it was his bedtime, "for I rise at the break of day."

Soon after sunrise Brooks was awakened by his host. Members of the family were gathering for breakfast. The General eyed with distrust and disfavor a pile of newspapers and letters on the table. (He was then receiving an average of twenty-four letters a day.) "What on earth will they say of me next? . . . There is scarcely anything I am not asked & if I were to answer all of this correspondence I should have no time for anything else." A roughly dressed stranger who came riding up was invited to come in. He asked to confer privately with the General and the two men repaired to another room. Harrison soon reappeared, exclaiming: "There is no need of having any private conversation about politics. If you will stop & dine I shall be very happy to welcome you." The stranger accepted. He remarked that he was from western New York and that his neighbors had wished him "kind of Committee like to call on the General and see what he thought of abolition."

A steamboat landed a party of visitors from Pittsburgh and a delegation of three men approached to pay their respects. Some remarks on cattle-raising were exchanged. Harrison proudly exhibited a Durham bull for which he had paid $850. After dinner a company of United States troops on their way to Fort Leavenworth arrived by steamboat, also a party of "ladies and gentlemen." The men plucked roses for their ladies and "a half hour was passed in social intercourse —in the playfulness and tact of which few men are the equal of General Harrison. He reviewed the troops, then they left."

Brooks summed up his impressions of Harrison for his readers: "His colloquial powers are remarkable, his memory wonderful, he has a fund of personal anecdote. He revealed that 'Where Madame Trollope's Bazaar now stands in Cincinnati many a time have I wheeled and marched my company in what was then Fort Washington. . . . I think I have personally obtained for the country from the Indians many more millions of acres of land than the sword of a conqueror ever permanently won.' Harrison seemed to remember not only all his officers, but his men."[31]

Thus was passed one day at North Bend. Harrison was allowed little time to devote to correspondence or farm work. The stranger from rural New York who had sought to discover what the General thought of abolition was quite possibly following up a letter mailed by the "Union Association" of Oswego which Harrison had not taken the trouble to answer. Most inquiries of this character were turned over to a committee of correspondence which managed certain details of Harrison's campaign. The committee, comprising Major David Gwynne, Judge John C. Wright, and Oliver M. Spencer, usually referred questioners to the General's published political views, adding that the candidate was to make no further declaration of his principles.[32] So the Democrats dubbed Harrison "General Mum," his commiteee of three his "Conscience-Keeping Committee."

The fact that a committee was relieving Harrison of much correspondence helped to foster another whispering campaign. Numerous inquiries were put to Cincinnati's famous physician, Dr. Daniel Drake, who answered them publicly. Far from being broken down in body and mind, he wrote, the General still possessed an accurate and full memory. "I have been surprised at the . . . vivacity and almost youthfulness of feelings. . . . His intellect is unimpaired. Bodily vigor as good as that of most men of his age. Subject to no disease but periodic headache. . . ." Somewhat against his own wishes, Harrison was persuaded to make a personal appearance at the Fort Meigs rally further to counteract the slander.[33]

Great Whig conventions and meetings already had been held that spring at Baltimore, on the Tippecanoe battleground, and in Springfield, Illinois, where Abraham Lincoln stood on a wagon to address a huge crowd. Everywhere log cabins and cider presses were being constructed. Cabins of wicker-work were set up on the decks of steamboats. A common sight at wood-yards along the rivers were signs bearing the words "Harrison Wood," "Whig Wood," or "Tippecanoe Wood." The General changed his tall silk hat for a broad-brimmed one, the rest of his garb a plain frock coat, bombazine stock, black silk vest and blue pantaloons. Crowds and cannon salutes greeted him at Dayton, Columbus, Delaware, and Sandusky on his way to Fort Meigs. The public enthusiasm served to cheer the General in spirit, he being somewhat cast down over the recent attacks on his military record. At Fort Meigs on the Maumee Whig delegations from fourteen states appeared with thousands of tents and wagons. It was like "ten or twenty camp meetings thrown into one." Crowds varying in size from one to five thousand people cheered stump speakers and sang Tippecanoe songs. On the midnight before Harrison's arrival the camp was aroused by an "Indian attack." The drums beat to quarters, the roar of cannon and musketry echoed from the woods, troops emerged from the fort in a gallant sortie. After an hour of "hard fighting" the Indians were driven back with the loss of a few captives. The sentinels resumed their positions, Whig citizens their repose.[34]

Arriving somewhat tardily on June 11 Harrison stood under a burning sun for an hour and spoke in "trumpet-like tones." Refutation of the slurs on his military reputation and a persistent charge of "federalism"[35] occupied most of his speech. The General's "keen piercing eye" and "elastic vigor" were hailed in the Whig press. Before turning homeward he addressed a log cabin rally at Cleveland, another at Columbus. Arriving at Springfield he received word of the death of his son Benjamin who had been in poor health for some months. Ten thousand people had gathered in a field to hear the General's scheduled address; as the change of program was announced they rushed in a body to Main Street to catch a glimpse of his carriage. There was hardly enough room for the horses to pass as the crowd maintained a "respectful silence."[36]

Following Benjamin's death on June 9 Anna Harrison became seriously ill. "Numerous visitors at North Bend," a Cincinnati paper admonished, "interrupt the quiet of the family and retard recovery of the invalid."[37] The General remained at home for a month. A "formidable array of letters" had accumulated. Meanwhile Webster, Clay, Tyler, Senator Tom Corwin, Hugh S. Legaré of South Carolina and other Whig orators were stumping the country. It was an inspirational campaign. Although admitting he had not been born in a log cabin, Webster related that his older brother and sisters had

From a contemporary drawing.

The May, 1840, National Convention of Whig Young Men at Baltimore, Md., assembled on the Canton Race Course.

The Log Cabin March.

From the Library of Congress.

been. "Its remains still exist. I make to it an annual visit. I carry my children to it . . . to teach them the hardships endured by the generations which have gone before them. I love to dwell on the tender recollections . . . which mingle with all I know of this humble abode."[38] Much to the surprise of his kinsfolk, Senator Legaré, of pompous and aristocratic manner, donned a coonskin cap and "engaged in cider drinking and general carousing."[39] Staid church-going farmers went about with canteens of hard cider hung about their necks. The buckeye tree of Ohio became the Whig emblem.[40] Buckeye canes were sold at stalls along the National Road, sprigs of buckeye waved from horses' bridles. A real Harrison log cabin had a live coon on the roof, a jug of cider and strings of buckeye nuts on the wall, the latchstring conspicuously out, ample living quarters inside. In 1840 a team of horses was named Tip and Ty, twin babies the same. Young ladies dubbed their sunbonnets "log cabins" and set their tea-cups in Sandwich glass plates with log cabins impressed on the bottom.[41] The "Buckeye Blacksmith," John W. Baer, an illiterate character of exceptional natural powers, practised Whig oratory at his forge, left his work to entertain crowds at Fort Meigs and then toured the East, appearing on one occasion with Webster. At an outdoor Whig meeting in Richmond a pickpocket was marched off to jail but was allowed an opportunity to speak. Mounting a box the prisoner advocated the election of those worthy patriots, "Tippecanoe and Tyler too."[42]

Campaign orators recalled Harrison's kind treatment of the men in his army, his generosity to families bereaved during the war, his donation of a horse and saddle to an itinerant missionary whose weary mount had died in the stable at North Bend. A great paper ball, ten feet in diameter, on which were inscribed names of states which had gone Whig in local elections, was set going in some eastern city and rolled through a dozen or more states. An illiterate return of a Whig victory bore the words "Oll Korrect" whereupon Whig editors adopted "O.K." as a victory sign.[43] "But the chief means of popular excitement," wrote a Harrison campaigner, "were the glee clubs, which never before or since have been so effectually used. Songs were written specially for them of the most patriotic and exciting character. . . . A good club of singers and new songs and airs, made the air thrill with popular excitement. . . .

> " 'What has caused this great commotion . . .
> All the country through?
> It is the ball a-rolling on
> For Tippecanoe & Tyler too!' "[44]

A Democratic editor discussed the perplexity of his party cohorts in combating the tuneful onslaught:

"Some of the songs I shall never forget. They rang in my ears wherever I went, morning noon and night. . . . Men, women and children did nothing but sing. It worried, annoyed, dumfounded, crushed the Democrats, but there was no use trying to escape. It was a ceaseless torrent of music, still beginning, never ending. If a Democrat tried to speak, argue, or answer anything that was said or done, he was only saluted with a fresh deluge of music. If a Democrat would say that John Tyler was no Whig, the Whigs would join in a derisive laugh and a song which ended with the chorus:

" 'And we'll vote for Tyler, therefore,
Without a why or wherefore.' "[45]

The original version of two chickens in every pot was set forth in this wise : "If you wish to be poor and trodden down and to see your wife starving and your children in ignorance, vote for Martin Van Buren. Vote for Harrison and get $2 a day and roast beef." And as far as Matty Van himself was concerned:

"Mr. Van Buren is not the choice of the people ; he was smuggled into the Presidential chair under the old general's popularity. We want no such bastard politicians foisted upon us. Let a man's own worth, talents, merit and popularity, father him—not another's."[46]

The songs, the emotion, the hurrahing were a proper answer to personal slander and irrelevant issues. Had the Democrats not commenced their vilification of the General in 1833, it is hardly likely that he would have been the Whig candidate.

Harrison was satisfied that his trip to Fort Meigs had "silenced the calumnies as to my bodily infirmities." He assured Daniel Webster : "My health is indeed better than it has been for many years."[47] Late in July he left North Bend to attend a celebration of the signing of the Indian treaties at Greenville. "I am and ever have been a Democratic Republican," declared Harrison at Greenville. "Being a child of the Revolution and bred in its principles, I believed in the right and the ability of the people to govern themselves. . . . It is not opprobrious to turn from a party to your country."[48] The haying season over, Whig meetings began to be measured in acres of men, the whole a great panorama of wagons, buggies, log cabins, moving masses of people, and military companies with sound. A conservative estimate of the Greenville crowd was 12,000 but a great rally held at

Dayton on the anniversary of the Battle of Lake Erie covered ten acres, with 10,000 Whig men and women, it was claimed, to the acre, "this grandest spectacle of all time."[49] Harrison visited some twenty towns in central and southern Ohio during the early fall. At Carthage he decried abolitionist activity, at Chillicothe he explained his principal purpose in extending his tour:

"I am here because I am the most persecuted and calumniated individual now living; because I have been slandered by reckless opponents to the extent that I am devoid of every qualification, physical, mental and moral, for the high place to which at least a respectable portion of my fellow-citizens have nominated me."

The incessant sniping of the opposition press allowed Harrison credit for only a blundering and pusillanimous military leadership. Recently the letters of Colonel Croghan deprecating Harrison's version of the defense of Fort Stephenson had appeared. Croghan himself was not wholly responsible. Some years ago Harrison had turned over the letters to Moses Dawson, his early biographer. Dawson, however, was a Jackson man who had fallen out with the General and the publication of the letters in the Washington *Globe* caused the Whigs some embarrassment. To atone for the mischief Croghan issued a statement that he had not authorized the use of his letters. From General Edmund P. Gaines, a colonel under Harrison, he secured an analysis of the whole plan of operations in 1812–13. The Gaines letter, in its calm statement of fact, merits the attention of the historian as well as the political partisan of that day. Gaines gave Harrison full credit for strong and sagacious leadership of an army which went undefeated because it was impossible of surprise.[50]

Determined efforts to get out the vote in Maine in September forecast augured bitter contests in local elections. The *Daily Evening Advertiser* of Portland issued the call: "Let it never be said that they staid at home, that they might save the profits of a day's labor, when by going to the Polls they would have saved the hard earnings of twenty years. To the Polls for HARRISON AND REFORM!" The election was close. For days the result was pure guesswork until "Laus Deo!" and "O.K. which . . . meaneth Old Kumberland [County]," Edward Kent of Bangor displaced Governor John Fairfield by a plurality of 67 votes.[51] This was not exactly "Hell-bent for Governor Kent" but it served. The Whigs then won in Pennsylvania and also in Ohio, Senator Tom Corwin becoming governor.

Suspicious of eleventh-hour Democratic tricks the Whig press endeavored to forestall reports that Harrison was in broken-down health or actually dead. "PRESIDENT HARRISON arrived in this city on Saturday last IN PERFECT HEALTH, in time to receive the congratulations of his friends in the evening," heralded the Cincinnati *Gazette* on November 2. The national election held some days later bore out the anticipation of victory. Harrison and Tyler carried nineteen states to seven for Van Buren and Johnson with an electoral vote of 234 to 60. Save in Pennsylvania and Maine where the margin was close, the Whigs gained very satisfactory majorities. Jackson's own state of Tennessee went Whig for the first time and by 12,000; New York, home state of Van Buren, elected Harrison by 13,000, Kentucky by this figure twice over. Among the most populous states only Virginia failed to support her two native sons, Van Buren receiving a 1400 majority. Excluding the vote of South Carolina, which cast her ballots through the legislature, Harrison's popular majority showed a gain of 170,000 over the previous campaign.[52]

The news was received with mixed feelings at North Bend. "I wish," Mrs. Harrison said, "that my husband's friends had left him where he is, happy and contented in retirement."[53]

XXV

JUBILATION AND MOURNING

HENRY CLAY had manfully supported the Whig cause even though it was necessary to say a few good words for his late opponent. Clay did not lose anything by this gesture. At Nashville, where he was once burned in effigy, Clay was "welcomed as a conqueror" by tens of thousands attending a southwestern convention.[1] Neither Clay nor Webster as a matter of fact could have shirked the contest and left a clear field to the other. More was at stake than the election of a one-term Whig President.

The pivotal issue in selecting Cabinet material was probably the bank question. Clay had yielded no ground in relation to the bank and he was preparing to reintroduce the subject in the next Congress. Daniel Webster, on the other hand, had declared that he considered the question of the bank charter as settled. "Public opinion has decided against it. . . . For myself I shall take no part in any attempt to renew the charter of the bank."[2] Harrison had expressed himself as willing to continue the "experiment" to carry on the government's finances without the aid of a bank. And when the General carried the anti-bank states of North Carolina, Georgia, Mississippi, Louisiana and Tennessee, he did not consider this any mandate to set up a new bank.

Escaping a flock of office hunters who came to feast at his table, Harrison visited Kentucky to see former Governor Charles A. Wickliffe, a prominent anti-bank Whig, his ostensible business "the old land company affair," of his brother Benjamin VI.[3] Harrison attempted to postpone an anticipated interview with Clay. The Kentucky Senator was forewarned: "Our personal meeting might give rise to speculation, and even jealousies, which it might be well to avoid."[4] But Harrison's conference with Wickliffe, whose son Robert was an intimate of the family, gave rise to speculation and jealousy. The word was passed that he planned to make Wickliffe Postmaster General and his son Robert his private secretary. Clay, argus-eyed, later positively declared that Harrison had offered Wickliffe a Cabinet post, but if the offer was made it was not accepted.

The expectation was that Harrison would take into the Cabinet some Kentuckian other than Clay. The matter of pride must be considered. The Senator would hardly accept any post which the General might offer him. Upon receiving Harrison's letter, however, Clay hastened to Frankfort to meet him and there was offered the State Department portfolio, which he refused. Harrison could not well decline an invitation to visit Clay's home at Ashland, near Lexington. He committed himself to no definite decisions during his visit although the probability was, his host wrote, that he would invite into his Cabinet John J. Crittenden of Kentucky and Thomas Ewing of Ohio.[5] Crittenden was a Thames campaign veteran and Whig orator who became United States Senator in December. Both Crittenden and Ewing were friends of Clay, the latter however more truly a Webster and Harrison man.

Harrison toasted Clay at a public dinner at Versailles and dined at Frankfort with Governor Robert P. Letcher and the Kentucky electors. He had Daniel Webster foremost in mind. On December 1, 1840, Harrison bid him take either the State Department or the Treasury post while Ewing was offered the Post Office. Webster replied that he would accept the State Department and recommended that Ewing be shifted to the Treasury.[6] Clay, meantime, had gone to attend the opening of Congress at Washington. So had Daniel Webster, but he was corresponding regularly with Harrison and had all the advantage. His suggestion as to Ewing blocked Clay's attempt some time later to obtain the Treasury place for Senator John M. Clayton of Delaware, a strong bank man, and the sequel bore out the character of the two most important Cabinet choices. Webster and Ewing in later months were to work out a plan for a bank which was in the nature of a compromise with the states' rights faction but entirely unacceptable to Clay.[7]

Returning to Cincinnati on December 10, Harrison resigned his office as Clerk of the Court. Suggestions as to all manner of official appointments were pouring in. Senator Crittenden, it was agreed, ought to become Attorney-General for surely Kentucky should receive a place in the Cabinet. Webster's suggestions regarding the War, Navy, and the Post Office were favorably considered except in regard to one man, who it is said, had a letter written in 1839, promising him a Cabinet post in event of the General's successful election.[8] This mythical letter has never been quoted or produced by the biographers of Thaddeus Stevens, but we find Harrison writing Webster on December 27: "I tell you . . . in confidence, that I have positively determined against S——; there is no consideration which would induce me to bring him into the cabinet. We should have no peace with his intriguing, restless disposition."[9]

And Governor Letcher of Kentucky wrote Crittenden that winter: "Don't speak of Thaddeus Stevens; rumor says he is to be one, but if the old gentleman talks over the matter, *Thad. can't succeed.*"[10] If Harrison had broken with the ideas originally expressed to the Anti-Masons, that he would promise no supporter rewards, it seems surprising that he would have committed himself to Stevens whom he personally disliked. In 1839, with Webster out of the picture, Stevens was bound to support some Whig candidate other than Clay who had long since disdained Anti-Masonic support. "I will come to no conclusion as to the treasury, war, and navy until I reach Washington," Harrison notified Webster. ". . . From the number of visitors which I have here, I have . . . [little] leisure."

In January the hordes of office-seekers began to converge upon the Capital where Cabinet-making was actually in progress. Harrison planned to leave Cincinnati the latter part of the month and spend two or three weeks in Virginia. Mrs. Harrison, who had been in poor health, was to follow in May when the weather had moderated. Meantime Jane Findlay Harrison, widow of William, Jr., would preside at the White House.[11] Jane's aunt, the widow of General James Findlay, was to accompany the party; also one of Harrison's nephews, a granddaughter and three grandsons. Colonels John Chambers and Charles S. Todd of Kentucky were members of his personal suite. As editor of the Cincinnati *Republican,* the official Harrison organ, Todd had made himself useful during the campaign.

"Monday, Jan. 25, 1841—Great Excitement in the city today." A young diarist noted the General's arrival at the Henrie House in Cincinnati where little comfort was obtained. Not until after midnight did Harrison escape the pressing mass of people and he had little sleep. "Tuesday, Jan. 26—Very fine morning. Great Excitement. Crowds all through the streets. Many from the country in wagons, on horse and on foot . . . black and white. Many down at the steam-boat. Many called to see him and to see the fine canes, with many other presents, that his black man had under his care. . . . General Harrison made a speech, closing: 'Gentlemen and fellow-citizens; perhaps this may be the last time I may have the pleasure of speaking to you on earth or seeing you. I will bid you farewell, if forever, fare thee well.' The steamboat *Ben Franklin* pushed out amidst shouts of joy. . . ."[12]

Yet the General had voiced a foreboding.

Cannon roared from both sides of the river as the *Benjamin Franklin* backed into midstream. Military companies aboard and on shore exchanged rifle salutes and a brass band was playing on deck. Hats, caps, handkerchiefs were waved from the crowd on the wharf, from windows, from housetops. A steamboat which had left earlier that morning carried the news of the General's approach and at every crossroads and town the river banks were crowded. Handkerchiefs were seen waving from distant windows; farmers waited along the bank with their guns, "firing and throwing up their hats and cheering for 'Tip.' " By night bonfires lighted the shore. At Maysville and Wheeling crowds boarded the boat to shake hands with the General. Approaching Pittsburgh the boat was delayed when it struck a rock and the crowd at the pier went without breakfast and dinner while it waited. The reception committee struggled with the dense mass for some time before the General could be escorted into a carriage.[13]

Lodged at the Pittsburgh House, Harrison was discovered that evening reading his Bible, a fixed habit for twenty years, he explained, before retiring. "At first . . . a matter of duty . . . it has now become a pleasure."[14] In the morning he addressed a crowd in front of the hotel, kissed a few ladies, and on Sunday attended church while his grandsons went to three services to look over the girls. The party sailed up the Monongahela as far as Brownsville where Harrison entered a shiny new coach decorated with interesting scenes from his life.

At McIlhenny's Tavern, Hagerstown, the General was warmly greeted by both Whigs *and* Democrats, a local sheet emphasized; a cake weighing 112 pounds and inscribed with appropriate mottoes was presented. "The General is in excellent health, speaks with the fluency and vigor of youth—his countenance is grave and contemplative," reported the *Herald of Freedom*.[15] Harrison reached Frederick on the evening of February 5. The streets were thronged; "all around betokened joy and exultation."[16] Following a reception at Dorsey's City Hotel, he took a train for Baltimore and Washington.

The President-elect entered the capital on his sixty-eighth birthday, Tuesday, February 9, 1841. His reception at Baltimore had been vigorous and he was forced to forego shaking hands. A pair of warm overshoes was provided, for it was snowing, but Harrison declined the offer of an umbrella and walked bareheaded to City Hall in the van of a hurrahing procession.[17] The new President had brought a snowstorm with him, the opposition paper pointed out, his arrival also signalized by the fall of a Senate Chamber scroll bearing the motto, "E Pluribus Unum." Another unfortunate omen, asserted the Washington *Globe,* was the breaking of a rope bearing the flags of all the states which had voted for Harrison, which stretched across Pennsylvania Avenue. "No sooner had he put his foot on the Avenue than the robbing commenced and a multitude had their pockets picked in the course of five minutes."[18] At City Hall speeches were exchanged with Mayor William W. Seaton and Harrison then repaired to Gadsby's Hotel where the dining room had been converted into a dormitory for office-seekers. A rude shed erected in the court accommodated the diners.

After resting, the General received Senators Webster, Crittenden, Ewing, Clay, and William C. Preston of South Carolina. Thurlow Weed was also in Washington and the new Cabinet was shaping up. Harrison readily agreed to Webster's choice of Ewing as Secretary of the Treasury and when Clay had a private interview with the General two days later he proposed Senator Clayton in such warm terms as to prompt the reply: "Mr. Clay, you forget that I am President."[19] Granger of New York, acceptable to Seward and Weed, was named Postmaster General; John Bell of Tennessee, a former Jackson Congressman who had voted for White four years ago, became Secretary of War. North Carolina's shift to the Whig column was likewise accorded recognition in the naming of George Badger Secretary of the Navy. Badger was another former Jackson man and a barrister of parts. Appointment of Granger and Badger occasioned some surprise, but the Cabinet was considered generally satisfactory by leading Whigs.[20]

Harrison promptly placed himself on a good footing with Martin Van Buren. Precedent was shattered when the President-elect called at the White House to chat pleasantly with his late rival for half an hour. Properly consoled over his defeat, Van Buren dismissed the old rule that the President should not return visits, taking his entire Cabinet with him to call on the General at Gadsby's.[21] An invitation to dine at the White House on Saturday found Harrison again in company with Democratic chieftains. Colonels Chambers and Todd were the only other Whigs present. Harrison spoke across the table to Senator Benton of Missouri: "Benton, I beg you not to be harpooning me in the Senate; if you dislike anything in my administration, put it into Clay or Webster, but don't harpoon me." Benton responded with jovial obeisance.[22]

The General's cheerful manner and ready repartee amazed the more sophisticated politicians who saw only grief ahead for the White House. The office-seekers were in full cry on Harrison's trail, the mail of every new Cabinet member bulked large with pleas and petitions. A Whig partisan as remote as Horace Greeley, editor of the *Tribune* and the *Log Cabin* of New York, declared he was "run down for letters, letters." The beggars were calling for "none of your half-way things. Write strong."[23] Senator Crittenden was believed to have influence. "If I had the sole disposal of all the *offices* and *honors* of the government," he notified a relative, "I could not be more hunted after, and *hunted down* than I am." But Harrison had postponed everything, save Cabinet appointments, in order to enjoy the happy ending as long as he could. Van Buren was reported as saying: "The President is the most extraordinary man I ever saw. He does not seem to realize the vast importance of his elevation. He talks and thinks with . . . much ease and vivacity. . . . He is as tickled with the Presidency as is a young woman with a new bonnet."[24] Visiting Congress, Harrison jested with members of both parties. "Let me introduce Mr. Williams of North Carolina to you General," some one remarked. "Mr. Williams is the oldest member and is called the Father of the House." "Mr. Williams," Harrison responded, "I am glad to see the Father of the House and the more so because you have a very unruly set of boys to deal with I know." The editor of the *Madisonian,* a young man of slight build, was led up. "Happy to see you Mr. Allen. You are a good-looking chap for these parts, but there is hardly enough raw material in you for the girls beyond the Alleghanies!"[25] At the dinner table, after listening to the claims of an eleventh-hour Whig, the General praised the ham.

On Monday the 15th, Harrison dined with Daniel Webster, General Van Rensselaer and a select company of other old soldiers and friends. He appeared at a Log Cabin ball at which 1800 wax candles were lighted, then departed to obtain a few days of rest in Virginia.

Escorted by the Major and "a large multitude" to the Powhatan House, Harrison refrained from making a speech but invited his friends to visit him next day. "General Harrison appears in decidedly better health than in 1836," commented the Richmond *Whig.*[26] On Saturday the Richmond Tippecanoe Club entertained the President at a spacious log cabin set up in the public square. Harrison and Tyler together watched a parade of volunteer corps and repaired to Military Hall for refreshments. Responding to a toast the new President denied what had been reported in opposition newspapers. He had never been, he said, nor could he ever become an abolitionist. He was proud, he added, to be surrounded by the chivalry of Virginia.[27] But most Southerners had found it difficult to distinguish between abolition and emancipation. Harrison's early membership in the Humane

Society of Richmond as well as his advocacy of negro colonization had probably cost him the vote of the state. Secluded in his mother's room at Berkeley, Harrison wrote an over-long inaugural message leavened with patriotic idealism and weighted with allusions to the ancient republics. John Tyler, Secretary of the Navy Badger, and a grand-nephew, Henry Harrison of Berkeley, secretary to the new President, accompanied Harrison on his return to the capital. The General's daughter, Anna Tuthill Taylor, came to assist Jane Findlay Harrison as White House hostess.

Politicians in Washington were discussing the feasibility of an extra session of Congress to consider pressing matters of revenue and finance. The Treasury was empty, the nation in debt, the rate of duty on imports down to its lowest point, 25 per cent. Little or nothing was being accomplished in the final session of the present administration. Harrison declined to enter into the argument nor to promise any further appointments. It had been his determination, he said, not to quarrel with any of his friends before March 4. Three more days of ease remained. Philip Hone, an influential Whig merchant of New York, recorded what he thought to be "a characteristic circumstance of which an American can be proud." It was the President-elect taking his morning walk.

"Passing through the crowd on Pennsylvania Avenue was . . . an elderly gentleman dressed in black, and not remarkably well dressed, with a mild benignant countenance, a military air, but stooping a little, bowing to one, shaking hands with another, and cracking a joke with the third. And this man was William Henry Harrison, the President-elect of this great empire, whose elevation has been procured by a severe throe which has been felt in the most remote corners of the land, which has destroyed and elevated the hopes of hundreds of thousands . . . and there he went unattended and unconscious of the dignity of his position—*the man* among men, the sun of the political firmament. People may say what they will about the naked simplicity of republican institutions. It was a sublime moral spectacle."[28]

Declining with thanks Van Buren's courteous offer to vacate the White House in advance of March 4, Harrison was lodged at the home of Mayor Seaton. He gave his inaugural address to Webster, who was also living at Seaton's, and examined another draft which the senator had outlined. After reading Harrison's speech, the story goes, Webster appeared at the dinner table looking a little weary. To Mrs. Seaton's inquiry as to what had happened he replied: "You would think that something had happened. . . . I have killed seventeen Roman proconsuls as dead as smelts, every one of them!"[29] In the nature of constructive criticism, Webster wrote in a penultimate paragraph expressing the President's reverence for the Christian religion, the foundation of the welfare of the republic.[30] Harrison accepted most of the changes and returned the speech which Webster had proposed. He then showed the address to Clay who suggested a few acceptable alterations but the few remaining historical allusions had become sacrosanct.

Inaugural Day dawned brisk and cold. Cannon saluted the sunrise and a dozen bands played as the military corps assembled. Although the Whigs of Baltimore had presented Harrison with a fine coach, the President rode his favorite mount, Old Whitey, down Pennsylvania Avenue. Two former aides at Tippecanoe and the Thames, Major Henry Hurst and Colonel Todd, were at the right and left behind him. Veteran soldiers, Tippecanoe Clubs bearing floats, army regulars and volunteer corps, and students from the Jesuit College at Georgetown marched in a grand procession which extended nearly two miles. Harrison wore no overcoat and his hat was in his hand as he bowed and waved to the crowd.[31]

Shortly before the noon hour Vice-President Tyler was installed in a well-packed Senate chamber. Harrison made his appearance, bowing easily, and exchanged formal greetings.[32] Following Tyler's address, which was brief, the assemblage moved to an outdoor platform where the Supreme Court judges, the diplomatic corps and Cabinet members took their places. The people, 50,000 in number, roared their greeting as Harrison came forward. Then silence fell as his address to the nation was awaited.[33]

Early March weather in Washington has dimmed the glory of many an inaugural. A chilly northeast wind nipped the extremities of the shivering multitude yet Harrison stood there bareheaded and without gloves or overcoat, his address one hour and forty minutes long. The only surviving Roman proconsul, introduced near the opening, was he who had marked the difference in the conduct of candidates for office before and after they attained power. As a check upon the abuse of presidential prerogative, Harrison advocated a single term. The privileges of the Chief Executive should be limited. There should be no executive encroachment upon the legislative branch of the government, no undue influence over elections. Control of the currency should rest entirely with Congress.

Against the wishes of some of his anti-slavery friends, Harrison brought up a subject upon which he had deep convictions. Congress had no right to abolish slavery in the District of Columbia, he re-iterated, without the consent of the people therein. "Our citizens must be content with the exercise of the powers with which the Consti-tution clothes them. The attempt of those of one State to control the domestic institutions of another can only result in feelings of dis-trust and jealousy, the certain harbingers of disunion, violence and civil war. . . ."[34]

A considerable portion of the crowd was not listening. Men left their seats to gossip over rumored appointments to office, and the sug-gestion of an extra session of Congress. Henry Clay, it was supposed, would introduce his plan for a new United States bank. And what turn would the tariff take? Would a new revenue law be based on the compromise of 1833 or would the influence of New England pre-vail? Daniel Webster would have something to say about that.

"As long as the love of power is a dominant passion of the human bosom," Harrison went on, "and as long as the understandings of men can be warped and their affections changed by operations upon their passions and prejudices, so long will the liberty of a people de-pend upon their own constant attention to its preservation. . . . Of all the great interests that appertain to our country, that of Union—cordial, confiding fraternal union—is by far the most important, since it is the only true and sure guaranty of all others." Violence of party spirit was deplored almost in the same breath as party sectionalism. For the sake of a united country the President promised to exert his influence against the shaping of an "executive party" in Congress. "Our aboriginal neighbors" were to be treated with justice and lib-erality. Peace, consonant with national honor, would be maintained with all foreign nations.[35]

Chief Justice Roger B. Taney administered the oath and the Presi-dent bid the crowd an affectionate farewell. A negro attendant came forward and helped him on with his hat and cloak, which were care-fully adjusted. The artillery boomed a parting salute. Although too long by half, the inaugural was considered a good one, and even Dem-ocrats acknowledged the President's sincerity, integrity, and "un-doubted sense of patriotism."[36]

A new public servant had been installed, the cares and burdens of office assumed. Upon entering the White House, Harrison lay down for half an hour while his head and temples were rubbed with alcohol. A mass of people filled the lower floor of the mansion and at three o'clock the President received them but refrained from shaking hands. His activity and stamina were remarked upon at the Inaugural Ball that evening. After attending two minor functions Harrison appeared at about 10:30 o'clock bringing a numerous retinue. According to one of the guests "the indefatigable President . . . for hours made the rounds of a hundred little circles, all so many eddies of delight in which he sported unrestrained."[37] Actually Harrison remained for a little over an hour, greeting Webster and Clay at the punch bowl and saluting General Scott resplendent in full dress uniform with heavy epaulettes and yellow plumes.

The Whig administration began. Day after day the White House was jammed with petitioners. Every one had letters. All of Harrison's friends and acquaintances had letters asking that they intercede with the President. Duff Green, editor of the *United States' Telegraph,* asked Harrison to give him the mission to Texas and was appointed Governor of Florida Territory. Thus encouraged he wrote again to beg an office for his son.[38] Harrison appointed his friend Colonel Chambers Governor of Iowa which caused a minor run-in with Daniel Webster, who wanted the place for General James Wilson of New Hampshire.[39] Colonel Todd was named Minister to Russia, Edward Everett of Massachusetts, a Webster cohort, Ambassador to Great Britain. Henry Clay undertook to insist upon some removals in order to create vacancies for personal friends. General Van Rensselaer, who once had hopes of becoming Secretary of War, his second choice the postmastership of New York, received back his Albany postoffice from which he had been ousted by President Van Buren. Van Rensselaer, something of a nuisance at the last, was now obviously disappointed.[40]

Harrison and his Cabinet received the foreign diplomatic corps one afternoon at the White House. A farewell dinner for General Van Rensselaer was the only other public function for which the President had any time. "I am glad with all my heart to see you," he greeted an old friend from Cincinnati, "for I know that you do not want an office." Another White House caller found the place full of people at a time when Harrison was to meet with his Cabinet. The clamorous crowd pressed after him. Expostulations of friends were in vain. Harrison called for order and made a little speech. Because of the demands of public business, he said, it was impossible to attend to every claim at this particular time. Still the intruders refused to leave unless the President "would *then* receive their papers and pledge himself to attend them." Harrison capitulated. First his pockets were filled, then his hat and his arms, and an attendant was loaded. Upstairs the men marched with as much as they could carry; finally, with much difficulty, the lower rooms were cleared.[41]

Foretaste of trouble between Clay and Harrison came in the appointment of Edward Curtis of New York as Collector of the Port. Curtis, an intimate of Webster and Weed, had helped to block Clay's nomination at Harrisburg. Clay used his every weapon against the appointment, but Harrison was moved to accord some recognition to the wishes of others. The prestige of a certain wealthy individual from Boston, friend and patron of Webster, accounts in some measure for Harrison's partiality for his Secretary of State. The Bostonian was Abbott Lawrence, a former Congressman and head of a syndicate which constructed a chain of cotton mills along the Merrimack River in New England. A few days after the inaugural Lawrence had loaned Harrison the sum of $5000, although the transaction in this case was a loan, not a gift.[42] Webster had received loans of a permanent nature from Lawrence; in later years the Bostonian also helped Clay. His presence in Washington at this time augured an upward revision of the tariff. And to secure the consent of the South to a high tariff, a policy of moderation, guided by Webster, was to be applied to the bank issue.

Was Henry Clay, also, a member of the White House inner circle? It would appear not. Although active elsewhere the Kentuckian was not mentioned as appearing at any of Harrison's dinners. On March 13, however, he addressed a "confidential letter" to the President suggesting the "propriety of a definite decision about an Extra Session," declaring broadly that time was rapidly passing away and that there existed "danger of the implication of vacillating counsels." Not satisfied with this, Clay enclosed his idea for a proclamation calling for the extra session.[43]

Harrison made emphatic response the same day:

"My dear friend,

"You use the privilege of a friend to lecture me and I take the same liberty with you.

"You are too impetuous. Much as I rely upon your judgment there are others whom I must consult and in many cases to determine adversely to your decision. In the matter to which your communication of this morning refers there is no difference of opinion as to the manner and there would be none as to the time but for the situation of Tennessee [its delegation incomplete and uninstructed] to whom we owe so much. Her feelings and interest must not be sacrificed if it can be avoided. The question will finally be settled on Monday having been adjourned over from a discussion which took place this morning.

"I prefer for many reasons this mode of answering your note to a conversation in the presence of others."[44]

For Henry Clay, who had expected to dine at the White House that evening, this was the most humiliating rebuke of his life. One of Clay's friends found him alone in his room, pacing the floor "in great perturbation." Crumbled in his hand was Harrison's note. "And it has come to this! I am civilly but virtually requested not to visit the White House, not to see the president personally but hereafter only communicate with him in writing. . . . Here is my table loaded with letters from my friends in every part of the Union applying to me to obtain offices for them, when I have not one to give, nor influence enough to procure the appointment of a friend to the most humble position!"[45] Clay mistakenly felt that political enemies had come between Harrison and himself, for he had predicted this very thing months ago. But Harrison rather did not wish to allow Clay to dictate the convening of a special session. Within certain limits he was taking advice first from Daniel Webster.

Replying, Clay misrepresented Harrison's letter as a suggestion that he had been "dictating" and defended himself against gossip that he had opposed the appointment of Curtis. This was shooting wide of the mark. "I do not wish to trouble you with answering this note," Clay ended his letter.[46] A day or two later he departed for Kentucky never to see Harrison again.

The President inaugurated what constructive measures he could. Attorney General Crittenden was assigned an international entanglement which threatened harmonious relations with England. This was the case of a loyalist Canadian named Alexander McLeod who had helped seize and destroy an American vessel, the *Caroline,* which had harbored revolutionists during the recent border outbreak. McLeod later boasted, while on American soil, that he had killed one of the crew and so he was arrested. The London press declared war was inevitable should McLeod be convicted and executed. To relieve our government of further embarrassment, Harrison sent Crittenden to New York to direct a *nolle prosequi* in the indictment and although Governor Seward considered the intervention as a piece of meddling in his own affair, he promised to pardon the offender.[47] Harrison issued a pardon to one William Johnston, who had been active in aiding the rebellion against England, and thus the book was closed.[48]

Carrying out the civil service ideas expressed on March 4, Harrison further rebuked the spoils system and countered the pressure of party patronage by requesting department heads that:

". . . information be given to all officers and agents . . . of the public service that partisan interference in popular elections . . . for whomsoever it may be exercised, or the payments of any contribution or assessment of salaries, or official compensation for party or election purposes, will be regarded by him as cause for removal."[49]

The President attempted to limit all department heads as well as himself to removals for cause. He visited every department to take stock of the personnel and obtained estimates of individual worth from former Cabinet officers. To guard against any defalcation of public funds (a Jackson appointee had stolen a cool million) punctuality was required of all collecting and disbursing officials in rendering accounts and paying balances.[50] Another presidential order called for detailed reports on the state of public works then under construction.[51] A special session of Congress to meet on May 31 was decided upon several days following the departure of Clay. The Kentuckian, who had attempted to force the issue, would have hardly come to an agreement in respect to such a late date.

The President did his own marketing in the early morning and generally brought a friend home to breakfast. Quite as informally he met delegations of Indian tribesmen on the White House grounds and escorted them in person to the War Office. His last letter, as far as is known, was addressed on March 26 to Edward Curtis, Collector of the Port of New York, urging the employment of a veteran seaman, a shipmate during the voyage from Colombia in the brig *Montilla*. "Having been several time shipwrecked within a few years, he says that himself and his family are now in such a situation that the humbliest employment would be acceptable. . . . I am persuaded that no one possesses, in a high degree, the virtues of fidelity, honesty, and indefatigable industry, and, I might add, of indomitable bravery."[52]

As a church-goer in Washington, Harrison occupied Pew 45 in St. John's Episcopal Church at 16th and H Streets.[53] He had purchased a new Bible and had announced his intention of becoming a communicant when he caught a severe cold. Overtaken by a shower during his usual walk, he again exposed himself by walking through the slush to offer a diplomatic post to Colonel John Tayloe, master of the Octagon House on Lafayette Square.[54] After dinner on March 27, he sent for a physician. Bleeding was not resorted to on account of his age. The President was "extensively cupped" but still the fever increased with symptoms of pneumonia and intestinal inflammation. The disease was announced as "bilious pleurisy."

After spending nearly a week in bed, Harrison appeared to feel better. He requested the 103d Psalm to be read, thanked the Lord for His goodness and seemed "overpowered with emotion."[55] A relapse soon came. Like his father, Benjamin V, on his death bed, Harrison confided his thoughts to a female attendant: "Ah, Fanny, I am ill, very ill, much more so than they think me."[56] At six o'clock on the same day, April 3, he was pronounced beyond recovery by the four attending physicians. Two others were even now hastening from Philadelphia and Baltimore.

The patient gradually sank into a stupor, his mind wandering in delirium: "It is wrong—I won't consent—'tis unjust. . . . These applications, will they never cease?"[57] Colonel George Croghan, who came to the bedside at Harrison's own request, testified to broken sentences: "I cannot stand it. . . . I cannot bear this. . . . Don't trouble me."[58] The spoils-seekers were buzzing with gossip. What of their fate should the President die? Should they return home or take their chances with Tyler? No one seemed to have the right answer. As a matter of fact it was every man for himself.

"Topical depletion, blistering and appropriate internal remedies, subdued, in a great measure, the disease of the lungs and liver, but the stomach and intestines did not regain a healthy condition," read the official report. Death came at 12:30 o'clock on the morning of Sunday, April 4. Doctor N. W. Worthington caught the last words of the President: "Sir, I wish you to understand the true principles of the government. I wish them carried out. I ask nothing more."[59]

Daniel Webster sent his son Fletcher to summon Vice President Tyler, then at Williamsburg, Virginia. The city of Washington wrapped itself in mourning. Badges and "habiliments of woe" appeared on the streets. Pennsylvania Avenue was hung with festoons and streamers of black; nearly every private dwelling had crape on the knocker or bell-handle. Newspaper columns were heavily leaded. Former Indian Agent John Johnston, appointed commissioner to purchase Wyandot holdings in Ohio and Michigan, discovered sorrow among those tribesmen who had known Harrison:

"They had promised themselves much from his administration. . . . Their confidence in his justice and humanity was unbounded. Poor fellows, his death fell upon them like the thunder which prostrates the loftiest oak. If the Indians had the privilege of voting in that last election for President, not one could be found to black-ball their old and faithful friend, Harrison."[60]

On Wednesday, April 7, heavy cannon boomed. Fourteen volunteer military companies assembled along Pennsylvania Avenue with marines and artillerymen. Harrison's horse, Old Whitey, was saddled to walk riderless in the last procession.

The body was laid in the East Room of a White House shrouded in black. A glass under the lid of the coffin, richly covered with velvet, disclosed the face of the President. "The expression was calm and natural; his white hair lying close to his head, and his features regular and peaceful."[61] Two score clergymen were gathered about the coffin. Behind them were seated the "faithful women," the attending physicians and twenty-four pall bearers wearing white sashes. Vice President Tyler, visibly affected, members of the Cabinet and Congressman John Quincy Adams formed another circle. The diplomatic corps appeared in gorgeous dress with stars, epaulettes, gold and silver lace. Further back sat members of the Senate and Congress with government officials and their ladies. Thousands stood outside at the gates; masses of people extended all the way to the Capitol where the body was to rest in state. Mourning coaches were drawn up about the front lawn.[62]

The frail scent of flowers filled the hushed East Room. At half-past eleven o'clock the rector of St. John's Church took his place in front of the coffin. He recalled the President's church-going habits, his recent purchase of a Bible and prayer book, his activity in the affairs of the church.

A portion of the fifteenth chapter of First Corinthians was read, and selections from the Psalms. *"I am the resurrection and the life,"* intoned the rector and the congregation arose seemingly in one movement, and joined in the service of the Episcopal Church.[63]

NOTES

CHAPTER I

[1]Henry Harrison Wilson, *Benjamin Harrison V*, unpublished address delivered at Richmond, Va., Oct. 20, 1931, contains a definitive account of the Signer. Copies are deposited in the Virginia State Library and the Library of Congress. See also, Silas Deane to his wife, Sept. 10, 1774, *Deane Papers*, 1 :25, New York Historical Society; Lyon G. Tyler, *Letters and Times of the Tylers*, 1 :67, 89, 124–25.

[2]Nell Marion Nugent (editor), *Cavaliers and Pioneers*, 1 :15–16. The signature on this early document places Benjamin Harrison in Virginia two years earlier than any date previously given. Charles Keith, *The Ancestry of Benjamin Harrison*, 41–43, and Dorothy Burne Goebel, *William Henry Harrison*, 2, give this date as 1634.

[3]Charles Campbell, *History of the Colony and Ancient Dominion of Virginia*, 654 n.; William G. and Mary Newton Stanard, *Colonial Virginia Register*, 62ff.

[4]W. S. Perry, *Historical Collections Relating to the American Church*, 70, 80–81, 92. Benjamin Harrison III was admitted to the Middle Temple, Inns of Court, London, Oct. 18, 1697. E. A. Jones, *American Members of Inns of Court*, 96.

[5]Mary Newton Stanard, *Colonial Virginia*, 351.

[6]Alexander Brown, *Genesis of the United States*, 2 :828, 1005.

[7]James A. Green, *The Berkeley Manor House* (privately printed), Mitten Collection, Indiana Historical Society; *Virginia Magazine of History*, 32 :96–101 ; Edith Tunis Sale, *Interiors of Virginia Houses of Colonial Times*, 435–36.

[8]*William & Mary College Quarterly*, 2: Second Series, 18–19; *Maryland Historical Magazine*, 17 :365; *Journals of the Virginia House of Burgesses*, 1619–49, 155. Colonel Benjamin Harrison IV was killed July 12, 1745 (O.S.).

[9]*Western Monthly Review* (1837–38), 1 :541.

[10]The account of the Harrison family in *Virginia Magazine of History*, 32 :299 states that Benjamin Harrison V was a member of the House from the session beginning April 10, 1749, to the last which began Jan. 1, 1775. Actually Harrison succeeded Edward Brodnax, deceased, in the fall of 1748. *Journals of the Virginia House of Burgesses*, 1742–49, ix.

[11]Woodrow Wilson, *George Washington*, 192; *Virginia Magazine of History*, 43 :431. An interesting early letter of Benjamin Harrison illustrates this point. Harrison to Colonel John Palfrey, March 14, 1733, Boston *Gazette*, April 12, 1773.

[12]William Henry Harrison to James Lyons, June 1, 1840, Washington *Globe*, July 7, 1840. John Adams pronounced this opinion several years after Harrison's death. During the sessions of Congress he entertained a

346 NOTES [pp. 3–10]

hearty dislike for the Colonel. C. F. Adams (editor), *Autobiography of John Adams* (*Works*), 3:25, 31.

[13]"When the time of hanging comes, I shall have the advantage over you," Harrison remarked to the lean Elbridge Gerry of Massachusetts. "It will be all over with me in a minute, but you will be kicking in the air for half an hour after I am gone." Hugh Blair Grigsby, *The Virginia Federal Convention of 1788*, 96. See also, Paul Wilstach, *Jefferson and Monticello*, 174–75.

[14]Benjamin Harrison to George Washington, Feb. 16, 1781, *Calendar of Virginia State Papers*, 1:523; John Graves Simcoe, *Journal of Operations of Queen's Rangers*, 159–60.

[15]*Virginia Magazine of History*, 6:346–48.

[16]Election day in Virginia was the third Thursday in April. Benjamin Harrison VII to Robert Waln, March 31, 1824, Mitten Collection.

[17]*Virginia Magazine of History*, 33:313.

[18]*Ibid.*, 6:235–36; Marion Harland, *Some Colonial Homesteads*, 15; Paul Wilstach, *Tidewater Virginia*, 129–30. Benjamin Harrison of Brandon was a contemporary of Benjamin V of Berkeley.

[19]*The '98 Kaleidoscope*, Hampden-Sidney College, 49–50.

[20]H. Boley, *Lexington in Old Virginia*, 17.

[21]Harrison to James Brooks, July 30, 1839, Harrison MSS., New York Historical Society.

[22]Thomas Jefferson to William Short, Paul L. Ford (editor), *The Writings of Thomas Jefferson*, 4:136; W. H. Foote, *Sketches of Virginia*, 412–13.

[23]Samuel Mordecai, *Richmond in By-Gone Days*, 531.

[24]Stephen B. Weeks, *Southern Quakers and Slavery*, 212.

[25]Harrison to Brooks, July 20, 1839, Harrison MSS., New York Historical Society.

[26]*Virginia Magazine of History*, 33:414. Colonel Harrison's personal estate amounted to £4286, 10s; also 110 negroes, 64 cattle, etc. *Ibid.*, 34:84–90.

[27]William Ogden Niles, *The Tippecanoe Textbook*, 4.

[28]Harrison to Brooks, July 20, 1839, Harrison MSS., New York Historical Society.

[29]Life of General Harrison in the *Portfolio* (Philadelphia, 1815), 5:No. 4, 309–10; H. Montgomery, *Life of William Henry Harrison*, 330–31.

[30]Henry Knox to Arthur St. Clair, Sept. 22, 1791, *American State Papers, Indian Affairs*, 1:82.

CHAPTER II

[1]Benson J. Lossing, *Pictorial Field-Book of the War of 1812*, 48 n.

[2]Harrison to Brooks, July 20, 1839, Harrison MSS., New York Historical Society.

[3]*Ibid.;* Jacob Burnet, *Notes on Northwest Territory*, 36–37.

[4]Harrison to A. B. Howell, April 7, 1838, Cincinnati *Daily Gazette*, May 19, 1838.

[5]Remarks of General Solomon Van Rensselaer, *ibid.*, July 4, 1840.

[6]A. E. Jones, *History of Cincinnati*, 123.

[7]James McBride, *Pioneer Biography, Ohio Valley Historical Series:* No. 4, 1:31–32.

[8]Robert Buntin to St. Clair, Feb. 13, 1792, J. B. Dillon, *Indiana,* 282–83.

[9]Harrison to Thomas P. Chilton, Feb. 17, 1834, Cincinnati *Daily Gazette,* May 10, 1834.

[10]Garrison Orders, May 11, 1792, Sargent Papers, Massachusetts Historical Society.

[11]Reverend Charles F. Goss, *Cincinnati,* 1:83.

[12]James Wilkinson to Winthrop Sargent, June 2, 1792, Sargent Papers; *Territorial Papers, Northwest Territory,* 2:400, 402; 3:377.

[13]*Pennsylvania Magazine of History,* 2:475.

[14]Anthony Wayne to Harrison, July 3, 1792, Wayne Papers, Pennsylvania Historical Society.

[15]Logan B. Esarey (editor), *Harrison's Messages & Letters,* 2:542.

[16]A. G. Bradley, *Lord Dorchester,* 231–32.

[17]*Historical & Philosophical Society of Ohio Quarterly,* 17: No. 3, 88–89.

[18]S. J. Burr, *Life of William Henry Harrison,* 33; see also *Ohio Valley Historical Series,* No. 4, 2:104–6.

[19]Wayne's Orderly Book," *Michigan Historical Collections,* 34:396–97.

[20]Memorandum, March 9, 1793, John Scott Harrison Collection. Harrison sold "all that part of the Berkeley Tract of Land lying in Charles City and Henrico Counties which has been given him . . . by the will of his late father . . . three thousand acres more or less."

[21]Harrison to John Tipton, *Messages & Letters,* 2:746.

[22]*American State Papers, Indian Affairs,* 1:352.

[23]Quoted in Thomas Boyd, *Mad Anthony Wayne,* 261.

[24]McBride, *Pioneer Biography,* 2:112.

[25]Harrison to Howell, April 7, 1838, Cincinnati *Daily Gazette,* May 19, 1838.

[26]George Will to John S. Williams, May 25, 1842, *Michigan Historical Collections,* 34:502–3.

[27]William Clark, "Journal of Wayne's Campaign" (R. C. McGrane, editor), *Mississippi Valley Historical Review,* 1:422.

[28]Harrison to Charles Scott, April 17, 1810, *Messages & Letters,* 1:414.

[29]O. W. Priddy, "Wayne's Strategic Advance," *Ohio Archæological & Historical Society Quarterly,* 39:50–54; Henry Howe, *Historical Collections of Ohio,* 1:545.

[30]William Henry Harrison, "Discourse on the Aborigines of the Ohio Valley," *Fergus Historical Series,* No. 26:18; C. V. R. Bonney, *A Legacy of Historical Gleanings,* 1:101; Lossing, *Pictorial Field-Book of the War of 1812,* 53–54 n.

[31]"Wayne's Orderly Book," *Michigan Historical Collections,* 34:545.

[32]Nevin O. Winter, *History of Northwest Ohio,* 1:85.

[33]Harrison to Tipton, Dec. 6, 1833, *Messages & Letters,* 2:746. In 1799, Harrison advertised his horse "Fearnaught" for sale.

[34] Bonney, *Legacy,* 2:133–34.

35Statement of Antoine Lassell, *American State Papers, Indian Affairs*, I :494.
36Lossing, *Pictorial Field-Book of the War of 1812*, 54–55; John Hyde Preston, *A Gentleman Rebel*, 242–43.
37Harrison to Carter Bassett Harrison, Nov. 27, 1794, Harrison Papers, I :21–22, Library of Congress.
38Bonney, *Legacy*, 2 :134.
39James Wilkinson to John Brown, Aug. 28, 1894, *Mississippi Valley Historical Review*, 16 :87.
40Harrison to Chilton, Feb. 17, 1834, Cincinnati *Daily Gazette*, May 10, 1834.
41*American State Papers, Indian Affairs*, I :494.
42"Wayne's Orderly Book," *Michigan Historical Collections*, 34 :547.
43Wayne to Henry Knox, Aug. 28, 1794, *American State Papers, Indian Affairs*, I :491.
44Journal of Lieutenant Thomas J. Underwood, Draper Collection, Wisconsin Historical Society.

CHAPTER III

1Harrison to Carter Bassett Harrison, Nov. 20, 1794, Harrison Papers, I :21–22.
2Two preliminary peace treaties were signed at Fort Greenville, Feb. 11 and 22, 1795. Wayne Papers, 2 :97; 39 :43.
3Ellis Paxson Oberholtzer, *Robert Morris*, 265–66.
4Andrew M. Sherman, *Historic Morristown*, 400; Bessie Smith, *Romances of the Presidents*, 128. An interesting letter from Harrison to Wayne, April 13, 1795, describes part of the trip. Dreer Collection, Presidential Autographs, Pennsylvania Historical Society.
5B. W. Bond (editor), *Correspondence of John Cleves Symmes*, 4–5; C. H.Winfield, "Life of John Cleves Symmes," New Jersey Historical Society, *Proceedings, Second Series*, 5 :37–38.
6Benjamin F. Thompson, *History of Long Island*, I :406.
7Harrison's *Messages & Letters*, 2 :637.
8*American State Papers, Indian Affairs*, I :562–63.
9Lossing, *Pictorial Field-Book of the War of 1812*, 572. Harrison's runaway marriage has been denied by a descendant (*Messages & Letters*, I :7), but in 1844 Captain Ellison Symmes declared that the lovers "concluded upon a clandestine marriage which was duly accomplished" at the home of a tenant of Judge Symmes. Francis Baxter, "Rafting on the Ohio and Alleghany Rivers," *Pennsylvania Magazine of History*, 51 :57–58.
10Charles S. Todd and Benjamin Drake, *William Henry Harrison*, 18. Lossing quotes a slightly different version of the incident. *Pictorial Field-Book of the War of 1812*, 572.
11Harrison to Wayne, July 11, 1796, American Art Association-Anderson Galleries (New York), *Catalogue*, December 5–6, 1934.
12Wayne to Harrison, July 11, 1796, *ibid*.
13John Cleves Symmes to Jonathan Dayton, Sept. 6, 1796, Bond (editor), *Correspondence of John Cleves Symmes*, 182–83; Howe, *Historical Collections of Ohio*, 2 :30–31.

[14]Harrison to James McHenry, May, 1797, and Aug. 13, 1797, B. C. Sterner, *Life of James McHenry*, 263–64.
[15]James Smith to James Findlay, Aug. 10, 1797, Torrence Papers, Historical & Philosophical Society of Ohio; Robert R. Jones, *Fort Washington*, 56.
[16]Sargent to Timothy Pickering, May 21, 1798, *Mississippi Territorial Archives*, 1:16.
[17]Harrison to Robert Goodloe Harper, May 26, 1798, Pickering Papers, 22:179, Massachusetts Historical Society.
[18]*Territorial Papers, Northwest Territory*, 3:508.
[19]William H. Smith, *Life of Arthur St. Clair* (*St. Clair Papers*), 2:207.
[20]Deposition of Griffin Yeatman, Cincinnati *Gazette*, July 15, 1840.
[21]Harrison to Brooks, July 20, 1839, Harrison MSS., New York Historical Society.
[22]Harrison to St. Clair, Sept. 23, 1799, St. Clair MSS., Ohio State Library; transcript in Indiana Historical Society Library.
[23]*The Hesperian* (Cincinnati, 1839) 3:366; J. P. Dunn, *Indiana*, 278; Caleb Atwater, *History of Ohio*, 163–64.
[24]*Annals, 6th Congress, 1st Session*, col. 537–38.
[25]*Ibid.*, col. 198, 209–10, 509–10, 625, 650–52; *Territorial Papers, Northwest Territory*, 3:48–50; *Western Monthly Magazine* (1835), 3:85–86.
[26]Harrison to constituents, May 14, 1800, *Messages & Letters*, 1:13.
[27]*Annals, 6th Congress, 1st Session*, col. 193, 198, 245–46, 374; Dunn, *Indiana*, 279; Harrison to Nathaniel Massie, Jan. 17, 1800, David Massie, *Life of Nathaniel Massie*, 155–56.
[28]St. Clair to Harrison, Feb. 17, 1800, Smith, *St. Clair Papers*, 2:489–91.
[29]*Ibid.*, 2:570; Dunn, *Indiana*, 279.
[30]St. Clair to James Ross, Dec., 1799, Smith, *St. Clair Papers*, 2:480–83.
[31]*Annals, 6th Congress, 1st Session*, col. 645, 649, 698–99; *Territorial Papers, Northwest Territory*, 3:76–77.
[32]*Annals, 6th Congress, 1st Session*, col. 1498–1500; Smith (editor), *St. Clair Papers*, 1:231.
[33]Caleb Swan to James Findlay, Jan. 11, 1800, Torrence Papers.
[34]Harrison to Thomas Jefferson, Aug. 8, 1802, *Messages & Letters*, 1:50.
[35]C. W. Byrd to Massie, Aug. 14, 1800, Massie Papers, Ohio Archæological & Historical Society; Harrison to Lyons, June 1, 1840, Washington *Globe*, July 7, 1840.
[36]Susan Symmes to Maria Short, June 21, 1801, Harrison Papers, 1:53.

CHAPTER IV

[1]Elias Pym Fordham, *Personal Narrative*, (F. A. Ogg, editor), 96–97; H. S. Cauthorn, *History of the City of Vincennes*, 17–22; George B. Catlin, "Early Travel on the Ohio," *Michigan Historical Magazine*, 20: No. 2, 158; Constantin F. C. de Volney, *A View of the Soil and Climate of the United States*, 368, 378–89; Lee Burns, "Life in Old Vincennes,"

Indiana Historical Society Publications, 8: 437–43; Dunn, *Indiana*, 295–96.

[2]Proclamation, Jan. 10, 1801, *Messages & Letters*, 1 :20–21.

[3]Susan Symmes to Maria Short, June 21, 1801, Harrison Papers, 1 :53.

[4]Harrison to Henry Dearborn, July 15, 1801, *Messages & Letters*, 1 :25–31.

[5]Proclamations of May 9, July 20, Aug. 31, 1801, *ibid.*, 1 :24, 31–32.

[6]Harrison to Dearborn, Oct., 1802, *ibid.*, 1 :60; same to same, March, 1802, Moses Dawson, *Life of William Henry Harrison*, 32–33; James Reynolds, *Pioneer History of Illinois*, 283; Proclamation offering a reward for a jail-breaker, May 5, 1802, *Messages & Letters*, 1 :48–49.

[7]Harrison to Findlay, Oct. 15, 1801, *ibid.*, 1 :34.

[8]Isaac Darneille, *Letters of Decius*, Oct. 10, 1805, Rare Book Room, Library of Congress.

[9]Harrison to Dearborn, Feb. 26, 1802, *Messages & Letters*, 1 :41–46.

[10]Address to the Indian Council, *ibid.*, 1 :52–55.

[11]Minutes of Council, Sept. 17, 1802, *ibid.*, 1 :56–57.

[12]Dunn, *Indiana*, 301.

[13]*Ibid.*, 307; Resolution and Petition of Vincennes Convention, Dec. 25–28, 1802, *Messages & Letters*, 1 :61–63.

[14]Harrison to Jonathan Dayton, Jan. 12, 1803, *Henkel's Catalogue of Autograph MSS.*, No. 663 :58, New York Public Library.

[15]Jefferson to Harrison, Feb. 27, 1803, *Messages & Letters*, 1 :70–73.

[16]Lossing, *Pictorial Field-Book of the War of 1812*, 132 n. 2.

[17]Harrison to Charles De Lassus, March 5, 1803, Harrison Papers, 1 :60; Commodore Grant to John Askin, May 17, 1803, *John Askin Papers* (Milo Quaife, editor), 2 :390; Darneille, *Letters of Decius*, Dec. 1, 1805; Dawson, *Harrison*, 47.

[18]*Ibid.*, 48–49.

[19]Harrison to Dearborn, March 3, 1805 (misdated 1803), *Messages & Letters*, 1 :83.

[20]C. J. Kappler (editor), *Indian Laws and Treaties*, 2 :64–65; C. C. Royce, "Indian Land Cessions," American Bureau of Ethnology, *18th Annual Report, 1896–97*, part 2 :257.

[21]Harrison to William Eustis, July 5, 1809, *Messages & Letters*, 1 :353–54.

[22]William O. Lynch, *Fifty Years of Party Warfare*, 144.

[23]Statement of Thomas McKee, Jan. 3, 1803, *Michigan Historical Collections*, 23 :20; Dawson, *Harrison*, 48.

[24]Harrison to John Armstrong, March 22, 1814, *Messages & Letters*, 2 :638.

[25]Kappler (editor), *Indian Laws and Treaties*, 2 :67–68; Dillon, *Indiana*, 419.

[26]Benjamin Parke (?) to Thomas Randolph, Sept. 5, 1808, W. W. Woollen, *Biographical & Historical Sketches of Early Indiana*, 6–7.

[27]Parke letter, *Indiana Gazette* (Vincennes), Sept. 5, 1804.

[28]Dunn, *Indiana*, 323–24.

[29]Kappler (editor), *Indian Laws and Treaties*, 2 :70–73.

[30]*Indiana Gazette*, Aug. 21, 1804. This newspaper was founded by Elihu Stout, July 4, 1804; later burned out, it was re-established as the *Western Sun*. See *Potter's American Monthly*, 12 :295.

[31]Harrison to Findlay, Sept. 22, 1804, Torrence Papers. This letter is reprinted in part in Harrison's *Messages & Letters*, 1:108. The omitted sentence should read: "She (Mrs. H.—) expects daily to be confined in the family way and is very much distressed at my being obliged to leave her." See also, Dawson, *Harrison*, 292.

[32]Harrison to Dayton, Oct. 29, 1804, *Henkel's Catalogue of Autograph MSS.*, No. 663:67, New York Public Library.

[33]Harrison to Editor of the *Ohio Confederate* (Columbus), Oct. 18, 1839, reprinted in Cincinnati *Gazette*, Nov. 10, 1839; Dawson, *Harrison*, 66.

[34]Anonymous letter, Nov. 4, 1804, F. C. Shoemaker, "Sketch of Missouri Constitutional History," *Missouri Historical Review*, 9:17-18.

[35]John Bruff to Dearborn, Nov. 5, 1804, Old Records Division, War Department.

[36]Milo Quaife, *Checagou*, 177; Cyrenus Cole, *History of the People of Iowa*, 59-61; Cole, *I Am a Man*, 30-32.

[37]Kappler (editor), *Indian Laws & Treaties*, 2:74-77; Dillon, *Indiana*, 419; Dawson, *Harrison*, 59. This cession of 15 million acres has always been misrepresented as 51 million, possibly a misprint copied without further investigation.

[38]Harrison to Dearborn, *Messages & Letters*, 1:132-34; Louis Houck, *History of Missouri*, 2:397; Cole, *I Am a Man;* 34; Moses M. Strong, "The Indian Wars of Wisconsin," *Wisconsin Historical Collections*, 8:265.

[39]Ben F. Sager, *The Harrison Mansion*, 12-13; George E. Greene, *History of Vincennes and Knox County*, 286-87.

[40]In 1801, Harrison paid $400 for a runaway slave from Kentucky and later freed him, according to an advertisement offering a reward for the kidnapers of his faithful servant. Cincinnati *National Republican*, June 27, 1823. In 1804, Harrison secured a court ruling releasing a slave from the hands of "kidnappers" and indentured him for a term of eleven years. This slave was about to be taken to Kentucky and sold.

[41]W. C. MacNaul, *The Jefferson-Lemen Compact*, 29. Apparently Jefferson had sent James Leman, an intimate friend, to Northwest Territory in order that he might combat slavery influence there through the organization of Baptist churches. Harrison's pro-slavery leanings have been denied (Logan Esarey, "Some Unsolved Questions of Our Early History," *Indiana History Bulletin*, extra number, Feb., 1924), but there is some further evidence to consider. See MacNaul, 15.

[42]Harrison to Jefferson, June 18, 1805, Jefferson Papers, Library of Congress.

[43]Proclamation, April 4, 1804, *Messages & Letters*, 1:94-95.

[44]Jefferson to Harrison, April 28, 1805, *ibid.*, 1:27.

[45]Darneille, *Letters of Decius*, May 10, 1805, Library of Congress.

[46]Address to Indiana General Assembly, July 29, 1805, *Messages & Letters*, 1:153.

[47]*Ibid.*, 1:154.

[48]Harrison to Edward Tiffin, Nov. 5, 1805, *Indiana Historical Society Publications*, 1:135.

⁴⁹Chief Billy Patterson to William Wells, April 5, 1805, *Messages &
Letters,* 1:122.
⁵⁰Harrison to Dearborn, March 3, 1805 (misdated 1803), *ibid.,* 1:76-
82; same to same, April 26 and July 10, 1805, *ibid.,* 125-26, 148; John
Johnston to Harrison, Feb. 26, 1806, Harrison Papers, 1:88.
⁵¹John Gibson and Francis Vigo to Harrison, July 6, 1805, *Messages
& Letters,* 1:141-47.
⁵²Harrison to Dearborn, Aug. 26, 1805, *ibid.,* 1:162-63.
⁵³Same to same, Aug. 26, 1805, *ibid.,* 164; Bill of Indian Goods, 1805,
ibid., 167; Kappler (editor), *Indian Laws and Treaties,* 2:80-82.
⁵⁴B. Chambers to Harrison, Oct. 17, 1805, English Collection, Indiana
Historical Society.
⁵⁵Dearborn to Harrison, Oct. 11, 1805, *Messages & Letters,* 1:169.
⁵⁶Harrison to Jefferson, Aug. 29, 1805, Jefferson Papers, Library of
Congress.
⁵⁷Same to same, Nov. 12, 1805, *ibid.;* Dawson, *Harrison,* 68.
⁵⁸Kappler (editor), *Indian Laws and Treaties,* 2:89; Dillon, *Indiana,*
419.

CHAPTER V

¹Harrison to Jefferson, Aug. 8, 1802, *Messages & Letters,* 1:50-51.
²*Indiana Magazine of History,* 17:132; *Americana,* 32:461-62.
³Jefferson's Second Inaugural Address, March 5, 1805, quoted in Gilbert Chinard, *Life of Thomas Jefferson,* 425. Chinard adds some perti-
nent comment.
⁴W. A. Galloway, *Old Chillicothe,* 163-65.
⁵*Ibid.,* 135-38.
⁶Harrison to William Eustis, Aug. 7, 1811, *Messages & Letters,* 1:549;
W. C. McLeod, *The American Indian Frontier,* 430.
⁷Benjamin Drake, *Life of Tecumseh,* 86-88; S. G. Drake, *Aboriginal
Races of North America,* 624-25; James Mooney, "The Ghost Dance
Religion," American Bureau of Ethnology, *14th Annual Report, 1892-
93:* part 2, 670-80; Galloway, *Old Chillicothe,* 139-44.
⁸L. A. Gipson (editor), "The Moravian Mission on White River,"
Indiana Historical Society Collections, 23:397.
⁹Arthur W. Brady, "The Moravian Mission in Indiana," Mississippi
Valley Historical Association, *Proceedings, 1919-20:* 286-97; Drake,
Tecumseh, 88-89.
¹⁰Harrison to Dearborn, July 11, 1807, *Messages & Letters,* 1:224;
Proclamation, June 21, 1806, *ibid.,* 190; Dawson, *Harrison,* 86.
¹¹Harrison to the Delawares, April (?), 1806, *Messages & Letters,*
1:183-84.
¹²Harrison to Jefferson, July 5, 1806, *ibid.,* 1:194-95.
¹³Message to Indiana Assembly, Nov. 3, 1806, *ibid.,* 199-200.
¹⁴Sager, *The Harrison Mansion,* 13.
¹⁵Walter F. McCaleb, *The Aaron Burr Conspiracy,* 35.
¹⁶Waller Taylor to Harrison, Jan. 12, 1807, *Messages & Letters,*
1:201-2.
¹⁷Harrison to Governor Robert Williams of Mississippi, *ibid.,* 1:205.
¹⁸Harrison to William Hargrove, Aug. 13, 1807, *ibid.,* 1:228.
¹⁹Beverley W. Bond, *The Civilization of the Old Northwest,* 179-80;

Jonathan Jennings to William Eustis, Feb. 7, 1812, "Unedited Letters of Jonathan Jennings," (Dorothy Riker, editor), *Indiana Historical Society Publications*, 10 : no. 4, 182–84.

[20]Harrison's *Messages & Letters*, 1 :209 n., 217.
[21]William Wells to Harrison, Aug. 20, 1807, *ibid.*, 1 :239.
[22]Harrison to Eustis, July 25, 1810, *ibid.*, 1 :451.
[23]Harrison to Hargrove, Oct. 12, 1807, *ibid.*, 1 :266.
[24]Harrison to Dearborn, July 11, 1807, *ibid.*, 1 :266; Deposition of Francois Ducharme, July 6, 1807, *ibid.*, 1 :245; Frederick Bates to Dearborn, Sept. 18, 1807, T. M. Marshall (editor), *Life and Papers of Frederick Bates*, 200–10.
[25]Message to the Indiana Assembly, Aug. 28, 1807, *Messages & Letters*, 1 :235–36.
[26]Harrison to Dearborn, Aug. 29, 1807, *ibid.*, 244.
[27]William Claus to Francis Gore, Feb. 27, 1808, *ibid.*, 287. Harrison's view concerning the possibility of war is found in an unpublished Special Message to the Indiana Assembly, Sept. 8, 1808, English Collection, Indiana Historical Society.
[28]Claus to Gore, Feb. 27, 1808, *Messages & Letters*, 1 :285.
[29]Drake, *Life of Tecumseh*, 92–93.
[30]Jefferson to Dearborn, Aug. 27, 1807, *Works* (Ford edition), 9 :131.
[31]James A. Craig to Gore, Dec. 6, 1807, *Canadian Archives Report, 1896*, 32–33.
[32]W. H. Roose, *Birthplace of Indiana*, 17–19. Harrison owned land in that sector later organized as Harrison County (Oct. 11, 1808). He named the town of Corydon, founded 1807, after a character in a favorite but lugubrious song.
[33]Harrison to Dearborn, May 19, 1808, *Messages & Letters*, 1 :291.
[34]Diary of William Claus, June 14, 1808, *Michigan Historical Collections*, 23 :53.
[35]Harrison to Eustis, June 26, 1810, *Messages & Letters*, 1 :434. Harrison quotes the testimony of an Iowa Indian : "Two summers ago . . . an agent from the British arrived at the Prophets Town and . . . delivered the message . . . [urging] the Prophet to unite as many Tribes as he could, against the United States, but not to commence hostilities, until they gave the signal." Trouble was, the Indians were not likely to wait.
[36]Diary of William Claus, July 12, 1808, *Michigan Historical Collections*, 23 :57.
[37]Craig to Secretary for War Castlereagh, July 15, 1808, *Canadian Archives Report, 1893*, 13.
[38]Harrison to Dearborn, Feb. 14, 1809 (misdated July), *Messages & Letters*, 1 :355.
[39]Same to same, Sept. 1, 1808, *ibid.*, 302.
[40]Claus to Prideau Selby, Jan. 18, 1809, *Michigan Historical Collections*, 23 :67.
[41]Message to Indiana Assembly, Sept. 27, 1808, *Messages & Letters*, 1 :307.

CHAPTER VI

[1]Dunn, *Indiana*, 366–67.
[2]Special Message to Indiana House, Oct. 25, 1808, *Messages & Letters*, 1 :320.

[3]Dunn, *Indiana,* 395–98.

[4]Jennings to William Duane, Dec., 1809, "Unedited Letters of Jonathan Jennings" (Dorothy Riker, editor), *Indiana Historical Society Publications,* 10:170–72; Dunn, *Indiana,* 400; Riker, "Jonathan Jennings," *Indiana Magazine of History,* 28:225–26.

[5]Bond, *The Civilization of the Old Northwest,* 324. Mr. W. C. Mason, president of Knox County Historical Society, writes me that Harrison founded the original organization in 1808.

[6]Harrison to Eustis, May 3 and 16, 1809, *Messages & Letters,* 1:345–46.

[7]*Ibid.,* 346.

[8]Same to same, July 5, 1809, *ibid.,* 1:341.

[9]Eustis to Harrison, July 15, 1809, *ibid.,* 1:356–57. Compare Madison's instructions with those of Sir George Prevost, Governor-General of Canada, May 1, 1812: "All Purchases of Land are to be made in Public Council with great solemnity and ceremony . . . the Principal Chiefs and leading men of the Nation, or Nations, to whom the Lands belong, being first assembled." *Michigan Historical Collections,* 23:93. This was also the American procedure.

[10]John Cleves Symmes to Anna Harrison, Sept. 11, 1809, Bond (editor), *Correspondence,* 297.

[11]Harrison to Eustis, Nov. 3, 1809, *Messages & Letters,* 1:389.

[12]Harrison to Indiana Assembly, Nov. 12, 1810, *Messages & Letters,* 1:489. The name of Hockingpomskon, a Delaware chief, is incorrectly interposed by the editor of this work. It was Blackhoof, the grand sachem of the Shawnees, who was present at the council. Blackhoof would not admit the rank of chief to either Tecumseh or The Prophet. Harrison to Editor of *The Hesperian* (Cincinnati), July, 1838, 259–60.

[13]Journal of the Proceedings at Fort Wayne, *Messages & Letters,* 1:363–64.

[14]*Ibid.,* 1:367–69.

[15]Harrison to Eustis, Nov. 3, 1809, *ibid.,* 1:389.

[16]Journal of the Proceedings at Fort Wayne, *ibid.,* 1:374.

[17]Harrison to Eustis, Nov. 3, 1809, *ibid.,* 1:389. The terms of the treaty are given in *ibid.,* 1:359–62. This was Harrison's most important land treaty.

[18]Resolutions of Oct. 21 (misdated Nov. 4), and Oct. 28, 1809, *ibid.,* 1:385, 391–92; *Western Sun* (Vincennes), Oct. 21 and Nov. 4, 1809.

[19]Kappler (editor), *Indian Laws and Treaties,* 2:103–4.

CHAPTER VII

[1]Message of Governor Charles Scott to Kentucky legislature, *Kentucky State Historical Society Register,* 1: No. 3, 16.

[2]Harrison's two letters to Governor Scott, dated March 10 and April 17, 1810, are respectively about 3800 and 2900 words long. *Messages & Letters,* 1:400–17. Harrison must have reviewed his history books during the winter. In these two letters he alludes to 32 military leaders and 15 battles of ancient and modern times, from the campaigns of Philip of Macedon to those of General Anthony Wayne.

[3]Deposition of Michel Brouillette, June 30, 1810, *ibid.,* 1:436–37.

[4]Harrison to Eustis, June 14 and 28, 1810, *ibid.*, 1 :424–25, 433.
[5]Same to same, June 15, 1810, *ibid.*, 1 :426.
[6]Same to same, June 19, 1810, *ibid.*, 429; *Western Sun* (Vincennes) June 30, 1810.
[7]Dillon, *Indiana*, 441; Lossing, *Pictorial Field-Book of the War of 1812*, 191.
[8]Harrison to The Prophet, July 19, 1810, *Messages & Letters*, 1 :447–48.
[9]Harrison to Eustis, Aug. 6, 1810, *ibid.*, 457.
[10]George R. C. Floyd to his wife, Aug. 14, 1810, Drake, *Tecumseh*, 125.
[11]William G. Hatch, *A Chapter of the History of the War of 1812*, 113–15; Lossing, *Pictorial Field-Book of the War of 1812*, 283 n.
[12]Drake, *Tecumseh*, 126.
[13]John Law, *Colonial History of Vincennes*, 84.
[14]Harrison to Eustis, Aug. 22, 1810, *Messages & Letters*, 1 :460. Tecumseh's are reprinted in *ibid.*, 1 :463–69.
[15]Dawson, *Harrison*, 156–57; Drake, *Tecumseh*, 126–27.
[16]Rose Schultheis, "Harrison and Tecumseh," *Indiana Magazine of History*, 27 :48; Harrison to Eustis, Aug. 22, 1810, *Messages & Letters*, 1 :461.
[17]Tecumseh's speech, Aug. 21, 1810, *ibid.*, 1 :468–69.
[18]William McIntosh, a native of Scotland and a former subaltern in the British army, was a prominent land speculator in Vincennes where he amused himself by cheating illiterate French settlers out of their property while at the same time fighting the advance to second grade government and the administration's policy of land acquisition. In 1801, he was a land partner of Harrison's but was ousted for rascality. Letter of Peter Paul & Pompey, *Western World* (Frankfort), March 3, 1808. See also the statements of Henry Vanderburgh, Luke Decker, William Prince and G. W. Johnston, Jan. 14, 1811, Appointment Files (State Department), National Archives.
[19]Dawson, *Harrison*, 158–59; Drake, *Tecumseh*, 128–29.
[20]Elmore Barce, "The Old Chicago Trail," *Indiana Magazine of History*, 15 :7.
[21]Harrison to Eustis, Aug. 22, 1810, *Messages & Letters*, 1 :460.
[22]Matthew Elliott to Claus, Oct. 16 and Nov. 16, 1810, *Canadian Archives Report, 1893, Calendar Q–114* :45.
[23]Craig to Francis Gore, Feb. 22, 1811, *ibid.*, 45–46; Craig to Lord Liverpool, March 29, 1811, William Wood (editor), *Select British Documents of the Canadian War of 1812*, 1 :164.
[24]Sir Isaac Brock to Craig, Feb. 27, 1811, F. B. Tupper, *Life of Sir Isaac Brock*, 80–81; Christopher B. Coleman, "The Ohio Valley in the Preliminaries of the War of 1812," *Mississippi Valley Historical Review*, 7 :45. Harrison was severely criticized by Federalists and Tories, the anti-administration party, for holding the British responsible for material support of Tecumseh and The Prophet. In recent years a number of scholars have rebuked him on rather shallow grounds. We have, for example, the statement of James Truslow Adams: "It has required

several generations of research to disprove utterly General Harrison's lies about the English having set Tecumseh on us." (Adams, *Epic of America*, 145.) A similar depreciation is expressed in a paper entitled: "The History of Events Resulting in Indian Consolidation West of the Mississippi River," by Annie Heloise Abel, Ph.D. (*American Historical Association Report, 1906*, 1:233–450.) Miss Abel severely criticizes Harrison's land treaty methods but her argument is weakened by errors of fact, omission and opinion. No American historian has yet made use of all the evidence of British intrigue furnished by the British Indian Agents themselves, and a great many statements presented as serious history indicate a sad lack of appreciation of actual conditions on the wilderness frontier. While Harrison gave the British credit for holding the Indians in check, he and other frontier governors were furnished pretty concrete evidence that the British were encouraging and assisting Tecumseh and his followers to the extent of thousands of dollars' worth of supplies yearly as well as inflammatory speeches. For several years Tecumseh and The Prophet played a double game, receiving supplies from both camps. Wrote Colonel Matthew Elliott at Fort Amherstburg, Nov. 18, 1810: "The Prophet's brother . . . said at first they intended to keep their plans secret but as Governor Harrison has pushed them to avow their intentions, they have decided now to disclose them." *Canadian Archives Report, 1893, Calendar Q–114*, 45. And as will be seen, Chief Shabonee, or Shaubena, Tecumseh's intimate friend, blamed the British for direct instigation of the Battle of Tippecanoe.

²⁵Jennings to Solomon Manwarring, Jan. 22, 1811, *Messages & Letters*, 1:501–02.

²⁶Harrison to Congressman John Eppes, Jan. 22, 1811, Appointment Files (State Department), National Archives; Harrison to Robert Smith, Jan. 10, 1811, *ibid*.

²⁷Deposition of G. W. Johnston, Speaker of the Indiana House, and Attorney William Prince, Jan. 16, 1811, *ibid*.

²⁸Harrison to Eustis, April 23, 1811, *Messages & Letters*, 1:509–10; *Western Spy* (Cincinnati), May 4, 1811; Dawson, *Harrison*, 176; Dunn, *Indiana*, 413.

²⁹*Ibid*., 413; *Western Sun* (Vincennes), Feb. 15, 1812; James Rariden to S. S. Tipton, Feb. 18, 1840, Tipton MSS., Indiana State Library. Harrison was notably generous to the families of soldiers who fell at Tippecanoe.

³⁰J. Snelling to Harrison, Jan. 18 and Feb. 17, 1812, *Messages & Letters*, 2:16–17, 24; Woollen, *Biographical and Historical Sketches of Indiana*, 379.

³¹J. Lalime to William Clark, May 26, 1811, *Messages & Letters*, 1:511 and note 2; Harrison to Eustis, June 6, 1811, *ibid*., 512–14, 517 n. 2; Harrison to Clark, June 19, 1811, *ibid*., 1:519–20.

³²Harrison to Eustis, June 6, 1811, *ibid*., 1:512–14.

³³Same to same, April 23, 1811, *ibid*., 1:507–08.

³⁴Same to same, June 19, 1811, *ibid*., 1:518; Harrison to Clark, *ibid*., 1:520.

³⁵Harrison to Tecumseh, June 24, 1811, *ibid*., 1:522–24.

[36]Law, *Colonial History of Vincennes*, 100–05; Harrison to Eustis, July 10, 1811, *Messages & Letters*, I :532–33.
[37]Same to same, July 2, 1811, *ibid.*, I :526–27.
[38]*Western Sun* (Vincennes), July 27, 1811.
[39]Harrison to Eustis, July 10, 1811, *Messages & Letters*, I :433.
[40]Same to same, Aug. 6, 1811, *ibid.*, I :546.
[41]Same to same, Aug. 13, 1811, *ibid.*, I :554.
[42]Same to same, Aug. 6, 1811, *ibid.*, 543–45.

CHAPTER VIII

[1]Harrison to Eustis, Aug. 6, 1811, *Messages & Letters*, I :546.
[2]Resolutions of Vincennes Citizens and Petition to President Madison, *ibid.*, I :538–43.
[3]Eustis to Harrison, July 17 and 20, 1811, *ibid.*, I :536–37.
[4]Harrison to Eustis, Sept. 17, 1811, *ibid.*, I :574.
[5]J. Wesley Wickar, "Shabonee's Account of Tippecanoe," *Indiana Magazine of History*, 17 :354.
[6]Harrison to Eustis, Aug. 7, 1811, *Messages & Letters*, I :550.
[7]Ninian Edwards to Eustis, Aug. 11, 1811, *ibid.*, I :553.
[8]Clark to Eustis, July 3, 1811, *ibid.*, I :529.
[9]Harrison to Eustis, Sept. 3, 1811, *ibid.*, I :564.
[10]Joseph Hamilton Daveiss to Harrison, Aug. 24, 1811, *ibid.*, I :558–59.
[11]"Funk's Narrative, Tippecanoe Campaign," *ibid.*, I :718; Alfred Pirtle, *The Battle of Tippecanoe* (*Filson Club Publications* No. 15) :17–18.
[12]E. Alexander Powell, *Gentlemen Rovers*, 6–16; Lossing, *Pictorial Field-Book of the War of 1812*, 194 n.
[13]Waller Taylor to Harrison, Sept. 15, 1811, *Messages & Letters*, I :560.
[14]Parke to Harrison, Sept. 13, 1811, *ibid.*, I :566.
[15]Harrison to Eustis, Sept. 17, 1811, *ibid.*, I :575.
[16]Journal of Private Adam Walker, *ibid.*, I :697. The dates given in this Journal are not to be trusted.
[17]General Orders, Sept. 20, 1811, *ibid.*, I :585–86; General Orders, Sept. 21, 1811, Harrison MSS., New York Historical Society.
[18]After Orders, Sept. 22, 1811, *Messages & Letters*, 587–88.
[19]Statement of Indiana militia officers, *Western Sun* (Vincennes), June 25, 1812.
[20]Harrison to Eustis, Sept. 25, 1811, *Messages & Letters*, I :590.
[21]Wickar, "Shabonee's Account," *Indiana Magazine of History*, 17 :354.
[22]Journal of Mrs. Lydia Bacon, Oct., 1811, New York Historical Society. Mrs. Bacon is likewise careless as to dates.
[23]*Indiana Magazine of History*, 15 :9.
[24]H. W. Beckwith, *History of Vigo and Parke Counties*, I :262; H. C. Bradsby, *History of Vigo County*, 115.
[25]Wickar, "Shabonee's Account," *Indiana Magazine of History*, 17 :355–56.
[26]Statement of Indiana militia officers, *Western Sun* (Vincennes), June 25, 1812.

[27]Walker's Journal, Harrison's *Messages & Letters*, 1:704.

[28]Statement of Indiana militia officers, *Western Sun*, June 25, 1812. Other stated opinions of Colonel (later General) Boyd appear to correspond. General Morgan Lewis called him: "A compound of ignorance, vanity and petulance, with nothing to recommend him but that species of bravery . . . which is vaporing, boisterous—stifling reflection, blinding observation, and better adapted to the bully than the soldier." Henry Adams, *History of the United States*, 7:162. Winfield Scott found Boyd "courteous, amiable and respectable as a subordinate; but vacillating and imbecile beyond all endurance, as a chief." Winfield Scott, *Memoirs*, 93–94.

[29]John Tipton, "Tippecanoe Journal," *Indiana Magazine of History*, 2:172–73.

[30]*Ibid.*, 174; *Fort Harrison* (pamphlet), 47, John Scott Harrison Collection.

[31]Harrison to Eustis, Oct. 13, 1811, *Messages & Letters*, 1:599; Walker's Journal, *ibid.*, 1:699.

[32]Eustis to Harrison, Sept. 18, 1811, Letter Book C, 112–13, Indian Office. This is the letter which Henry Adams states was "never published but often referred to . . . [and] not found in the records of the Government." Adams, *History of the United States*, 6:95–96. This letter can be easily located by any one at any time.

[33]Harrison to Eustis, Oct. 13, 1811, *Messages & Letters*, 1:599–600.

[34]Lossing, *Pictorial Field-Book of the War of 1812*, 195. Lossing says the fort was christened on Oct. 28 but Ensign John Tipton, who was there, says Oct. 27. Tipton's "Tippecanoe Journal," *Indiana Magazine of History*, 2:178. Tipton is fairly accurate.

[35]Harrison to Eustis, Oct. 29, 1811, *Messages & Letters*, 1:605; Harrison to Governor Charles Scott, Oct. 25, 1811, Philadelphia *Aurora*, Nov. 28, 1811.

[36]Dr. John M. Scott to the *Argus of Western America*, Oct. 23, 1811, Philadelphia *Aurora*, Nov. 15, 1811.

[37]Walker's "Journal," *Messages & Letters*, 1:700.

[38]Harrison to Eustis, Nov. 2, 1811, *ibid.*, 1:606.

[39]S. J. Burr, *Life of General Harrison*, 135–36.

[40]Harrison to Eustis, Nov. 18, 1811, *Messages & Letters*, 1:618–19; Robert B. McAfee, *History of the Late War*, 30–31.

[41]*Ibid.*, 32; Harrison to Governor Scott, Dec. 13, 1811, *Messages & Letters*, 1:670.

[42]Harrison to Eustis, Nov. 18, 1811, *ibid.*, 1:620; "Polke's Tippecanoe Narrative," *ibid.*, 1:716.

[43]Harrison to Governor Scott, Dec. 13, 1811, *ibid.*, 1:670.

[44]"Polke's Tippecanoe Narrative," *ibid.*, 1:716–17; Harrison to Eustis, Nov. 18, 1811, *ibid.*, 1:621; Taylor to *National Intelligencer* (Washington), Feb. 22, 1817, *ibid.*, 1:613–14; Taylor to Moses Dawson, July 15, 1823, *ibid.*, 1:710; Elmore Barce (editor), "Naylor's Narrative," *Indiana Magazine of History*, 2:164.

[45]Harrison to Eustis, Nov. 18, 1811, *Messages & Letters*, 1:621; McAfee, *History of the Late War*, 37–38.

CHAPTER IX

[1]Wickar, "Shabonee's Account," *Indiana Magazine of History*, 17:356–57.

[2]Snelling to Harrison, Nov. 20, 1811, *Messages & Letters*, 1:643–44.

[3]Wickar, "Shabonee's Account," *Indiana Magazine of History*, 17:353, 57.

[4]Statement of William Brigham, Walker's Journal, *Messages & Letters*, 1:703.

[5]Barce (editor), "Naylor's Narrative," *Indiana Magazine of History*, 2:165.

[6]Statements of Captains Barton, Snelling, etc., Jan. 8, 1812, *Messages & Letters*, 2:7–11.

[7]Harrison to Dr. Scott, Dec., 1811, *ibid.*, 1:691–92.

[8]George Pence, "General Joseph Bartholomew," *Indiana Magazine of History*, 14:292; Harrison to Eustis, Nov. 18, 1811, *Messages & Letters*, 1:630; Journal of Mrs. Lydia Bacon, New York Historical Society.

[9]Charles Moore, "Old Corydon," *Indiana Magazine of History*, 3:27.

[10]Woollen, *Biographical & Historical Sketches of Early Indiana*, 189.

[11]Dunn, *Indiana*, 410.

[12]Harrison to Editor of *Kentucky Reporter*, Jan., 1812, Philadelphia *Aurora*, Feb. 25, 1812.

[13]Walker's "Journal," Harrison's *Messages & Letters*, 1:704.

[14]Harrison to Eustis, Nov. 18, 1811, *ibid.*, 624; "Funk's Narrative," *ibid.*, 721–27; "Naylor's Narrative," *Indiana Magazine of History*, 2:166; Parke to Harrison, Aug. 8, 1831, Harrison Papers, 7:1152–53; McAfee, *History of the Late War*, 39–40. Parke points out several errors in the McAfee work.

[15]Harrison to Eustis, Nov. 18, 1811, *Messages & Letters*, 1:628.

[16]John P. Boyd to Richard Cutts, Dec. 16, 1811, Mitten Collection, Indiana Historical Society.

[17]David Turpie, *Sketches of My Own Times*, 66; Harrison to Eustis, Nov. 18, 1811, *Messages & Letters*, 1:625.

[18]Walker's "Journal," *ibid.*, 1:702.

[19]Statement of Indiana militia officers, *Western Sun* (Vincennes), June 25, 1812.

[20]Harrison to Governor Scott, Dec. 13, 1811, *Messages & Letters*, 1:668.

[21]Adjutant James Hunter to (?), Nov. 8, 1811, Philadelphia *Aurora*, Dec. 3, 1811.

[22]Harrison to Eustis, Dec. 4, 1811, *Messages & Letters*, 1:657.

[23]Barce (editor), "Naylor's Narrative," *Indiana Magazine of History*, 2:168.

[24]Snelling to Harrison, Nov. 20, 1811, *Messages & Letters*, 1:644.

[25]"Funk's Narrative," *ibid.*, 1:722.

[26]Harrison to Dr. Scott, Dec. 2, 1811, Pirtle, *The Battle of Tippecanoe*, 99–100.

[27]Walker's "Journal," *Messages & Letters*, 1:705–06; Tipton's Journal, *Indiana Magazine of History*, 2:182–83.

[28]Letter of Louisville man to Stephen Ormsby, Nov. 19, 1811, Philadelphia *Aurora*, Nov. 29, 1811.

[29]Harrison to Governor Scott, Dec. 13, 1811, *Messages & Letters*, 1:660; Harrison to Eustis, Dec. 28, 1811, *ibid.*, 1:687.

[30]Regimental Order, Nov. 20, 1811, *ibid.*, 1:646.

[31]Boyd and Prescott to Eustis, Dec. 11, 1811, *Western Sun* (Vincennes), Feb. 8, 1812; Boyd to Cutts, Dec. 16, 1811, Mitten Collection, Indiana Historical Society; Boyd to Eustis, Nov. 20, 1811, Philadelphia *Aurora*, Jan. 4, 1812.

[32]Vanderburgh to Boyd, Nov. 25, 1811, *Messages & Letters*, 647–48; Indiana Legislature to Boyd, Dec. 4, 1811, *ibid.*, 1:654–55.

[33]Anonymous to Congressman Lewis, Dec. 26, 1811, *Western Sun*, Feb. 8, 1812. Harrison's offer of a reward appears in the issue of Feb. 15, 1812.

[34]Resolutions, Dec. 7, 1811, *Messages & Letters*, 1:678–79.

[35]Samuel G. Hopkins to Harrison, Jan. 15, 1812, Harrison Papers; Lossing, *Pictorial Field-Book of the War of 1812*, 208.

[36]Resolutions, Dec. 27, 1811, *Messages & Letters*, 1:680–82.

[37]Harrison to Governor Scott, Dec. 13, 1811, *ibid.*, 1:669–72.

[38]Statements of officers, Jan. 8, 1812, *Messages & Letters*, 2:5–6.

[39]Account of a "patriotic dinner" at Hagerstown, Md., Philadelphia *Aurora*, March 11, 1812.

[40]*Ibid.*, Aug. 15, 1812. This lengthy editorial gives Colonel Boyd the entire credit for the victory at Tippecanoe while Harrison is blamed for all sorts of military errors. The *National Intelligencer* (Washington) supported Harrison. See editorial of Dec. 3, 1811.

[41]Harrison to Governor Scott, *Messages & Letters*, 1:671.

[42]Wickar, "Shabonee's Account," *Indiana Magazine of History*, 17, 361–6.

[43]*Western Sun*, Dec. 7, 1811; Harrison to R. J. Meigs, Feb. 20, 1812, Thomas F. Madigan *Autograph Catalogue* (1935), 50; Harrison to Eustis, March 4, 1812, Harrison Papers, 1:158. The British were still active in recruiting Indians although denying any participation in the late frontier warfare. See notes unaddressed and without signature reprinted in *Michigan Historical Collections*, 15:80.

[44]Journal of Mrs. Lydia Bacon, New York Historical Society; Walker's "Journal," *Messages & Letters*, 1:707.

[45]*Ibid.*, 1:707–08; Harrison to Meigs, March 11, 1812, Presidential Autographs, 4:13, Pennsylvania Historical Society; George Beck to Harrison, April 13, 1812, *Messages & Letters*, 2:30; Harrison to Eustis, April 14, 15, 22, 26 and May 6, 1812, *ibid.*, 2:33–34, 41–42, 44; James Miller to Stephen Ranney, April 24, 1812, *Freeman's Journal* (Philadelphia), July 3, 1812.

[46]*Ibid.*; General Hopkins to Governor Scott, May 9, 1812, Philadelphia *Aurora*, July 17, 1812.

[47]*Kentucky Gazette*, May 26, 1812.

[48]Harrison to Eustis, Jan. 3, 1812, *Messages & Letters*, 2:59.

[49]Speeches of Indians, May 15, 1812, *ibid.*, 2:50–53; Tecumseh to Elliott, June 8, 1812, *ibid.*, 2:60–61.

[50]Claus to Brock, June 16, 1812, *ibid.*, 2:62.

CHAPTER X

[1]Lossing, *Pictorial Field-Book of the War of 1812*, 255.
[2]John H. De Witt, "General James Winchester," *Tennessee Historical Magazine*, 1 :No. 2, 79–80; McAfee, *History of the Late War*, 148–49.
[3]Elias Darnell, *Journal of the Kentucky Volunteers*, 20.
[4]*Argus of Western America* and *The Palladium* (Frankfort), July 1, 1812.
[5]Henry Clay to Monroe, July 29, 1812, Monroe Papers, 5 :1635, Library of Congress.
[6]Harrison to Governor Scott, July 14, 1812, *Messages & Letters*, 2 :74.
[7]Scott to James Madison, July 30, 1812, Madison Papers, 5 :48, Library of Congress.
[8]Cincinnati *Gazette*, Aug. 3, 1840. The Harrison dinner was held July 9, 1812.
[9]H. Montgomery, *Life of William Henry Harrison*, 109–10.
[10]Harrison to Eustis, July 5, 1809, *Messages & Letters*, 1 :349–56.
[11]Same to same, Aug. 12, 1812, *ibid.*, 2 :84–88.
[12]Clay to Monroe, Aug. 12, 1812, Monroe Papers, 13 :1638, Library of Congress.
[13]Mann Butler, *History of Kentucky*, 344.
[14]John C. Parish (editor), *Robert Lucas Journal*, 92.
[15]Philadelphia *Aurora*, Oct. 8, 1812.
[16]Extract from a letter from Canada, Aug. 4, *ibid.*, Sept. 9, 1812.
[17]Harrison to Eustis, Aug. 28, 1812, *Messages & Letters*, 2 :98; Hopkins to John J. Crittenden, Aug. 24, 1812, Mrs. Chapman Coleman, *Life of John J. Crittenden*, 16. Sentiment for Harrison was revealed also at public meetings in Ohio. *Democratic Press* (Philadelphia), Sept. 14, 1812.
[18]General Orders, Aug. 25, 1812, Philadelphia *Aurora*, Sept. 10, 1812.
[19]Clay to Monroe, Aug. 25, 1812, Monroe Papers, 13 :1641, Library of Congress.
[20]Harrison to John Gibson, Aug. 26, 1812, War Department Records, National Archives.
[21]W. A. Brice, *History of Fort Wayne*, 217–18.
[22]Winchester-Harrison correspondence, Aug. 27–28, 1812, Harrison Papers, 2 :226–33.
[23]"A Diary of the War of 1812," *Mississippi Valley Historical Review*, 1 :274; Philadelphia *Aurora*, Sept. 18, 1812; Winchester to *National Intelligencer*, Sept. 16, 1817.
[24]Harrison to Eustis, Aug. 24, 1812, *Messages & Letters*, 2 :100.
[25]*Ibid.*
[26]Darnell, *Journal*, 10.
[27]Winchester to Harrison, Aug. 31, 1812, *National Intelligencer*, Sept. 1, 1819; Eustis to Harrison, Aug. 22, 1812, *Messages & Letters*, 2 :92.
[28]Harrison to Eustis, Sept. 3, 1812, *ibid.*, 2 :110.
[29]Letters dated Sept. 13 and 26, 1812, Philadelphia *Aurora*, Oct. 14, 1812.
[30]Brice, *History of Fort Wayne*, 219–20.

[31]Letter of a volunteer, Sept. 13, 1812, Philadelphia *Aurora*, Oct. 14, 1812.

[32]McAfee, *History of the Late War*, 147.

[33]Harrison to Isaac Shelby, Sept. 18, 1812, *Messages & Letters*, 2:138.

[34]Same to same, Sept. 22, Lossing, *Pictorial Field-Book of the War of 1812*, 326 n.

[35]Richard M. Johnson to Madison, Sept. 18, 1812, Madison Papers, 49:46.

[36]Waller Taylor to Harrison, Sept. 16, 1818, Dawson, *Harrison*, 443–44; Statement of Joshua Barbee, July 8, 1814, *National Intelligencer*, Sept. 16, 1817.

[37]Madison to Monroe, Sept. 6, 1812, Monroe Papers, 13:1648.

[38]Jonathan Monroe to James Monroe, Sept. 2, 1812, Monroe Papers, New York Public Library.

[39]Jonathan Monroe to Dr. Thomas Monroe, Sept. 6, 1812, *ibid.*

[40]Thomas Todd to Madison, Sept. 2, 1812, Harrison Letters, Chicago Historical Society.

[41]Shelby to Monroe, Sept. 5, 1812, Harrison's *Messages & Letters*, 2:115.

[42]Monroe to Jefferson, June 7, 1813, Stanislaus M. Hamilton (editor), *Writings of James Monroe*, 6:260–61.

[43]Eustis to Harrison, Sept. 17, 1812, *Messages & Letters*, 2:136–37.

[44]Zachary Taylor to Harrison, Sept. 10, 1812, *ibid.*, 2:126.

[45]Harrison to Eustis, Sept. 27, 1812, *ibid.*, 127.

[46]Harrison to the Citizens of Kentucky, Sept. 25, 1812, *Kentucky Reporter* (Lexington), Sept. 26, 1812. Harrison also addressed the ladies of Dayton, Ohio, on the same subject and as a result 1800 shirts were made from Indian Department calico. A. B. Norton, *Reminiscences of the Great Revolution of 1840*, 139.

[47]Harrison to Eustis, Sept. 27, 1812, *Messages & Letters*, 2:156 n.

[48]William Jennings to Harrison, Sept. 26, 1812, *ibid.*, 152–53.

[49]Burr, *Harrison*, 174–75.

[50]McBride, *Pioneer Biography*, 1:255–56.

[51]Winchester's Orderly Book, *Michigan Historical Collections*, 31:261.

[52]McAfee, *History of the Late War*, 164–65; Howe, *Historical Collections of Ohio*, 1:546.

[53]Letter from Camp Defiance, Oct. 11, 1812, Philadelphia *Aurora*, Nov. 12, 1812.

[54]Harrison to Shelby, Oct. 8, 1812, Harrison MSS., New York Public Library.

[55]Deposition of Thomas Bodley, Oct. 24, 1819, Dawson, *Harrison*, 447.

[56]Winchester to Harrison, Oct. 26, 1812, Harrison Papers, 2:339–40.

[57]James Morrison to Monroe, Jan. 19, 1813, Monroe Papers, New York Public Library.

[58]Harrison to William Piatt, Oct. 22, 1812, Harrison Papers, 2:324–25.

[59]Harrison to Eustis, Oct. 22, 1812, *Messages & Letters*, 2:184; letter of John O'Fallon, J. T. Scharf, *History of St. Louis*, 348–49.

[60]Philadelphia *Aurora*, Nov. 25, 1812, quoting Harrison letter of Nov. 1, 1812.

[61]General Orders, Nov. 27, 1812, *ibid.*, Dec. 1, 1812.

[62]Major Hardin to Shelby, Nov. 15 (?), 1812, McAfee, *History of the Late War*, 186–87; Harrison to Eustis, Dec. 12, 1812, *Messages & Letters*, 2:241; Bodley to Harrison, Dec. 11, 1812, *ibid.*, 2:238–39.

[63]Harrison to Meigs, Nov. 21, 1812, Harrison Papers, Draper Collection, 5X:19.

[64]Harrison to Eustis, Nov. 15, 1812, *Messages & Letters*, 2:211; *Freeman's Chronicle* (Franklinton), Nov. 17, 1812.

[65]General Orders, Jan. 2, 1813, *Messages & Letters*, 2:290; Harrison to Monroe, Jan. 3, 1813, *ibid.*, 2:293.

[66]John B. Campbell to Harrison, Dec. 25, 1812, *ibid.*, 2:256–57.

[67]Same to same, Dec. 25, 1812, Harrison Papers, 3:444.

[68]Account of Mississinewa Expedition, *Messages & Letters*, 2:273.

[69]General Orders, Jan. 2, 1813, *ibid.*, 2:290.

[70]Thomas Worthington to Harrison, Nov. 28, 1812, Harrison Papers, 3:279–81. Harrison's commission as brigadier-general was confirmed by the Senate Dec. 2, 1812, as of Aug. 22, 1812. U. S. Senate *Executive Journal*, 2:303–308; Philadelphia *Aurora*, Dec. 11, 1812.

[71]Duncan McArthur to Worthington, Nov. 21, 1812, Worthington Papers, Ohio State Library.

[72]Harrison to Monroe, Dec. 26 (?), 1812, *Western Sun*, Jan. 30, 1813. The date of this letter, written at Delaware, is quoted in some accounts as Dec. 28 but Harrison was at Chillicothe, a two days' ride away, on that date. The General's '6's' were likely to be mistaken for '8's,' his '2's' for '3's.'

CHAPTER XI

[1]Julius W. Pratt, *Expansionists of 1812*, 52–58, 153, 156.

[2]Monroe to Harrison, Dec. 26, 1812, *Messages & Letters*, 2:265–69.

[3]Harrison to Eustis, Dec. 12, 1812, *ibid.*, 2:240–43.

[4]*Ibid.*, 2:242–43.

[5]Harrison to Monroe, Jan. 6, 1813, *ibid.*, 2:302.

[6]Same to same, Jan. 4, 1813, *ibid.*, 2:298.

[7]McAfee, *History of the Late War*, 222.

[8]Monroe to Harrison, Jan. 17, 1813, *Messages & Letters*, 2:313.

[9]Winchester's Orderly Book, *Michigan Historical Collections*, 31:286–97; Darnell, *Journal*, 41.

[10]William Atherton, *Narrative*, 26.

[11]Darnell, *Journal*, 38.

[12]Winchester's Orderly Book, *Michigan Historical Collections*, 31:303; Darnell, *Journal*, 39.

[13]*Ibid.*, 39–40.

[14]*Ibid.*, 40.

[15]*Ibid.*, 43.

[16]*Freeman's Chronicle* (Franklinton), Dec. 5, 1812.

[17]Harrison to Simon Perkins, Dec. 16, 1812, Harrison Papers, 3:416.

[18]McAfee, *History of the Late War*, 219.

[19]Lossing, *Pictorial Field-Book of the War of 1812*, 350; Speech of Leslie Combs, July 4, 1871, H. S. Knapp, *History of the Maumee Valley*, 215.

[20]Harrison to Winchester, Jan. 16, 1813, *Messages & Letters*, 2:311.

[21]McAfee, *History of the Late War*, 222–23, 249; Harrison to Monroe, Jan. 24, 1813, *Messages & Letters*, 2:335–36; Dawson, *Harrison*, 55–56.

[22]Harrison to Winchester, Jan. 16, 1813, *Messages & Letters*, 2:311–12.

[23]Isaac Day to Harrison, Jan. 12, 1813, *ibid.*, 307–08. The 3000 barrels of flour said to be at Frenchtown actually numbered 300. Winchester to Harrison, Jan. 13, 1813, *ibid.*, 314.

[24]Darnell, *Journal*, 46; Perkins to Meigs, Jan. 28, 1813, *Western Reserve Historical Society Tracts*, No. 92:104–05. See also the criticism of Winchester in the "Journal of Colonel Eleazar D. Wood," reprinted in George W. Cullum, *Campaigns of the War of 1812*, 367–68; also, A. B. Woodward to Monroe, Jan. 31, 1813, *Michigan Historical Collections*, 8:647–48.

[25]William Lewis to Winchester, Jan. 20, 1813, *Messages & Letters*, 2:321.

[26]E. Whittlesey to his wife, Jan. 25, 1813, *Western Reserve Historical Society Tracts*, No. 92:100–04; Darnell, *Journal*, 49–51.

[27]Major McClanahan to Harrison, Jan. 26, 1813, *Messages & Letters*, 2:339; Statement of Major George Madison, Kentucky Reporter (Lexington), March 13, 1813.

[28]Winchester to Harrison, Jan. 21, 1813, *Messages & Letters*, 2:325.

[29]Lossing, *Pictorial Field-Book of the War of 1812*, 353 n. 5.

[30]Harrison to John Tupper, Jan. 21, 1813, Harrison Papers, 3:516.

[31]Harrison to Meigs, Jan. 19, 1813, *Messages & Letters*, 2:315; to Shelby, Jan. 19, 1813, Harrison Papers, 5X:22, Draper Collection.

[32]McAfee, *History of the Late War*, 32.

[33]W. W. Cotgreave to Harrison, Jan. 21, 1813, *Western Reserve Historical Society Tracts*, No. 92:99–100; Cotgreave to his father, Jan. 25, 1813, Philadelphia *Aurora*, Feb. 19, 1813.

[34]Harrison to Monroe, Jan. 20, 1813, *Messages & Letters*, 2:317.

[35]John Meek to John S. Gano, Jan. 21, 1813, Gano Papers, Historical & Philosophical Society of Ohio.

[36]Lossing, *Pictorial Field-Book of the War of 1812*, 354; *Ohio Archæological & Historical Society Publications*, 9:272.

[37]Statement of Francis Navarre, Aug. 22, 1818, Harrison Papers, 6:1053–54.

[38]Nathaniel G. S. Hart to Harrison, Jan. 19, 1813, Dawson, *Harrison*, 456.

[39]John Richardson, *Richardson's War of 1812*, 134.

[40]Thomas P. Dudley, "Account of the Battle of the River Raisin," *Western Reserve Historical Society Tracts*, 1:2.

[41]John Richardson to Charles Askin, Feb. 4, 1813, *Richardson's War of 1812*, 303.

[42]Statement of Francis Navarre, Aug. 22, 1818, Harrison Papers, 6:1053–54.

[43]McClanahan to Harrison, Jan. 26, 1813, *Messages & Letters*, 2:340.

[44]Richard M. Gano to John S. Gano, Jan. 25, 1813, Gano Papers.

[45]*Ibid.*

[46]*Richardson's War of 1812*, 135.

[47]Deposition of Joseph Robert, Aug. 22, 1818, Harrison Papers,

6:1055; McAfee, *History of the Late War*, 237; Darnell, *Journal*, 54 n.
[48]*Ibid.*, 54.
[49]*Ibid.*
[50]E. A. Cruikshank, "Harrison and Procter," Royal Society of Canada, *Proceedings and Transactions, Series 3*, 4:165.
[51]McAfee, *History of the Late War*, 248.
[52]*Richardson's War of 1812*, 140.
[53]Cotgreave to (?), Jan. 21, 1813, *Western Reserve Historical Society Tracts*, No. 92:101.
[54]Harrison to the Secretary of War, Jan. 24, 1813, *Messages & Letters*, 2:331.
[55]Richard M. Gano to John S. Gano, Jan. 25, 1813; Gano Papers.
[56]*Ibid.*, 35–36.
[57]Harrison to Meigs, Jan. 24, 1813, *Messages & Letters*, 2:330.
[58]*Richardson's War of 1812*, 7–8.
[59]Report of Nimrod Doyell, May 3, 1813, *American State Papers, Indian Affairs*, 1:843; *Richardson's War of 1812*, 159. "Each warrior had a piece of string hanging over the edge [of a kettle] and to this was suspended a food which . . . consisted of a part of an American."
[60]*Ibid.*, 7.
[61]Quoted in "Reminiscences of B. F. H. Witherell," *Wisconsin Historical Collections*, 3:308.
[62]*Richardson's War of 1812*, 7–8.
[63]Statements of Major George Madison and other surviving officers, *Kentucky Reporter* (Lexington), March 13, 1813.
[64]Affadavit of Medard Labbadi, Feb. 11, 1813, *Messages & Letters*, 2:361.
[65]Darnell, *Journal*, 60–61.
[66]Statement of J. M. Donnell, *Niles' Register* (Baltimore), April 10, 1813.
[67]Testimony of Isaac Baker, *ibid.*, March 27, 1813.
[68]A. G. Tustin to his mother, Jan. 23, 1813, Lossing, *Pictorial Field-Book of the War of 1812*, 355 n.
[69]Harrison to Samuel McKeehan, Jan. 31, 1813, *Messages & Letters*, 2:346; McKeehan's Narrative, *ibid.*, 2:461–63.
[70]"Reminiscences of B. F. H. Witherell," *Wisconsin Historical Collections*, 3:307–08.

CHAPTER XII

[1]Harrison to Monroe, Jan. 24, 1813, *Messages & Letters*, 2:333.
[2]Unsigned and undated statement, Harrison Papers, 5:922–23.
[3]J. Woodbridge to Worthington, Jan. 27, 1813, Worthington Papers, Ohio State Library.
[4]Memoir of Luther Harvey, *Michigan Historical Collections*, 1:408–09.
[5]Letter of a Petersburg (Va.) volunteer, Dawson, *Harrison*, 369.
[6]E. Whittlesey to Polly Whittlesey, Jan. 25, 1813, *Western Reserve Historical Society Tracts*, No. 92:104.
[7]A. L. Langham to Worthington, Jan. 30, 1813, Worthington Papers, Ohio State Library.
[8]Harrison to Shelby, Feb. 11, 1813, Harrison Papers, 5X:24, Draper Collection.

[9]Journal of Colonel Wood, Cullum, *Campaigns of the War of 1812*, 373; George Tod to Meigs, Feb. 11, 1813, Meigs Papers, Ohio State Library.

[10]Harrison to the Secretary of War, Feb. 11, 1813; *Messages & Letters*, 2:357.

[11]Harrison to Shelby, Feb. 11, 1813, Harrison Papers, 5X:24, Draper Collection.

[12]J. Carpenter to J. S. Gano, Feb. 5, 1813, Gano Papers.

[13]Ohio militia officers to Harrison, Feb. 20, 1813, *Messages & Letters*, 2:366–67.

[14]Journal of Ensign William Schillinger, March 2, 1813, MSS. in Cincinnati Public Library.

[15]Journal of Colonel Wood, Cullum, *Campaigns of the War of 1812*, 371.

[16]Harrison to James Morrison, Feb. 28, 1813, *St. Louis Globe-Democrat*, Aug. 13, 1811. Photostat in New York Public Library.

[17]Harrison to John Armstrong, Feb. 24, 1813, *Messages & Letters*, 2:368.

[18]Howe, *Historical Collections of Ohio*, 1:526; Wood's "Journal," Cullum, *Campaigns*, 375; Philadelphia *Aurora*, March 27, 1813.

[19]McAfee, *History of the Late War*, 269–70.

[20]Harrison to Shelby, Feb. 11, 1813; Harrison Papers, 5X:24, Draper Collection.

[21]Same to same, Feb. 18, 1813, Harrison Papers, New York Public Library.

[22]Philadelphia *Aurora*, April 9, 1813; Harrison to editor of the *Western Spy* (Cincinnati), Aug. 24, 1816, *ibid.*, Aug. 30, 1816.

[23]"John Armstrong," *Dictionary of American Biography*, 1:355–58.

[24]Henry Adams, *Albert Gallatin*, 471; Gaillard Hunt, *James Madison*, 329.

[25]Monroe to Madison, July 25, 1813, Hamilton (editor), *Writings of James Monroe*, 5:244–49.

[26]James C. Fitzpatrick (editor), *Autobiography* of Martin Van Buren, 42.

[27]Adams, *History of the United States*, 7:35.

[28]Philadelphia *Aurora*, March 2 and 30, 1813.

[29]Morrison to Harrison, April 25, 1813, Harrison Papers, 4:722.

[30]John Armstrong to Harrison, March 5, 1813, *Messages & Letters*, 2:379–81.

[31]Harrison to Armstrong, March 17, *ibid.*, 2:389.

[32]Armstrong to Meigs, March 28, 1813, Armstrong, *Notices of the War of 1812*, 1:248–50.

[33]Harrison to Armstrong, March 27, 1813, *Messages & Letters*, 2:401.

[34]Harrison to Green Clay, April 1, 1813, Harrison Papers, 4:678.

[35]Army officer to a friend, April 15, 1813, *National Intelligencer*, May 6, 1813.

[36]Harrison to Armstrong, April 21, 1813, *Messages & Letters*, 2:422.

[37]Darnell, *Journal* (Timothy Mallary's Narrative), 86–87.

[38]Journal of Adam Walker, *The Log Cabin* (New York), May 9, 1840.

[39]Harrison to Shelby, April 21, 1813, Harrison Papers, 5X:34, Draper Collection.

[40]Walker's "Journal," *The Log Cabin*, May 9, 1840.
[41]Wood's "Journal," Cullum, *Campaigns*, 389.
[42]McAfee, *History of the Late War*, 280–81.
[43]Wood's "Journal," Cullum, *Campaigns*, 387.
[44]Walker's "Journal," *The Log Cabin*, May 9, 1840.
[45]Narrative of the Rev. A. M. Lorraine, Howe, *Historical Collections of Ohio*, 1 :531.
[46]Lossing, *Pictorial Field-Book of the War of 1812*, 478–79.

CHAPTER XIII

[1]*Richardson's War of 1812*, 138.
[2]Wood's "Journal," Cullum, *Campaigns*, 387–88.
[3]Winter, *History of Northwest Ohio*, 1 :122.
[4]Walker's "Journal," *The Log Cabin*, May 9, 1840.
[5]Wood's "Journal," Cullum, 389.
[6]Lossing, *Pictorial Field-Book of the War of 1812*, 483 n.
[7]William S. Hatch, *A Chapter in the War of 1812*, 115.
[8]Winter, *History of Northwest Ohio*, 1 :123.
[9]*Ibid.*
[10]Walker's "Journal," *The Log Cabin*, May 9, 1840.
[11]*Ibid.*
[12]Winter, *History of Northwest Ohio*, 1 :124.
[13]Wood's "Journal," Cullum, 394.
[14]Narrative of Thomas Christian, *Western Reserve Historical Society Tracts*, No. 23 :4–5.
[15]Green Clay to Harrison, May 9, 1813, *Messages & Letters*, 2 :400–41.
[16]Wood's "Journal," Cullum, 395; J. H. Hawkins to J. J. Crittenden, Aug. 6, 1813, Crittenden Papers, 1 :82–83, Library of Congress.
[17]Winter, *History of Northwest Ohio*, 1 :125.
[18]Harrison to Tipton, Dec. 6, 1833, *Messages & Letters*, 2 :747.
[19]McAfee, *History of the Late War*, 289.
[20]Hawkins to Crittenden, Aug. 6, 1813, Crittenden Papers, 1 :82, Library of Congress.
[21]Narrative of Thomas Christian, *Western Reserve Historical Society Tracts*, No. 23 :5.
[22]*Ibid.*, 6.
[23]Hatch, *A Chapter in the War of 1812*, 115; Letter of Leslie Combs reprinted in *American Historical Record*, 1 :26–27.
[24]McAfee, *History of the Late War*, 289–90; Speech of General Harrison, Dec. 26, 1833, *Celebration of the 45th Anniversary of the Settlement of Cincinnati* (pamphlet, Cincinnati, 1834), 27–28.
[25]Wood's "Journal," Cullum, 399.
[26]John O'Fallon to his mother, May 17, 1813, Scharf, *History of St. Louis*, 349.
[27]Harrison to Armstrong, May 9, 1813, *Messages & Letters*, 2 :446.
[28]Same to same, May 13, 1813, *ibid.*, 2 :443.
[29]Walker's "Journal," *The Log Cabin*, May 9, 1840; McAfee, *History of the Late War*, 296. McAfee lists 81 killed, 189 wounded. Other accounts of the siege of Fort Meigs are to be found in the letter of Samuel Cushing, June 8, 1813, *Mississippi Valley Historical Review*, 19:No. 2,

262–64; also in *Ohio Archæological & Historical Society Publications,* 10:315–30.

CHAPTER XIV

[1]Hawkins to Crittenden, Aug. 6, 1813, Crittenden Papers, 1:82, Library of Congress.

[2]General Orders, May 16, 1813, *Messages & Letters,* 2:449.

[3]Armstrong to Harrison, April 14, 1813, Harrison Papers, 4:697.

[4]Harrison to Armstrong, May 13, 1813, *Messages & Letters,* 2:445.

[5]Johnson to Harrison, May 23, 1813, *ibid.,* 2:460–61; L. W. Meyer, *Richard Mentor Johnson,* 110.

[6]Harrison to Johnson, June 11, 1813, *Messages & Letters,* 2:468–70.

[7]*Register of Debates, 19th Congress, 1st Session,* col. 42.

[8]Winchester's Orderly Book, *Michigan Historical Collections,* 31:281.

[9]Caleb Atwater, *History of Ohio,* 240; Letter of General Edmund P. Gaines, Louisville *Journal,* Oct. 9, 1840.

[10]John McDonald, *Life of General Duncan McArthur,* 175.

[11]Atwater, *History of Ohio,* 240.

[12]General Orders, Nov. 22, 1812, Harrison Papers, 3:368.

[13]*Freeman's Chronicle* (Franklinton), June 16, 1813.

[14]*Ohio Archæological & Historical Society Quarterly,* 34:203.

[15]Harrison to General Vincent, Nov. 3, 1813, *Messages & Letters,* 2:592.

[16]Harrison to Editor of *The Hesperian* (Cincinnati, July, 1838); 1:359–60.

[17]Daniel J. Ryan, Ohio in Four Wars, 41; *Ohio Archæological & Historical Society Quarterly,* 37:186.

[18]Harrison to Meigs, June 23, 1813; *Messages & Letters,* 2:476; to Armstrong, June 24, 1813; *ibid.,* 2:478.

[19]"Journal of Robert G. McAfee," *Kentucky State Historical Society Register,* 26:15.

[20]Harrison to Armstrong, July 6 and 9, 1813, *Messages & Letters,* 2:484–85; Charles J. Dutton, *Oliver Hazard Perry,* 92–95.

[21]Oliver Hazard Perry to Harrison, July 19, 1813, Ernest A. Cruikshank, *Documentary History of the Niagara Frontier,* part 8:14.

[22]Perry to Chauncey, July 23, 1813, Lossing, *Pictorial Field-Book of the War of 1812,* 513.

[23]Alfred Brunson, *A Western Pioneer,* 1:119–20. Brunson quotes Little Crow, head chief of the Sioux. McAfee, *History of the Late War,* 322–23.

[24]Procter to Sir George Prevost, July 13, 1813, *Michigan Historical Collections,* 15:339–40.

[25]O'Fallon to his mother, July 25, 1813, Scharf, *History of St. Louis,* 349.

[26]*Richardson's War of 1812,* 177.

[27]Hawkins to Crittenden, Aug. 6, 1813, Crittenden Papers, 1:82, Library of Congress.

[28]Green Clay to Harrison, Aug. 3, 1813, Harrison Papers, 5X:41, Draper Collection.

[29]*Richardson's War of 1812,* 118.

[30]Lossing, *Pictorial Field-Book of the War of 1812*, 498–99; Harrison to Armstrong, July 28, 1813, *Messages & Letters*, 2:501.

[31]McAfee, *History of the Late War*, 347.

[32]Brunson, *A Western Pioneer*, 1:114–15.

[33]McAfee, *History of the Late War*, 348.

[34]Brunson, *A Western Pioneer*, 1:116.

[35]Croghan to Editor of *Liberty Hall*, Aug. 27, 1813, *Messages & Letters*, 2:529.

[36]Joseph Duncan to C. F. Mercer, March 25, 1836, *Illinois State Historical Library Publications*, No. 26:111.

[37]Lossing, *Pictorial Field-Book of the War of 1812*, 501.

[38]Croghan to Harrison, Aug. 5, 1813, *Messages & Letters*, 2:515.

[39]Statement of Joseph Anthony and David G. Cowan, Aug. 27, 1814, Jackson Papers, Library of Congress.

[40]Procter to Prevost, Aug. 9, 1813, *Richardson's War of 1812*, 187.

[41]Harrison to Croghan, July 21, 1818, Croghan MSS., New York Public Library.

[42]Harrison to Meigs, Winter, *History of Northwest Ohio*, 1:139.

[43]W. L. G. Smith, *Life and Times of Lewis Cass*, 69.

[44]Joseph Wheaton to Monroe, Aug. 13, 1813, Monroe Papers, New York Public Library; Lossing, *Pictorial Field-Book of the War of 1812*, 505 and notes 3, 5.

[45]Armstrong to Harrison, July 14, 1813, Harrison Papers, 5:792.

[46]Harrison to Shelby, July 20, 1813, *Messages & Letters*, 2:493.

[47]Harrison to Meigs, Aug. 27, 1813, Harrison Papers, 5:817; Cass to Duncan McArthur, Sept. 10, 1813, McArthur Papers, 3:571, Library of Congress.

[48]McArthur to Harrison, Aug. 13, 1813, Harrison Papers, 5X:44. Draper Collection; Letters of Samuel Williams, Aug. 25 and 29, 1813, *Ohio Valley Historical Series*, No. 7:51–52.

[49]Joseph Kerr to Worthington, Jan. 29, 1814, Worthington Papers, Ohio State Library.

[50]Lossing, *Pictorial Field-Book of the War of 1812*, 514.

[51]Perry to Harrison, Aug. 5, 1813, Alexander Slidell MacKenzie, *Life of Commodore Oliver Hazard Perry*, 1:179–80.

[52]Harrison to Armstrong, Aug. 22, 1813, *Messages & Letters*, 2:526; Dutton, *Oliver Hazard Perry*, 119.

[53]*Ibid.*, 124; MacKenzie, *Oliver Hazard Perry*, 1:203.

[54]*Ibid.*, 1:206–07.

[55]Josiah Meigs to Jefferson, Nov. 5, 1813, Jefferson Papers, Library of Congress.

[56]Shelby to Harrison, Sept. 1, 1813, *Messages & Letters*, 2:532.

[57]Harrison to Meigs, Sept. 4, 1813, *ibid.*, 2:533–35. Upon receipt of this letter Governor Meigs issued a stern proclamation warning against any wrong-doing or violence upon the peaceful Indians. See *Niles' Register* (Baltimore) Oct. 12, 1813.

[58]Howe, *Historical Collections of Ohio*, 3:248, 459.

[59]Harrison to Armstrong, Sept. 8, 1813, *Messages & Letters*, 2:538–39; to Speaker of the House, Dec. 20, 1815, *ibid.*, 705–08.

[60]Brunson, *A Western Pioneer*, 1:120.

[61]Harrison to Shelby, Sept. 12, 1813, *Messages & Letters*, 2:539.

[62]Perry to Harrison, Sept. 10, 1813, Lossing, *Pictorial Field-Book of the War of 1812*, 530, 531 n. Lossing presents a facsimile of Perry's famous message.

CHAPTER XV

[1]Edward Baynes to Procter, Sept. 18, 1813, *Messages & Letters*, 2:582–84.
[2]Procter to General De Rottenburg, Sept. 12, 1813, *Michigan Historical Collections*, 15:377–78.
[3]Speech of Tecumseh, Sept. 18, 1813, *Messages & Letters*, 2:542.
[4]*Richardson's War of 1812*, 205–06.
[5]Speech of Tecumseh, Sept. 18, 1813, *Messages & Letters*, 2:543.
[6]*Richardson's War of 1812*, 207.
[7]Matthew Elliott to Claus, Oct. 24, 1813, *Niagara Historical Society Publications*, No. 9:40–43.
[8]Letter of a British officer, Sept. 26, 1813, New York *Commercial Advertiser*, Nov. 18, 1813.
[9]Brunson, *A Western Pioneer*, 1:120; *Western Monthly Magazine* (1836), 5:520.
[10]McAfee, *History of the Late War*, 393.
[11]*Ibid.*, 414–15.
[12]Samuel R. Brown, *History of the Second War*, 1:116; Brunson, *A Western Pioneer*, 1:129.
[13]*Ibid.*, 1:130.
[14]Wood's "Journal," Cullum, 409.
[15]McAfee's "Journal," *Kentucky State Historical Society Register*, 26:119–20.
[16]Brown, *History of the Second War*, 1:118.
[17]General Orders, Sept. 27, 1813, *Messages & Letters*, 1:546–50; Lossing, *Pictorial Field-Book of the War of 1812*, 546.
[18]Wood's "Journal," Cullum, 410.
[19]Dutton, *Oliver Hazard Perry*, 196. The eagle in question may have been seen instead at the mouth of the Thames River. McAfee, *History of the Late War*, 414.
[20]Brunson, *A Western Pioneer*, 1:134.
[21]Harrison speech, Feb. 3, 1819, *Annals, 15th Congress, 2nd Session*, col. 1029.
[22]McAfee, *History of the Late War*, 405–06.
[23]Brown, *History of the Second War*, 1:120.
[24]Proclamation, Sept. 29, 1813, *Messages & Letters*, 2:554.
[25]Silas Farmer, *History of Detroit*, 283; E. M. Sheldon, *Early History of Michigan*, 407–08.
[26]Harrison to Armstrong, Sept. 30, 1813, *Messages & Letters*, 2:555.
[27]McAfee's "Journal," *Kentucky State Historical Society Register*, 26:121.
[28]Harrison to Armstrong, Sept. 30, 1812, *Messages & Letters*, 2:555.
[29]This point later gave rise to one of the many political arguments which arose from the Thames campaign. Sound facts are presented in the letters of Shelby to Harrison, April 21, 1816, and Perry to Harrison, Aug. 18, 1817, *Messages & Letters*, 2:567–70.

[30]*Ibid.* Also Joseph Desha to Harrison, June 28, 1816, Washington *Globe,* April 10, 1840; James Simrall to Harrison, *Kentucky Reporter* (Lexington), April 14, 1816.

[31]Statement of Thomas Bodley, July 17, 1816, *National Intelligencer* (Washington), Aug. 12, 1816.

[32]James C. Mills, *Oliver Hazard Perry,* 181.

[33]McAfee's "Journal," *Kentucky State Historical Society Register,* 26:123.

[34]*Ibid.,* McAfee, *History of the Late War,* 413–14.

[35]Brunson, *A Western Pioneer,* 1:136–37.

[36]Thomas Boyd, *Simon Girty,* 242–43.

[37]Elliott to Claus, Oct. 24, 1813, *Niagara Historical Society Publications,* No. 9, 40–43; *Richardson's War of 1812,* 224–25. General Procter was reported at Moraviantown, or Fairfield, on Sept. 29 and again on Oct. 3. Moravian Historical Society, *Transactions,* 5:33–34.

[38]Brown, *History of the Second War,* 1:124–25; McAfee's "Journal," *Kentucky State Historical Register,* 26:123; McAfee, *History of the Late War,* 416–17.

[39]Elliott to Claus, Oct. 24, 1813, *Niagara Historical Society Publications,* No. 9, 42.

[40]McAfee's "Journal," *Kentucky State Historical Society Register,* 26:124.

[41]*Ibid.,* 125.

[42]Brown, *History of the Second War,* 1:166.

[43]Bennett H. Young, *The Battle of the Thames,* 73–86, *passim.*

[44]Speech of Colonel Johnson, May 19, 1843, *Illinois State Historical Society Journal,* 13:202–05.

[45]Harrison to Armstrong, Oct. 9, 1813, *Messages & Letters,* 2:560.

[46]*Richardson's War of 1812,* 222–23, 226.

[47]*Ibid.,* 228.

[48]Agnes M. Machar, "Historical Sketch of the War of 1812," *Canadian Monthly* (July, 1874), 15.

[49]*Richardson's War of 1812,* 212.

[50]McAfee's "Journal," *Kentucky State Historical Society Register,* 26:126.

[51]Harrison to Armstrong, Oct. 9, 1813, *Messages & Letters,* 2:561. Harrison states here that his aggregate force amounted to "something above three thousand," but a few days later he wrote Armstrong: "Govr Shelby . . . has convinced me that I have greatly overrated our force . . . and that it fell short of two thousand five hundred of every description." *Messages & Letters,* 2:576.

[52]McAfee, *History of the Late War,* 420; O'Fallon to Moses B. Corwin, Feb. 26, 1840, Scharf, *History of St. Louis,* 347–48; Harrison to Corwin, July 2, 1840, Rufus King, *Ohio,* 412–14; Henry H. Fuller to Boston *Atlas,* Aug. 22, 1840; *The Log Cabin* (New York), Sept. 19, 1840.

[53]Harrison to Armstrong, Oct. 9, 1813, *Messages & Letters,* 2:562.

[54]Samuel Theobald to B. J. Lossing, Jan. 16, 1861, Mitten Collection, Indiana Historical Society. Although of a rather late date, this letter presents an accurate view of an eye-witness and a member of the "Forlorn Hope."

⁵⁵Johnson to Armstrong, Dec. 22, 1834, Armstrong's *Notices of the War of 1812*, 1 :222–24; Same to same, Nov. 21, 1813, War Department Records, National Archives; Harrison to Armstrong, Oct. 9, 1813, *Messages & Letters,* 2 :562–63.

⁵⁶McAfee's "Journal," *Kentucky State Historical Society Register,* 26 :127.

⁵⁷*Ibid.;* Brown, *History of the Second War,* 1 :127–28.

⁵⁸Meyer, *Richard Mentor Johnson,* 128–30; Lossing, *Pictorial Field-Book of the War of 1812,* 554–56.

⁵⁹Letter of John Speed Smith, Cincinnati Daily *Gazette,* July 10, 1840. See also the eyewitness testimony of John Chambers and C. S. Todd in *Harrison Pamphlets* 1 :No. 1, appendix, Historical & Philosophical Society of Ohio Library.

⁶⁰McAfee's "Journal," *Kentucky State Historical Society Register,* 26 :128.

⁶¹Lossing, *Pictorial Field-Book of the War of 1812,* 555 n. 2.

⁶²*Ibid.,* note 1.

⁶³Harrison to Armstrong, Oct. 9, 1813, *Messages & Letters,* 2 :565; McAfee, *History of the Late War,* 425; *Richardson's War of 1812,* 218. Harrison reported a total of 601 enemy prisoners with 12 killed and 22 wounded; Richardson says that the British army comprised a total of 634 men. These figures compare rather closely. A few dragoons, however, escaped with General Procter.

⁶⁴*Ibid.,* 213.

⁶⁵Harrison to Tipton, May 4, 1834, *Messages & Letters,* 2 :750–51.

⁶⁶Theobald to Lossing, Jan. 16, 1861, Mitten Collection, Indiana Historical Society.

⁶⁷Statement of Chief Black Hawk, *Scioto Gazette* (Chillicothe), Nov. 29, 1836. The death of Tecumseh was the most discussed incident of the war. A list of "eye-witness" and other accounts in the possession of this writer would fill nearly a page.

⁶⁸Brunson, *A Western Pioneer,* 1 :140.

CHAPTER XVI

¹Jacobson, Moravian Historical Society, *Transactions,* 5 :35–36; Brown, *History of the Second War,* 1 :136.

²*Ibid.,* 433.

³Harrison to Armstrong, Oct. 10, 1813, *Messages & Letters,* 2 :574.

⁴Armistice terms, Oct. 14, 1813, *ibid.,* 577–78.

⁵Proclamation, Oct. 16, 1813, *ibid.,* 579.

⁶Adams, *History of the United States,* 7 :197–200; John Bach McMaster, *History of the United States,* 4 :50–53.

⁷Armstrong to Harrison, Sept. 22, 1813, *Messages & Letters,* 2 :544–45.

⁸Same to same, Oct. 30, 1813, Harrison Papers, 5 :899.

⁹*Erie Gazette* (Extra), Oct. 23, 1813.

¹⁰*Ibid.,* Dutton, *Oliver Hazard Perry,* 213.

¹¹Todd and Drake, *William Henry Harrison,* 108.

¹²Bacon to Daniel D. Tompkins, Oct. 31, 1813, Cruikshank, *Documentary History of the Niagara Campaign,* part 8 :110–11.

[13]George McClure to Tompkins, Nov. 1, 1813, *ibid.*, 114–15; Harrison to Tompkins, *ibid.*, 116–17; P. B. Porter to Harrison, Nov. 3, 1813, Harrison Papers, 5:902; letter dated Nov. 14, 1813, *New York Evening Post*, Nov. 29, 1813.

[14]Armstrong to Harrison, Nov. 3, 1813, *Messages & Letters*, 2:594–96.

[15]Armstrong to Madison, Nov. 14, 1813, Madison Papers, 53:87.

[16]McClure to Harrison, Nov. 15, 1813, *Messages & Letters*, 2:604.

[17]Harrison to McClure, Nov. 15, 1813, *ibid.*, 2:605.

[18]McClure, *Causes of the Destruction . . . on the Niagara Frontier*, 14.

[19]Franklin B. Hough, *History of Jefferson County* (New York), 506–07; Commodore Chauncey to Secretary of the Navy, Nov. 21, 1814, Cruickshank, *Documentary History of the Niagara Campaign*, part 8:224.

[20]John S. Gano to Harrison, Sept. 20 and Oct. 6, 1813, Gano Papers.

[21]Harrison to Gideon Granger, Nov. 2, 1813, Harrison papers, 5:901.

[22]Alvin F. Harlow, *Old Post Bags*, 298.

[23]*Memoirs of General Joseph Gardner Swift*, 121–22.

[24]*Ibid.*, 123; *Albany Argus*, Nov. 30, 1813; *National Advocate* (New York), Nov. 29, 1813.

[25]R. S. Guernsey, *New York City During the War of 1812*, 1:29.

[26]James Ross to James McHenry, Sept. 20, 1813, Sterner, *James McHenry*, 609.

[27]Guernsey, *New York City During the War of 1812*, 1:359–61.

[28]*Ibid.*, 1:363–64; *Memoirs of General Swift*, 123.

[29]*National Advocate* (New York), Dec. 3, 1813.

[30]Dawson, *Harrison*, 434.

[31]*Niles' Register* (Baltimore), Dec. 18, 1813.

[32]Joseph Desha to Harrison, Dec. 11, 1813, Harrison Papers, 5X:49, Draper Collection.

[33]*National Advocate* (New York), Dec. 21, 1813.

[34]*Kentucky Reporter* (Lexington), Jan. 15, 1814 (from Richmond *Compiler*).

[35]Letter to *Freeman's Journal* (Philadelphia), Dec. 16, 1813. See also O'Fallon letter, Dec. 17, 1813, Scharf, *History of St. Louis*, 347.

[36]David Buell to his father, Nov. 25, 1813, reprinted in Augustus C. Buell, *Andrew Jackson*, 1:379–82.

[37]Harrison to Armstrong, Dec. 21, 1813, *Messages & Letters*, 2:610–11.

[38]Dawson, *Harrison*, 435.

[39]Jacob Burnet, *Notes on Northwest Territory*, 55.

[40]Winfield, "John Cleves Symmes," New Jersey Historical Society, *Proceedings, Second Series*, 5:39; Speech of Timothy Walker, Cincinnati *Daily Gazette*, April 7, 1838; Howe, *Historical Collections of Ohio*, 2:137–38.

CHAPTER XVII

[1]Communication from "A Military Man," Philadelphia *Aurora*, Jan. 4, 1814. See also editorials in *ibid.*, Jan. 11 and 13, 1814.

[2]Monroe to Madison, Dec. 27, 1813, Hamilton (editor), *Writings of James Monroe*, 5:275–77.

[3]Charles R. King (editor), *Life of Rufus King*, 5:370–71.

[4]J. W. Taylor to Tompkins, Jan. 14, 1814, Washington *Globe*, Aug. 29, 1840; Memorandum, Jan. 12, 1814, Taylor Papers, New York Historical Society.

[5]Shelby to Harrison, April 21, 1816, *Messages & Letters*, 2:567-69.

[6]Adams, *History of the United States*, 7:407-08.

[7]Gano to Harrison, Jan. 27, 1814, *Messages & Letters*, 2:620.

[8]Armstrong to Harrison, Dec. 29, 1813, and Jan. 8, 1814, *ibid.*, 2:614, 617. On Dec. 31, Armstrong ordered Howard to report at Cincinnati. See Military Books, 7:89, National Archives.

[9]*Kentucky Reporter* (Lexington), Jan. 15 and Feb. 5, 1814.

[10]McArthur to Harrison (undated letter), Dawson, *Harrison*, 464.

[11]Harrison to Armstrong, Feb. 13, 1814, War Department Records, National Archives.

[12]Armstrong to Harrison, Feb. 5 and March 2, 1814, *Messages & Letters*, 2:628-31.

[13]John Miller to Worthington, Feb. 24, 1814, Worthington Papers, Ohio State Library.

[14]John B. Walbach to Harrison, Feb. 16, 1814, McArthur Papers, 5:858.

[15]A. H. Holmes to Robert Butler, March 10, 1814, *Messages & Letters*, 2:632-36.

[16]Citizens of Fleming County to James Clark, March, 1814, Mitten Collection.

[17]Harrison to Shelby, March 20, 1814, Harrison Papers, Indiana Historical Society.

[18]Worthington to McArthur, Feb. 7, 1814, McArthur Papers, 5:810.

[19]Statement of B. G. Orr, March 10, 1814, *American State Papers, Military Affairs*, 1:648-49.

[20]Statement of John H. Piatt, Nov. 6, 1813, *Niles' Register*, Nov. 13, 1813.

[21]Harrison to *National Intelligencer*, April 2, 1814, *ibid.*, May 10, 1814.

[22]13th Congress, 2nd Session, *House Report No. 205*, April 8, 1814.

[23]Armstrong to Harrison, April 22 and 29, 1814, *Messages & Letters*, 2:644-46.

[24]Same to same, April 25, 1814, *ibid.*, 645. Armstrong sent a copy of the order (not found) to Harrison.

[25]Croghan to Harrison, May 27, 1814, McArthur Papers, 9:1594-96.

[26]Todd to Shelby, May 9, 1814, Mitten Collection.

[27]Harrison to Armstrong, May 11, 1814, *ibid.*

[28]Harrison to Madison, May 11, 1814, *Messages & Letters*, 2:647-48.

[29]Shelby to Madison, May 15, 1814, *ibid.*, 2:649-51.

[30]Adams, *History of the United States*, 7:410; *Writings of James Madison* (J. B. Lippincott edition), 3:373-81. The material herein is spiced by Monroe's comment.

[31]Armstrong memorandum, *ibid.*, 3:405-06.

[32]Armstrong to Harrison, March 3, 1814, *Messages & Letters*, 2:631.

[33]Harrison to Armstrong, March 20, 1814, War Department Records, National Archives.

[34]Same to same, March 22, 1814, *Messages & Letters*, 2:636-41.

[35]Armstrong to Harrison, June 11, 1814, *American State Papers, Indian Affairs*, 1:827.

[36]Johnston to Harrison, June 26, 1814, War Department Records, National Archives.
[37]*American State Papers, Indian Affairs*, 1:829.
[38]Howe, *Historical Collections of Ohio*, 2:138.
[39]*American State Papers, Indian Affairs*, 1:829.
[40]*Ibid.*, 1:830.
[41]*Ibid.*, 1:835. W. L. G. Smith, *Life of Lewis Cass*, 100–01, presents a fanciful and inaccurate view of the council.
[42]Kappler, *Indian Laws & Treaties*, 2:105–07.
[43]Lossing, *Pictorial Field-Book of the War of 1812*, 937 n. 3.

CHAPTER XVIII

[1]Deposition of James Findlay and Jacob Burnet, Jan. 20, 1816, *American State Papers, Military Affairs*, 1:658.
[2]Howe, *Historical Collections of Ohio*, 2:138; Fannie G. Hendryx, "Biographical Sketch," *Messages & Letters*, 1:8.
[3]Gorham A. Worth, *Recollections of Cincinnati*, 22–23.
[4]Hendryx, "Biographical Sketch," *Messages & Letters*, 1:8–9.
[5]Timothy Flint, *Recollections of the Past Ten Years*, 50.
[6]Deposition of Findlay and Burnet, Jan. 20, 1816, *American State Papers, Military Affairs*, 1:658.
[7]Frank P. Goodwin, "Building a Commercial System," *Ohio Archæological & Historical Society Quarterly*, 16:329–330, 337.
[8]McAfee, *History of the Late War*, 479–89.
[9]Woodbridge to Worthington, April 29, 1815, Harrison Papers, Draper Collection, 5X:60; B. Parke to Thomas Posey, May 25, 1815, *Messages & Letters*, 2:691–92.
[10]Harrison to Alexander J. Dallas, June 26, 1815, Mitten Collection.
[11]Dallas to Harrison, McArthur and John Graham, *American State Papers, Indian Affairs*, 2:13.
[12]William James to Harrison, Aug. 29, 1815, *ibid.*, 2:15–16.
[13]Journal of the Proceedings at Spring Wells, *ibid.*, 2:17–24.
[14]Harrison to Congressman Fisk (New York), Sept. 17, 1814, Harrison Papers, 5X:52, Draper Collection.
[15]Fisk to Harrison, Oct. 3, 1814, *ibid.*, 53.
[16]Harrison to Hawkins, Sept. 17, 1814, *ibid.*, 50.
[17]Depositions of James Reed, Eli Bond and Elisha Norton, July 29 and Oct. 16, 1815, *American State Papers, Military Affairs*, 1:654. A number of unpublished depositions and statements concerning Northwestern Army transport and supply are to be found in the Mitten Collection.
[18]One of these drafts is dated Nov. 2, 1815. Harrison Papers, 5X:62, Draper Collection.
[19]John McLean to Harrison, Jan. 7, 1816, *ibid.*, 64. Harrison's letter to the Speaker of the House is reprinted in *Messages & Letters*, 2:700–710. See also *Annals, 14th Congress, 1st Session*, cols. 1196–99, 1456.
[20]The *Kentucky Gazette* (Lexington), Feb. 12, 1816, describes one of the dinners held in honor of the General. Another took place in Vincennes. See *Western Sun*, March 2, 1816.
[21]*Kentucky Gazette*, May 13, 1816.

[22]*Annals, 14th Congress, 1st Session,* col. 1273; War Department to Harrison, Oct. 30, 1815, Indian Office Letter Book C, 270-71, National Archives; Harrison to same, Dec. 23, 1815, Harrison Papers, 5X:63, Draper Collection. Jennings's formal motion to investigate Harrison's accounts was not placed on record however until early in 1816.

[23]Todd and Drake, *Harrison,* 27.

[24]*Annals, 14th Congress, 1st Session,* col. 253, 316, 334; Harrison to McLean, March 22, 1816, Harrison Papers, 5X:65, Draper Collection; Todd to Harrison, *ibid.,* 69.

[25]Shelby to Harrison, May 16, 1816, Harrison Letters, Chicago Historical Society.

[26]Todd to Harrison, April 23, 1816, Harrison Papers, 5X:68, Draper Collection.

[27]*Liberty Hall* (Cincinnati), June 17, 1816.

[28]Harrison to Desha, June 22, 1816, Washington *Globe,* April 10, 1840.

[29]Desha to Harrison, June 28, 1816, *ibid. The Globe,* a newspaper opposed to Harrison in 1840, reprints a number of testimonials representing Desha's point of view.

[30]Shelby to Harrison, April 21, 1816, *Messages & Letters,* 2:568-69. Perry substantiated Shelby's testimony in a letter to Harrison, Aug. 18, 1817. *Ibid.,* 2:569-70.

[31]Harrison to officers, etc., July 10, 1816, Cincinnati *Gazette,* Aug. 12, 1816. Original draft in Harrison Papers, 5X:74, Draper Collection.

[32]Jones to Harrison, Aug. 12, 1816, *ibid.,* 75.

[33]Address to electors, Aug. 24, 1816, *Western Spy* (Cincinnati), Aug. 30, 1816.

[34]Glyndon G. Van Deusen, *Henry Clay,* 116; Adams, *History of the United States,* 9:120-22.

[35]*Western Spy,* Aug. 30, 1816.

[36]James Heaton to E. A. Brown, Sept. 4, 1816, Brown Papers, Ohio State Library.

[37]*Liberty Hall* (Cincinnati), Oct. 21, 1816.

[38]*Washington, City and Capital,* American Guide Series, 211.

[39]*Congressional Directory,* 1816, 23.

[40]*Annals, 14th Congress, 2nd Session,* col. 245-46, 293, 368, 372, 444, 761, 942.

[41]*Ibid,* col. 270, 275; Burr, *Harrison,,* 243-44.

[42]*Annals, 14th Congress, 2nd Session,* col. 567-74.

[43]*Ibid.,* col. 692-93; Harrison to Findlay, Jan. 24, 1817, Torrence Papers.

[44]*Annals, 14th Congress, 2nd Session,* 874, 922, 934; William O. Lynch, *Fifty Years of Party Warfare,* 256.

[45]*American State Papers, Military Affairs,* 1:644-61; *Annals, 14th Congress, 2nd Session,* col. 394.

[46]*Ibid.,* col. 709-11.

[47]Harrison to Findlay, Jan. 24, 1817, Torrence Papers; to Thomas Willing, Jan. 13, 1817, Simon Gratz Collection, Pennsylvania Historical Society; to William Jones, Jan. 23, 1817, Mitten Collection.

[48]Shelby to Monroe, Feb. 16, 1817, Monroe Papers, New York Public Library; Todd to Monroe, Feb. 9, 1817, Monroe Papers, 16:4757; Library of Congress.

[49]Lynch, *Fifty Years of Party Warfare*, 253–54; Hamilton (editor), *Writings of James Monroe*, 6:1–2, 4–5, 33.

[50]*Annals, 14th Congress, 2nd Session*, col. 1024, 1041.

[51]Margaret Bayard Smith, *First Forty Years of Washington Society*, 137.

[52]*Ibid.*, 139.

CHAPTER XIX

[1]Richmond *Enquirer*, March 29, 1817.

[2]Worth, *Recollections of Cincinnati*, 19–22.

[3]*Ibid.*, 26–27; Farnsworth's *Directory of Cincinnati, 1819*, 47.

[4]W. H. Venable, *Centennial History of Christ Church, Cincinnati*, 11–12.

[5]Winchester letters, *National Intelligencer*, Sept. 12, 16, 20, 23, Dec. 13 and 17, 1817; Dawson to Croghan, Sept. 14, 1840, Croghan MSS., New York Public Library.

[6]Harrison to *Kentucky Reporter*, Nov. 4, 1817, reprinted in *Liberty Hall*, Nov. 24, 1817; *National Intelligencer*, July 17, Sept. 1, and Dec. 21, 1819.

[7]James C. Mills, *Perry*, 235–45.

[8]Marquis James, *Andrew Jackson*, 279–80.

[9]*Annals, 15th Congress, 1st Session*, col. 450–51.

[10]*Ibid.*, col. 575, 583–84.

[11]*Ibid.*, 794–97; Montgomery, *Harrison*, 270.

[12]Harrison to Judge Peters, Jan. 23, 1818, Peters MSS., Pennsylvania Historical Society.

[13]Smith, *St. Clair Papers*, 1:251–52; *Annals, 15th Congress, 1st Session*, col. 851–53.

[14]Harrison to George P. Torrence, Jan. 17, 1818, Torrence Papers.

[15]Harrison letter in *Liberty Hall*, March 25, 1818.

[16]*Annals, 15th Congress, 1st Session*, col. 894.

[17]*Ibid.*, col. 283–85, 298, 1648.

[18]*Ibid.*, col. 1770.

[19]*Ibid.*, col. 1781.

[20]Croghan to Harrison, July 1, 1818, Croghan MSS., New York Public Library.

[21]Harrison to Croghan, July 21, 1818, *ibid.*

[22]Croghan to Harrison, May 24, Aug. 5, and Sept. 25, 1825; Harrison to Croghan, Aug. 13 and Oct. 24, 1825, *ibid.*

[23]Harrison to Todd, Aug. 10, 1819, *A. J. Scheuer Autograph Catalogue, 1929*, No. 5; Frank P. Goodwin, "Manufactures in the Miami Country," *American Historical Review*, 12:773.

[24]Ernest L. Bogart, "Taxation of the Second Bank of the United States by Ohio," *American Historical Review*, 17:312–18.

[25]Harrison to (?), Dec. 16, 1818, *Historical & Philosophical Society of Ohio Quarterly*, 3:No. 3, 73 n. See also *Annals, 15th Congress, 2nd Session*, col. 376–87, 393–97.

[26]*Ibid.*, col. 377–78.

[27]*Ibid.*, col. 310–11.

[28]*Ibid.*, col. 1272, 1280–82.

[29]James, *Andrew Jackson*, 286.

[30]Harrison to John Cleves Short, Aug. 3, 1829, transcript in Mitten Collection.

[31]*Annals, 15th Congress, 2nd Session,* col. 1025.

[32]*Ibid.,* col. 1135–37; Harrison to Findlay, Feb. 8, 1819, Torrence Papers.

[33]Harrison to W. H. Harrison Jr., Jan. 15 and May 4, 1820, John Scott Harrison collection.

[34]Same to same, July 8, 1819, *ibid.*

[35]Harrison to Editor of *National Republican* (Cincinnati), June 27, 1833, *ibid.,* July 1, 1833.

[36]Theodore Greve, *Centennial History of Cincinnati,* 1 :512.

[37]Harrison to Todd, Aug. 10, 1819, *A. J. Scheuer Autograph Catalogue, 1929,* No. 5

[38]Harrison to Electors of Hamilton County, Oct. 6, 1819, Cincinnati *Gazette,* Oct. 8, 1819.

[39]Worth, *Recollections of Cincinnati,* 34.

[40]*Scioto Gazette* (Chillicothe), Oct. 22, 1819.

[41]C. C. Huntington, "History of Banking and Currency Before the Civil War," *Ohio Archæological & Historical Society Quarterly,* 24 :No. 3, 316, 319.

[42]*Ohio Senate Journal, 1819–20:*113–14; *Scioto Gazette,* Jan. 27, 1820.

[43]*Ohio Senate Journal, 1820–21:*43–44, 86–118, 173–75, 306–07, 332; Bogart, "Taxation of the Second Bank of the United States by Ohio," *American Historical Review,* 17 :329–30.

[44]*Ohio Senate Journal, 1820–21:*137.

[45]*Scioto Gazette,* Jan. 25, 1821. On the fourth and last ballot, Ruggles had 52 votes, Harrison 43.

[46]*Western Spy* (Cincinnati), Jan. 12, 1822.

[47]In the only recent life of Harrison (Goebel, *Harrison,* 235), appears the statement that the General was "overwhelmingly defeated for the governorship," receiving not a single vote in his own county. As a matter of fact Harrison was not a candidate, a fact well known near home. Brown, the only avowed candidate in the election, naturally received an overwhelming plurality while Senator Jeremiah Morrow polled 9424 votes, Harrison, 4330. See *Western Spy,* Dec. 21, 1820; *Scioto Gazette,* Dec. 14, 1820. Harrison also received a complimentary vote in 1824 and again in later years.

[48]Greve, *Centennial History of Cincinnati,* 1 :608; *Ohio Senate Journal, 1819–20:*241, 277; *1820–21:*187.

[49]Harrison to W. H. Harrison Jr., Feb. 24, 1820, Harrison Papers, 6 :1091; Anna Harrison to same, April 4, 1820, John Scott Harrison Collection.

[50]*Western Sun* (Vincennes), Nov. 17, 1821.

[51]Harrison to constituents, Feb. 14, 1822, Todd and Drake, *Harrison,* 133.

[52]*Ibid.*

[53]W. H. Harrison Jr. to George P. Torrence, June 13, 1834, *Historical & Philosophical Society of Ohio Quarterly,* 3 :No. 3, 81.

[54]*Ibid.,* 2 :No. 3, 113 n.; Greve, *Centennial History of Cincinnati,* 1 :577–78.

⁵⁵*Western Spy*, Oct. 19, 1822.

⁵⁶Dawson to Findlay, May 11, 1823, Torrence Papers.

⁵⁷Harrison to Monroe, June 16, 1823, Monroe Papers, 20:2609, Library of Congress.

⁵⁸*Liberty Hall*, Oct. 5, 1824.

⁵⁹*Cincinnati Daily Gazette*, Oct. 8, 1824.

⁶⁰Allen Trimble to Duncan McArthur, Dec. 22, 1824, McArthur Papers, 33:6395–96.

⁶¹L. Goodale to E. A. Brown, Jan. 24, 1825, Brown Papers, Ohio State Library.

⁶²Trimble to McArthur, Jan. 25, 1825, McArthur Papers, 33:6438.

⁶³Testimony of William Greene and the Rev. J. L. Wilson, *The Log Cabin* (New York), Sept. 12, 1840. On the final ballot of the election Harrison polled 58 votes and Silliman 34. Cincinnati *Gazette*, Feb. 8, 1825.

⁶⁴Harrison to James Heaton, March 6, 1825, Forrest G. Sweet Collection.

⁶⁵Charles Francis Adams (editor), *Memoirs of John Quincy Adams*, 6:523–24.

⁶⁶Ben Perley Poore, *Perley's Reminiscences*, 1:71; Anne Royall, *The Black Book*, 3:115.

⁶⁷Thurlow Weed, *Autobiography*, 535.

⁶⁸Clay to Francis Brooke, April 19, 1826, Calvin Colton (editor), *Works of Henry Clay*, 4:139.

⁶⁹*National Crisis* (Cincinnati), Feb. 2, 1826; *Register of Debates, 19th Congress, 1st Session*, col. 42.

⁷⁰*Ibid.*, col. 373; Theodore D. Jervey, *Life of Robert Y. Hayne*, 209–10.

⁷¹Harrison to his wife, March 9, 1824, Mitten Collection.

⁷²Harrison to James Barbour, Dec. 1, 1825, *ibid.;* C. F. Adams (editor), *Memoirs of John Quincy Adams*, 7:105.

⁷³Goebel, *Harrison*, 244–45.

⁷⁴*Literary Gazette* (Providence), Dec. 29, 1827.

⁷⁵Harrison to W. H. Harrison Jr., Jan. 16, 1828, Harrison Papers, 6:1117.

⁷⁶Same to same, Dec. 4, 1827, and Jan. 26, 1828, John Scott Harrison Collection.

⁷⁷Morgan Neville to Findlay, March 4, 1828, Torrence Papers.

⁷⁸*Literary Gazette* (Providence), March 8, 1828; *Scioto Gazette* (Chillicothe), April 3, 1828.

⁷⁹C. F. Adams (editor), *Memoirs of John Quincy Adams*, 7:507.

⁸⁰*Ibid.*, 8:4–5.

CHAPTER XX

¹Francis P. Weisenburger, "Life of Charles Hammond," *Ohio Archæological & Historical Society Quarterly*, 43:413.

²Harrison to W. H. Harrison Jr., undated fragment in Harrison Papers, 6:1478.

³Harrison to Clay, July 3, 1828, Colombia Dispatches, vol. 5, National Archives.

[4] Letter from Caracas, July 6, 1828, Cincinnati *Daily Gazette,* Aug. 28, 1828.

[5] Letter from "an esteemed correspondent in Colombia," July 22, 1828, *ibid.,* Aug. 22.

[6] Carleton Beals, *America South,* 200–04; T. Y. Ybarra, *Bolivar,* 335–39; Hildegarde Angell, *Bolivar,* 250–57; Henry Kittredge Norton, "South America Pays Honor to Bolivar," *New York Times Magazine,* July 23, 1933.

[7] Clay to Harrison, Oct. 13, 1828, Instructions to Minister, 12:152–55, National Archives.

[8] Joseph B. Lockey, *Pan-Americanism,* 129–30.

[9] Harrison to Thomas Taylor, Nov. 3, 1828, *American Art Association– Anderson Galleries Catalogue,* May 6, 1935, No. 160.

[10] Harrison to W. H. Harrison Jr., Nov. 7, 1828, Harrison Papers, 7:1145.

[11] Harrison to Solomon Van Rensselaer, Nov. 8, 1828, Bonney, *Legacy,* 1:436–37.

[12] William R. Manning, "Poinsett's Mission to Mexico," *American Journal of International Law,* 7:781–822, *passim.*

[13] Harrison to Clay, Dec. 28, 1828, Colombia Dispatches, 5:No. 1, National Archives.

[14] *Ibid.*

[15] Letter of Rensselaer Van Rensselaer, Jan. 1, 1829, Bonney, *Legacy,* 1:447–49.

[16] Harrison, *Remarks of General Harrison . . . on certain charges,* etc. (pamphlet), 4.

[17] *Ibid.,* 43–44.

[18] Vergara to Bolivar, Feb. 8, 1829, Goebel, *Harrison,* 262.

[19] Same to same, March 15, 1829, *ibid.*

[20] Lynch, *Fifty Years of Party Warfare,* 357.

[21] James A. Hamilton to Martin Van Buren, Feb. 27, 1829, Van Buren Papers, 8:1939.

[22] Bonney, *Legacy,* 1:463–64.

[23] Solomon Van Rensselaer to his son, March 23, 1829, *ibid.,* 1:470–71.

[24] Jackson to Van Buren, May 23, 1829, Van Buren Papers, 9:60. See also same to same, March 31, 1829, John Spencer Bassett (editor), *Correspondence of Andrew Jackson,* 4:18–19.

[25] Van Buren to Jackson, June 9, 1829, Donelson Papers, Library of Congress; to Harrison, June 9, 1829, Instructions to Ministers, 12:204–05.

[26] Rensselaer Van Rensselaer to his father, July 12, 1829, Bonney, *Legacy,* 1:502–03.

[27] *Ibid.,* 503, 517; Harrison to Clay, March 28, 1829, Colombia Dispatches 5:No. 7.

[28] Harrison to Clay, Feb. 12, 1829, *ibid.,* No. 3.

[29] *Ibid.;* Ybarra, *Bolivar,* 338–39.

[30] Harrison to Van Buren, May 27, 1829, Colombia Dispatches, 5:No. 13.

[31] Jesus Maria Henao and Gerado Arrubla (Fred Rippy, translator), *History of Colombia,* 410; Lockey, *Pan-Americanism,* 121–22.

[32]A. B. Nones to Van Buren, June 25, 1829, Consular Letters, Carthagena, vol. 1.

[33]Harrison to Short, Aug. 3, 1829, transcript in Mitten Collection.

[34]Van Rensselaer to his father, July 12, 1829, Bonney, *Legacy*, 1 :505–06.

[35]Harrison, *Remarks*, etc., 38.

[36]*Ibid.*, 39.

[37]*Ibid.*, 40; Harrison to Van Buren, July 28, 1829, Colombia Dispatches 5 :No. 18.

[38]Harrison, *Remarks*, etc., 32.

[39]Harrison to Van Buren, Sept. 7, 1829, Colombia Dispatches, 5 :No. 22.

[40]Van Rensselaer to his father, Sept. 21, 1829, Bonney, *Legacy*, 1 :522–23.

[41]H. Montgomery, *Harrison*, 289–305.

[42]Van Rensselaer to his father, Nov. 17, 1829, Bonney, *Legacy*, 1 :524–30; to Harrison, Oct. 9, 1830, *ibid.*, 2 :33–35.

[43]Harrison's *Remarks*, 7.

[44]Van Rensselaer to his father, Nov. 17, 1829, Bonney, *Legacy*, 2 :203; Edward Tayloe Diary, reprinted in Harrison's *Remarks*, 9.

[45]*Ibid.*, 13; Thomas P. Moore to Van Buren, Oct. 19, 1829, Colombia Dispatches, 6 :No. 6.

[46]Van Rensselaer to his father, Nov. 17, 1829, Bonney, *Legacy*, 2 :5. Harrison's side of the story is related in his letter to Van Buren, March 8, 1830, Colombia Dispatches, 5 :(unnumbered letter).

[47]Van Rensselaer to his father, Jan. 31, 1830, Bonney, *Legacy*, 2 :14–19.

[48]Considerable newspaper space was devoted to the discussion. See the *New York American*, Feb. 8 and 10, 1831; *Morning Courier and Enquirer*, Jan. 26, Feb. 12, July 24, 1830; *Commercial Advertiser*, Feb. 9, 10, 11, 27, etc., 1830; *Niles' Register*, April 10, 1830, also current newspapers of Ohio, Virginia, and Kentucky.

[49]Moore to Van Buren, Oct. 19, 1829, Colombia Dispatches, 6 :No. 6, and enclosures; Vergara to Moore, Jan. 17, 1830, enclosed with Moore Letter of March 27, 1830, *ibid.*

[50]Madison to Harrison, June 5, 1830, Madison Papers, 83 :1071.

[51]C. F. Adams (editor), *Memoirs of John Quincy Adams*, 8 :189, 212.

[52]*Ibid.*, 8 :194.

CHAPTER XXI

[1]W. H. Harrison Jr. to Torrence, March 5, 1830, Torrence Papers. See also *Historical & Philosophical Society of Ohio Quarterly*, 3 :No. 3, 77 n. 30.

[2]Cincinnati *Daily Gazette*, Nov. 29, 1830; June 15, 1840. The amount of Symmes's debt is herein stated to be $9000 but in a letter to James Findlay, Dec. 7, 1830, Harrison gives the sum as $12,803.63.

[3]Harrison to W. H. Harrison Jr., Feb. 19, 1830, John Scott Harrison Collection.

[4]Statement of James A. Green of Cincinnati to the writer.

[5]Lewis Whiteman to Mrs. Jane Findlay, April 25, 1830, Torrence Papers.

[6]Harrison's share of the foundry loss "exceeded $30,000," according to an account of his financial history in the *Sentinel of Freedom* (Newark, N. J.), Sept. 27, 1836 (from the Cincinnati *Daily Gazette*). Certain notes possibly arising from this debt are listed in Harrison Papers, 7:1142. These show that on Aug. 25, 1828, Harrison had borrowed $10,336.46 from the United States Bank of Philadelphia and had another note outstanding for $8702.89. His personal drafts on the United States Bank where his salary checks were deposited are to be found in the MacAlester Collection, Library Company of Philadelphia.

[7]Bonney, *Legacy*, 2:28.

[8]Edward Tayloe to R. Van Rensselaer, July 16, 1830; Harrison to Van Rensselaer, Aug. 15, 1830; Van Rensselaer to Harrison, Oct. 9, 1830; "Mr. Henderson's Memorandum," *ibid.*, 29–37. Wrote Mr. Henderson: "To effect his diabolical purpose of party spirit against Gen. Harrison he [Moore] recklessly involves myself . . . whom then he had never seen because I was a friend of Gen. Harrison, and gets Colonel Torrens and Mr. Leidendorf expelled and his own countryman Gooding thrown into prison. That Moore was the occasion of all this, Gen. Urdaneta has openly declared in all companies."

[9]Advertisement in Cincinnati *Advertiser*, June 2, 1830; letter of Mrs. Jane Findlay, Dec. 28, 1830, *Historical & Philosophical Society of Ohio Quarterly*, 3:No. 3, 79 n.

[10]*Indiana Republican* (Madison), Sept. 2, 1830; *Niles' Register*, Oct. 23, 1830.

[11]*Ibid.*, Nov. 27, 1830.

[12]Cincinnati *Daily Gazette*, Nov. 2, 1830.

[13]Harrison to Findlay, Dec. 7, 1830, Torrence Papers.

[14]Harrison to Van Rensselaer, Nov. 4, 1830, Bonney, *Legacy*, 2:36.

[15]Cincinnati *Daily Gazette*, Nov. 24 and Dec. 1, 1830; also succeeding issues.

[16]Harrison to Findlay, Dec. 7, 1830, Torrence Papers.

[17]Todd and Drake, *Harrison*, 132.

[18]*Register of Debates, 21st Congress, 2nd Session*, Appendix, 48–49.

[19]Todd & Drake, *Harrison*, 131.

[20]Fannie G. Hendryx, "Biographical Sketch," *Messages & Letters*, 1:10.

[21]W. H. Harrison Jr. to Findlay, March 21, 1832, Torrence Papers.

[22]Harrison to Cass, April 24, 1832, Emmet Collection, No. 1425, New York Public Library.

[23]Harrison to Findlay, April 23 and Dec. 2, 1832, Torrence Papers.

[24]W. H. Harrison Jr. to Findlay, July 4, 1832, *ibid.*

[25]Harrison to Findlay, Dec. 2, 1832, *ibid.*

[26]James, *Andrew Jackson*, 611–12.

[27]Harrison to Cass, Feb. 16, 1833, transcript in Mitten Collection.

[28]*Ibid.; Indiana Journal* (Indianapolis), Jan. 16, 1833.

[29]James, *Andrew Jackson*, 620.

[30]Greve, *Centennial History of Cincinnati*, 588–89.

[31]Thomas Ewing to William Dearborn, Aug. 20, 1833, Mitten Collection.

[32]*New York Spectator*, Dec. 27, 1833.

[33]Harrison's "Speech at Cheviot," July 4, 1833, pamphlet, Mitten Collection.

[34]Lew Wallace, *Life of General Ben Harrison*, 47; letter of James A. Green of Cincinnati in *Life*, Aug. 13, 1839.

[35]Elliott Coues (editor), *Forty Years a Fur Trader*, 1:16–17.

[36]Meyer, *Johnson*, 408.

[37]Hamilton (Ohio) *Intelligencer*, March 2, 1833; Harrison to Indianapolis Committee, Sept. 27, 1834, *Niles' Register*, Nov. 13, 1834, 173–75.

[38]*Ibid.;* Harrison to Tipton, Dec. 6, 1833, *Messages & Letters*, 2:745.

[39]Harrison to Committee, Sept. 27, 1834, *Niles' Register*, Nov. 15, 1834, 173–75.

[40]Harrison to Tipton, Dec. 6, 1833, *Messages & Letters*, 2:748–49.

[41]Same to same, May 2, 1834, *ibid.*, 2:748–54.

CHAPTER XXII

[1]Letter of "A Friend to Truth," in William Emmons, *Colonel R. M. Johnson,* 82–85.

[2]Harrison to Committee, Sept. 27, 1834, *Niles' Register,* Nov. 15, 1834, 174. Colonel Johnson was also made the hero of "Tecumseh, or the Battle of the Thames, a National Drama in Five Acts," which played to crowded houses in Washington, Baltimore and Annapolis. See Meyer, *Johnson,* 401–02.

[3]Harrison to Tipton, May 2, 1834, *Messages & Letters,* 2:749–54; to John O'Fallon, April 9, 1834, Galloway, *Old Chillicothe,* 160–61.

[4]Harrison to Thomas Chilton, Feb. 27, 1834, Cincinnati *Daily Gazette,* May 10, 1834.

[5]Charles Hammond to Harrison, June 16, 1834, Harrison Papers, 7:1162–63.

[6]W. H. Harrison Jr. to Torrence, June 13, 1834, Torrence Papers.

[7]William Henry to J. B. Gardner, June 23, 1834, Harrison Papers, 7:1166.

[8]Harrison to Committee, Sept. 27, 1834, *Niles' Register,* Nov. 15, 1834, 173–75.

[9]Harrison to Edward King, Oct. 9, 1834, Welsh Collection, Pennsylvania Historical Society; Cincinnati *Daily Gazette,* Oct. 22, 1834. Harrison was serving as Grand Jury foreman at the time.

[10]Michel Chevalier (French economist), *Society in the United States,* 196.

[11]*Pennsylvania Intelligencer* (Harrisburg), Dec. 14, 1834; *Ohio State Journal* (Columbus), Dec. 20, 1834.

[12]Harrison to William Ayres, Jan. 2, 1834, Henkels' Catalogue, 1368, New York Public Library.

[13]Pennsylvania *Intelligencer,* Jan. 31, 1835.

[14]Harrison to Van Rensselaer, Jan. 15, 1835, Bonney, *Legacy,* 2:55–56.

[15]Salmon P. Chase to Samuel F. Vinton, Feb. 8, 1835, R. B. Warden, *Life of Salmon Portland Chase,* 246–48.

[16]*Pennsylvania Intelligencer,* Feb. 12, 1835; *Ohio State Journal,* Feb. 13, 1835, *Cincinnati Gazette,* Feb. 3 and 21, 1835.

[17]Nancy N. Scott (editor), *Memoir of Hugh Lawson White*, 329–32.
[18]Register of the Union Inn, Indianapolis, Indiana Historical Society.
[19]Dennis Tilden Lynch, *An Epoch and a Man*, 382–83.
[20]Quoted in Meyer, *Johnson*, 419.
[21]*United States' Telegraph*, June 3, 1835.
[22]Webster to Biddle, May 12, 1835; Everett to Biddle, June 3, 1835, R. C. McGrane (editor), *Correspondence of Nicholas Biddle*, 251–53.
[23]Webster to Everett, July 2, 1835, Webster Papers, Massachusetts Historical Society.
[24]James Truslow Adams, *Epic of America*, 142.
[25]William McDonald, *Jacksonian Democracy*, 298.
[26]Biddle to Herman Cope, Aug. 11, 1835, McGrane (editor), *Correspondence of Nicholas Biddle*, 255.
[27]Harrison to Joseph Wallace and Samuel Shock, April 22, 1835, *Richmond Whig*, Oct. 30, 1835.
[28]Harrison to William Ayres, May 13, 1835, Henkel's Catalogue, 1368, New York Public Library.
[29]Harrison's Vincennes Speech, May 25, 1835, Todd and Drake, *Harrison*, 135–39; *The Commonwealth* (Frankfort), June 30, 1835.
[30]Terre Haute *Courier*, June 11, 1835; *Indiana Democrat*, June 19, 1835; A. A. Leonard, "Personal Politics in Indiana," *Indiana Magazine of History*, 19:152–53.
[31]Cincinnati *Daily Gazette*, July 25, 1835.
[32]Letter signed "Shelby," in *ibid*.
[33]The Kentucky papers were *The Commonwealth* of Frankfort, the Lexington *Observer and Reporter*. See also the *Indiana Democrat* (Indianapolis), July 17 and 24; the Louisville *Journal*, Aug. 8; *Republican Banner* (Madison), Aug. 13; *Kentucky Gazette*, Aug. 15, *Niles' Register*, Oct. 3, 1835.
[34]A. L. Kohlmeier, *The Old Northwest*, 22–33.
[35]*Ibid.*, 28–29; T. D. Jervey, *Robert Y. Hayne*, 385; J. Fred Rippy, *Joel Roberts Poinsett*, 163.
[36]Clay to John Bailhache, Sept. 13, 1835, Colton (editor), *Private Correspondence*, 4:399–400.
[37]Cincinnati *Whig*, Sept. 30, 1835, reprinted in Richmond *Whig*, Oct. 16, 1835.
[38]Richmond *Whig*, Oct. 9, 1835.
[39]*Ibid.*, Oct. 20, 1835.
[40]The New York *Evening Post*, Oct. 10, and *Niles' Register*, Oct. 24, 1835, describe the Thames celebrations in New York.
[41]Unsigned and undated letter in Harrison's handwriting in the Thomas M. Madigan collection. Judging by the context the letter must have been written in November, 1835.
[42]Harrison-Stevens correspondence quoted in T. F. Woodley, *Thaddeus Stevens*, 38; James A. Woodburn, *Thaddeus Stevens*, 24.
[43]Webster to Harmar Denny, Nov. 20, 1835, *Writings and Speeches of Daniel Webster*, 18:12–13; to J. Wallace, etc., Nov. 28, *ibid.*, 16:259; to W. W. Irwin, *ibid.*, 16:260.
[44]Henry L. Mueller, *The Whig Party in Pennsylvania*, 29; *Ohio State Journal*, Dec. 22, 1835, Jan. 1, 1836.

[45]Charles Miner to Webster, Dec. 17, 1835, Webster Papers, 4:16234, Library of Congress.

CHAPTER XXIII

[1]Richmond *Whig,* Jan. 7, 1836.
[2]Tyler, *Letters & Times of the Tylers,* 1:519–20.
[3]Robert Ware to Tyler, Feb. 24, 1836, *ibid.,* 1:521.
[4]Miller to Tyler, Feb. 23, 1836, *ibid.,* 1:520–21.
[5]Thomas Ewing, *The Ohio Presidents,* 519; *Niles' Register,* March 5, 1836.
[6]J. Pearce to J. Bailhache, June 27, 1836, Harrison Papers, 7:1190.
[7]Harrison to W. B. Tyler, Feb. 9, 1836, *National Intelligencer,* Feb. 24, 1836.
[8]Harrison to John W. Taylor, Feb. 20, 1836, *Autograph Album,* 1:No. 2.
[9]Cincinnati *Daily Gazette,* May 25, 1836.
[10]Sherrod Williams to Harrison, April 7, 1836; Harrison to Williams, May 1, 1836, *National Intelligencer,* July 4; *Niles' Register,* Sept. 10, 1836.
[11]Holmes Alexander, *The American Talleyrand,* 329–30.
[12]Harrison to Williams, May 1, 1836, *Niles' Register,* Sept. 10, 1836.
[13]Cincinnati *Whig,* May 24, 1836; *Niles' Register,* June 18, 1836.
[14]C. B. Harrison to his father, June 1, 1836, Harrison Papers, 7:1183. The date of this letter is incorrectly quoted as 1839 in Goebel, *Harrison,* 340 n.
[15]Harrison to John Sargeant, etc., June 24, 1836, Harrison Letters, Pennsylvania Historical Society.
[16]Henry H. Simms, *Rise of the Whigs in Virginia,* 107–09.
[17]Edward Tayloe to Harrison, Oct. 20, 1836, Harrison Papers, 7:1215–16.
[18]Harrison to Van Rensselaer, Aug. 25, 1836, Bonney, *Legacy,* 2:56–57.
[19]Newark (N. J.) *Sentinel of Freedom,* Sept. 2, 1836. "This distinguished gentleman is travelling in a public stage . . . in that plain, unostentatious republican manner which becomes his own admirable character, and is so well suited to the genius of his countrymen." *Ibid.,* Aug. 30, 1836.
[20]Quoted in *Sentinel of Freedom,* Sept. 20, 1836.
[21]Simms, *Rise of the Whigs in Virginia,* 110–11. Editor Duff Green placed Van Buren in contrast with "plain, republican" Harrison in this wise: "We do not like to see a proud rich nabob . . . in a fine coach . . . attended by English waiters, *dressed in livery* after the fashion of an English lord, attempt to pass himself off as a true workingman's democrat." *United States' Telegraph,* Sept. 7, 1836.
[22]John H. Pleasants to Harrison, Sept. 15, 1836, *Niles' Register,* Oct. 8, 1836.
[23]Harrison to Hamilton (Ohio) *Intelligencer,* Dec. 22, 1821, quoted in Burr, *Harrison,* 247–52.
[24]Harrison to Pleasants, Sept. 15, 1836, *Niles' Register,* Oct. 8, 1836; *Senate Journal, 19th Congress, 2nd Session,* 325; *20th Congress, 1st Session,* 101–02.

²⁵Richmond *Whig*, Sept. 20, 1836.

²⁶*Sentinel of Freedom*, Sept. 27, 1836.

²⁷Baltimore *Chronicle*, Sept. 23, 1836; *National Intelligencer*, Sept. 24, 1836.

²⁸*Ibid.*, Sept. 28, 1836; Philadelphia *Commercial Herald*, Sept. 25; *National Gazette* (Philadelphia), Sept. 26, 1836.

²⁹John Frelinghuysen Hageman, *History of Princeton*, 1 :264.

³⁰Quoted in *Sentinel of Freedom*, Oct. 11, 1836.

³¹*Ohio People's Press* (Columbus), Oct. 19, 1836, Forrest G. Sweet Collection. See also, New York *American*, Sept. 30, and New York *Morning Courier*, Oct. 1, 1836.

³²*Sentinel of Freedom*, Oct. 11 and 18, 1836.

³³*Ibid.*, Oct. 18, 1836.

³⁴*Lancaster County Historical Society Papers*, 27 :168.

³⁵Quoted in Lynch, *An Epoch and A Man*, 395.

³⁶*Ohio People's Press* (Columbus), and *National Intelligencer*, Oct. 26, 1836; Richmond *Enquirer*, Nov. 1, 1836.

³⁷Harrison to William Sheets, Oct. 27, 1836, *Virginia Magazine of History*, 18 :109. Mr. Sheets, Indiana Secretary of State, married the daughter of Thomas Randolph who fell at Tippecanoe. Miss Randolph had been raised as a member of the Harrison household.

³⁸James, *Andrew Jackson*, 706–07, 730–31.

³⁹Edward Stanwood, *A History of the Presidency:* 184. Maine elected a Democratic Governor by 9000 votes that year but there was "no choice of a Congressman . . . in any one of the eight districts."

⁴⁰*Ibid.*, 1 :185; Lynch, *Fifty Years of Party Warfare*, 472; Greeley, *Recollections of a Busy Life*, 112–13; Meyer, *Johnson*, 427; Alexander, *The American Talleyrand*, 331–32.

⁴¹Harrison to Noah Noble, Dec. 2, 1836, *Indiana Magazine of History*, 22 :205.

⁴²New York Whigs to Harrison, Jan. 9, 1837, Harrison Papers, 7 :1229–30.

⁴³Clay to W. Thompson, July, 1837, *The Collector*, vol. 22, Mss. Division, Library of Congress.

⁴⁴E. Hulse to Harrison, Dec. 29, 1837, Miscellaneous Harrison Letters, Historical & Philosophical Society of Ohio.

⁴⁵*Scioto Gazette*, Feb. 1, 1838.

⁴⁶Cincinnati *Daily Gazette*, April 3, 1838 (from *United States' Gazette*).

⁴⁷Harrison to A. B. Howell, April 7, 1838, Cincinnati *Daily Gazette*, May 16, 1838.

⁴⁸*Ibid.*, May 22, 1838.

⁴⁹*Scioto Gazette*, June 7, 1838.

⁵⁰*Ibid.*, July 19, 1838; *Niles' Register*, Aug. 18, 1838.

⁵¹Quoted in *Scioto Gazette*, Aug. 2, 1838.

⁵²Cincinnati *Daily Gazette*, Aug. 3, 1838.

⁵³Harrison to Harmar Denny, Dec. 2, 1838, *National Intelligencer*, Feb. 14, 1839.

⁵⁴Harrison to N. P. Tallmadge, Feb. 22, 1840, Tallmadge MSS., Wisconsin Historical Society.

CHAPTER XXIV

[1]Alexander, *The American Talleyrand*, 357.

[2]*Ibid.*, 355; Thurlow W. Barnes, *Memoir of Thurlow Weed*, 76–77.

[3]O. W. Smith to Clay, Sept. 28, 1839, O. H. Smith, *Early Indiana Trials and Sketches*, 252–53. Clay's letter is reprinted in *ibid.*, 251.

[4]Millard Fillmore to Weed, May 1, 1839, *Buffalo Historical Society Publications*, 11:191.

[5]P. B. Porter to Gulian C. Verplanck, July 24, 1839, Verplanck Papers, New York Historical Society.

[6]Todd to William H. Seward, June 17, 1839, Gratz Collection, Pennsylvania Historical Society.

[7]Harrison to Clay, Sept. 20, 1839, Harrison Papers, 7:1251.

[8]Same to same, Sept. 21, 1839, Indiana Historical Society Mss.

[9]Harrison to Miller, Oct. 18, 1839, Cincinnati *Daily Gazette*, Nov. 10, 1839.

[10]Harrison to Van Rensselaer, Nov. 19, 1839, Bonney, *Legacy*, 2:115.

[11]C. H. Peck, *The Jacksonian Epoch*, 424–25.

[12]Alexander McClure, *Our Presidents*, 68 n. 2.

[13]Harriett A. Weed (editor), Autobiography of Thurlow Weed, 481. A day-by-day account of the convention proceedings is given in Julia Perkins Cutler, *Life of Ephraim Cutler*, 234–36.

[14]Carl Schurz, *Henry Clay*, 2:179.

[15]A. Porter to Crittenden, Dec. 18, 1839, Crittenden Papers, 6:1166.

[16]C. F. Adams (editor), *Memoirs of John Quincy Adams*, 10:151–52.

[17]Johnson to Crittenden, Dec. 11, 1839, Crittenden Papers, 6:1164.

[18]Abraham Lincoln to John T. Stuart, Jan. 20, 1840, Nicolay and Hay, *Works of Abraham Lincoln*, 1:39–40.

[19]Horace Greeley, *Recollections of a Busy Life*, 132.

[20]Cincinnati *Daily Gazette*, Cincinnati *Chronicle*, Jan. 3, 1840.

[21]Harrison to John Owen, Dec. 29, 1839; Tyler to John Owen, Dec. 16, 1839, Cincinnati *Daily Gazette*, July 2, 1840.

[22]Rives statement in Richmond *Whig*, Feb. 27, 1830. See also, Harrison to Clay, Feb. 25, 1840, Indiana Historical Society Collection. John C. Calhoun expressed another Southerner's point of view: "How can I, who am anti abolition, go on a ticket, headed by one, who has expressed an opinion in favour of appropriating money to emancipate our slaves by purchase; and whose main support is in a state chiefly tainted by abolitionism . . . ? Calhoun to Duff Green, July 27, 1837, American Historical Association *Report*, 1899, 2:376. Green wanted Calhoun to run with Harrison.

[23]Harrison to J. M. Berrien, Nov. 4, 1836, Todd and Drake, *Harrison*, 169–70.

[24]Raynor G. Wellington, *Political & Sectional Influence of the Public Lands*, 95–96.

[25]*Ohio Confederate* (Columbus), Feb. 26, 1840; Cincinnati *Daily Gazette*, Feb. 25, 1840; A. B. Norton, *Reminiscences*, 44–58.

[26]Richard S. Elliott, *Notes Taken in Sixty Years*, 120.

[27]Current attacks on Harrison in Congress appear in the *Congressional Globe, 26th Congress, 1st Session* (see index to the appendix, 860, 862).

The gibes of the defense kept administration orators busy and vice versa. See reply of Corwin to Crary, *ibid.*, 200–01 ; also Poore, Perley's *Reminiscences*, I :235–37.

[28]St. Louis *Daily Argus*, March 3, 1840.

[29]Catherine V. Rensselaer, to her brother, July 4, 1840, Bonney, *Legacy*, 2:140–41.

[30]Quoted in Peck, *Jacksonian Epoch*, 451 n. 2.

[31]James Brooks in the *New York Express*, May 23, 1840.

[32]The *Congressional Globe, 26th Congress, 1st Session*, appendix, 572, prints the Oswego letter and the committee's reply. Harrison declared he tossed "half of the letters I receive in the fire without replying to them." Harrison to Clay, May 7, 1840, Indiana Historical Society.

[33]Harrison to Webster, June 25, 1840, transcript in Mitten Collection.

[34]Todd and Drake, *Harrison*, 165–66. See also, *The Republican, The Chronicle,* and the *Daily Gazette* of Cincinnati, issues of June 12 to 18, 1840.

[35]Harrison's Fort Meigs Speech, Norton, *Reminiscences,* 178–87.

[36](?) to Horace Greeley, *The Log Cabin,* June 27, 1840.

[37]Cincinnati *Daily Gazette,* June 26, 1840.

[38]Webster's Saratoga Speech, *Writings and Speeches* (National edition), 3 :30.

[39]Linda Rhea, *Hugh S. Legare,* 191–92.

[40]"Ohio's Storied Tree Lives On," *New York Times Magazine,* Dec. 6, 1936.

[41]Harriet H. Robinson, *Loom and Spindle,* 86–87. Dr. Charles W. Green of New York kindly showed me a number of Harrison items in his collection of early American glass.

[42]Mary Newton Stanard, *Richmond,* 144.

[43]E. D. Mansfield, *Personal Memories,* 324.

[44]*Ibid.,* 318.

[45]Statement of Lecky Harper, Norton, *Reminiscences,* 374.

[46]*Ibid.,* 363.

[47]Harrison to Webster, June 27, 1840, transcript in Mitten Collection.

[48]Speech at Fort Greenville, July 28, 1840, Norton, *Reminiscences,* 249.

[49]Mansfield, *Personal Memories,* 319. The crowd was also estimated at 60,000 and at 78,000 on a smaller acreage while a total of 100,000 was reported in and about the town. Cincinnati *Chronicle,* Sept. 12, 1840; Howe, *Historical Collections of Ohio,* 2 :289–90.

[50]Gaines-Croghan correspondence reprinted in Cincinnati *Daily Gazette,* Oct. 16, 1840. See also Gaines letter in Louisville *Journal,* Oct. 9, 1840.

[51]Portland *Daily Evening Advertiser,* Sept. 12 and 15, 1840; Harrie B. Coe (editor), *Maine, A History,* 111.

[52]Stanwood, *History of the Presidency,* I :203–04; Simms, *Rise of the Whigs in Virginia,* 157–58.

[53]Cincinnati *Daily Gazette,* April 13, 1841.

CHAPTER XXV

[1]Norton, *Reminiscences,* 269.

[2]Claude Fuess, *Daniel Webster,* 2 :27.

[3]Harrison to Clay, Nov. 2, 1840, Indiana Historical Society Collection. Harrison here refers to the land he bartered in 1793 for his legacy of 3000 acres.

[4]Same to same, Nov. 15, 1840, Colton (editor), *Works of Henry Clay,* 4:446.

[5]Clay to Brooke, Dec. 8, 1840, *ibid.,* 4:446–47. The situation is also discussed in G. P. Poage, *Henry Clay and the Rise of the Whig Party,* 16–18.

[6]Webster to Harrison, Dec. 11, 1840, *Writings and Speeches,* 18:93–94.

[7]Van Deusen, *Henry Clay,* 346.

[8]McClure, *Our Presidents,* 68 n. 2; J. A. Woodburn, *Thaddeus Stevens,* 65–66.

[9]Harrison to Webster, Dec. 27, 1840, *Writings and Speeches,* 18:97.

[10]Letcher to Crittenden, Feb. 9, 1841, Coleman (editor), *John J. Crittenden,* 145.

[11]*Sentinel of Freedom,* March 30, 1841. Harrison lost four grown sons, Symmes, William Jr., Carter and Benjamin. William Jr., intemperate to the last, died Feb. 6, 1838, and on Aug. 12, 1839, Carter "was suddenly and mysteriously" taken away. (Cincinnati *Daily Gazette,* Aug. 16, 1839.) In other words his ailment was not properly diagnosed. Son John Scott and three married daughters still survived. Daniel Webster, incidentally, lost four out of five children; Clay six daughters and one son, while his eldest son was insane.

[12]John Findlay Torrence Diary, reprinted in *Kentucky State Historical Society Register,* 7:No. 20, 60.

[13]*Ibid.,* 62. (Jan. 29, 1841 entry.)

[14]*National Intelligencer,* April 13, 1841.

[15]T. J. C. Williams, *History of Washington County* (Maryland), 237.

[16]*National Intelligencer,* Feb. 8, 1841.

[17]Catharina Van Rensselaer to her brother, Feb. 18, 1841, Bonney, *Legacy,* 2:154–55.

[18]Washington *Globe,* Feb. 9, 1841.

[19]Tyler *Letters & Times of the Tylers,* 2: n. 4.

[20]Crittenden to Letcher, Feb. 20, 1821, Coleman (editor), *John J. Crittenden,* 146–47.

[21]Lynch, *An Epoch and a Man,* 470.

[22]Mrs. E. F. Ellet, *Court Circles of the Republic,* 284.

[23]Greeley to Weed, Feb. 19, 1841, Barnes (editor), *Thurlow Weed,* 93.

[24]Ellet, *Court Circles of the Republic,* 286.

[25]*Ibid.,* 287.

[26]Richmond *Whig,* Feb. 19, 1841.

[27]*Ibid.,* Feb. 23, 1841; John A. Cutchins, *A Famous Command,* 49.

[28]Allan Nevins (editor), *Diary of Philip Hone,* 1:529.

[29]Peter Harvey, *Reminiscences and Anecdotes of Daniel Webster,* 160–63.

[30]Fuess, *Daniel Webster,* 2:408.

[31]Poore, *Perley's Reminiscences,* 1:251.

32Smith, *Early Indiana Trials,* 148–49; Thomas C. Grattan, *Civilized America,* 1 :340.

33Bonney, *Legacy,* 2 :161.

34Harrison's Inaugural Address, Montgomery, *Harrison,* 357.

35*Ibid.,* 358–65.

36Nevins (editor), *Diary of Philip Hone,* 1 :530; Thomas Hart Benton, *Thirty Years' View,* 2 :210.

37Grattan, *Civilized America,* 1 :342.

38Green to Harrison, Feb. 28 and March 23, 1841, Harrison Papers, 8 :1373, 1418.

39Poore, *Perley's Reminiscences,* 1 :258.

40Bonney, *Legacy,* 2 :168.

41Francis P. Blair to Jackson, April 4, 1841, J. F. Jameson (editor), *Correspondence of Andrew Jackson,* 6 :97–98.

42Charles MacAlester to Todd, March 19, 1841, Harrison Papers, 8 :1411. On July 12, 1841, Abbott Lawrence wrote Judge Jacob Burnet suggesting repayment of the loan from a $25,000 Congressional grant to Harrison's family. Lawrence MSS., New York Public Library.

43Clay to Harrison, March 13, 1841, quoted in Poague, *Henry Clay,* 30.

44Harrison to Clay, March 13, 1841, *ibid.,* 30–31.

45Nathan Sargent, *Public Men and Events,* 2 :115–16.

46Clay to Harrison, March 15, 1841, Colton (editor), *Works of Henry Clay,* 4 :452–53.

47Coleman, *John J. Crittenden,* 1 :149–55; James Schouler, *History of the United States,* 4 :397; Webster to Seward, March 17, 1841, C. H. Van Tyne (editor), *Letters of Daniel Webster,* 231; Beckles Willson, *America's Ambassadors to England,* 224–26.

48Lossing, *Pictorial Field-Book of the War of 1812,* 663 n.

49Circular to All Cabinet Officials, March 20, 1841, Todd and Drake, *Harrison,* 204–05; original in State Department Papers, National Archives. A member of Congress from Indiana described a scene at the White House in revealing Harrison's earnest endeavors to counter the spoils-seekers. During a conference between the President and "three or four leading Whigs" on March 22, 1841 :

"These men were urging the indiscriminate discharge of Democratic office-holders. All the parties appeared warm and eager in the controversy until at length General Harrison started up, and with a warmth and energy he rarely exhibited, he extended his arms, exclaiming . . . 'So help me God, I will resign my office before I can be guilty of such iniquity.' After they were gone the President turned to me and remarked, 'Proffit, I am glad to see you. The Federal portion of the Whig party are making desperate efforts to seize the reins of government. They are urging the most unmerciful proscription, and if they continue to do so much longer, they will drive me mad!' " Tyler, *Letters & Times of the Tylers,* 2 :11, (reprinted from the Washington *Madisonian,* July 8, 1842.)

50Todd and Drake, *Harrison,* 204–05.

51Webster to St. Clair, Clark, etc., March 27, 1841, *ibid.,* 205–06.

52Harrison to Curtis, March 26, 1841, *ibid.,* 207–08.

53*Washington City and Capital,* 491.

54Bowers, *Party Battles of the Jackson Period,* 14 n.

[55]Bonney, *Legacy*, 2:173.

[56]Nevins (editor), *Diary of Philip Hone*, 1:535.

[57]Letter of "A Personal Friend," *National Intelligencer*, April 17, 1841, answering editorial in the Washington *Globe* of April 15.

[58]Croghan to Washington *Globe*, April 14, 1841, *ibid.*, April 16, 1841.

[59]Report of the attending physicians, Todd and Drake, *Harrison*, 208. The Mitten Collection has several bulletins scribbled by Colonel Todd conveying sick-bed news to the *National Intelligencer*.

[60]Johnston to Cutler, June 19, 1842, Cutler, *Ephraim Cutler*, 248.

[61]Montgomery, *Harrison*, 448.

[62]*Ibid.*, 449.

[63]*Ibid.*, 456. See also *Perley's Reminiscences*, 1:267–68. John Quincy Adams wrote a detailed account of the funeral in his *Memoirs*, 10:456–59. A few weeks following Harrison's death, comment was rife concerning the steamer *President* which sailed from New York for Liverpool on March 11, 1841, and was never again heard from. An interesting account of Harrison's last days is the communication of the Rev. William Hawley to the *National Intelligencer* of April 24, 1841.

BIBLIOGRAPHY

MANUSCRIPT SOURCES

Appointment Office Files (State Department), National Archives, Washington.

Mrs. Lydia Bacon Journal, New York Historical Society.

James Barbour Papers, New York Public Library.

Nicholas Biddle Papers, Library of Congress, Washington.

Ethan Allen Brown Papers, Ohio State Library, Columbus.

The Collector, Library of Congress.

Colombia Dispatches, volumes 4–6, National Archives.

Consular Letters, La Guayra, volume 2; Maracaibo, volume 1, National Archives.

John J. Crittenden Papers, Library of Congress.

George Croghan Manuscripts, New York Public Library.

Silas Deane Papers, New York Historical Society, New York City.

Domestic Letters, volume 16 (State Department Bureau of Indexes and Archives), National Archives.

Andrew Jackson Donelson Papers, Library of Congress.

Draper Collection, Wisconsin State Historical Society, Madison.

Dreer Collection, Pennsylvania Historical Society, Philadelphia.

Emmet Collection, New York Public Library.

English Collection, Indiana Historical Society, Indiana.

Flagg Collection, New York Public Library.

John S. Gano Papers, Historical and Philosophical Society of Ohio, Cincinnati.

Gratz Collection, Pennsylvania Historical Society.

James A. Green, *The Berkeley Manor House,* Mitten Collection.

William Henry Harrison Letters and Manuscripts, Chicago Historical Society, Indiana Historical Society, Historical and Philosophical Society of Ohio, National Archives (War Department Records), New York Historical Society, New York Public Library, Ohio State Library.

Harrison Papers (eight volumes), Library of Congress.

Instructions to Ministers, 1828–30 (State Department), National Archives.

Andrew Jackson Papers, Library of Congress.

Thomas Jefferson Papers, Library of Congress.

Abbott Lawrence Manuscripts, New York Public Library.

Letter Books "A," "B," and "C" (Office of Indian Affairs), National Archives.

Duncan McArthur Papers, Library of Congress.

James Madison Papers, Library of Congress.

Nathaniel Massie Papers, Ohio Archæological and Historical Society, Columbus.

Return Jonathan Meigs Papers, Ohio State Library.

Mitten Collection, Indiana Historical Society.

James Monroe Papers, New York Public Library, Library of Congress.

Richard Peters Manuscripts, Pennsylvania Historical Society.

Presidential Autographs, New York Public Library, Pennsylvania Historical Society, Wisconsin State Library.

St. Clair Manuscripts, Ohio State Library, Indiana Historical Society.

Winthrop Sargent Papers, Massachusetts Historical Society, Boston.

William Schillinger Journal, Cincinnati Public Library.

Nathaniel P. Tallmadge Papers, New York Public Library, Wisconsin State Historical Society.

John W. Taylor Papers, New York Historical Society.

George P. Torrence Papers, Historical and Philosophical Society of Ohio.

Thomas J. Underwood Journal, Draper Collection, Wisconsin State Historical Society.

Martin Van Buren Papers, Library of Congress.

Gulian C. Verplanck Papers, New York Historical Society.

Anthony Wayne Papers, Pennsylvania Historical Society.

Daniel Webster Papers, Massachusetts Historical Society, Library of Congress.

Henry Harrison Wilson, *Address,* "Benjamin Harrison V," Library of Congress.

Thomas Worthington Papers, Ohio State Library.

PRIVATE COLLECTIONS

Walter R. Benjamin, New York City.

John Scott Harrison IV, Helena, Montana.

Thomas F. Madigan, New York City.

Forrest G. Sweet, Battle Creek, Michigan.

PUBLISHED SOURCES

Henry Adams, *Life of Albert Gallatin* (1880) : *History of the United States* (1890–91).

James Truslow Adams, *Epic of America* (1931).

394 BIBLIOGRAPHY

John Adams, *Autobiography* (edited by Charles Francis Adams), (1850).

John Quincy Adams, *Memoirs* (edited by Charles Francis Adams), (1876).

Holmes Alexander, *The American Talleyrand* (1935).

Clarence W. Alvord, *The Illinois Country, 1673–1818* (1920).

American Historical Record.

American Historical Association Report, 1902, 1906, 1918.

American Historical Review.

American Pioneer.

American State Papers, Foreign Affairs, volume 3; *Indian Affairs,* volumes 1–2; *Military Affairs,* volume 1.

Hildegarde Angell, *Bolivar* (1930).

John Armstrong, *Notices of the War of 1812* (1840).

William Atherton, *Narrative of the suffering and defeat of the northwestern army under General Winchester* (1842).

Caleb Atwater, *A History of the State of Ohio* (1838).

Thurlow W. Barnes, *Memoir of Thurlow Weed* (1884).

John Spencer Bassett (editor), *Correspondence of Andrew Jackson* (1926–35).

Carleton Beals, *American South* (1937).

H. W. Beckwith, *History of Vigo and Parke Counties* (1880).

Thomas Hart Benton, *Thirty Years' View* (1854–56).

Henry Boley, *Lexington in Old Virginia* (1936).

Beverly W. Bond, *The Civilization of the Old Northwest* (1934).

Beverly W. Bond (editor), *Correspondence of John Cleves Symmes* (1926).

Catharina V. R. Bonney, *A Legacy of Historical Gleanings* (1875).

Claude G. Bowers, *Party Battles of the Jackson Period* (1922).

Thomas Boyd, *Mad Anthony Wayne* (1929); *Simon Girty, The White Savage* (1928).

A. G. Bradley, *Lord Dorchester* (1907).

H. C. Bradsby, *History of Vigo County* (1891).

W. A. Brice, *History of Fort Wayne* (1868).

Alexander Brown, *Genesis of the United States* (1890).

Samuel R. Brown, *History of the Second War of Independence* (1815).

Alfred Brunson, *A Western Pioneer* (1872–79).

Augustus C. Buell, *A History of Andrew Jackson* (1904).

Buffalo Historical Society Publications.

Jacob Burnet, *Notes on Northwest Territory* (1847).

Samuel J. Burr, *Life and Times of William Henry Harrison* (1840).

Mann Butler, *History of Kentucky* (1834).

Calendar of Virginia State Papers, 1652–1781.
Charles Campbell, *History of the Colony and Ancient Dominion of Virginia* (1860).
Canadian Archives Report, 1893, 1896.
H. S. Cauthorn, *History of the City of Vincennes*, 1902.
Celebration of the 45th Anniversary of the Settlement of Cincinnati (pamphlet), (1834).
Clara Longworth de Chambrun, *Cincinnati* (1939).
Michel Chevalier, *Society, Manners and Politics in the United States* (1839).
Gilbert Chinard, *Thomas Jefferson* (1929).
Henry Clay, *Works* (edited by Calvin Colton and others), (1897).
Mrs. Chapman Coleman, *Life of John J. Crittenden* (1873).
Harrie B. Coe, *Maine, A History* (1928).
Cyrenus Cole, *History of the People of Iowa* (1921); *I Am a Man; the Indian Black Hawk* (1938).
Elliott Coues (editor), *Forty Years a Fur Trader* (1898).
Ernest A. Cruikshank, *Documentary History of the Niagara Frontier* (Lundy's Lane Historical Society, *Publications*, 1886–1907).
George W. Cullum, *Campaigns of the War of 1812* (1879).
John A. Cutchins, *A Famous Command* (1934).
Julia Perkins Cutler, *Life and Times of Ephraim Cutler* (1890).
Isaac Darneille, *Letters of Decius* (1805).
Elias Darnell, *Journal of the Kentucky Volunteers. . . .* (1854).
Moses Dawson, *A Historical Narrative of the Civil and Military Services of Major-General William H. Harrison* (1824).
J. B. Dillon, *Indiana* (1843).
Benjamin Drake, *Life of Tecumseh* (1841).
S. G. Drake, *Aboriginal Races of North America* (1880).
J. P. Dunn, *Indiana* (1888, revised 1905).
Charles J. Dutton, *Oliver Hazard Perry* (1935).
Mrs. E. F. Ellett, *Court Circles of the Republic* (1869).
Richard S. Elliott, *Notes Taken in Sixty Years* (1883).
William Emmons, *Colonel Richard M. Johnson* (1833).
Logan B. Esarey (editor), *Harrison's Messages and Letters* (1922).
Silas Farmer, *History of Detroit and Michigan* (1889).
Farnsworth's Directory of Cincinnati, 1819–40.
Filson Club Publications (Louisville, Kentucky).
Timothy Flint, *Recollections of the Past Ten Years* (1826).
W. H. Foote, *Sketches of Virginia* (1850–55).
Henry A. Ford, *History of Cincinnati* (1881).
Elias Pym Fordham, *Personal Narrative* (edited by F. A. Ogg), (1906).

Claude Fuess, *Daniel Webster* (1923).
W. A. Galloway, *Old Chillicothe* (1934).
Rev. Charles F. Goss, *Cincinnati* (1912).
Dorothy Burne Goebel, *William Henry Harrison* (1926).
Thomas C. Grattan, *Civilized America* (1859).
Horace Greeley, *Recollections of a Busy Life* (1868).
George E. Greene, *History of Old Vincennes and Knox County* (1911).
Theodore Greve, *Centennial History of Cincinnati* (1904).
Hugh Blair Grigsby, *The Virginia Federal Convention of 1788* (1890–91).
R. S. Guernsey, *New York City During the War of 1812* (1889–95).
Hampden-Sidney College, *The '98 Kaleidoscope* (1898).
Marion Harland, *Some Colonial Homesteads* (1897).
Alvin F. Harlow, *Old Post Bags* (1928).
William Henry Harrison, *Discourse on the Aborigines of the Ohio Valley* (1839) ; *Remarks of General Harrison, late envoy . . . to Colombia* (1831) ; *Speech at Cheviot* (1833).
Peter Harvey, *Reminiscences and Anecdotes of Daniel Webster* (1890).
William G. Hatch, *A Chapter of the History of the War of 1812* (1872).
Jesus Maria Henao and Gerado Arrubla (Fred Rippy, translator), *History of Colombia* (1938).
The Hesperian, 1838–39.
Historical and Philosophical Society of Ohio Quarterly Publications.
Louis Houck, *History of Missouri* (1908).
Franklin B. Hough, *History of Jefferson County* (1854).
Henry Howe, *Historical Collections of Ohio* (1847).
M. A. D. Howe, *Life and Letters of George Bancroft* (1908).
Gaillard Hunt, *Life of James Madison* (1902).
Illinois State Historical Society Journal.
Illinois State Historical Library Publications.
Indiana Historical Collections.
Indiana Historical Society Publications.
Indiana History Bulletin, extra numbers Feb., 1924; Feb., 1925.
Indiana Magazine of History.
Marquis James, *Andrew Jackson* (one volume, 1938).
Thomas Jefferson, *Writings* (edited by Paul L. Ford) (1892–99).
Theodore D. Jervey, *Robert Y. Hayne and His Times* (1909).
A. E. Jones, *History of Cincinnati* (1888).
Edward A. Jones, *American Members of Inns of Court* (1924).
Robert R. Jones, *Fort Washington at Cincinnati* (1902).
C. J. Kappler (editor), *Indian Affairs, Laws and Treaties*, volume 2 (1904).

Charles Keith, *The Ancestry of Benjamin Harrison* (1893).
Kentucky State Historical Society Register.
Charles R. King, *Life of Rufus King* (1894).
Rufus King, *Ohio* (1888).
H. S. Knapp, *History of the Maumee Valley* (1872).
A. L. Kohlmeier, *The Old Northwest* (1938).
John Law, *Colonial History of Vincennes* (1858).
Joseph B. Lockey, *Pan-Americanism* (1920).
Benson J. Lossing, *Pictorial Field-Book of the War of 1812* (1869).
Dennis Tilden Lynch, *An Epoch and a Man* (1929).
William O. Lynch, *Fifty Years of Party Warfare* (1930).
Robert B. McAfee, *History of the Late War* (1816).
James McBride, *Pioneer Biography* (1869–71).
Walter F. McCaleb, *The Aaron Burr Conspiracy* (1903).
Charles McCarthy, *The Antimasonic Party* (1902).
Alexander McClure, *Our Presidents* (1900).
George McClure, *Causes of the Destruction . . . on the Niagara Frontier* (1817).
John McDonald, *Biographical Sketches of General Nathaniel Massie, General Duncan McArthur, etc.* (1852).
William McDonald, *Jacksonian Democracy* (1906).
R. C. McGrane (editor), *Correspondence of Nicholas Biddle* (1919).
Alexander Slidell MacKenzie, *Life of Commodore Oliver Hazard Perry* (1840).
W. C. McLeod, *The American Indian Frontier* (1928).
John Bach McMaster, *History of the United States* (1893–1913).
W. C. MacNaul, *The Jefferson-Lemen Compact* (1915).
James Madison, *Writings* (J. B. Lippincott edition), (1865).
E. D. Mansfield, *Personal Memoirs* (1879).
T. M. Marshall, *Life and Papers of Frederick Bates* (1926).
Maryland Historical Magazine.
David Massie, *Nathaniel Massie, A Pioneer of Ohio* (1896).
William Meade, *Old Churches, Ministers and Families of Virginia* (1878).
Leland W. Meyer, *Richard Mentor Johnson* (1932).
Michigan Historical Collections.
Michigan History Magazine.
James C. Mills, *Oliver Hazard Perry* (1913).
Mississippi Territorial Archives.
Mississippi Valley Historical Review.
Missouri Historical Review.

James Monroe, *Writings* (edited by Stanislaus M. Hamilton), (1898–1903).

Leander J. Monks, *Courts and Lawyers of Indiana* (1916).

H. Montgomery, *Life of Major General William Henry Harrison* (1852).

James Mooney, "The Ghost-Dance Religion," *14th Annual Report, Bureau of American Ethnology.*

Moravian Historical Society Transactions.

Samuel Mordecai, *Richmond in By-Gone Days* (1856).

Henry L. Mueller, *The Whig Party in Pennsylvania* (1922).

Allan Nevins (editor), *The Diary of Philip Hone* (1927).

New Jersey Historical Society Proceedings, Second Series.

Niagara Historical Society Publications.

Niles' Weekly Register.

William Ogden Niles, *The Tippecanoe Textbook* (1840).

A. B. Norton, *Reminiscences of the Great Revolution of 1840* (1888).

Nell Marion Nugent (editor), *Cavaliers and Pioneers* (1934).

Ellis Paxson Oberholtzer, *Robert Morris* (1903).

Ohio Archæological and Historical Society Publications.

Ohio Archæological and Historical Society Quarterly.

Ohio Valley Historical Series.

Ohio Senate Journal, 1819–20, 1820–21.

Old Northwest Genealogical Quarterly.

John C. Parish (editor), *The Robert Lucas Journal* (1906).

C. H. Peck, *The Jacksonian Epoch* (1899).

Pennsylvania Magazine of History.

W. S. Perry, *Historical Collections Relating to the American Church* (1870–78).

Alfred Pirtle, *The Battle of Tippecanoe* (1900).

G. P. Poage, *Henry Clay and the Rise of the Whig Party* (1936).

Ben Perley Poore, *Perley's Reminiscences* (1866).

The Portfolio (Philadelphia, 1815).

E. Alexander Powell, *Gentlemen Rovers* (1913).

Julius W. Pratt, *Expansionists of 1812* (1925).

John Hyde Preston, *A Gentleman Rebel* (1934).

Milo M. Quaife (editor), *The John Askin Papers* (1928).

James Reynolds, *Pioneer History of Illinois* (1887).

Linda Rhea, *Hugh Swinton Legaré* (1934).

John Richardson, *Richardson's War of 1812* (1902).

J. Fred Rippy, *Joel R. Poinsett* (1935).

Harriet Jane Robinson, *Loom and Spindle, or Life Among the Mill Girls* (1898).

W. H. Roose, *Birthplace of Indiana* (History of Harrison County), (1911).

Royal Society of Canada, *Proceedings and Transactions*.

Daniel J. Ryan, *Ohio in Four Wars* (1917).

Charles C. Royce and Cyrus Thomas, "Indian Land Cessions," *Eighteenth Annual Report*, Bureau of American Ethnology.

Ben F. Sager, *The Harrison Mansion* (1928).

Edith Tunis Sale, *Interiors of Virginia Houses of Colonial Times* (1927).

Nathan Sargent, *Public Men and Events* (1875).

J. T. Scharf, *History of St. Louis* (1883).

James Schouler, *History of the United States* (1913).

Nancy N. Scott (editor), *Memoir of Hugh Lawson White* (1856).

Winfield Scott, *Memoirs* (1864).

Carl Schurz, *Henry Clay* (1887).

William Seward, *Autobiography* (edited by Frederick W. Seward), (1877).

Mrs. Electa M. Sheldon, *Early History of Michigan* (1856).

Andrew M. Sherman, *Historic Morristown* (1905).

John Graves Simcoe, *Journal of Operations of the Queen's Rangers* (1787).

Henry H. Simms, *Rise of the Whigs in Virginia* (1929).

Bessie W. Smith, *Romances of the Presidents* (1932).

Margaret Bayard Smith, *First Forty Years of Washington Society* (1906).

O. H. Smith, *Early Indiana Trials and Sketches* (1856).

William H. Smith, *Life and Public Services of Arthur St. Clair* (1882).

W. L. G. Smith, *Life and Times of Lewis Cass* (1856).

Mary Newton Stanard, *Colonial Virginia* (1917); *Richmond, Its People and Its Story* (1923).

William G. and Mary Newton Stanard, *Colonial Virginia Register* (1902).

Edward Stanwood, *A History of the Presidency* (1898).

B. C. Sterner, *Life of James McHenry* (1907).

Joseph Gardner Swift, *Memoirs of Gen. Joseph Gardner Swift* (1890).

Tennessee Historical Magazine.

Territorial Papers, Northwest Territory (edited by Clarence E. Carter), (1935).

Benjamin F. Thompson, *History of Long Island* (1843).

Charles S. Todd and Benjamin Drake, *Sketches of the Civil and Military Services of William Henry Harrison* (revised by James H. Perkins), (1847).

Ferdinand B. Tupper, *Memoirs of Major-General Sir Isaac Brock* (1835).
David Turpie, *Sketches of My Own Times* (1903).
Lyon G. Tyler, *Letters and Times of the Tylers* (1896).
U. S. Congress: *Debates and Proceedings, Register of Debates.*
U. S. Congress: *House Report* 205.
U. S. Congress: *Congressional Globe* (26th Congress).
U. S. Congress: *Journal of the Executive Proceedings of the Senate.*
Martin Van Buren, *Autobiography* (edited by James C. Fitzpatrick), (1920).
Glyndon G. Van Deusen, *Henry Clay* (1937).
Virginia Historical Collections.
Virginia Magazine of History and Biography.
Virginia House of Burgesses, *Journals, 1619–1776* (edited by John P. Kennedy and H. R. McIlvaine), (1905–15).
Constantin F. C. de Volney, *A View of the Soil and Climate of the United States* (1804).
R. B. Warden, *Life of Salmon Portland Chase* (1874).
Daniel Webster, *Letters* (edited by C. H. Van Tyne), (1902).
Daniel Webster, *Writings and Speeches* (National Edition), (1903).
Thurlow Weed, *Autobiography* (edited by Harriet A. Weed), (1883).
Stephen B. Weeks, *Southern Quakers and Slavery* (1896).
Raynor G. Wellington, *Political and Sectional Influence of the Public Lands* (1914).
Western Monthly Magazine.
Western Monthly Review.
Western Reserve Historical Society Tracts.
William & Mary College Quarterly.
T. J. C. Williams, *History of Washington County* (1906).
Beckles Willson, *America's Ambassadors to England* (1928).
Woodrow Wilson, *George Washington* (1896).
Paul Wilstach, *Jefferson and Monticello* (1925); *Tidewater Virginia* (1929).
Nevin O. Winter, *History of Northwest Ohio* (1917).
Wisconsin Historical Collections.
William Wood (editor), *Select British Documents of the Canadian War of 1812* (1920–23).
James A. Woodburn, *Life of Thaddeus Stevens* (1913).
T. F. Woodley, *Thaddeus Stevens* (1934).
Lew Wallace, *Life of General Ben Harrison* (1890).
W. W. Woollen, *Biographical and Historical Sketches of Early Indiana* (1900).

Works Progress Administration, *Washington, City and Capital* (1938).
Gorham A. Worth, *Recollections of Cincinnati* (1916).
T. Y. Ybarra, *Bolivar* (1930).
Bennett H. Young, *The Battle of the Thames* (1903).

N. B. This bibliography would include newspapers save for the fact that a list of those consulted would be rather lengthy. In general, this writer followed Harrison on his numerous travels by consulting newspapers published in every town and city he passed through; also city and county histories. Altogether, newspapers and other sundry publications of twelve states and the Dominion of Canada were consulted. Copies of a resulting subsidiary work, a "Harrison Chronology," have been deposited with the Indiana State Historical Commission, the Library of Congress, and the New York Public Library. This "Chronology," a twenty-page typewritten manuscript, contains a day-by-day and week-to-week tabulation, with dates, of arrivals and departures and other various events in Harrison's life.

INDEX